ORIGEN
SPIRIT AND FIRE

ORIGEN

SPIRIT AND FIRE

A Thematic Anthology of His Writings

by

Hans Urs von Balthasar

Translated by

Robert J. Daly, S.J.

The Catholic University of America Press
Washington, D.C.

Originally published as *Origenes GEIST UND FEUER: Ein Aufbau aus seinen Schriften*, übersetzt und mit einer Einführung von Hans Urs von Balthasar, © 1938 by Otto Müller Verlag, Salzburg (2nd revised edition, 1956)

Library of Congress Cataloging in Publication Data

Origen.
  Origen, spirit and fire.

  Translation of: Origenes, Geist und Feuer.
  Includes index.
  1. Theology—Addresses, essays, lectures.
I. Balthasar, Hans Urs von, 1905–
II. Title.   III. Title: Spirit and fire.
BR65.053E5   1984   230'.1'30924   83-14368
ISBN 0-8132-0591-3

I WANT TO BE A MAN OF THE CHURCH. I DO NOT WANT TO BE CALLED BY THE NAME OF SOME FOUNDER OF A HERESY, BUT BY THE NAME OF CHRIST, AND TO BEAR THAT NAME WHICH IS BLESSED ON THE EARTH. IT IS MY DESIRE, IN DEED AS IN SPIRIT, BOTH TO BE AND TO BE CALLED A CHRISTIAN.

IF I, WHO SEEM TO BE YOUR RIGHT HAND AND AM CALLED PRESBYTER AND SEEM TO PREACH THE WORD OF GOD, IF I DO SOMETHING AGAINST THE DISCIPLINE OF THE CHURCH AND THE RULE OF THE GOSPEL SO THAT I BECOME A SCANDAL TO YOU, THE CHURCH, THEN MAY THE WHOLE CHURCH, IN UNANIMOUS RESOLVE, CUT ME, ITS RIGHT HAND, OFF, AND THROW ME AWAY.

ORIGEN

CONTENTS

Translator's Foreword xi
Introduction 1
Prologue 25

I. SOUL

The World and the Soul 37
    Self-Knowledge 37
    Between Matter and Spirit 42
    Sliding Middle 46
The Image of God 51
    Participation in God 51
    Image of God 54
    Image of the WORD 57
Fall and Return 60
    Spiritual Death 60
    The Sin of the Race 61
    Wandering through the Desert 64

II. WORD

Word with God 77
    The Word of Revelation 77
    The Knowledge of God 82
Word as Scripture 86
    The Scripture as Body 86
    The WORD Which Comes 88
    Mystery 89
    Image Upwardly Open 91
    From WORD-Scripture to WORD-Spirit 94
    On Interpreting the Scripture 100
    Water and Wine 108

Word as Flesh 113
  Christ 113
    Old Covenant and New Covenant 113
      Demolition of What Was Preliminary 113
      The Definitive in What Was Preliminary 117
    The Life of Jesus as Parable 120
      Incarnation 120
      Childhood 124
      Humility 126
      Suffering 128
    The Eternal Christ 133
      Consumption of the Earthly 133
      Mystery of the Transitus........................... 138
      Body and Super-Body 141
      Human Being and Super-Human Being 144
      Universal Salvation 146
  Church 148
    The Church in the Old Covenant..................... 148
    The Church in the New Covenant 152
    Harlot and Holy 156
    Heresy 169
  The Law of Sublation 175

III. SPIRIT

Life in the Spirit 183
  The Spiritual God 183
  Awakening... 186
  Voice 188
  Initiation 189
  Grace 192
    Faith as Grace 192
    Work from Nature and Work from God 198
    Human Wisdom and Divine Wisdom 203
  The Inner Human Being 208
    Doubly Human 208
    Fall of the Idols 209
    Law of Love.. 213
  The Inner Senses..................................... 218
  Spiritual Sense and Spirit-Discernment................. 218

Senses for God 218
The Spiritual Battle 223
The Nature and Discernment of Spirits 225
Hearing 232
Sight 235
Inner Sight 235
Faith, Deed and Vision 239
Faith as Seeing 244
Touch 249
Smell 254
Taste 257
Food 258
Spiritual Nourishment 258
WORD as Flesh and Blood 261
Transformation of the Nourishing WORD 265
Generation 268
Generation by God 268
Fidelity 271
The Great Canticle 273
Divine Birth 278
Mystical Body 280
One Body 280
One Sacrifice 287
Christ the Priest 287
Royal Priesthood 290
Co-Redemption 297
One Meal 302
One Life 305

IV. GOD

The Mystery of God 317
God-Fire 320
Spiritual End of the World 320
Fire 325
The Salvific Significance of Punishment 330
Unjudgeable Guilt 334
The Salvific Significance of Guilt 336
The Cunning of Love 342
Fear and Love 349

God, All in All 351
   The Sacraments of Truth 351
   Super-World 356
   Union in and with God 360
Epilogue 367
Appendix: The Paschal Mystery 368

Translator's Epilogue 371
   I. Recent Origen Studies 371
   II. This Translation 373
Index of Abbreviations 377
Index of Passages Translated 379
Index of Biblical References 401

TRANSLATOR'S FOREWORD

Despite a fairly strong consensus among patristic scholars that Origen might well be the greatest of all the early Christian writers, he remains relatively inaccessible for contemporary Christians. A desire to do something about this "scandal of inaccessibility" has been the motivation behind this translation. Von Balthasar's introduction, although written in 1938, still remains the best brief introduction to the heart, soul and spirit of Origen's writings. The brief bibliographic update provided in the Translator's Epilogue will meet the initial needs of the serious reader or scholar who is eager for further study. Beyond that, it seems appropriate to add here some comment on Origen's interpretation of scripture. For modern readers, while less likely than their forebears to be upset by speculations which have proven to be erroneous or inadequate, are more likely to be alienated by Origen's manner of interpreting the bible which is often so badly misunderstood as to make it difficult to hear and understand what Origen was really saying and doing.

Our basic problem in reading Origen today is that we tend to read him in terms of the standards of scholarly exegesis. How well does Origen measure up to these? But this is far from the most important question in coming to an understanding of what Origen was really about. For if we are thinking of modern exegesis when we ask: "Was Origen an exegete?", "No" is a far more correct answer than "Yes."

Now Origen obviously did many of the things a modern exegete does, and in some of these, such as textual criticism and sensitivity to the significance of differences between the evangelists, his accomplishments were not surpassed until the modern age. However, most of the methods of modern exegesis were simply not available to scholars in Origen's time. But most important of all, his central conception of what he was doing as he interpreted the bible was quite different from what the modern exegete or biblical theologian thinks he or she is doing. The modern exegete[1]

---

[1] By "modern exegete" we mean someone committed to scientific or "critical" exegesis, and working in the context of a theology which accepts the inspiration

applies a sophisticated blend of philosophical, historical and literary tools to uncover the "literal meaning" of the bible, i.e., the meaning intended by its human authors, or the meaning contained, by denotation or connotation, in the text itself. Practically all the work of the modern biblical scholar is directed towards or proceeds from this central goal. Origen would have regarded such a conception of theology (at that time, all Christian theology was essentially biblical theology), if indeed anyone could have formulated it at that time, as curious, misguided, or even pernicious. For although he was constantly looking to see precisely what Moses, David, Jeremiah, Matthew, John, Paul, etc., were saying and why they were saying it, this was always done with a view to hearing and understanding what God, the WORD, was saying.

One way of putting this is to point out that in commenting and preaching on the bible, Origen was really doing theology (as opposed to exegesis). At first glance, the modern reader might well conclude that Origen simply used the bible as a means or catalyst to bring his theology to expression, or, put more bluntly, that Origen used the bible as a handy frame on which to hang the various elements of his theology. For the educated modern reader, this is a misuse of the bible; it may be more elegant and sophisticated, but in the end it does not essentially differ from the way some modern sects selectively quote the bible to support their own particular view of Christian reality.

There is a vitally important grain of truth in such an observation, and we will return to it later. But for the moment, let us examine some of its unacceptable consequences. The most striking of these is that it logically pushes us to dismiss patristic theology as something irrelevant for the modern Christian. It is reduced, at its worst, to a naively unscientific biblicism, and at its best to an elegant glass bead game. However, reducing Origen's exegesis to an elegant "game" does not adequately explain his ability to inspire a whole series of great theologians from his own day (Athanasius, Basil, the Gregorys) down to ours (K. Rahner, de Lubac, von Balthasar). To make sense of this fact we must obviously look more deeply. Our suggestion on how to do this will consist of a brief presentation of the following three points: (1) a description of Origen's conception of the biblical WORD

---

of scripture, the reality of the incarnation, and the life of the Spirit in the church —i.e., a serious, critical scholar who accepts the bible as the word of God.

of God, (2) an indication of how this determines his methods of interpreting scripture, and (3) an attempt to put all this in the context of
his *rule of faith*.

(1) Jesus Christ, the WORD incarnate, is central to Origen's concept of scripture — because for him, the WORD was incarnated not
only in the flesh of the historical Jesus, but also in the very words of
scripture. This is what Origen has in mind when he says that the
meaning of all scripture, of the Old as well as of the New Testament,
is Jesus Christ. Thus, he means much more than what comes to our
minds when we hear the statement that the Old Testament points to
the New. For Origen, the WORD is already there, incarnated, as it
were, in the words of Moses, David and the prophets. Thus the real
meaning or, as he liked to express it, the ultimate *spiritual* meaning of
every biblical text is Christ. Hence, every text, every word of the bible is
important and worthy of reverence and study. This is strikingly illus-
trated in the famous homily passage where, after reminding his
listeners of the care and reverence with which they handle every particle
of the consecrated bread, Origen asks: "But if you exercise such concern in taking care of his body — and indeed with every right —
how can you think it a lesser crime to neglect the WORD of God than
his body?" (No. 721).

Thus, when a Christian prays the Psalms, the eternal Logos is
speaking to that soul. In the Song of Songs, the bridegroom is the
WORD, conversing with his spouse, the soul. And, perhaps most
revealing of all, the historical, Egyptian passover is not an image or
type of Christ's suffering, but of Christ's *transitus* to the Father — *a
reality that is still taking place in us* (cf. Nos. 1035-1039). The words of
the bible are not just signs and symbols and images of Christ; in a
very real sense they *are* Christ; the eternal Logos is present in them by
an incarnation which is different, of course, but hardly less real than
his historical, bodily incarnation. But just as many who encountered
the man Jesus in the flesh did not, because of their lack of faith, encounter the eternal WORD, so too is it with the biblical WORD:
many do not see beyond the flesh of the letter or historical meaning;
they do not see beyond these externals to the internal reality of the
eternal WORD already present and active within themselves, calling
and leading their souls to make progress toward perfect unity with the
Father who is all in all.

(2) Once one sees Origen's concept of the biblical WORD as the
letter of history in which the eternal WORD has become incarnate,

the main aspects of Origen's method of interpreting scripture fall fairly readily into place. The text, the literal or historical meanings, are by no means unimportant, for they are the "body" or the "flesh" in which the Logos becomes incarnate. But in relation to the inner, spiritual reality of the eternal Logos, God the WORD, these external realities tend to pale into insignificance. This alone would account for the impression that Origen undervalues the historical meaning. This is indeed an obvious tendency in Origen, and it is all the more heightened by the Platonizing cast of his thought.[2]

But when Origen speaks of the biblical WORD, the WORD incarnate in the scriptures, at least four interconnected levels of meaning are in play. *First,* this WORD is the pre-existent, eternal, divine Logos, the Logos proclaimed in the prologue of John's gospel and expounded in extraordinary detail and depth in Origen's commentary on this prologue. *Second,* this same divine Logos is the one who took flesh of the Virgin Mary, lived and worked among us, suffered, died, rose again and ascended to the Father, where he continues to intercede for us and to work until all things have become subjected to the Father who is all in all. *Third,* this same eternal WORD who took flesh of Mary has also become incarnate in the words of scripture. *Fourth,* this same divine WORD, born of Mary and also incarnate in the scriptures, also dwells and is at work within us, espoused to our souls, calling us to make progress toward perfection, and to work with him in ascending to and subjecting all things to the Father.

At any time Origen may have one of these levels of meaning more in mind than another, but at no time is any one of them very far from his consciousness. But clearly dominating, and thus constituting his central hermeneutical principle, is the fourth level of meaning which includes the other three. It is thus that one can speak of "existential interpretation" in describing Origen's hermeneutics; but in doing so one must locate it within Origen's conception of the *real* incarnation and hence "real presence" of the eternal WORD in the scriptures. It is thus not mere metaphorical language but precise theological description to

---

[2] The mere fact that Origen's thought can be described as "Platonizing" is, in itself, only a sign that he was a Christian thinker in the third century. There was at the time no thought system better suited to help Christians in the theological reflection. The real question is not whether Origen thinks as a Platonist, but whether in so doing he gives sufficient place to the incarnational aspects of Christianity.

speak of the "sacramentality of the biblical word" according to Origen. This enables us to see, for example, that where Origen seems to speak of or favor a "WORD-presence" of Christ in the Eucharist over against a *mere* physical or bodily presence, this is not a downgrading but an upgrading of the reality and mystery of the eucharistic real presence.

An interesting contrast between the modern exegete and Origen the biblical theologian can be drawn by locating where each of them sees what we now call diachronic complexity. The modern exegete locates this in the complicated processes, sometimes extending over centuries, by which the biblical text came to take its final form. Origen had access to none of the information and methods which would have afforded him a view into this process. But he does find complex diachronic reality in the scriptures; not, however, in how they came to be, but in the way they reveal how the soul is making progress towards God, and in the way they document how the Logos, who is already incarnated in the scriptures, is coming to be in us. Thus, much of what Origen is doing in his commentaries and homilies would, in today's classifications, be called spiritual theology.

This outline of Origen's understanding of the biblical WORD enables us to make sense of Origen's particular techniques for approaching the biblical text, some of which are quite foreign or even alienating to modern scholarly sensitivities. First, the extraordinary reverence and meaning attached to each particular word and phrase is the logical consequence of Origen's understanding of the real incarnation of the eternal Logos in *all* of scripture, in both Testaments, and not just in the more important or elevated passages of either. In particular, variations and inconsistencies (as between the different evangelists), or passages whose literal or historical meanings seem unworthy of the WORD, are obvious signs that one should search for the deeper, spiritual meaning behind these words. This, of course, tends to annoy the modern exegete who can explain most of these variations, inconsistencies and "unworthinesses" as part of the process of the human authorship of the bible. Equally annoying to the modern exegete, especially if one is unaware of what Origen is about, is his habit of ranging freely across the entire bible in order to interpret any particular passage. Since the WORD, as explained above, is incarnate in all of the bible and in all of its parts, such a procedure is not only allowable but necessary.

Up to this time we have been speaking of the difference between the literal or historical and the higher or spiritual sense. This is indeed the simplest schema which applies to all cases in Origen. But beyond this, Origen quite often speaks of or uses a triple schema, and he does so in two distinguishable variations. In the *first variation*, there is (1) a *historical* or *literal* meaning: facts recorded, or the texts of the Law; then (2) a *moral* meaning, which is an application to the soul (but not yet talking about Christian grace); and finally (3) a *mystical* meaning relating to Christ, the church and all the realities of faith. In the *second variation*, there is (1) a *historical* or *literal* meaning relating to the things of Israel; then (2) a *mystical* meaning relating to the mystery still to be fulfilled, i.e., Christ and the Church; and finally (3) a *spiritual* meaning relating to the soul—but here it is the soul not just in its psychological reality as in the first variation, but the soul as "spouse of the WORD" in its graced progress toward full union with God.[3] Origen will use (without apparent rule or consistent method of application—method in this sense is a modern invention) sometimes only the basic letter-spirit schema, sometimes one or the other of its more elaborate triple variations, and sometimes other variations of these possibilities. Allegory and typology simply fit in as techniques to be used within these schemas. And although the triple schemas were often more helpful in dealing with some of the apparently more "Christ-distant" realities of the Old Testament, Origen apparently never made a significant attempt to be consistent in these matters. But such inconsistency was itself fully consistent with his overall conception of what was happening as he interpreted scripture: it was the Christian soul following the guidance of the Spirit to look beyond the literal and historical meaning to catch some glimpse of the humanly incomprehensible mystery of the WORD.

This is what Origen thought he was about as he interpreted scripture. It is not what the modern scholar would call exegesis. But once modern readers see what Origen was doing and attempting to do, it becomes possible for them too to be captivated by the brilliance and range of insight which flashes from the pages of the great Alexandrian. But if this captivation is to become more than just a fascinating glimpse into an elaborate game, once played but now dead, two interrelated objections remain to be faced. The first and more obvious is the charge of *arbitrariness:* one can see what Origen is doing and why,

---

[3] Cf. H. de Lubac, *Histoire et Esprit: L'intelligence de l'Écriture d'après Origène* (Theologie 16; Paris: Aubier, 1950), esp. 139–43.

but in the end, there often seem to be no firm and consistent rules and regulations as to how and why Origen comes up with one particular interpretation, especially in his allegorizing, rather than another. The second objection is that of *irrelevance:* one can marvel at the brilliance of his interpretations; but because his fundamental conception of the bible is so different from that of a modern theologian, one is tempted to concede antiquarian significance to the study of Origen, and then dismiss him as of little relevance for the modern Christian. To meet these objections, one has to see Origen's biblical theology in the context of his concept of the Christian faith or, more precisely, the *rule of faith.*

(3) Origen's faith and biblical theology is radically and profoundly ecclesiastical. Notwithstanding the famous difficulties with his own bishop, Demetrios, in Alexandria, or the questionable use to which some of the Origenists later put his work, no one familiar with Origen's work as a whole can have any doubt about this. The two texts selected by von Balthasar to serve as the epigraph of this book are fully typical of his attitude of total adherence to the church.

One aspect of Origen's church-oriented faith is his insistence that all of the bible must be kept in mind when interpreting any particular passage. On the one hand, this corresponds to the church's insistence on the sacredness of the whole bible over against the heretics, especially the gnostics, who accepted only parts of it as inspired. On the other hand, it removed much of the danger of arbitrariness from his interpretations. Indeed, the fact that Origen's interpretations made so much sense in the context of the whole bible is a major reason for his massive influence on the development of the golden age of patristic theology. But in the end, it was Origen's ecclesiastical *rule of faith* that was decisive. This is what provided the structure and substance of his particular hermeneutical circle; this is what, in effect, determined his interpretations of the bible.

As becomes perfectly clear from the prologue to *On First Principles,* Origen is not affected by the hermeneutical naiveté of those who believe that they are taking all their faith and theology directly from the bible, but who in fact are only reading into a select part of the bible the narrow rule of faith that reigns in their own sectarian community. But there is one point of parallel: Origen is, as a modern scholar would put it, reading into the bible. *But,* he is with the utmost conscientiousness reading into the *whole* bible, and doing so with unparalleled skill and insight. And also, *what* he is, so to speak, "reading into" the bible is the broad rule of faith of the whole Christian community. This is

Origen's hermeneutical circle (of which he himself, for an ancient writer, seems to be impressively conscious): he studies and interprets the bible in order to know and understand his Christian faith; but it is his already possessed ecclesiastical Christian faith which tells him what to look for and find in the bible.

Now hermeneutical circles can be concentric, that is, limiting or confining, as is the case with sectarians or heretics in the classical sense, or they can be opening and expansive in order to embrace as much of reality as possible. Origen's circle was of the latter type in at least three different ways. First, he was an avid, curious, dedicated and daring biblical "scientist." All that could be known about the bible he took pains to learn. Second, he was a philosopher of apparently considerable ability and dedicated to the idea that Christian faith, although not answerable to human reason, was not inconsistent with it, because true human reason is always a participation in divine reason. Properly approached, he saw philosophy and reason not as a danger but as a help to faith. Third, he brought his own personal and practical experience to bear on his theological reflection and interpretation of the bible.

Thus, to say that the Christian *rule of faith* as handed on from the apostles and as received in the church of his day determined how Origen interpreted the bible is far from the whole story. From his constant research, from his incessant questioning and speculating, and from his own personal and spiritual experience, he was continually bringing in new insight and understanding to the church's understanding both of the bible and of its own rule of faith. His was not only the vision and insight to broaden and deepen, not only the courage to admonish and correct, but also the boldness and adventuresomeness to question and speculate. It was this unique combination of knowledge and curiosity, insight and eagerness to teach, fidelity to the *rule of faith* as well as the boldness to correct misconceptions of it, and finally, absolute faithfulness to the WORD, that enabled him to captivate the minds and hearts of so many of the Fathers to follow. And he will captivate ours too if we do not smother him with erroneous presuppositions.

ROBERT J. DALY, S.J.

INTRODUCTION

1

It is all but impossible to overestimate Origen and his importance for the history of Christian thought. To rank him beside Augustine and Thomas simply accords him his rightful place in this history. Anyone who has given long hours to studying the Fathers will have had the same experience as 'a mountain climber: the slow, steady receding of the seemingly still-threatening peaks all around him, until, beyond them, the hitherto-hidden dominant central massif rises majestically before him. None of the great Fathers, from the Cappadocians to Augustine, and on up to Dionysius, Maximos, Scotus Eriugena and Eckhart, could escape an almost magical fascination for the "man of steel," as they called him. Some were completely swept away. For if you remove the Origenian brilliance from Eusebius, there is nothing left but a semi-Arian theologian of dubious merit and an industrious historian. Jerome, when commenting on scripture, continues to copy straight from Origen's pages, even after outwardly breaking in anger the chains and fiercely denying the bond that linked him to the master. Basil and Gregory of Nazianzen, in their enthusiastic admiration, make a collection of the most fascinating passages from the inexhaustible works of the one to whom they continually returned when their day-to-day struggles allowed them a moment of peace. Gregory of Nyssa was even more thoroughly captivated. The Cappadocians transmit him practically intact to Ambrose, who also knew and copied from him firsthand. In fact, many of the breviary readings of Ambrose (as well as of Jerome and Bede) are practically word-for-word from Origen. Thus, flowing simultaneously from several directions, the heritage of Origen, already become the common possession of the Church, poured over Augustine and through him into the middle ages. But in the East, he is the subject of wave upon wave of enthusiasm. There, the stream of Origenism, as it became wider and wider, also became more and more shallow. It fell into the hands of obscure communities of monks who tenaciously and thickheadedly defended the "letter" of the master's teaching — the exact opposite of what Origen himself would have desired. And the more the spirit of the master departed, leaving behind only the dull dregs of the "system," the more distorted it stood before the bar of Church teaching. The doubt and suspicion which the embarrassing quarrel between Jerome and Rufinus had long ago cast over Origen's name fell upon it even more heavily in the East; for with the condemnations of the emperor Justinian, the power of Origenism (as something public or official) was thoroughly shattered.

But what was the point of rendering completely harmless this half-desiccated system of theses, of attacking the pre-existence of souls, the angelic incarnation of the Logos, the soul-existence of the heavenly bodies, the spherical form of the resurrection-bodies (which Origen actually never held), and finally the dissolution of hell at the end of time, what was the point of it when, from these miserable remains of a brilliant whole — one is tempted to compare them to the scraps of a fallen airplane — the spirit, the drive and the fascination had long since disappeared? But this was only the open occurrence of what had long since taken place unnoticed: while the jar was breaking into a thousand pieces and the name of the master was being overwhelmed and stoned, the fragrance of the ointment was coming forth and "filling the whole house." For there is no thinker in the Church who is so invisibly all-present as Origen. He himself hardly ever wrote, but dictated, practically day and night, tirelessly, to a team of stenographers. Thus his works — the six thousand books that Epiphanius mentions are a legend, but Eusebius and Jerome know of almost two thousand — are really only the sound of a voice. But it is a voice that drives straight through everything, always pushing on, without fanfare and without fatigue, almost, it seems, without an obvious goal, possessed almost to the point of insanity, and yet with a cool, unapproachable intellectual restraint that has never again been equaled. It is not the voice of a rhetorician (there are enough of these among the Fathers so that the difference is immediately obvious), for this voice is not even trying to persuade; nor is it the enthusiastic voice of a poet (although the images and comparisons fly up in swarms everywhere); it is too brittle, too dry and too plain for that, even to the point of poverty. But neither is it the voice of an enchanter: there is nothing of the captivating chiaroscuro and baroque glitter of the Areopagite, nothing of the magical verbal geometry of the bishop of Nazianzen. Everything here is unpremeditated, unforced, and expressed with a modesty that never ceases to amaze; with little formulas of apology like "if you want to venture a daring explanation," or with a little smile and a "you might consider whether perhaps," thus leaving the solution up to the listener. Not a trace of the Augustinian pathos which, without asking, breaks open the doors of the heart and is accustomed, like a doctor, to look upon it naked and place it before God. But no less distant is the sagacious and, in the best sense of the word, humanistic balance of the great pastoral bishop Basil, who was born to rule and in whom moderation is second nature. The voice of the Alexandrian is more like that glowing, rainless desert wind that sometimes sweeps over the Nile delta, with a thoroughly unromantic passion: pure, fiery gusts. Two names come to mind in comparison: Heraclitus and Nietzsche. For their work too is, externally, ashes and contradiction, and makes sense only because of the fire of their souls which forces their unmanageable material into a unity and, with a massive consumption of fuel, leaves behind it a fiery track straight across the earth. Their passion, however, stems only from the Dionysian mystery of the world. But here, in Origen, the flame shoots out and darts upward to the mystery of the super-worldly Logos-WORD which fills the face of the earth only to be itself baptized in this fire, to be ignited and transformed into the Spirit. In its inner form, then, the thought of Origen is a contribution to the consummation of its one single object, and that is the voice, the speech, the WORD of God and nothing else. But it is *voice* which cuts into the heart like a fiery sword, *speech* which whispers with other-worldly tenderness one mystery of love after another, and WORD which is the flash and reflection of the hidden beauty of the Father. Into the anonymity of this WORD Origen's voice, too, has been drawn, and in this form it has attained that universal presence in Christian thought of which we have been speaking.

2

But, despite all this, after long and desperate opposition, Origen was rejected and condemned by Christian theology. And even if this judgment, as we explained, touches only the dry skeleton of his thought, Origen has remained a marked man. For the figure is held upright by the bone structure, and when deprived of this, it collapses powerlessly. No great system allows form and content to be separated, even when they don't come together all that well, as in Hegel. Of course, it is always possible that certain aspects of a thought-system are truer than others, so that one can accept some and reject others. But the more purely such a choice can be made, the less do the parts suffer loss; and the "more material" the original structure really was, the less did it possess a forceful, centripetal unity, a style. It is not easy to be a Hegelian in logic without also being one in the philosophy of history and of government. One can't accept the *Critique of Pure Reason* and reject the *Critique of Practical Reason*. Indeed, you really can't even accept the first movements of the Ninth Symphony and forget about the last. For the truth of all great things rests less in the what than in the how; the spirit of the whole gives sense and unity to the whole. And all the members first take part in the truth of the indivisible idea.

This consideration brings us right to the middle of the most questionable part of our undertaking. Many before us have tried to "Christianize" Origen in the mechanical way we have described. You switch off pre-existence and restoration, moderate here and there some extravagant views, and end up with a flat, dull product which is full of nice, harmless things, but in which no one senses any longer the breath of genius. Another way is the edition of the complete works of the master, as is now being done so very well by the commission on the Church Fathers of the Prussian Academy of Sciences. It goes without saying that this massive work merits the greatest admiration and gratitude, since it makes an undeniably reliable tool available to the scholar. But even that is only a means. With its help the philosopher and the theologian have to carve out, compare and evaluate the form that lies dormant within like a statue within the rock. Somewhat the same thing has to be said of the exemplary German translations of Koetschau in the Kösel Library of the Church Fathers which have given us new access to the great tract *Against Celsus*, the treatise *On Prayer* and the *Exhortation to Martyrdom*. They provide openings for the modern-day thinker, invitations — but you don't see anyone accepting these invitations. Furthermore, the treatise *Against Celsus*, full of boring passages and partly also full of rubbish, can today count on only a few readers; and the two other short works do not lead into the heart of Origen's thought. This heart becomes audible only to the person who delves deep into the commentaries on the bible. It isn't in the early work *Peri Archōn* (*On First Principles*), but in his comments on the Old and New Testament that one finds the living spirit of this thought.

But to present these works in their entirety to a modern reader would be a hopeless task. Not only do many of them consist only of a disordered heap of fragments, and others only of modified Latin translations, but they are themselves, as dictated works, often full of digressions, without subdivisions and structure, full of repetitions and passages that would be distasteful to the uninitiate. So, we have decided to make a selection, from all of his works, of what still makes sense today, and in such a way that out of the interconnection of these central passages the true face of Origen could shine forth as from a mosaic. For basically, "what still makes sense today" is also the living heart that did so then and always, so that when we are in contact with this no essential misrepresentation need be feared.

But in so far as this inner "spiritual bond" in Origen's thought is being sought out, we are obviously, already, placing ourselves beyond purely historical interest (as, to some extent, the Kösel editions have) and are erecting in the arena of intellectual investigation a statue for whose validity we are responsible. Now we already observed above that it would be hopeless to try to separate in a purely material way the "heterodox" from the "orthodox" in Origen; thus it is unavoidable that both will be represented in our picture. So it is superfluous to note that we in no way identify ourselves with everything that must be taken up into this selection in order to give shape to the true, inner picture of the master. What we are primarily concerned about is the truth itself of this picture. Even the colossus of Daniel consisted of different metals and stood on clay feet; this did not keep it from being a colossus. And only when this objective correctness of the picture we are sketching has been assured can we look to our second goal.

For in view of this figure the unavoidable question arises: If it is really true that in Origen, who is all-present in Christian theology, form and content stand in the most intimate relationship, what conclusion can we draw from that for Christian theology? If Origen flowed for centuries like a broad stream through the riverbed of Christian thought — and so powerfully that even bitter opponents like Methodius submit almost completely to his authority — what, in relation to that, do those bars mean that are supposed to keep his "heterodoxy" from penetrating into the sanctuary? Nothing or almost nothing, says Harnack's well-known answer. Origen is for him the decisive importation of what is worldly and Greek into the spirit of the Gospel from which the Catholic Church never again freed itself. The *Peri Archōn* is for Harnack the first theological Summa, the original attempt to master and get control of revelation by means of human logic. Theology has since then been powerless to resist the seduction of this most powerful gnosis. It would be superficial to dispose of Harnack with references to pre-Origenian theology. He had too fine a feel for things not to be aware that at this point elements which as such did not come from the gospels were pushing their way into Christianity. Our argument with Harnack must begin at another point: with his, in our opinion, unjustified denial of every possibility of a human development and unfolding of evangelical revelation in theology, and his denial of every supernatural direction of the Church in the area of the theoretical formulation of its deposit of faith. The religious world view of Harnack lacks the concept of a WORD living on and continuing to give witness in the church as its Body. This explains why he falsely formulated what he rightly sensed. It isn't just the fact that a Hellenistic spirit infiltrated the church through Origen that gives one pause, but rather the concrete way in which this appropriation takes place.

For clarity's sake, it is possible to divide the whole of Origen's thought (prescinding completely, for the time being, from its relationship to Christianity) into three strata. This doesn't mean a material division of thought content, but rather three cross-sections at different depths.

In the *first stratum* we find those "heterodox" opinions which, obviously influenced by Platonic myths, never found a home in the church and finally were openly and energetically rejected by her. In this place of course belongs also what, in Origen, suggests the subordination of the three Divine Persons, which was common in the time before Nicaea, and which got taken care of through the struggles with Arianism. Besides, no one took objection to Origen on this point because of the way in which, much more clearly than did Justin or Tertullian, he insisted on the equal eternity of the Son with the Father. Here too belongs the strong separation of roles which the Divine Persons take on in salvation history, above all the almost excessive and exclusive relationship of creatures to the Son in God. The unique shape of Origen's Logos-mysticism was possible only in this not yet fully developed stage of trinitarian doctrine. The idea that the soul is in a direct way only "image and likeness" of the Logos, and only, because the Logos himself is only image and likeness of the Father, also an indirect image of the Father—this opinion, after the trinitarian teaching of the first general council, becomes obsolete of itself. The whole tendency to trinitarian subordination (Son under Father,

Spirit under Son) is obviously of Greek-gnostic origin and is connected with the attempt to bridge the gap between God and world by means of "emanations," "spheres," stages and rungs on which the soul in need of salvation tries to climb up to heaven. — Belonging consequently to this group is also the idea that the Logos incarnated himself on all these stages and rungs so that he, just as he was human to humans, was also angel to angels; and consequently, the soul which climbs on these rungs to the Father becomes a living ladder to heaven, a cosmic "true way." Indeed the very rise of the soul through various heavenly stages, and thus the in-principle equality of essence in humans and angels (both are, as creatures, of a body-soul nature), also belongs in this essentially Hellenistic world of ideas. But this upward journey is only the counterpart of that first mythical sin from which comes not precisely the (numerical) individuation of souls, but rather their qualitative difference. For to each of them, according to its particular turning away from the primordial light, God gave in the ensuing world age a thicker and heavier or a more spiritual body. This is how the circle is closed which connects pre-existence, subordination, incarnation on all levels, upward movement, and becoming an angel.

The second stratum, which cuts across the whole of Origen's thought, is harder to characterize. It concerns the, so to speak, purely formal influence on the whole of his thought of the doctrines we have just described. It is more a question of attitude than of content and can be almost completely separated from those material doctrines. There was very little barrier to the acceptance of such a formal attitude into the church, since the whole age of waning of antiquity breathed in it as in a common atmosphere. Thus the filter we spoke about above was not strong enough to keep out this stratum of Origen's thought, and this is what has become invisibly all-present in Christian theology.

This manifestation has been given different names. There has been mention, for example, of the Platonism of the Fathers. And to the extent that one can find in Plato the model of the fall and the rising again as well as the thoroughgoing separation of idea and appearance, some Platonic elements actually do get into the Fathers. But in thinking so, one forgets that in the third and fourth centuries the great schools were already irrevocably mixed. Even in Philo there is as much of the Stoa as of Platonism. If one looks a bit more closely at Gregory of Nyssa who has been stamped as a Platonist, one discovers far more Aristotelian and Stoic than Platonic elements. Somewhat

the same is true of Basil. But Clement and Origen have already become gathering basins for the whole philosophical culture of their
time. "Platonism" thus does not describe the true situation.

There has also been talk of the Fathers' flight from the world—that
they had gotten infected by the Gnostic disdain for the body and marriage, by Encratism and all kinds of influences from the desert fathers.
But this doesn't get at the real heart of the matter either. Irenaeus is
the great advocate of the earth against Gnosticism. Origen himself
never gave a thought to denying the resurrection of the body; against
Celsus he emphatically defended the worth of the body, and more
than later Fathers he pointed to the positive value of the physical emotions. His ideal of knowledge is expressly this-worldly: an unlimited
thirst to see to the bottom and to the essence of all things. The sight
(vision) of the Logos is the sight of the personal richness of the one
world-idea, and the sight (vision) of the Father is practically only the
outer limit [*Grenzfall*] of this cosmic (comprehending earthly and
heavenly things) wisdom.

Flight from the world is thus not the word which describes Origen's
customary attitude. Rather, this attitude would best be characterized
by the formal directional movement which can be read from the contents of the first sphere: the way to God as (re-) ascension. In this
sense there has been talk of the pronounced *theologia gloriae* of the
Greeks in general and of Origen in particular. In this everything is
actually graded upwards, everything directed to the *ascensiones in corde*,
everything turned upward from the concealing lowliness to the ra-
diant light of Tabor, to the transparency of the garments and to the
cloud of light out of which breaks the revealing voice. Not that cross,
grave, grief and pain are suppressed; they are there, but always only
like just-vanishing clouds, just-raised curtains, and one never dwells
on them. Certainly Origen knows that all Christian life must be persecution; he himself wrote the fiery exhortation to martyrdom and
suffered martyrdom himself. He had certainly thought out the
beautiful theory of *aporia* according to which insight into a word of the
Logos is never given until that moment in which the spirit seems to
have lost its way in hopelessness and perplexity. Certainly he understands too that the higher one climbs, the stronger becomes the attack
of the enemy powers and one's own inner death—but these are for
him epic battles and heroic opportunities for higher trials, an adventure in one's cosmic career, something like what a Mithras-believer
could experience in his journey through the spheres. So it is, in his

profound idea of the co-redemption of the world with Christ, that it is always the "stronger," the "more advanced," who is allowed to fight for the weaker members of the mystical body; it is always also the wiser (not necessarily the externally more learned, but the one more richly endowed with the gift of wisdom) who mediates to those on the lower steps the light received immediately from Christ. This ascension-model has often been confused with Pelagianism and a self-empowered piety of works. Falsely, we believe, for according to Origen (as later according to Augustine) every step upwards entails being lifted and drawn. That is why we find joined in Origen in such a naive and obvious way the status-consciousness of the "advanced" together with a fully unhypocritical humility and consciousness of sin. All that he is, he is solely by the grace of Christ. That is the only reason we are here insisting that he, in any way at all — is something.

We are not concerned here with criticism but only with description — and only with the affirmation that it is *this* Origen who entered without reserve, as it were, into the broadest ranges of the thinking of the Church. Not only did all the Alexandrians after him, not only did Pamphilius, Gregory the Wonder-Worker, Didymus, Eusebius and the Cappadocians, Jerome, Hilary, Ambrose and, through all these, Augustine accept his model of the *ascensiones in corde*, but also, mediated through these dominant figures, the little thinkers, the preachers, the people. How often does the priest and the monk, even today, read in his breviary the words of Ambrose: "Pay close attention, how Christ climbs up with the apostles, how he climbs down to the masses. For how else could the masses look upon Christ if not as humbled? They don't follow him up to the heights, they don't climb up to the sublime. But where he climbs down, there he finds the weak, for the weak are unable to be on the heights." If these words have not been copied directly from the master, as they seem to be, they at any rate reflect his noblest spirit. Harnack has put together from Jerome's commentaries on Paul [some of the] lost commentaries of Origen. In the Berlin edition of Origen's commentary on Matthew the often word-for-word copied texts of Jerome are supplied. But also for Augustine (to say nothing of Gregory of Nyssa's mysticism of the journey to heaven) the Origenian starting point is clear: the life of the Lord as *transitorium Domini* and thus, for the upward-climbing Christian, as the (absolutely, completely indispensable) "lowest" stage; and thus faith as the (again completely indispensable) starting point of insight, precisely in the sense in which Origen calls gnosis "perfect faith" and calls faith "initial insight"; and thus finally, on the other hand, the (certainly never clearly expressed) tendency to let the gnostic grow out of the domain of faith solely from hearing. In these things lies the almost boundless Origenism of the Fathers.

But, at the deepest level, there is still a *third stratum* in Origen which, just like the first, has not been taken up by the tradition. This is not because, like the first, it proved to be inconsistent with the tradition, but simply because, as the uniquely personal, mysterious and inimitable aspect of this great spirit, it wasn't the kind of thing that could be handed on. The "model," the formal habits of thought, can always be restamped into a school form. But the passion, the breath of genius, necessarily escape this form. Thus it is quite striking how quickly the most vital core in the thought of the Master was overlooked even by his most devoted blind adherents. Ideas which actually still touch this innermost core, but which only take on their full brilliance when they are seen and interpreted out of this center and not transplanted as loosely hanging, "edifying" ideas into another spiritual milieu, such ideas still buzz about for a long time in the air before they disappear for lack of earth and climate, so to speak, or experience another brief flowering in later offshoots like Eriugena. The sustaining ground and middle point of this innermost circle is the equally passionate and tender love for the WORD. Because of this love many things were transformed for Origen from an everyday into an infinitely mysterious mystical reality accessible almost to him alone. In this inwardness of glowing love the miraculous happens: the meaning of the second stage seems to be suspended and reversed. From the most immediate oneness with the God-WORD, and not obscured by the medium of any philosophy, sudden insights break through like flashes of lightning which are among the most unforgettable and yet most forgotten of the history of Christian thought.

There is first, occupying a broad range in his thought, his insight into the essence of scripture as the great sacrament of the real presence of the divine WORD in the world. Only the person who understands what this presence means for Origen will also find some access to what today is often with such utter shallowness and superficiality written off as "allegorizing." For was not Origen also the greatest philologist of Christian antiquity, the one to whom we owe the Hexapla? Are we to think that he didn't know how to take the measure and weight of the letter? His writings teem with highly valuable grammatical remarks, concordance attempts and explanations of the verbal meaning of the text. But if all that was for him only a means, if he touched it only like a body, feeling for the inwardly beating heart of the WORD incarnated in this "body of lowliness" made up of letters and scrolls, one will in the end have to learn to see that this is something quite different from a futile and by now long-outmoded game. The later Fathers knew far better than that. But even with them the "allegorical" method was no longer always surging up from the innermost source, and so, here and there, it had already turned into a routine "technical skill." The immeasurable fruitfulness of this method can be unfolded only when the bible is understood in its immediate relationship with the incarnation and the same laws of understanding are applied to both. We are not saying this in order to defend the allegories of Origen in their individual detail. There could even be somewhere in him a fundamental misunderstanding over the application of the method—more about that later. But a misunderstanding in application already belongs to a secondary zone and doesn't touch the innermost, true intuition.

Next to his scriptural mysticism stands a second doctrine, just as misunderstood today, which, without being understood in its profundity, was handed on only superficially even by his former students, and thus also soon withered away: the truth of the spiritual communion of the WORD. Ferdinand Ebner recently picked up a few splinters of this in his *Word and Love*. But in Origen everything was grounded in the most profound knowledge of an absolute Being which is both WORD and at the same time the substantial nourishment of the created and needy spirit. Separated from this sustaining ground, this doctrine immediately turns into an imaginative and edifying metaphor. Even in Basil and Augustine it has no more meaning than this. To Jerome and Ambrose belongs the merit of having taken over the texts of Origen in their undiminished sharpness and transmitted them to the middle ages where, here and there, among those who could see more deeply (as in the Eucharistic treatise of a William of Saint Thierry), they enjoy an unnoticed resurrection.

One final thought from the circle of his word-mysticism, and that the innermost: the passion of the WORD. This is the insight that the thrust of the lance on Golgotha was only the sacramental likeness of another spear which spiritually struck the WORD and caused it to flow out. It is the presentiment that every word of God poured out in this world is due to this lance. None of his disciples has crawled into this corner of Origenism. That is why, after him, similar lightning-like insights into the mystery of the kenosis and self-emptying of God are rare. Even in Origen they surface only briefly, and then only against the grain and direction of his stream of thought. These are the insights that emptying is wisdom, descent wisdom, fruitlessness wisdom, weakness and powerlessness wisdom. — But it was emptied-out, poured-out, crucified wisdom that had to dawn in rare moments even upon this most intense lover of wisdom. But then wasn't it necessary, in order to follow the direction of God's wisdom, for *descensiones in corde* to be prepared? And indeed *descensiones* which were not already hidden means and preparations for a complex sophisticated ascent, but the genuine pouring out of one's substantial spiritual blood?

This possibility is rarely findable in the vision which Origen had of the Church of his time. The primitive Christian dream of the sinless bride of Christ had come to an end. Origen was the first to look the whole truth in the eye: this spotless one is pure only because she is daily, hourly absolved by the blood of Christ from her daily, hourly new faithlessness and harlotry. If *ascensio* takes place here, then it is only in an always simultaneous descension, right down to the gutter. Again and again Origen applied the tears of the Savior over Jerusalem to his grief over the Church. Later, this grief deeply troubled Augustine too. But although Augustine laments more lyrically and painfully, he did not express the unforgettably hard image that Origen dared to apply.

Through these few briefly mentioned thoughts which stand about and guard the sanctuary of Origen's thought we finally look within with some inkling into the innermost mystery of this soul. *Spirit and Fire* is what we have called this book, because both, spirit as fire and fire as spirit, still glow only in this center: "Flame is what I truly am!" It is a fire that is simultaneously love and Wisdom, simultaneously pure heat and pure light, in the same duality in which this soul experiences her God: as the "consuming fire" and as "the light in which there is no darkness." As love this fire is pure impatience that is content with nothing that is preliminary or imaged, but is immediately consumed, purified and elevated to spirit. As insight it is like an X ray that pierces through finite things until their essence becomes visible. In this center of pure ardor, in the greater fire of God, we reach so to speak the place which comes before every theory of the *ascensiones in corde*, the process which is explained only afterwards with a view to this *ascensio*. For the fire is certainly a leaping and licking upwards, something stretching out of the consumed material of finitude into the boundless. But as God's fire which consumes the bowels of the spirit, it simultaneously involves being burned down ever more deeply, the progressive dredging out of the heart until it has become the pure space and pure ether of the light alone which is radiating through it. But when this final stage is recognized as the decisive one, then the flames of longing can thrust only upwards: this ascent is then no longer a heaven-storming clambering by stages, but a spiritual, cosmic conflagration, a spiritual torch of sacrifice to God.

3

The division of Origen's thought into three strata now reveals the second purpose of this selection. In its attempt to sketch out the Alexandrian's spiritual form without dress and ornament, it will try at the same time to demonstrate his significance for the history of theology. We do not say with Harnack that Origen led theology down a false path from which it never found its way back. But we believe that through his massive influence elements came into theology which, in this form, are not to be found in the bible and which we attempted to sketch out as the second stratum, the *theologia ascendens*. We emphasized that this stratum was not so much a matter of content (and thus not something that directly touches dogma as such) as it was the formal residue of the contents, more an attitude than contents. And because this attitude is maintained anonymously, so to speak, and unnoticed through the whole history of theology, it seemed to be to us important to retrace this path once up to the point where this attitude made its appearance in pure form and where it is still directly united with its (rejected by the church) contents.

Our selection will thus take up from the first stratum only what is needed to make this unity visible. We decided, after some hesitation, not to include the well-known principal texts on the myth of the pre-existence of souls. Instead, we presume knowledge of this. However, we do not hesitate to include texts which openly allude to this myth, but which are important for other reasons, whether because they allow a glimpse into the massive cosmic consciousness of Origen which, for the first and last time in the history of [= before Chardin] Christian thought expands beyond measure the horizon of the historical and opens up a view into an immeasurable series of outcomes [*Schicksalsebene*] with judgments, redemptions, first sins (but always within one single world-epoch which closes with the "God all in all"), or simply because these texts illustrate the attitude of the *ascensio* or the concept of mystery. For the same reason the ex professo subordinationist Trinity texts are also excluded. What they say brings no enrichment to our contemporary image of the world and of God. But that this subordination still broke through in many places, because it was inseparably mingled with the basic structure of Origen's world synthesis, was unavoidable. But, as already indicated, one should not exaggerate this subordination of the Divine Persons. Origen is, even in this matter, the most orthodox of the pre-Nicene theologians. He clearly distinguishes the internal divine processions from the creation of the world. The Son is not, as he was for Arius and many before him, a "means" of creation but the eternal birth of love of the Father. Subordination in Origen has a stronger salvation-history aspect and thus can be better brought into harmony with Nicaean theology. The unequivocal line of subordination is broken by means of this. For on the one hand that the Father is thereby the most known in God, the Son the more mysterious and the Spirit the most inward becomes a mystery known only to Christians (PA 1, 3, 1). On the other hand the way to salvation leads from the objective revelation of the Son, through the subjective appropriation in the Spirit to life made perfect in the Father. This final trinitarian model which places the Spirit between Son and Father seems to us to represent so nicely the internal, implicit form of Origen's whole picture of the world that we have used it as our principle of classification. For what was still lacking in Origen's inner-trinitarian theology he makes up for with his magnificent salvation-history trinitarianism.

Consciously excluded is also his teaching on the sacraments, above all on penance. Although for baptism, Eucharist, matrimony (*Fragments on 1 Corinthians* in Cramer!) and confession Origen is one of the most significant witnesses of early Christianity, still everyone familiar with the period knows how difficult it is to present clearly and unambiguously Origen's idea of baptism in its relationship to the baptism of John and to the baptism of fire, Spirit and blood, how difficult to separate out his doctrine of the Eucharist in its (unquestionably present) realism from his so-called allegorization as spiritual WORD-communion, and above all how difficult it is to disentangle the very serious problems of the unforgivable sins and the power of confession for the laity.[1] But indirectly, as in his trinitarian theology, many of our text selections will have to do with these sacraments. If then the "spiritual" interpretation of the sacraments seems in many places to be the only one represented, let us remember that Origen everywhere, even on the Eucharist, sets the foundation of sacramental realism and at times emphasizes it more strongly than later Fathers such as Gregory of Nazianzen, Basil, Augustine. The reason for this lies in the fundamentally sacramental character of the whole plan of salvation (which in its turn rests on a quasi-sacramental structure of being itself), which will be expressly brought out in the selection.

The idea of pre-existence, inner-divine trinitarian speculation and the doctrine of the sacraments are the only thoroughgoing thought-motifs which will not be treated thematically. The whole tone should lie with the second and third strata: the setting out of the formal theological attitude on the one hand, and of the innermost personal essential heart of the thinker and mystic on the other hand. But critical judgment must make its way right through these two strata.

4

It will be left to the reader to make this critical judgment in depth. We will satisfy ourselves with a few pointers and question marks. In the first instance it seems to be important to indicate in what direction the criticism of Origen (we are no longer talking here about the first group of motifs) should not go. There is today no longer any doubt that Jerome, in his passionate polemic against his once-idolized master, abused his ideas and often completely reversed their meaning. In his works Origen often spoke *gymnastikōs* [with complete openness], developing various hypotheses which he himself did not hold but which he still considered to be worthy of attention and consideration. Such a doctrine was, for example, the transmigration of souls, something which Origen sharply opposed in all his writings. The same is

---

[1] For confession we refer to the works of Poshmann (*Die Sündenvergebung bei Origenes*, 1912) and A. d'Alès (*L'Edit de Calliste*, Paris, 1914). For baptism cf. Hugo Rahner, "Taufe und geistliches Leben bei Origenes" (*Zft. f. Aszese u. Mystik*, 1932) and also my article in *Recherches de science religieuse*, 1936 and 1937: "Le Mysterion d'Origène." The same work contains also a critique of the usual interpretation of the Eucharist. [This work was later published independently as: *Parole et mystère chez Origène* (Paris: Cerf, 1957). — R.J.D.]

true of the doctrine that the soul, at the height of its ascent, gets rid of the body, an opinion that strikes against all principles of Origen's ontology and against his, at core, thoroughly orthodox doctrine of the resurrection. There belongs, finally, to this group the doctrine falsely (in our opinion) attributed to him that, after the completion of the world process (extending over many aeons and countless years), and when the end has come and God is all in all, a new falling away will be possible. This doctrine is placed by Origen among those which are philosophically discussable (this is how C Cels 8, 72 is to be interpreted), but not among those which are to be held.

Criticism of Origen, therefore, has no need to become agitated against a raw, literally understood spiritualism. The way from body to spirit, from material image to ideational truth is a way not to the destruction of body and image, but to its transfiguration, eclipse and "sublation" ['Aufhebung'] only in the Hegelian sense. The statement (falsely) attributed to Maximos the Confessor: "Everything of a phenomenal nature has need of the cross, . . . everything spiritual has need of being buried" (PG 90, 1108B), could be placed over Origen's whole teaching on sublation [Aufhebungslehre]. "No one sees my face and lives," said God to Moses, and so also has "no eye seen" what God has prepared for his chosen ones. All that is only sentient must be consumed by God's fire when it stands before his face, and only by passing through this fire, quasi per ignem, is it saved. That Origen applies this fundamental law to every situation where there is a likeness-truth relationship gives witness only to his consistency. No one has understood more deeply than he the sublation of the old covenant, of the Law with its image-like multiplicity and its visible priesthood, into the unity of Christ. "The law is spiritual," said Paul, and: "There is no law for the spiritual person." But Christ had himself sublated the plurality of earlier moral rules and commandments into the unity of his law of love, just as he replaced the plurality of priesthoods with his eternal priesthood. But to this belongs also the sublation of the "letter" of scripture into the unity of its unique meaning: Christ. To attack Origen for this spiritualizing of image-like materiality would be to miss the point of Christianity itself and turn back "to Jewish fables." But the fact that, even in Christianity, not only is the full content of the sublated preserved in this unity, but also the signs and images and sense-forms keep their signifying function — to argue with this is far from Origen's mind. Just consider for a moment the almost exaggerated significance, even for the simple Christians, which he attributes to knowledge of the Old Testament, or the necessity for salvation which he sees in baptism and confession.

A second error in criticism would seem to be the fundamental rejection of Origen's esotericism. This esotericism is grounded in his doctrine of being itself and is thus not to be disposed of by an external comparison with pagan mystery cults. The esotericism of Origen is rather only the consequence he has fearlessly drawn from the Christian idea that true knowledge is only attained by action, and that consequently the anticipation of a higher knowledge by someone still unpurified and unprepared can be harmful and even existentially false for such a person. For every stage of maturity in existence has its corresponding stage of truth. But to this philosophical truth corresponds the theological one that the WORD of God in its incarnation adapts itself to each of these stages of existence and thus becomes all to all. That a kind of truth-relativism can come from this, that in the adventure of its divine metamorphoses the WORD can go astray and "lie," Origen was already accused of this by Celsus. But the fact of this existential relativism of truth is, as such, not to be denied, not even the esotericism of truth that follows from it. But Origen correctly emphasizes that the WORD, the personal, absolute and sole truth, does not become a liar by its adaptation to different stages of maturity. Otherwise childhood and the age of youth would be lies as such because they are not adulthood. Otherwise "milk" would be poisonous because it is not "solid food." Or, as Origen once said in a paradoxical and Hegelian way: because something is not true does not automatically mean that it is false. For there is a third possibility: to be an indicator or analogy pointing to the truth. Later theology gave up this esotericism. It could do this only at the price of a progressive separation between school theology and mystical (or existential experience-) theology, both of which form a strict unity in Origen.

Criticism of Origenism will begin successfully only when it takes as its object the formal attitude of the *ascensio in corde* and the broad sphere of its consequences in content. Although Origen discovered the unfathomable dictum: "But since he emptied himself in coming into this life, this very being-empty was wisdom" — he never drew the last consequences from this statement. The Alexandrian idea of incarnation always reminds one of the action of a ball which, thrown from great height, in an instant strikes against the ground only to spring up from the earth with tremendous force and return to its starting point. But kenosis — to remain with images for the moment — is more properly to be compared with a wave of the sea which, rushing up on the flat beach, runs out, ever thinner and more transparent, and does not return to its source but sinks into the sand and disappears. The sinking in and the disappearing of the emptied-out WORD is as such, immediately and without any degrees of difference, regression, the "giving over of the kingdom to the Father." The emptying of death and its humiliation is as such already the elimination of the multiplicity of the images and letters, of the law and the prophets, and is the transitory process of making room for the Glory of the Lord. This "I must decrease" is the growth of Christ in us, and only in this form does the whole Pneuma-theology and spiritualizing theology in Origen have its fundamental right to existence.

But in contrast to this, it is part of the model of the *ascensus*-theology to understand the "I must decrease" only as applying to the "outer" human being, while in the "He must increase" the inner, pneumatic is also growing. One encounters here the real danger of the doctrine of mystical inhabitation, according to which in the "depth of the soul" Pneuma and created spirit are in immediate contact and (in the mystery of grace as participation in God) merge flowingly so to speak into one another. Incessantly Origen repeats the words of Paul: "Whoever relies on the Lord" — literally: sticks to, is melted into — "he is one Spirit with Him." But the concrete way in which this unity takes shape is taught only by that other word of Paul: "The world is crucified to me and I to the world," and is illuminated by this word: "I live, no longer I, but Christ lives in me." Origen, who otherwise can look right into the eye and heart of scriptural texts with incomparable candor, not uncommonly, before the decisive words about the "folly of the cross," the "helplessness" and "weakness" of the Christian, begins to blink and squint. For, like so many today, he confuses in the end the heroic and the Christian. The heroic is an exalted form of natural virtue; the Christian, however, is the supernatural form of the death and resurrection of Christ extended to the whole natural world of values. For Origen there exists between the "simple Christian" and the "gnostic" a clear *ascensus*, because in the "gnostic" (from grace and only from grace) the inner pneumatic Life lives higher, stronger and more full of life. These levels are for him an essential law, not something empirical. In the empirical realm it can well be that the apparently spiritual person really isn't so interiorly, that he is proud or in constant danger of becoming proud, while the "poor widow" in reality is much more humble, i.e., is living out her Christianity much more existentially, i.e., stands much "higher" than the seemingly pneumatic person. Thus only the empirical reality is turned around by 180 degrees, while the law of being remains unchanged. One can see here that the theology of the *ascensus* ties in very neatly with "humility," "self-abasement," "self-denial" and the strictest form of monastic asceticism. The irrefutable proof of this is the whole Eastern monastic culture, up to the "high light of Athos," where everywhere, in the genuine dying off of the "outer human being," the "inner human being" rises up to participation in the ever fuller transfiguration of Christ on Tabor. The descent of the cross is only the falling of the shell of the sensual away from the resurrection-reality of the Spirit.

It is not our task here to investigate the influence of this *ascensus*-theology of Origen on the history of the ensuing centuries. We will content ourselves with mentioning that under the primacy of this idea those parts of the system which we earlier said we were not going to criticize were also modified and, so to speak, colored.

Assuredly, Origenism is not "Spiritualism." The body maintains its rights; the world is not pantheistically cursed. But under the tendency to bring together human-spirit and God-Spirit into the infinite, the material pole of creation inevitably suffered devaluation. Oversimplified, it is only the material pole that is subject to death on the cross. Of course, everything material in the spirit itself is "pathic" (subject to suffering). It is indication enough that Origen in his marvelous fountain [*Brunnen*] homily compares the restoration of the image of God in the soul with the cleansing of a painting from extraneous overpainting. Movement is so to speak only in the material pole of the creature, while the innermost point of the spiritual and divine remains unmoved. And if that already quoted statement of Maximos says that the spirit too is in need of being buried, this burial will immediately be explained as "the immovability" in relation to all "natural activities." We have oversimplified, because the whole situation has to do only with a tendency, not with any propositional formula with a definite content. But a tendency is more mobile than a proposition and can creep into the last little crevices of an idea.

But the influence of this formative attitude extends also to the "esotericism" of Origen. For just as there the (God-) Spirit lies unmoved behind the change of material things, so here does the esoteric spiritual meaning lie ready, clear and motionless so to speak behind the image of the letter. Instead of understanding the one body-spiritual, ensouled reality of the world as a unified image that points beyond itself to the infinity of God, the body, the letter, becomes of itself the image that really points to the truth of the sphere of the spirit. Thus it is that Origen seeks in the biblical, earthly history for the image of the heavenly history, instead of interpreting the one body-soul human history as image of the divine history descending to us. And there also follows from this that that heavenly cosmic history of the soul has to function less as true "spirit" than as a second letter behind the first. Thus it is right here and not with the "allegorical" method that criticism should have started. But still, even here, where Origen doesn't go too far in allegorizing, but enters into a false bypath, one has to stand in constant admiration for his unique feeling for the spiritual sense of scripture. His interpretations have so much moderation, so much sound sense and taste (and thus stand out clearly from those of many other allegorizing exegetes) that a totally negative criticism completely misses the point. But few today know, in the age of philological precision and analysis, that the bible has God as its author and that as Origen can't help repeating, it must have a meaning that is worthy of God — or none at all.

That is how it is everywhere in Origen. Shining through every objective mistake and deviation there is always an ultimate Christian and ecclesiastical sense which again and again disarms the critics and leaves them standing in astonishment before so much genuine value. That third stratum we uncovered breaks new trails everywhere and, in the end, overcomes the gnostic tendencies. Only in penultimate things is Origen "heterodox." In ultimate things he is catholic. His childlike attachment to the visible church, to its dogma and its tradition, its priesthood and its sacraments, demonstrates this. It was the fundamental mistake of the otherwise so excellent book of Walther Völker: *Das Vollkommenheitsideal des Origenes* [Origen's Ideal of Perfection] (1931) to have overlooked this thoroughgoing sacramental structure of the whole cosmic system of Origen. We hope, without applying the least force to the intellectual gestalt of the master, to be able to illustrate this sacramental structure in the arrangement of the whole book that lies before us. Church itself is for Origen so little a merely inner community that it was precisely the fundamental tension between ritual church and hierarchical church on the one hand and the *corpus mysticum* on the other that became for him a tragic experience. But he never gave a thought to striking his way out of this conflict by denying the first aspect of the church. The church is for him the great total sacrament which continues the "sacrament" of the Body of Christ, preserves in itself the "sacrament" of the scriptural word, and activates the sacraments of baptism, Eucharist, confession and matrimony as its distinctive marks and functions.

5

At the end of this introduction a few remarks on the arrangement of the selections is in order. The texts were selected evenly from all the works that have come down to us. Most scholars today agree that the translations of Rufinus which used to be so suspect do not deserve this rejection. That he painted over some especially heterodox passages in the *Peri Archōn* and freely reworked the *Commentary on Romans* for which even he didn't have the complete text is quite obvious. But even for the latter work, the catena fragments show that he went about his work conscientiously.[2] That the other homilies almost without exception are translated truly and accurately is revealed both by the Greek fragments and the possible comparisons with other works preserved in Greek. Thus, like everyone else, we made use of the Latin translations. Only in two significant places did we actually have to advert to the authenticity of the Greek passages because of the likelihood of a cover-up by Rufinus (485–487 and 1030).

Apart from the Berlin edition and the works in Migne, we made use of Harnack's edition of the *Commentary on the Apocalypse* (Texte und Untersuchungen 38, 3), the critical edition by Gregg of the *Fragments on Ephesians* which had been published earlier by Cramer (*Journal of Theological Studies* 3, 1902), the rich fragments from Vatican Catenae published by Pitra (*Analecta sacra* 2, 349–483; 3, 1–588) even if they seem to be doubtful for internal and text-critical reasons, the critical edition of an Athos manuscript by E. v. der Goltz (*Eine textkritische Arbeit des 10. bzw. 6. Jahrhunderts*, Texte und Untersuchungen 17 [1899]), and finally the rich treasures still to be found in the *Catena Patrum Graecorum* by Cramer (8 volumes, 1838–1844), as well as the small but worthwhile edition of fragments by Cadiou: *Commentaires*

---

[2] Subsequent studies, and especially the publication and analysis of the extensive Greek papyrus fragments of the *Commentary on Romans* discovered at Toura — cf. Jean Scherer, *Le commentaire d'Origène sur Rom. III.5–V.7. d'après les extraits du papyrus N° 88748 du Musée du Caire et les fragments de la Philocalie et du Vaticanus Gr. 762* (Cairo: Institut français d'archéologie orientale, 1957) — tend only to strengthen this basically positive assessment of the reliability of Rufinus's translations. — R.J.D.

inédits des Psaumes: Étude sur les textes d'Origène contenus dans le manuscrit Vindobonensis 8 (Paris, Les Belles-Lettres 1936).

In choosing and arranging the texts we gave as much preference as possible to brevity and precision of thought so that there is some cutting even within the texts (recognizable by three dots: . . .). The text will be rather strongly broken up by this brevity and perhaps seem tiresome in its terseness. We have tried to make good this disadvantage by the most natural possible arrangement of the texts as well as by brief summaries which can put the reader's hand so to speak on the thread of Ariadne to lead him through the labyrinth of the fragments.

The quoted scripture passages, to the extent that they clearly stand out as such, will be indicated by double quotation marks. Nevertheless, Origen's style is so thoroughly saturated with the language of scripture that there is really no way to draw clear lines between quotation, vague reminiscence and his personal manner of speaking.[3]

We have made no artificial attempts to clean up Origen's dry, unembellished, factual and sentimentality-disdaining style. Origen is effective precisely by contrast between form and thought. He himself mistrusted the art of the rhetoricians, and also occasionally expressed this mistrust.

Finally, not wishing to coin a new word for the untranslatable term *Logos*, we decided to represent it simply with WORD. The capital letters remind us that our English expression isn't intended as a translation but only as a reference to a more comprehensive concept. Only in a few places was the translation SPEECH or reason-WORD unavoidable.[4]

Literature about Origen and a scholarly apparatus have been left out because the purpose of this anthology will have been achieved if it makes a broader and not only theologically educated circle of readers familiar with the basic thought of the Alexandrian, and awakens in them either the curiosity to venture independently into the work of the master, or the satisfaction of having once gazed into that forge in

---

[3] As a further aid to the reader, and especially to those who might wish to use this translation as the starting point for more serious study, I have added in parentheses the actual scriptural references to the passages quoted or obviously alluded to. For further details on how this translation differs from von Balthasar's first and second editions (1938 and 1956), cf. the Translator's Epilogue below. — R.J.D.

[4] It was not always possible to carry out this convention in English in precisely the same way that von Balthasar did in German. — R.J.D.

which, two hundred years after the death of Christ and two hundred before the death of Augustine, the shape of Christian theology was hammered out.

PROLOGUE

OF TENTS AND WELLS

The distinctive characteristic in Origen's thought is the eros of an unquenchable thirst for wisdom. Works are finite, knowledge is infinite (1). But, unlike the ascending eros of Plato, this infinity is conditioned less by the creature's ineradicable orientation to God than by the personally infinite essence of God himself (2–3). Thus, for all eternity, hope is upwardly open (4–6).

True wisdom is life: an eternally bubbling source. It is the living soul of the body of the WORD: the scriptures. But this interiority is at the same time the inner space of every soul (7). Wisdom is wholly fulfilled only as a co-flowing and co-bubbling over of life together with Christ (8–10). The ultimate ground of this source is the Trinity (11–12).

1   "How fair are your houses, O Jacob, your tents, O Israel" (Num 24:5). If you ask about the difference between "house" and "tent," and between "Jacob" and "Israel," even here there is a certain distinction to be made. A house is a solidly grounded, permanent thing, set on a definite plot of ground. Tents, on the other hand, serve as shelter for those who are always on the road, always moving, and who have not yet come to the end of their wandering. Thus, Jacob represents those who are perfect in work and deed. Israel, however, stands for those who labor for wisdom and knowledge. Therefore, because the doing of works and deeds will one day come to a definite end (for the perfection of works is not without end), they who have done all they should and come to perfection in their works, that very perfection will be called a "fair house" (Num 24:5). But they who labor for wisdom and knowledge, because there is no end to that task — for what could ever put a limit on God's wisdom? Indeed the more one enters into it, the deeper one goes, and the more one investigates, the more inexpressible and inconceivable it becomes, for God's wisdom is incomprehensible and

immeasurable — thus he does not praise the houses of those who enter upon the path of wisdom — for they never come to an end — , but he admires their "tents" in which they continually wander and make progress; and the more progress they make the more does the road to be travelled stretch out into the measureless. And so, contemplating in the Spirit these progressions, he calls them the "tents of Israel." And true it is, when we make some progress in knowledge and gain some experience in such things, we know that when we have come to a certain insight and recognition of the spiritual mysteries, the soul rests there, in a certain sense, as in a "tent." But when it begins to make fresh sense again of what it finds there and moves on to other insights, it pushes on with folded tent, so to speak, to a higher place and sets itself up there, pegged down by strong conclusions; and again the soul finds in the place another spiritual meaning, for which the conclusions from earlier insights have doubtless prepared the way, and so the soul seems always to be pulled on toward the goal that lies ahead (cf. Phil 3:14), moving on, so to speak, in "tents." For once the soul has been struck by the fiery arrow of knowledge, it can never again sink into leisure and take its rest, but it will always be called onward from the good to the better and from the better to the higher.

2   When they who are humble occupy themselves with great and marvelous things which are too great for them (cf. Ps 131:1), that is, with those doctrines that are truly "great" and in those thoughts that are "marvelous," they humble themselves "under the mighty hand of God" (1 Pet 5:6).

3   "O the depths of the riches and wisdom and knowledge of God!" (Rom 11:33). To see that Paul uttered this in desperation of ever coming to understand it fully, listen to what he then says: "How unsearchable are his judgments and how impossible to discover his ways!" For he does not say "hard to discover" but "impossible to discover." . . . For however far one may advance in speculation and make progress by unremitting study, even assisted by God's grace and with one's mind "enlightened" (cf. Eph 1:18), one cannot get to the end of what one is searching for. Nor is this possible for any created mind, for as soon as it has found something of what it was looking for, it catches sight of something new to inquire about. . . . Therefore it is to be desired that everyone, according to one's strength, should "forget what lies behind and push forward to what lies ahead" (Phil 3:14), both to "better works" and to a purer sense and understanding "through Jesus Christ our Savior" (Tit 3:8, 6).

4   Those who hope do not maintain the same hope they had in the beginning. Rather when they make progress as God wants, they thus grow
in hope, and the more their love is expanded the stronger becomes their
hope as well . . . and out of God's love their hope grows stronger.

5   And I will not only hope but "hope beyond hope" in the progress of
love. For "love hopes all things" (1 Cor 13:7).

6   "But I will hope always" (Ps 71:14). Now it is quite possible that
God will always be praised in song, always be blessed, and that there
will always be chaste living and just conduct. But who can "hope
always"? Because the person who always hopes will never reach what
he hopes for. Thus, someone might say that this "always" refers not to
the length of eternity but only to this life. Someone else will, on the
other hand, understand this "always" of the periods of eternity, but in
such a way that the limit of hope is knowledge of the Trinity. But a
third reader will say that this "always" is spoken precisely with the Holy
Trinity in mind; but such insight is of course limitless.[1]

7   The patriarchs always had a lot to do with wells. For the scripture
tells us that Isaac, after the Lord "blessed him and made him very
great" (cf. Gen 26:12f, 15), undertook a great work. He began, it is
written, to dig wells, "wells which his father's servants had dug in the
time of Abraham his father, but which the Philistines had stopped and
filled with earth." And so first "he dwelt at the well of vision" (cf. Gen
25:11), and illuminated by the well "Vision" he went from there to
open other wells, and not new ones at first, but those which his father
Abraham had dug. And when he had dug the first well, "the
Philistines," it is written, "were envious of him" (Gen 26:14). But he
didn't allow himself to be deterred by their jealousy and he did not give
in to their envy but, as it is written, "dug the wells again" (Gen 26:18)
. . . , and also dug other new ones in the "valley of Gerar," not he of
course, but his servants, "and he found there," it is written, "a well of living
water" (Gen 26:19-20). But then the shepherds of Gerar began to quarrel
with the shepherds of Isaac, saying that this was their water; so he called
the well "Contention" because they had dealt contentiously with him
there. But Isaac drew back from their quarrelsomeness and

---

[1] The idea of a progress that lasts through all eternity is common among
the Greek Fathers of the first centuries. Irenaeus allows faith to continue in
the midst of the vision of God because God always has ready new revelations
of His glory. Gregory of Nyssa shifts even the essence of beatitude into the
moved and still blessed longing for the ever-unattainable and escaping God.

dug yet another well and they quarrelled, it is written, over that too, and he called that "Enmity." And he drew back from there and dug yet another well, over which they did not quarrel, and gave it the name "Broad Places," for he said: "Now the Lord has made room for us and spread us out over the land" (Gen 26:21–22).

As the holy Apostle well said somewhere when contemplating the greatness of the mysteries: "Who is sufficient for these things?" (2 Cor 2:16). In the same way, or rather in a far different way—as far beneath him as we are—do we also say as we see so much depth in the mysteries of the wells: "Who is sufficient for these things?"; for who would be worthy to explain the mystery [*sacramentum*] of such wells or the deeds told about them, unless we call upon the Father of the living WORD and He Himself deigns to put His WORD in our mouth so that we may be able to draw out for you in your thirst a little living water from such rich and varied wells as these?

There are thus wells which the servants of Abraham dug, but which the Philistines had filled with earth. Isaac undertook to clean these first. Philistines hate water and love the earth. Isaac loves water; he is constantly looking for wells; he cleans out old ones and opens new ones. Gaze now on our Isaac, who was offered up as a victim for us, as he comes into the "valley of Gerar" (Gen 26:17) . . . : he wants first of all to dig those wells which the servants of his father Abraham had dug, that is he wants to renew the wells of the Law and the Prophets which the Philistines had filled with earth. Who are they who fill wells with earth? They are without doubt those who put an earthly and fleshly understanding on the Law and block up its spiritual and mystical meaning so that they neither themselves drink nor allow others to drink. Listen to our Isaac, the Lord Jesus, saying in the gospels: "Woe to you Scribes and Pharisees, for you have taken away the key of knowledge, and you neither enter yourselves nor permit others to enter" (Lk 11:52 and Mt 23:13). . . . He "departs from them" (Gen 26:22); for he cannot be with people who want no water in the well but only earth, and he says to them: "Behold, your house will be left desolate" (Mt 23:38). Thus Isaac digs new wells, and even the servants of Isaac dig. Isaac's servants are Matthew, Mark, Luke, John; his servants are Peter, James, Judas; his servant is the apostle Paul; all these dig the wells of the New Testament. But also because of this, "Contention" (Gen 26:21) springs up among those who have their minds set on earthly things (Phil 3:19) and allow neither new wells to be dug nor old ones to be cleaned. They contradict the wells of the gospel, they oppose the Apostles. And because they oppose everything and are in everything contentious, it is said to them: "Because you have made yourselves unworthy of the grace of God, we will from now on turn to the Gentiles" (cf. Acts 13:46).

After this, then, Isaac dug a third well and called the name of that place: "Broad Places". . . . For truly Isaac has now been extended and "his name is increased over all the earth" (Gen 26:22), since he has filled us with knowledge of the Trinity. . . . For the servants of Isaac, going out across the whole face of the earth, dug wells and showed the living water to all, "baptizing all nations in the name of the Father and of the Son and of the Holy Spirit" (cf. Mt 28:19). For "the earth is the Lord's and the fulness thereof" (Ps 24:1). But also each one of us who ministers to the word of God digs a well and searches for living water with which to refresh his hearers. If therefore I too begin to analyze the sayings of the Old Testament and to search for their spiritual meaning, if I will try to take away the veil of the Law . . . I will indeed be digging wells, but right away friends of the letter will calumniate me and plot against me; they will immediately prepare for war and persecution denying that truth can stand anywhere but on the earth. . . . But we will never stop digging wells of living water. . . . But if, from among those who are now listening to me speak, someone familiar with secular letters should say: what you are saying is ours, and it is learned from our skill; these very things which you are discussing and teaching are our art of eloquence! And should he come at me with "Contention" like a Philistine and say: you are digging the well on my land, and should he seem to demand justly for himself what is of his own earth, I will still reply to this that all earth contains water; but they who are Philistines and have their minds set on earthly things (Phil 3:19) do not know that water is found in all the earth, do not know that a rational sense and the image of God is found in every soul, do not know that faith, piety and religion can be found in everyone. What good does it do you to have knowledge and not know how to use it, to have words and not be able to speak? That, now, is the proper work of the servants of Isaac who dig "wells of living water" (cf. Gen 26:19) in all the earth, that is, they speak the WORD of God to every soul and find fruit. . . .

This, then, is how the wells which Abraham dug, i.e., the scriptures of the Old Testament, were filled with earth by the Philistines, whether by bad teachers, Scribes and Pharisees, or even by the enemy powers; and their veins were blocked up lest they provide drink for the descendants of Abraham. For that people cannot drink from the scriptures; they suffer thirst for the WORD of God until Isaac comes and opens them so that his servants may drink. . . . HE was opening the wells to them, for they were saying: "Did not our heart burn within us while he opened to us the scriptures?" (Lk 24:32). He thus opened these wells and "gave them the names," it is written, "which his father Abraham had given them" (Gen 26:18). . . . For he did not change the titles of the wells. Now it is remarkable that Moses is called Moses even by us, and every one of the prophets is called by his own name. For Christ did not change their names but their understanding. But He makes this change that we might no longer give heed to "Jewish fables" and "interminable genealogies" (cf. Tit 1:14; 2 Tim 1:4), because they turn away from truth and turn instead to fables. He therefore opened the wells and taught us not to look for God in a particular place but to know that "in all the earth is offered a sacrifice to his name" (cf. Mal 1:11). For now is that time when "true worshippers will worship the Father" neither in Jerusalem nor on Mount Gerizim but "in spirit and in truth" (cf. Jn 4:20–23). Thus God does not live in a place nor on the earth, but in the heart. And if you are looking for the place of God, a clean heart is his place. For in this place he said he would live when he spoke through the prophet: "I will be their God, says the Lord" (2 Cor 6:16; Lev 26:12). Look, therefore, to see whether there is not in the soul of each of us a "well of living water" (Gen 26:19), a certain heavenly sense and hidden image of God, and whether the Philistines, i.e., the adversary powers, have filled this up with earth. With what kind of earth? With carnal feelings and earthly thoughts, and for that reason we have borne "the image of what is earthly" (cf. 1 Cor 15:49). At that time, then, since we were bearing "the image of what is earthly," the Philistines filled up our wells. But now, because our Isaac [Christ] has come, let us accept his coming and dig our wells, let us throw the earth out of them, let us purify them of every dirty thing and from all worthless and worldly thoughts, and we will find in them that "living water," of which the Lord speaks: "He who believes in me, rivers of living water will flow from his body" (Jn 7:38). See how great the generosity of the Lord is: wells are what the Philistines filled up, envying our poor little veins of water, and in place of this, wells are turned into rivers for us!

And so if you, hearing this today, are faithfully taking what you hear, Isaac [Christ] is at work in you too; he is purifying your hearts from earthly feelings. And as you see so many great mysteries hidden in

the divine scriptures, you are making progress in understanding, you
are making progress in the spiritual perception of things. You yourselves will also begin to be teachers and "rivers of living water" will
flow from you (cf. Jn 7:38). For the WORD of God is present and
this is now His work, to remove the earth from each of you and open
up your fountain. For he is within you and does not come from outside, just as "the kingdom of God is within you" (cf. Lk 17:21). And
that woman who had lost a drachma did not find it outside but in her
own house after she "lit a candle and cleaned the house" (cf. Lk 15:8)
of the dirty and unclean things which the sloth and idleness of a long
time had piled up, and there she found the drachma. And you too, if
you light a candle, if you apply to yourself the illumination of the Holy
Spirit and "in His light you see the light" (cf. Ps 35(36):10). For
within you is set the image of the heavenly King. For when God made
man in the beginning, "in his image and likeness he made him" (cf.
Gen 1:26; 5:1); and this image he did not place outside but within
him. This image could not be seen in you while your house was dirty
and filled with unclean things and rubbish. This fountain of knowledge was located in you, but it could not flow because the Philistines
had filled it with earth and made in you an "image of earthly things"
(cf. 1 Cor 15:49). But now, purified by the WORD of God through
hearing this, let the "heavenly image" shine forth in you. . . . The
Son of God is the painter of this image. And because He is so great a
painter, his image can be obscured by lack of care, but it can never be
wiped out by evil. For the image of God always remains even if you
yourself paint over it an "image of earthly things." That is a picture
which you paint yourself. For when concupiscence has darkened you,
you have added an earthly color; if you are seething with greed, you
have mixed in another color. And when anger makes you bloody you
have added still a third color. Pride adds yet another dark color, and
godlessness another. And thus with each and every type of evil, collected
so to speak in the different colors, you paint on yourself an "earthly
image" which God did not make in you. Therefore we must beseech
him who said through the prophet: "Behold, I sweep away your transgressions like a cloud, and your sins like mist" (Isa 44:22).

8   Let us also try to do as Wisdom encourages us with the words:
"Drink water from your own cisterns and from your own wells, and
let them be for yourself alone" (Prov 5:15, 17). Make an effort, you
too, my hearer, to have your own well and your own fountain. . . .
There is within you the nature "of living water," there are inexhaustible

veins and irrigating streams of the spiritual sense, if only they are not blocked with earth and rubbish. Get up, then: dig out your earth and clean out the dirt; that is, get rid of the sloth of your nature and shake out the hardness of your heart.

9   But let us go back to Isaac and dig with him "wells of living water" (Gen 26:19). . . . Let us persevere with him in digging until our wells are overflowing and our fields are soaked so that the knowledge of the scriptures may not only be enough for ourselves, but that we might also instruct others so that the people can drink, and also the flocks. Let the wise hear, and also the simple . . . while our hearts are being illumined and purified by the Lord Jesus Christ our Savior Himself, to whom be glory and power, for ever and ever. Amen.

10   Come, I pray, Lord Jesus, Son of God, "lay aside your garments" which you have put on for my sake, and gird yourself for me and "pour water into a basin and wash the feet" of your servants (cf. Jn 13:3–15); rinse away the filth of your sons and daughters. "Wash the feet" of our souls so that, imitating you and following you we may put off our old "garments" and say: "At night I had put off my garment, how could I put it on?" and that we may further say: "I had bathed my feet, how could I soil them?" (Cant 5:2, 3). For as soon as you have washed my feet you also make me lie down beside you to hear you say: "You call me Teacher and Lord; and you are right, for so I am. If I then, your Lord and Teacher, have washed your feet, you also ought to wash one another's feet" (Jn 13:13–14). And therefore I take water which I draw from the fountains of Israel . . . and pour it into the basin of my heart, receiving its meaning in my heart, and I take the feet of those who come forward and prepare themselves for washing, and, as far as in me lies, I desire to wash the feet of my brothers . . . so that all of us, purified together through the WORD in Christ, may not be ejected from the bridal chamber of the bridegroom because of dirty garments, but clothed in white, and with washed feet and a "clean heart," we might lie down at the banquet of the bridegroom, our Lord Jesus Christ.

11   "As the deer thirsts for springs of water, so does my soul thirst for you, O God" (Ps 42:1). If we do not thirst for the three sources of water, we will not find even one source of water. The Jews seemed to have thirsted for one source of water, God. But because they did not thirst for Christ and the Holy Spirit, they were unable to drink even from God. The heretics seemed to have thirsted for Christ Jesus, but because they did not thirst for the Father who is God of the Law and

the Prophets, they do not for this reason drink of Jesus Christ either. Those who honor one God but think little of the prophecies, they have not thirsted for the Holy Spirit which is in the prophets, and for this reason they drink neither from the source of the Father nor from him who cried out in the temple the words: "If anyone has thirst, let him come to me and drink" (Jn 7:37). "The breasts of the rock," therefore, "did not run dry" (cf. Jer 18:14); but they "left the source of living water" (Jer 2:13), the source of living water did not leave them. For God does not separate himself from anyone, but "those who separate themselves from him are lost" (cf. Ps 73:27). Instead, God comes close to some and goes to meet everyone who comes towards Him . . . for he says: "I will come closer to them than the tunic on their skin" (cf. Jer 13:11), because "I," it is written, "am a God who comes close and not a God afar off, says the Lord" (cf. Jer 23:23). . . . The water of the Holy Spirit does not flee; it is, rather, each one of us who, in sinning, runs away instead of drinking from the Holy Spirit.

12   This discourse is a song of praise — and that is what theology is all about.

I

SOUL

THE WORLD AND THE SOUL

SELF-KNOWLEDGE

The never-ending thirst for wisdom (13) must be chosen by souls as their first object. This necessarily means first of all a strong orientation inward involving the closing of one's eyes to the outer world. But the soul is itself the center point of the world; directly before its inner eye dimensions are unrolled which are unknown to the external world of bodies. To ask about the soul means to cast one's gaze into the abyss of eternal eons and immeasurable waves of fate (14). Since in this event, spilling over far beyond the boundaries of time, the salvation and damnation of the soul is played out, self-knowledge becomes an absolute requirement (15).

The inner space is a new, spiritual world (16) which, in the miracle of memory, comprehends the whole breadth of the bodily world (17), but which still possesses a completely different power of comprehension: to be the place where God dwells and acts (18–20).

13   Just as when our eyes rest upon something made by an artist, . . . our mind burns to know how and in what way and to what purpose it was made, far more and beyond all comparison with such things does our spirit burn with an unspeakable longing to know the why and wherefore of the works of God which we see. This longing, this love, we believe, has been without doubt planted in us by God. And just as the eye naturally seeks light and sight, and our body naturally desires food and drink, so does our spirit have its own natural desire to know God's truth and the causes of things. But we have received this desire from God not just so that it never should or could be gratified; for otherwise "the love of truth" (2 Thes 2:10) would seem to have been planted in our spirit by the Creator in vain.

14   "Be still, and know that I am God" (Ps 46:10). It is the principal duty of "knowledge" to acknowledge the Trinity. But after that, it is to recognize his creatures according to him who said: "For it is he who

gave me unerring knowledge of what exists, to know the structure of the world and the activity of the elements; the beginning and end and middle of times" and so forth (WisSol 8:17–18). Thus there will also be in this a certain self-knowledge of the soul by which it should know what its substance is, whether corporeal or incorporeal; whether it is simple, or composed of two or three or even more parts. But the soul should also know, according to the questions that some ask, whether it has been made or not made by anyone at all; and, if made, how it was made. It should know whether, as some think, its very substance is contained in its bodily seed and it has its beginning together with the beginning of the body; or whether, coming finished from outside, it puts on a previously prepared and formed body within the female womb. And if that's the way it is, whether it comes newly created and then is made only when the body is formed (so that the necessity of animating a body is seen to be the cause of its being made) or whether, having been previously made, it is for some reason thought to come to take on a body. And if for some reason it is thought to be brought about in this way, it should know what this reason is. For all this to be knowable, "knowledge" is necessary.

But the question also has to be asked whether the soul takes on a body only once and, after it has left it, does not go back to it, or, after it has once left the body it has taken, it will take it up again; and if so, whether it will always have the body it has taken, or will lay it aside again at some time. And if, according to the authority of scripture, the consummation of the world is still to come and this corruptible state will be changed into an incorruptible state, there would seem to be no doubt that a soul cannot come a second or third time into a body in this state of life. For if this were held, it would necessarily follow that, because of these never-ending successions, the world would have no end.

In addition, the soul in its self-knowledge should also ask if there exists some order of spirits, that is, certain spirits of the same substance as itself, and others not of the same substance but different, that is, whether there are other rational spirits like itself, and others which do not have reason; and also ask if its own substance is the same as that of the angels, since there is thought to be no distinction between rational and rational. It should ask further whether it is not this way by substance, but will be this way by grace, if it has merited it, or whether it cannot be made altogether like the angels unless it has received this as a quality and likeness of its nature. For it seems possible for it to be given back what it has lost, but not to be granted what the Creator has not given from the beginning.

And in its self-knowledge the soul should also ask about this: whether the power of its spirit can come and go and is changeable, or, once acquired, is never lost again. But what need is there to go on mentioning the reasons why the soul should know itself, except that, should it neglect "to know itself" perfectly, it might be commanded to "go out and follow in the tracks of the flock and pasture your kids," and to do this not beside its own tent but "beside the shepherds' tents" (Cant 1:8), while for the soul which is ready there are prepared all sorts of opportunities for it to become proficient, according to its ability, in the "utterance of knowledge" (1 Cor 12:8)? But these things might be said by the WORD of God to the soul which is indeed set on the paths of progress but has not yet risen to the height of perfection. Because it is progressing, it is called "beautiful." But for it to be able to come to perfection, it is necessary for it to be threatened. Because unless it comes to know itself, through the things I have mentioned, and becomes proficient in the WORD of God and the divine law, it will suffer the fate of taking in various of these opinions and of following men who have said nothing of note, nothing from the Holy Spirit. This is what it means to "follow the tracks of the flocks" and follow the teachings of those who have themselves remained sinners and can provide no remedy for sinners. Whoever follows these, yes "goats," whoever follows the judgment of sinners, will seem, in their "pasturing," to be passing by "the shepherds' tents," that is, "pasturing" on the various sects of the philosophers. Consider then more fully what a terrible reality is contained in this figure. It says: "Go out in the tracks of the flocks" (Cant 1:8); as if the soul were already inside and residing within the mysteries, but, because it is neglectful of "knowing itself" and of inquiring what it is and how it should act and what it ought to do or not do, it is told: "Go out," as if, because of the guilt of this slothfulness, it were being cast out by the one in charge. Thus it is a terribly great danger for the soul to neglect the study of itself and its self-knowledge. But perhaps, since we gave a twofold explanation of the self-knowledge of the soul, it will seem, according to that interpretation by which it neglects to examine its own actions and seek after its own progress or guard against vices, that it is rightly told: "Go out," by which it seems as if it were driven outside from within. But if one follows the second interpretation in which we said that the soul must acknowledge its own nature and substance, and its state whether past or future, then the situation is serious. For how easily will one find such a soul which is so perfect, so superior, that the meaning and understanding of all these things are open to it? To this we will reply that the words we are talking about are not directed to all souls, and that the spouse is not speaking here to the "maidens," nor to the other "women" nor to the "eighty concubines" or "sixty queens," but to the one who alone among all "women" is called "beautiful" and "perfect" (Cant 6:7-8). To certain beloved souls, therefore, is this spoken.

15   One of those seven who had the reputation among the Greeks of being unique in wisdom, is said to have uttered, among other things, this marvelous maxim: "Know yourself" or "Recognize yourself." But Solomon, of whom we noted in our preface that he preceded all these in time and wisdom and in factual knowledge, speaking to the soul as if to a woman with a certain threat, says: "If you do not know yourself, O fairest among women" (Cant 1:8), and acknowledge that the causes of your beauty stem from the fact that "you have been made in the image of God" (cf. Gen 1:27) by which you possess a wealth of natural comeliness, and acknowledge how beautiful you were from the beginning (even if you now still excel over the rest of the "women" and you alone are called "beautiful" among them), nevertheless, "if you do not know yourself," what you are — for I do not wish your beauty to seem good by comparison with inferiors, but from the fact that you stand up to careful comparison with yourself and your beauty — if you do not do this, I order you "to go out" and take your place in the worst "tracks of the flock" (Cant 1:8) — until you understand from the experience of these things how great an evil it is for the soul not to know itself and its beauty.

16   You must understand that you are another world in miniature, and that there is in you sun and moon and also stars. If this were not so, the Lord would never have said to Abraham: "Look toward heaven and number the stars, if you are able to number them; so shall your descendants be" (Gen 15:5). . . . Hear something else that the Lord says to his disciples: "You are the light of the world" (Mt 5:14). Do you still doubt that there is sun and moon in you, you to whom is said that you are the "light of the world"? Do you want to hear still more about yourself, lest perchance by thinking small and humbly of yourself you might neglect your life as of little worth? This world has its own governor, it has someone who rules it and lives in it, the almighty God, as he himself says through the prophet: "Do I not fill heaven and earth? says the Lord" (Jer 23:24). Listen then to what the almighty

God also says about you, that is, about human beings: "I will live in them," he says, "and move among them" (2 Cor 6:16). He adds something more regarding you yourself: "And I will be a father to them, and they shall be my sons and daughters, says the Lord Almighty" (2 Cor 6:18). This world possesses the Son of God, it possesses the Holy Spirit, as the prophet says: "By the WORD of the Lord the heavens were made, and all their host by the breath of his mouth" (Ps 33:6). . . . Hear too what Christ says to you: "And lo, I am with you always, to the close of the age" (Mt 28:20). And of the Holy Spirit it is said: "And I will pour forth of my spirit on all flesh, and they shall prophesy" (Joel 2:28).

17   "Prepare the way of the Lord" (Luke 3:4). What "way of the Lord" should we prepare? A bodily way? But is it even possible for the WORD of God to travel along such a route? Is not an internal road to be prepared for the Lord, and straight and even paths built up in our heart? This is the way by which came in the WORD of God which dwells in the capacity of the human heart. Great and spacious is the human heart, and capable of holding a great deal, if only it is clean. . . . Whatever cities we pass through, we have them in spirit; and their qualities and the locations of their streets and walls and buildings dwell in our heart. The road by which we entered we hold in the picture and description of memory; the sea over which we sailed we embrace in silent thought. Not small, I said, is the human heart which can hold so much. But if it is not small, which holds so much, then the way of the Lord must be prepared in it and the path made straight so that the WORD of God and wisdom might walk on it.

18   Holy things are not to be sought in a place but in actions and life and customs. If these are found to be in accord with God and in accord with God's commandment, even if you are at home, even if in the market—in the market do I say?—even if you should be in the theater but devoted to the WORD of God, do not doubt that you are in a holy place. Or don't you think that Paul, when he entered the theater or when he came into the Areopagus and preached Christ to the Athenians, was in a holy place? And also when he was walking among the altars and idols of the Athenians where he found the inscription: "To an unknown god" (Acts 17:23) which he made the starting point of his preaching of Christ, even there, while "passing by" the "altars" of the gentiles, he was in a holy place because he was thinking holy things.

19   I do not seek a "holy place" (cf. Lev 24:9) on earth but in the heart. For the spiritual soul is called a "holy place." That is why the Apostle says: "Give no room to the devil" (Eph 4:27).

20   I think that we have received our very soul and our body as a deposit from God. And would you like to see an even greater deposit that you have received from God? God has entrusted to your very soul his own "image and likeness" (cf. Gen 1:26–27). That therefore which was loaned to you must be returned in the same undamaged condition in which you received it. . . . Was not this the sacred commission the apostle was giving to his chosen disciple when he said: "O Timothy, guard what has been entrusted to you" (1 Tim 6:20)? And I will also add this, that we have received Jesus Christ as a "deposit" and have the Holy Spirit as a "deposit."

BETWEEN MATTER AND SPIRIT

In self-knowledge, the soul is given a glimpse of its own position in the cosmos and its most common structure: Everything which is creature is inseparably spirit-body (21), and in such a way that bodiliness, although distinguished from spirit, is still only its accompanying appearance (22–23) and shadow (24–25). But the fundamental relationship of both poles is that of unity-plurality (27–29), truth-likeness (26, 30), core-shell (31), thought-feeling (32). Because this structure is the most pervasive and most common, the soul can move on from anything sensible to something spiritual, and understand all bodily reality as expression and image (33).

21   God created two general natures of things: visible nature, that is, corporeal, and invisible nature, which is incorporeal. These two natures are subject to all kinds of changes. The invisible nature which is endowed with reason changes itself by plan and intention because it is endowed with freedom of will, and thus sometimes does good and sometimes the opposite. But the corporeal nature is subject to substantial change; and thus matter is offered as an obedient instrument for all that God, the maker of all things, wishes to form and build or reshape.

22   Some things are made for their own sake, others by consequence and for the sake of the former. Made for its own sake is the living being endowed with reason; made for its use are the animals and the plants of the earth.

23   Logic and reason compel us to understand that rational natures
were created first of all, and that material substance can really be distinguished from them only in theory, and that it seems to have been
made for them or after them, and that they neither live nor have lived
without it. For only the life of the Trinity can be properly considered
to be incorporeal.

24   When someone gives us some bodily object or other, we do not say
that so-and-so has given us the shadow of the object. (For it was not
with the intention of giving us two things, the object and its shadow,
that he gave us the object; rather, the intention of the giver is to give
the object, and it follows from the giving of the object that we also receive the shadow.) So too, if we consider, with our minds fixed on
higher things, the nobler gifts given us by God, we will say that what
follows upon the great and heavenly spiritual gifts (cf. 1 Cor 12:1, 4,
7) are the corporeal things that go with them, given "to each" of the
saints "for the common good" (1 Cor 12:7) or "in proportion to our
faith" (Rom 12:6) or "as" the giver "wills" (1 Cor 12:11).

25   All material and corporeal things, whatever they may be, have the
nature of a fleeting and frail shadow.

26   The "likeness [ornament] of gold" (Cant 1:11) was, for example,
that "tabernacle made with hands" of which the Apostle speaks: "For
Jesus has entered, not into a sanctuary made with hands, a copy of
the true one, but into heaven itself" (Heb 9:24). Therefore the things
which are in heaven, invisible and incorporeal, they are the true
things; but those which are on earth, visible and bodily, they are called
not true things but "copies of the true things."

27   And truly one must marvel at how all the things that are of this
world are in flux, fleshly things too, and how fleeting and fragile are
the things which among unbelievers are thought to be lasting and permanent. But whoever considers the true nature of things and reflects
upon the supposed goods of this life, how things continually change
and pass away, that one might well say: "How fleeting it is."

28   For nothing that is material and bodily is one, but everything that
is thought to be one is split and cut up and divided into several things,
thus losing its unity. For the good is one, and shameful things are
many; and truth is one, but lies are many; and true righteousness is
one, but many the ways of counterfeiting it; and wisdom is one, but
many are the wisdoms "of this age or of the rulers of this age, who are
doomed to pass away" (1 Cor 2:6); and the WORD of God is one, but
many the words opposed to God.

29   He who is one, when he sins, becomes many, cut off from God and divided in parts, and fallen away from the unity.

30   Even though nothing sensible is true, one cannot say that, because the sensible is not true, the sensible is therefore false; for the sensible can have an analogy to the actual.

31   Rational beings which occupy the place of honor have reason when they are formed as children; but non-rational and soulless beings have only the outer shell which is created along with the child.

32   There is, next to this visible and sensible world which consists of heaven and earth (or, of heavens and earth), another world of things not seen. And all this is a world unseen, an invisible and intelligible world where the clean of heart will look upon its aspect and beauty and, by this viewing, be made ready to move on to the very vision of God himself, to the extent that God can be seen.

33   The Apostle Paul teaches us that "the invisible things of God are understood" from the visible things, and "the unseen through the seen . . . " (cf. Rom 1:20 and 2 Cor 4:18), thus pointing out that this visible world contains instruction about the invisible world and that this earthly condition contains "images of the heavenly things" (cf. Heb 9:24), so that from the things that are below we can ascend to the things which are above, and that from what we see on earth we can perceive and understand something of what is in heaven. A certain similarity to these heavenly things was given by the Creator to earthly creatures by means of which their varieties could more easily be comprehended. And perhaps, just as God "made man in his image and likeness" (Gen 1:27), he also furnished other creatures with a similarity to certain other heavenly images. Perhaps each earthly thing has an image and likeness of heavenly things to such an extent that even "a grain of mustard which is the smallest of all the seeds" (Mt 13:31–32) has something of an image and likeness in heaven; and in this case, because the composition of its nature is such that, while being the "smallest of all the seeds it becomes the greatest of shrubs so that the birds of the air can come and dwell in its branches," it contains the likeness not just of any heavenly image, but of the "kingdom of heaven" itself. Thus it is possible for the other seeds of the earth also to contain some kind of heavenly likeness and meaning. If this is true of seeds, then certainly also of bushes; and if of bushes then certainly also of animals, whether winged or creeping or quadruped. But this can also be understood further in such a way that, just as the "grain of mustard" contains not just the one similitude of the

"kingdom of heaven" because of the dwelling "of the birds in its branches," but also has another image of perfection, namely, of faith, so that "if" anyone "has faith" "like a grain of mustard," he can say "to a mountain to move" itself, and "it will move" (1 Cor 13:2), so is it possible that the other things too, not just in one particular respect but in many, bear an "image and likeness of heavenly things." And since, for example, there are in "the grain of mustard" many virtues which contain "images of heavenly things," the very last of these is that practice which takes place among human beings in bodily ministry. Thus it can also be seen in other things, whether seeds or bushes or roots of herbs, or even in animals, that they are indeed of bodily use and service to human beings, but still have the forms and images of incorporeal things by which the soul can be instructed to contemplate also those things which are invisible and heavenly. And perhaps this is what that writer of divine wisdom has in mind when he says: "For it is he who gave me unerring knowledge of what exists, to know the structure of the world and the activity of the elements; the beginning and end and middle of times, the alternations of the solstices and the changes of the seasons, the cycles of the years and the constellations of the stars, the natures of animals and the tempers of wild beasts, the powers of spirits and the reasonings of men, the varieties of plants and the virtues of roots; I learned both what is secret and what is manifest" (WisSol 7:17–21). Look now whether we cannot more clearly explain from these words of scripture what we have been discussing. For this writer of divine wisdom, after listing each of these things, says at the end that he has received "knowledge of what is secret and what is manifest," and he shows in this way that everything that is "manifest" is related to one of those things which are in "secret"; that is each individual visible thing has some likeness and relationship of meaning to invisible things. Therefore because it is impossible for a human being living in the flesh to recognize something that is secret and invisible without conceiving some image and likeness of it from visible things, it is my conviction that he who "made all things in wisdom" (cf. Ps 104:24) created each species of visible things on earth in such a way as to put in them a certain teaching and recognition of invisible and heavenly things by which the human mind would ascend to a spiritual understanding and seek out the causes of things among heavenly things so that, instructed by the divine wisdom, it might itself be able to say: "All that is secret and is manifest is known to me" (cf. WisSol 7:21).

SLIDING MIDDLE

But the soul is neither spirit nor body, but the transitional middle between both. This is not of course meant as an essential definition. Because for Origen (as for most of the early Fathers) the human being is invariably made up of body, soul and spirit. Spirit is the heavenly, graced element which will indeed one day be taken away from the damned, but remains eternally united to the soul in the blessed. Soul is the vital middle between matter and spirit, but as such it is at the same time the place of the choice whether the human being will be fleshly or spiritual. If the soul chooses the spiritual as its form of life, it is changed into "spirit"—not according to its essence but according to its most profound mode of being. It becomes "flesh" if it chooses the material.

This choice is unavoidable (34) and is, ultimately, the only religious act (35). This alone decides over good and evil (36). Good is the movement of the (in itself indifferent) middle from likeness to truth, from matter to spirit (37–39). This choice is fateful: Salvation is not necessary (40–41), but rests in our hands (42). Its realization is free act (43).

True order comes from this: body under soul, soul under (God-) spirit (43–45). The body is to be commanded and used sensibly; its instincts are not bad (46–49), but they are to be made spiritual (48). To this end the soul itself must be fixed on the spirit (50). Only in the spirit is it what it should be; in itself it is imperfect (52). The spirit of the human being is not "the divine in it" (51), but, in its own being, the immediate participation, consisting of grace and bestowed as grace, of the soul in the divine life which will be taken away from the damned (53).

34   Every soul is either of God or of whoever it is who has received power over human beings.

35   Each one is under the reign of sin or of justice.

36   Human wisdom is not capable of knowing and understanding the Lord nor of acknowledging the judgments and mercy and justice which he has accomplished on earth; it is, therefore, indifferent and "in the middle." . . . But if those things which are in the middle are applied to the virtue of the soul and to the fruit of good work, they become worthy of praise, or of the opposite if they are applied to a

bad deed (as when one oppresses a poor person through wealth or strikes down a weak person through strength). In this case they are no longer thought to be in the middle, but bad. Therefore, they are for this reason called indifferent or in the middle, because they can be called both evil when associated with an evil deed and good when joined to good deeds. But without this inclination to the latter of these, whoever calls them good is thought to be inexperienced and ignorant of rational definitions and terminology.

37   You can see, then, that a deed which is thought to be one and the same, such as abstention from adultery, is really not the same but different; for the intentions of those abstaining can come either from sound doctrine or from the most perverse and impious of motives.

38   Everything that is or is done is either good or bad or indifferent. . . . It is certain that things which relate to the virtues of the soul are called good in the proper sense; they are labeled bad only if they incline to evil and work against God's law; the rest are indifferent. That is, they are to be called neither good nor bad, such as wealth, beauty of body, courage or tall stature, and things which are of service to the body. Should we be ignorant of this distinction and take glory in things which are not truly good and do not relate to the virtue of the soul, we do so culpably.

39   Just as there is a certain indifferent life which is neither good nor bad, according to which we call both the wicked and irrational animals "living," and just as there is another life which is not indifferent but good, about which Paul says: "Your life is hid with Christ in God" (Col 3:3), and our Lord himself speaking about himself: "I am the life" (Jn 11:25), so too you could say that there is, over against the indifferent life, an indifferent death; but it is an evil and harmful death at enmity with the one who says: "I am the life."

40   But because the divine fire can sometimes die out even in the saints and the faithful, listen to how the Apostle Paul exhorts those who have merited to receive the grace and the gifts of the Spirit: "Do not quench the Spirit" (1 Th 5:19).

41   Sanctity is something that can come to every creature. But if it is something that can come to it, it is also something that can leave it.

42   For the body to grow and to become great lies not within our power. For the body takes its material size, whether large or small, from its genetic origin; but our soul has its own causes and its free will to make it large or small.

42a "God did not make death" (WisSol 1:13) nor did he make evil; he bestowed on human beings and angels a free will for everything. What needs to be understood in this is how, through free will, some climbed to the pinnacle of good things and others fell into the depth of evil. But you, O man, why do you wish to be deprived of your free will? Why is it too much for you to strive, to work, to struggle, and by good works to become yourself the cause of your salvation? Or will it please you more to enjoy eternal happiness in a state of slumber and ease? "My Father," it is written, "is working still, and I am working" (Jn 5:17). And you who were created to work do not like to work?

43 "He who sows to his own flesh will from the flesh reap corruption; but he who sows to the Spirit will from the Spirit reap eternal life" (Gal 6:8). Because it is one person who sows but another person in whom it is sown (it is sown "to one's own flesh" when one sins, so that corruption is reaped, or it is sown "to the Spirit" when one lives according to God, so that "eternal life" is reaped) it is clear that it is the soul which sows "to the flesh" or "to the Spirit," and which can fall into sin or turn from sin. For the body is the follower to whatever the soul should choose; and the spirit is the soul's guide to virtue, if it is willing to follow it.

44 God did not make us in his image that we should be subject to the needs of the flesh, but that the soul, in the service of its creator, should itself make use of the help and service of the flesh.

45 The bodies of human beings are the instruments of the soul. When the soul commands, the body obeys, and the soul makes use of it as it wills. But the WORD of God wishes our bodies no longer to be energized by our souls but by Christ himself. This is why Paul says: "It is no longer I who live, but Christ who lives in me" (Gal 2:20). We thus become members of Christ (cf. 1 Cor 6:15) when we do all things according to his WORD.

46 For it is God's will that that great "product" of God, the human being, for whose sake the world was created, should not only remain pure of the [animal] things we have been discussing, but should also rule over them.

47 It seems to me that concupiscence and anger, because they are in every soul, are necessarily said to be evil to the extent that they lead us to sin; but to the extent that posterity cannot be assured without concupiscence, nor any improvement take place without anger and punishment, they are said to be necessary and to be preserved.

48   Things give joy to the spirit because it passionately longs for them. Thus water gives life to those who are thirsty, because of their thirst, and to those who are hungry, because of their hunger. What does the Physician of Souls say about this? He neither destroys the things of which he himself is the Creator nor does he force the soul to pass over these things as if they were not there, for they were created in order to be known. Rather, through spiritual instruction and direction, he puts an end to those passions which are foreign to our thoughts and self-controlled deeds, and thus frees the soul from its bonds.

49   "Male and female he created them" (Gen 1:27). But let us also see by allegory how the human being was created male and female in the likeness of God. Our human being is made up internally of spirit and soul. . . . When there is concord and harmony among these, they grow in union with each other and they are multiplied and they bring forth offspring: good perceptions and understandings or useful thoughts by which they fill the earth and are masters of it; that is, they put the sense of the flesh, which is subject to it, to better use and exercise mastery over it. . . . But if the soul which is joined to the spirit and united to it in matrimony as it were, at times yields to bodily pleasures and inclines its senses to fleshly delight, and at times seems to listen to the salutary advice of the spirit, but at still other times gives in to carnal vices — it cannot be said of such a soul, defiled as it were with an adultery of the body, that it is increasing and multiplying rightly.

50   In one way, soul and spirit and power are in the body, but looked at in another way, the body of the just person is in these better parts as if leaning on them and clinging to them. "Those who are in the flesh cannot please God. But you are not in the flesh, you are in the Spirit, if the Spirit of God really dwells in you" (Rom 8:8–9). For the soul of the sinner is in the flesh, while that of the just is in the Spirit.

51   One must ask whether the spirit of Elijah is the same as the Spirit of God which is in Elijah (cf. 2 Kgs 2:9), or whether they are different. . . . But the Apostle has clearly indicated that the Spirit of God, although it is in us, is different from the spirit which is by nature in each human being, for he says: "The Spirit himself bears witness with our spirit that we are children of God" (Rom 8:16); and in another place: "No one knows a man's thoughts except the spirit of the man which is in him. So also no one comprehends the thoughts of God except the Spirit of God" (1 Cor 2:11).

52   The soul is defined as an imaginary and reacting [*phantastikē et hormētikē*] substance. . . . Paul the Apostle indeed speaks of an "animal man" [*anthrōpos psychikos*] who "does not receive the gifts of the Spirit of God," but says that the teaching of the Holy Spirit seems "folly" to him and that "he is not able to understand them because they are spiritually discerned" (1 Cor 2:14). But in another place he says that "it is sown a physical body" and "raised a spiritual body," thus showing that in the resurrection of the just there will be nothing physical [*animale*] in those who have merited beatitude. And so we ask whether there is not a certain substance which, as soul, is imperfect. . . . Let us consider whether the following answer might not be true: that just as the Savior came "to save the lost" (Lk 19:10), and when once the lost is saved it is no longer lost, so too, if he has come to save the soul just as he came "to save the lost," the soul, now that it has been saved, no longer remains soul. . . . The spirit [*nous*], in its falling, became soul; and the soul, when formed again in virtues, will become spirit again.[1]

53   ["He will divide them in two" (cf. Mt 24:50 var).] For they who have sinned are divided: one part of them is put "with the unfaithful" (cf. Lk 12:46), but the part which is not from themselves "returns to God who gave it" (Eccl 12:7). . . . He will divide them in two when "the spirit returns to God who gave it," but the soul goes with its body to hell. The just, however, are not divided; instead their soul goes with their body to the heavenly kingdom. . . . But they who are divided, and who put off the spirit which returns to him who gave it, and no longer have any part which comes from God, they are left with the part that is their own, their soul, which will be punished with their body.

---

[1] Origen clearly derives the name of the soul (*psychē*) from "coolness" (*psychros*): the soul is the "spirit" which, in its pre-existence, turned away from the warmth of God's love and fell. But that does not claim that the pre-existent soul (which even in its pre-existence is at times already called "soul" by Origen) has by its sin become another substance, but only that "soul," when it does not dwell in God, when it lives wholly in itself, is necessarily imperfect, indeed "lost." It is a being made in such a way that it can fulfill its essential destination only in a higher medium, just as the fish can live only in water.

THE IMAGE OF GOD

PARTICIPATION IN GOD

If "spirit" is participation of the soul in God, then its ultimate essence is determined precisely from this participation. Only in orientation towards God is it immortal (54), only in derivation from God is it ever new in being (55–57), only through relationship to him is it good and blessedly happy (56–61). Thus everything the soul has is "grace" (64) and every relationship of righteousness is encompassed by a relationship such as mercy (62–63). Thus the soul must strive for this participation with the most absolute of commitments (65), and build its life on the foundation of this unmerited grace (66).

54   Everyone who participates in something is doubtless of one substance and one nature with whoever participates in the same thing. For example, all eyes share in the light, and thus all eyes which share in the light are of one nature. . . . Every spirit which participates in intellectual light must doubtless be of one nature with every spirit which similarly participates in intellectual light. . . . Thus [human beings] seem to have a certain familial relationship with God. And, while God knows all things and no spiritual being is of itself concealed from him (for only God the Father with his only-begotten Son and the Holy Spirit possess self-knowledge as well as knowledge of what is created), a reason-endowed spirit can still, by progressing from small things to greater and from "visible" to "invisible" (Col 1:16), come to a more perfect understanding. . . . God possesses a spiritual and reasonable nature, as does also his only-begotten Son and the Holy Spirit; the angels and dominations and the rest of the heavenly powers possess this nature, as does also the "inner human being" (cf. 2 Cor 4:16) who has been grounded in God's image and likeness (cf. Gen 1:26). It follows from this that God and these beings are in some

208844

way of the same substance. . . . But the heavenly powers are incorruptible and immortal; and also, without doubt, is the substance of the human soul incorruptible and immortal. But there is even more to it than that: because the very nature of the Father and Son and Holy Spirit, in whose purely intellectual light the whole of creation shares, is incorruptible and eternal, it follows quite logically and necessarily that every substance which shares in that eternal nature will itself also remain forever and be incorruptible and eternal, so that the eternity of the divine goodness would also be recognized in the fact that those beings which receive its benefits are also eternal. . . . Does it not seem even impious to think that a spirit which is capable of receiving God could ever be reduced in substance to nothingness? As if the very fact that it can understand and perceive God could be insufficient to assure it eternity!

55   For God made all things so that they would exist; and what has been made in order to exist is incapable of not existing.

56   "Be holy, for I also am holy" (cf. Lev 20:26; Mt 5:48). But however much one might advance in sanctity, however much purity and sincerity one might acquire, a human being cannot be holy like the Lord, because he is the bestower of sanctity, the human being its receiver, he is the fountain of sanctity, the human being a drinker from the fountain, he is the light of sanctity, the human being the contemplator of the holy light; and thus "there is none holy like the Lord, there is none besides thee" (1 Sam 2:2). What it means to say: "There is none besides thee," I do not understand. If it had said: "There is no God but you" or "There is no creator but you," or had added something like this, there would be no problem. But if it now says "There is none besides thee," this is what it seems to me to mean here: none of those things which are possess their existence by nature. You alone, O Lord, are the one to whom your existence has not been given by anyone. Because all of us, that is the whole of creation, did not exist before we were created; thus, that we are, is [due to] the will of the Creator. And because there was a time when we were not, it is not wholly right if it is said of us, without qualification, that we exist. . . . For the shadow is nothing in comparison with the body; and in comparison with the fire, smoke too is nothing.

57   It is God alone who says: "I am who I am" (Ex 3:14); and one only is the substance of God which always is. Whoever is joined to him "becomes one spirit with him" (1 Cor 6:17) and is said to be through the one who always is. But whoever is far from him and has no part in

him, is said not even to be, just as we were when we were heathens before we came to the recognition of divine truth. And thus is it said that God "calls into existence the things that do not exist" (Rom 4:17) as well as those that do exist.

58   Every creature endowed with reason has a need for participation in the Trinity.

59   "Who alone has immortality" (1 Tim 6:16). Implied in this is the assumption that no other being gifted with reason possesses blessedness as an essential or inseparable part of its nature.

60   Justice is in us like an echo; it comes to us by reverberation from the first justice.

61   And it is not possible for someone who participates in life, and for this reason is called living, ever to become life itself, and for someone who participates in righteousness, and for this reason is called just, to become equal to righteousness itself.

62   Each human being, as human being, needs the mercy of God.

63   Even the most just person, when faced with the rigor of God's judgment, has need of God's mercy, because the very fact of seeming to have become just is due to the mercy of God. For what has anyone done that could be worthy of eternal blessedness?

64   Grace therefore is whatever that person has who was not, and now is, is receiving from him who always was, and is, and will be forever.

65   Each of you should strive to become a divider of that water which is above and which is below, that is to say, by gaining an understanding and a share in that spiritual water which is "above the firmament" (Gen 1:7), and draw forth "from his heart rivers of living water" (Jn 7:38) "welling up to eternal life" (Jn 4:14), separated, of course, and distinguished from the water which is below, the water of the abyss in which the darkness is said to be.

66   For we must depend on God alone and on no other, even if someone is said to come forth from God's paradise. As Paul says: "Even if we, or an angel from heaven, should preach to you . . . let him be accursed" (Gal 1:8).

67   It is impossible that, in a human being who has already reached the age of understanding and of distinguishing between good and evil, there should be neither injustice nor justice. If this is so, then a soul cannot be found without one of these two; and it is certain that if it is turning away from evil, it is already in good. . . . And thus the Apostle is right in saying (where he treats of the forgiveness of sins and the covering over of guilt and points out that God does not reckon

sins) that this "is reckoned" to man "as righteousness" (cf. Rom 4:5) even though he has not yet performed just works, but solely because he has believed in him who justifies the unjust. For the beginning of being justified by God is the faith which believes in the justifier. And this faith, when it has been justified, like a root that has received rain, clings to the foundation of the soul so that, when it begins to be cultivated by the law of God, branches which bear the fruit of works grow from it. Not therefore from works does the root of justice grow, but from the root of justice grows the fruit of works.

IMAGE OF GOD

Of all creatures, only the soul endowed with reason "participates" in the life of God. The human being is thus both "participating" in God (as spirit-soul: "inner man") and "created" by God (as living soul and body: "outer man") (68–70). This twofold aspect is connected in Origen, in the context of the myth of prior life, with the twofold aspect of the "heavenly" (pre-) existence and the "earthly" existence caused by sin (71), and thus also with the Pauline "pneumatic" and "psychic" human being as well as with the twofold Genesis account: human being according to "God's image and likeness" and human being of "dust from the ground" (69, 72). One must note here that the soul (as created) also had a body in heaven, although a spiritual one. Thus body is not in itself the consequence of sin, but only the gross, disordered earthly body.

Made manifest to us in Christ is the primal image of the heavenly human being; by living according to this model we can restore the obscured "image of the heavenly" in us (72–74). Indeed by our free effort the final state will be even higher than the beginning: the freely gained "likeness" turns into an "image" become reality (75) (a motif which, through Origen, came to have great significance among the later Fathers).

68   First God created the heavens, of which he says: "Heaven is my throne" (Isa 66:1). But after this he made the firmament, that is, the bodily heavens . . . for, since everything that God was to make would consist of spirit and body, it is thus said that "in the beginning" and before everything else the heavens were made, that is, every spiritual substance above which, as on a throne or chair, God sits. But this heaven here below, the firmament, is corporeal. Consequently

that first heaven, which we have called spiritual, is our mind, which is itself spirit; it is our spiritual human being who sees and gazes upon God. But this corporeal heaven, which is called firmament, is our external human being, which sees corporeally.

69 That eminence I find is even more pronounced in the condition of the human being which I do not find mentioned elsewhere: "And God created man, in the image of God he created him" (Gen 1:27). We do not find this written in the heavens or on earth or on the sun or moon. Indeed this human, made "in the image of God," we do not understand as bodily. For no figment of the body contains the image of God, nor is the corporeal human said to be created but formed, as is written in what follows. For it says: "God formed man," that is, shaped him "of dust from the ground" (Gen 2:7). But the one who was made "in the image of God" is our internal human, invisible and incorporeal and incorrupt and immortal.

70 The human being made by God in his image and likeness was the first to be so named, and is thus human being in the true sense.

71 There are two images in the human being: the one which he received when made by God in the beginning as written in Genesis: "according to the image and likeness of God" (Gen. 1:27), and the other which he received later when, because of disobedience and sin, he was expelled from paradise after yielding to the allurements of the "ruler of this world" (Jn 12:31).

72 All those who come to [Christ] and try to become sharers of the intelligible image are, through their progress, "daily renewed in inner nature" (2 Cor 4:16) unto the image of him who made them, so that they might become like his glorious body (cf. Phil 3:21), but each one according to his strength. . . . He himself had already prayed to the Father for his disciples, for the original likeness to be returned to them, when he said: "Father grant that just as I and You are one, so also may they be one in us" (cf. Jn 17:21–22). Let us therefore always fix our gaze on this image of God so that we might be able to be reformed in its likeness. For if the human who has been made in the image of God, by contemplating against his nature the image of the devil, becomes like him through sin, so much more will he, by contemplating the divine image in whose likeness God has made him, receive through the WORD and his power that form which had been given him by nature.

73 We are not commanded to tear out and destroy the natural impulses of the soul, but to purify them, that is, to purge and drive out

the dirty and impure things which have come to them by our negligence so that the natural vitality of its own innate power might shine forth.

74 It is written: "Who is like thee, O Lord, among the gods?" (Exod 15:11). . . . "Gods" he calls those who by grace and participation in God are given the name of gods. . . . And yet although these are capable [of being] God and seem to be given this name by grace, none of them is found to be like God in power or nature. And even though the Apostle John says: "Beloved, . . . we do not yet know what we shall be, but we know that when he appears"—he is indeed speaking of the Lord—"we shall be like him" (cf. 1 Jn 3:2), this likeness is not due to nature but to grace. For example if we say that a portrait is like the one whose image is seen expressed in the portrait, the similarity is due to the quality of the expression—grace—, while in substance the two remain quite different. For in the one is the beauty of the flesh and the comeliness of a living body, and in the other only the appearance of colors and wax applied to lifeless wood. Therefore no one is "like the Lord among the gods"; for no one is invisible, no one incorporeal, no one unchangeable, no one without beginning and without end, no one the creator of all except the Father with the Son and the Holy Spirit.

75 The highest good towards which every rational creature is hurrying, also called the end and goal of all things, . . . is to become like God as much as possible. . . . This is indeed what Moses is pointing out above all when he describes the original creation of humankind with the words: "Then God said: 'Let us make man in our image, after our likeness,'" and then continues: "And so God created man, . . . in the image of God he created him; male and female he created them. And God blessed them" (Gen 1:26–28). Thus when he said: "In the image of God he created him" and said nothing more about the likeness, he is actually indicating that while the human being did indeed receive the dignity of God's image in the first creation, the dignity of his likeness is reserved for the consummation. This is so that human beings would work to acquire it by their own industrious efforts to imitate God; for in the beginning only the possibility of perfection is given them by the dignity of the "image," while in the end they are to acquire for themselves the perfect "likeness" by the carrying out of works.

But John the Apostle describes this situation even more clearly and lucidly when he says: "Beloved, we do not yet know what we shall be; but when he is revealed to us" (obviously speaking of the Savior) "we shall be like him" (1 Jn 3:2). . . . And in the gospel the Lord himself describes this same reality not only as something which is to come but also as something which is to come through his intercession, since he himself deigns to request this of the Father for his disciples when he says: "Father, I desire that they may be with me where I am," and: "Even as I and you are one, that they also may be one in us" (cf. Jn 17:24, 21). This indicates that the likeness itself makes progress, so to speak, and grows from likeness into unity, in the sense, obviously, that at the consummation or end "God is everything to everyone" (1 Cor 15:28).

IMAGE OF THE WORD

But the "image of God" in the soul is, on closer examination, the image of the Logos (76). For in him the Father has created all things, formed all other images according to his ideal. The Logos is primal reason, primal spirit, primal life, and only in a thoroughly personal and dynamic relationship to him does the inner human live and grow (77–84). The fundament of the soul is like an open window through which enter the illuminating rays of the Logos who is also present in each spirit as personal conscience (83). The question whether Logos and human spirit are different Origen avoids by means of the scriptural image of "nearness" (82). But not for an instant was he thinking of pantheism (84).

76   "So God created man . . . in the image of God he created him" (Gen 1:27). We must see what this image of God is. . . . What else could this image of God be . . . except our Savior who is "the first-born of all creation" (Col 1:15)?

77   It is clear that the source of that life which is pure and unmixed with anything else resides in him who is "the first-born of all creation" (Col 1:15). Drawing from this source, those who have a share in Christ truly live that life. But those who try to live apart from him, just as they do not have the true light, neither do they have the true life.

78   For, since he is the invisible "image of the invisible God" (Col 1:15), he himself grants participation in himself to all rational creatures in such a way that the participation each of them receives from him is commensurate with the passionate love with which they cling to him.[1]

---

[1] Many formulations in Origen as well as in other pre-Augustinian Fathers sound Pelagian without really being so. What is meant here is only the transition

79 "He was the true light that enlightens every man who comes into the world" (Jn 1:9). Whatever is of rational nature has a share in the true light; and every human being is of rational nature. But while all human beings share in the word, the power of the WORD increases in some and decreases in others. If you see a soul full of passion and sin, you will see there the power of the WORD decreasing. If you see a holy and just soul, you will see the power of the WORD bearing fruit day by day, and what was said of Jesus you will apply to the just: for it was not just for himself that "Jesus increased in wisdom and in age, and in favor with God and man" (Lk 2:52).

80 Just as those who have departed this life and gone on to better things have a life which is more real, now that the body of death and the incentives to all vices have been put aside; so those who "carry in their body the death of Jesus" (2 Cor 4:10) certainly do not live by the flesh but by the Spirit; they live in him who is life, and in them lives Christ of whom it is written: "The word of God is living and active" (Heb 4:12).

81 The saints are the living and the living are the saints.

82 The question arises whether the word in us is to be declared the same as the WORD which was in the beginning with God and is God, especially since the Apostle does not seem to make it something different from the WORD which was in the beginning with God when he teaches: "Do not say in' your heart, 'Who will ascend into heaven?' (that is, to bring Christ down) or 'Who will descend into the abyss?' (that is, to bring Christ up from the dead). But what does the scripture say? The WORD is near you, on your lips and in your heart" (Rom 10:6-8).[1]

83 Since the WORD is in a sense law and commandment, and there would be no sin if there were no law, . . . there would also be no sin if there were no WORD ("For if I had not come and spoken to them,

---

of the potential presence of the WORD in the soul into an actual and living presence. This transition is accomplished only through cooperating appropriation by the soul itself (cf. Nos. 682-684). For Origen's doctrine of grace, cf. Nos. 474-488.

[1] The concept of creation is much too clearly expressed in Origen to leave him open to the charge of pantheism. In reality his idea is somewhat like Eckhart's doctrine of the soul as a little spark, which only by gross misunderstanding can be interpreted as pantheism (cf. Alois Dempf, *Meister Eckhart*, 1934). Actually, Eckhart is both directly and indirectly dependent on Origen.

they would have no sin"—Jn 15:22). For every excuse is taken away from those who want to make excuses for their sin, for although the WORD is in them and showing them what to do, they do not obey him. . . . For just as the master is inseparable from the disciple, so the WORD dwells in the nature of rational beings always suggesting what is to be done even if we pay no heed to his commandments.

84   Therefore, just as there are "many gods, yet for us one God, the Father, and many lords, yet for us one Lord, Jesus Christ" (1 Cor 8:5-6), so there are many "words"; but we pray that the one WORD who was with God in the beginning may be with us, God the WORD (cf. Jn 1:1). . . . [Just as we] are called gods because of our participation in him, without really being so, . . . so [are we], so to speak, wordless WORDS [or reasonless REASON].

FALL AND RETURN

SPIRITUAL DEATH

*Sin is a turning away from this source of light, life and holiness,
a fall into essential non-being and thus, so to speak, out of the
knowledge of God. Sin is the real death, of which bodily death is
only an image (85–90).*

85   One just person counts as much as the whole world; but the unjust,
even if they are many, are considered to be worthless and counting
for nothing before God.

86   The Apostle appears not to count the things which "are not" among
those things which have no existence whatever, but rather among the
things which are evil, considering non-being to be evil. For it is written: "God calls into existence the things that do not exist" (Rom 4:17).
. . . Therefore the good is the same as the one who "is" (cf. Ex 3:14).

87   "For the Lord knows the way of the righteous, but the way of the
wicked will perish" (Ps 1:6). Nothing evil is recognized by God, but
only the way of the just. For "the Lord knows those who are his"
(2 Tim 2:20). The "way of the righteous" is he who said "I am the
way" (Jn 14:6). . . . He has no cognizance or knowledge of evil, not
that there is anything which he cannot comprehend or understand
(for it is blasphemous to think this of God), but that it is unworthy of
his knowledge.

88   We say therefore with confidence that according to scripture God
does not know all things. God does not know sin and God does not
know sinners; he does not know those who are alien to him. . . .
Listen to the Savior as he says: "Depart from me all you evil doers; I
never knew you" (Mt 7:23). And Paul too, who says: "If any one
thinks that he is a prophet, or spiritual, he should acknowledge that
what I am writing to you is a command of the Lord. If any one does
not recognize this, he is not recognized" (1 Cor 14:37–38).

89 Dead is the soul which has sinned; and the serpent is proven to have lied for saying "You will not die the death" (Gen 3:4).

90 "The power of death" which the devil is understood to have (Heb 2:14) does not refer to that intermediate or indifferent death by which those composed of body and soul die, when the soul leaves the body, but to that death which is opposed and inimical to the one who says: "I am the life" (Jn 11:25; 14:6).

THE SIN OF THE RACE

Even if it is true that the myth of (individual) sin in a prior life makes the theological concept of original sin impossible, Origen still had a deep insight into the universal solidarity of all humans in guilt. All, with the exception of Christ, have slipped from truth (91). Adam signifies man, signifies the original unity of human nature which in the primordial time fell as a whole from heaven (92–97). Thus original sin for Origen signifies not a temporal, horizontal relationship back to an original parent, but a vertical relationship to the super-worldly, common fall (98–99).

Christ is the one who restored the human race (100) which, only through the fall, gained its so to speak experiential insight into God's grace (101); but the second things are always more lasting than the first (102).

91 I ask myself whether "having to do with the truth" (Jn 8:44) is not something monolithic and unified while variety and multiplicity are characteristic of not having to do with it. Some really try to stand in the truth, but their feet shake, so to speak, and they waver, and do not succeed; others do not have this experience but are in danger of finding themselves in the situation of the one who says: "My feet had almost stumbled" (Ps 73:2). . . . And if one looks rather carefully at human nature, . . . one will see that just as "every man is a liar" (Ps 115:2 LXX), so also does no one stand completely in the truth.

92 Those persons will have a philosophical understanding of Adam and his sin who know that in [Hebrew] the word Adam means man, and that in those things which seem to be about Adam, Moses is discoursing upon the nature of man. For "in Adam all die" (1 Cor 15:22), as the scripture says, and "were condemned in the likeness of Adam's transgression" (Rom 5:14). This was said not so much about one individual as about the whole human race. For the context shows

that the curse of Adam apparently spoken over one man really applies to all, nor is there any woman against whom what was spoken against the woman does not apply. And also the expulsion of the man with the woman from paradise and their being clothed with "garments of skins" (Gen 3:21) which, because of the transgression of men, God made for those who had sinned, contain a certain secret and mystical doctrine quite superior to Plato's doctrine about the descent of the soul which has lost its wings and is swept downwards "until it can catch hold of something solid" (*Phaedo* 246b–c).

93   But consider the text: "In Adam all die, so also in Christ shall all be made alive" (1 Cor 15:22). In these words it is not the intermediate death that is meant according to which "in Adam all die," nor is it the indifferent life which is neither good in itself nor bad according to the text: "in Christ shall all be made alive." You will find in this the life of the human being "according to the image" (cf. Gen 1:26). Understand his life and you will understand in what way the murderer has killed the living human being, and that it is not because of one individual but because of the whole race that he committed murder (this is the meaning of "in Adam all die"), and why he is rightly called the "murderer of men."

94   "He has set the world aright in his wisdom" (Jer 10:12 LXX). We too want to have set aright our own world which may have fallen. For this world has fallen . . . because "we have sinned and acted wickedly and unjustly" (Dan 9:5), and thus it needs setting aright. God is the one who sets the world aright. But if you do not follow this interpretation, . . . but take the more common meaning of "world," search out how the world is to be set aright. Look for the fall of the world, so that from finding its fall you might come to see its setting aright. . . . "In Adam all die." Thus the whole world has fallen and needs setting aright, so that "in Christ all might be made alive" (1 Cor 15:22). I have thus spoken of "world" in two ways: in one way as individual soul . . . and in the other according to its ordinary meaning.

95   And at the same time it is clearly shown that, as far as the underlying nature is concerned, just as the potter begins with one basic piece of clay, from which mass come "vessels for beauty and for menial use" (Rom 9:21), so too is there in the hands of God the one underlying nature of every soul, from which one mass, so to speak, and following already existing causes, he formed rational beings, "one for beauty and another for menial use" (cf. Rom 9:21).[1]

---

[1] Cf. below, No. 789.

96   "And I was among the exiles by the river Chebar" (Ez 1:1), which means "heavy." But heavy is the river of this world, as is said elsewhere in a secret interpretation (and for the simple this is only a historical fact; but for those who hear the scripture spiritually, it signifies the soul which has fallen into the toils of this life): "By the waters of Babylon, there we sat down and wept, when we remembered Zion . . . " (Ps 137:1ff). It is the heavenly fatherland for which they are mourning and weeping.

97   For every human being sins. "There is not a righteous man on earth who does good and never sins" (Eccles 7:20). No one is free from uncleanness, even if his life last only a day (cf. Job 14:4–5).

98   It is quite clear that every soul, when it first comes of age and a kind of natural law within it begins to defend its own rights, produces as its first carnal movements those emotions which take their driving force from the furnace of concupiscence and anger. This is why the prophet mentions it of Christ as something unusual and not commonly found in others, that "he shall eat curds and honey; before knowing how to do or speak evil, he will choose the good, because before the boy knows good or evil" (cf. Isa 7:15), he resists evil to choose what is good. But another prophet, as if speaking of himself, says: "Remember not the sins of my youth, or my transgressions" (Ps 25:7). This is because those first movements of the soul, borne forward according to the desires of the flesh, fall into sin.

99   And so it seems to me that one of those followers of wisdom was not at all wrong in determining that, when anyone from the race of mortal human beings comes to the age when the natural law enters in and is able to distinguish right from wrong, it is first of all evil that gets aroused; and it is only after this that it is gradually beaten down and won over to virtue by means of instruction, education and exhortation. For it seems to me that Paul too was saying something similar when he said: "But when the commandment came, sin revived" (Rom 7:9).

100   We are all indeed creatures of God, but all of us, one and all, have been sold through our sins and been separated from our own creator by our sin. We are God's, therefore, because we have been created by him; but we have become slaves of the devil, because we have been sold by our sins. . . . And so [Christ] can receive as his own those whom he has created; he can win possession of them as if they were strangers who had sought a foreign master for themselves.

101   Reason-endowed beings . . . do not recognize God's beneficence unless they have first had to condemn themselves. This applies to all.

The purpose of it all is for them to become aware of what comes from themselves and what from the grace of God. For they who are not aware of their own weakness and the grace of God, even if they receive this beneficence but still have no experience of themselves from which they have to condemn themselves, will consider as their own heroic achievement what has really come to them as grace from heaven. This creates in them a vain swell-headedness (cf. 1 Cor 4:6; 8:1; 13:4) which becomes the cause of their fall.

102 "And [God] showed [Abraham] the stars of heaven and said: so shall your descendants be" (cf. Gen 15:5; 22:17). And then he adds the reason why he strengthens this firm future promise with an oath. He says: "because you have done this and not withheld your son" (Gen 22:17). He thus shows that because of the sacrificing and suffering of the son the promise stands firm, obviously meaning that the people that comes from heathenism and "is of the faith of Abraham" (cf. Rom 4:16) remains assured of the promise because of the passion of Christ. And is not in this alone the second firmer than the first? In many things of this kind you will find sacraments hinted at. The first tablets of the law in the letter Moses broke and threw away; the second law he receives in the spirit, and the second things are firmer than the first. It is the same thing again when he has put together the whole law in four books; he then writes Deuteronomy which is called the second law. Ishmael is first, Isaac second, and a similar form of preference is found in the second. You will find this hinted at in this way in Esau and Jacob, in Ephraem and Manasseh and in a thousand other places.

WANDERING THROUGH THE DESERT

Climbing back up to the heavenly homeland, the leveling out of "image" and "likeness," the return to God, is the history of every soul, but also the history of all humanity and the world itself, a history in which this age of the world represents only a fading episode: wandering through the desert of the millions of years in which rising and falling are still possible, until more and more souls, guided by tireless providence out of the Samsara of the ways of the world, come together in the super-heavenly place, and the mystical body of Christ finally comes to "maturity."

The pathos of the departure, of the wandering, of the ever-new upward movement from the material and the letter to the spirit, the pressure, the haste that inexorably presses on through all that is passing, the passion of the macrocosmic adventure, the consuming longing to pierce through the image to the real, but at the same time the mounting state of being seized by the pull and allurement of grace, the prayerful insight that the endless path in the desert is no one else but "Christ the way," and the blind surrender of his self to this way — : that is Origenian existence (103–122).

103   From the "land of the Chaldaeans" (cf. Gen 15:7) . . . (because they attribute most earthly events to the influence of the stars and reduce both our sins and our virtues to the influence of their movements) come the kind of people who are given to such convictions. . . . But God, calling Abraham to better things, said to him: "I am he who leads you out of the land of the Chaldaeans" (cf. Gen 15:7).

104   Therefore we must move out of Egypt; we must leave the world if we wish to "serve the Lord." But I mean leaving not with reference to a place but with reference to the soul, not by moving along a road but by moving along in faith.

105   For it is on account of certain hidden and mystical reasons that the people is visibly led out of this earthly Egypt and makes its way "through the desert with its fiery serpents and scorpions and thirsty ground where there was no water" (Dt 8:15), and all the rest that has been written on this.

106   The figure of the exodus from Egypt can be understood in two ways. . . . For when someone is led from the darkness of error to the light of recognition and changes from earthly converse to a spiritual way of life, he seems to have come out of Egypt and to solitude, i.e., to that state of life in which, by peace and quiet, he becomes practiced in the divine laws and imbued with heavenly thoughts. Formed and guided by these things, when he has crossed the Jordan, he hastens to the Promised Land, i.e., through the grace of baptism to a life according to the gospel. But the exodus from Egypt is also a figure of the soul which leaves the darkness of this world and the blindness of bodily nature and is transferred to that other world which, in the story of Lazarus, is spoken of as the "bosom of Abraham" (Lk 16:32) or, in the story of the thief who received faith on the cross, is called "paradise" (Lk 23:43), or to whatever other places or mansions there might be which are known to God. Passing through these and coming to that "river" which "makes glad the city of God" (Ps 46:4), the soul takes unto itself the heritage promised to the fathers.

107   "And the people made haste and crossed over the Jordan" (Jos 4:10).
Now I do not think that the Holy Spirit was speaking idly when it said
"that the people made haste to go across." Thus it also seems to me
that in our case too, when we are coming to saving baptism and are
receiving the sacraments of the WORD of God, we should not act
slowly and lazily but with haste and urgency until we all get across.
For to "go across" everything is to fulfill everything that is commanded.
Let us therefore make haste to "go across," which means first of all to
fulfill what is written: "Blessed are the poor in spirit" (Mt 5:3), in order
that, having put aside all arrogance and put on the humility of Christ,
we might deserve to come to the beatitude promised us. But even when
we have fulfilled this, we cannot stand and rest on our laurels but must
cross over the other things which follow, so that we might "hunger and
thirst for righteousness" (Mt 5:6). And we must cross over what follows,
so that we might "mourn" (Mt 5:4) in this world. The rest are also to be
crossed over quickly, that we might become "meek" (Mt 5:5) and also
remain "peacemakers" and thus become able to hear the name "sons
of God" (Mt 5:9). We must also make haste so as to cross over the
burden of persecutions by the power of patience. And when we are
struggling through all these things which belong to the glory of virtue,
not lazily or neglectfully but with all urgency and speed, this, it seems
to me, is what it means to "cross over the Jordan" in haste.

108   It is better for the one who is seeking the perfect life to die along the
way than never to have started on the search for perfection.

109   If you only understood how much repose is found in the way of
wisdom, how much grace and how much sweetness! Don't go into
hiding, don't be neglectful, but take up this journey and do not be
afraid of the loneliness of the desert. For when you live in tents of this
kind, the manna from heaven will come and you will "eat the bread of
angels" (Ps 77:25). Just get started and do not, as we said, let the solitude of the desert frighten you.

110   For those who follow a spiritual and elevated sense [of scripture and
nature] and understand that there is more truth in "the things that are
unseen" than in "the things that are seen" (2 Cor 4:18), and that invisible and spiritual things are closer to God than visible and corporeal, it will doubtless seem that an understanding of this kind is to
be embraced and followed; for they recognize that this is the way of
understanding the truth by which one comes to God.

111   The WORD of God spoke to this beautiful and well-endowed soul to
which, through its bodily senses (i.e., through contemplating scripture

and the hearing of doctrine), it appeared "through the window" and demonstrated the height of its stature so that it was speaking to it while resting on it, and then calling it forth to come outside and, outside of the senses of the body, to be no more in the flesh so that it might deserve to hear the words: "But you are not in the flesh, you are in the Spirit" (Rom 8:9). For the WORD of God would not otherwise call it "next to" itself unless it were joined to it and it became "one spirit" (Eph 4:4) with itself. Nor would it call the soul "beautiful" unless it saw its image "being renewed every day" (2 Cor 4:16); and unless it saw that the soul was capable of the Holy Spirit which descended on Jesus in the form of a dove at the Jordan (Mt 3:16 par), it would not call it "my dove."

12   For the soul has freedom of choice and the option of moving in whatever direction it wants; and thus God's judgment is just for, whether its advisors are good or bad, the soul follows them of its own accord. Do you want me to show you something still more from holy scripture, namely how much more care God has for the salvation of human beings than the devil has for their damnation? Wouldn't the care of the angels have been enough help against the snares of the demons and against those who draw men into sin? The only-begotten Son himself, the very Son of God is here; he himself defends, he himself watches over, he himself draws us to himself. Listen to the way he himself says: "And lo, I am with you always, to the close of the age" (Mt 28:20). Nor is it enough for him to be with us, but he even uses a kind of force in order to draw us to salvation; for he says elsewhere: "When I am lifted up from the earth, I will draw all things to myself" (Jn 12:32). You see how he not only invites the willing but also "draws" all. Do you want to hear how he also "draws" all? He did not give permission to the one who wanted "to go and bury his father" (cf. Mt 8:21), nor give him any time, but said to him: "Leave the dead to bury their own dead; but you, follow me" (Mt 8:22). And elsewhere he says: "No one who puts his hand to the plow and looks back is fit for the kingdom of God" (Lk 9:62). Now if you want to know still more about this mystery, I will show you from the scriptures that even God the Father himself does not neglect the management of our salvation; he himself not only calls us to salvation but also "draws" us. For this is what the Lord says in the gospel: "No one comes to me unless my heavenly Father draws him" (Jn 6:44). . . . Thus it is that we are not only invited by God, but also drawn and forced to salvation.

13   Consider unto what great hope you have been called, O man, you who, surrounded by flesh, say: "Didst thou not pour me out like milk

and curdle me like cheese? Thou didst clothe me with skin and flesh, and knit me together with bones and sinews" (Job 10:10-11). You then, who were describing your own fate . . . are called [as Gentile] into that hope from which he [the Jew] fell. "Through the trespass [of Israel] salvation has come to the Gentiles." I will dare to say something even more mystical: in place of the angels who "fell," you are to rise, and the mystery which was once entrusted to them will be entrusted to you. . . . You have become the "light of the world" (cf. Mt 5:14), you in his place have become "Lucifer"; one of the stars which fell from heaven was Lucifer (cf. Lk 10:18) and you, if you are of the "seed of Abraham," will be reckoned among the stars of heaven (cf. Gen 15:5).

114   But when the soul takes its departure from the Egypt of this life in order to move to the promised land, it necessarily goes by certain paths . . . and through certain stopping places. These, I think, are what the prophet had in mind when he said: "These things I remember, as I pour out my soul, because I am walking to the place of the wonderful tent, to the house of the Lord" (Ps 41:5 LXX; cf. Ps 42:4). . . . That is why the same prophet says in another place: "My soul has wandered much" (cf. Ps 120:6). Understand then, if you can, what those wanderings of the soul are in which it bewails its wandering so long with groaning and sorrow. But the understanding of these things becomes dull and obscured as long as the wandering continues. Only when it has returned to its repose, that is, to its home in paradise, will the soul be taught more fully and understand more deeply what the reason for its wandering is. Gazing into the mystery of this the prophet said: "Return, O my soul, to your rest; for the Lord has dealt bountifully with you" (Ps 116:7). But meanwhile, it is journeying along its way and past its stopping places, doubtlessly provided for through these things by the providence of God for the sake of some benefit. . . .

The soul also has a guide — not Moses (for he himself did not know where he was going) — but "a pillar of fire and a cloud" (Ex 13:21), which is the Son of God and the Holy Spirit, as the prophet says in another place: "The Lord himself was leading them" (cf. Ps 78:14). Such then will be the ascent of the blessed soul when all the Egyptians have been drowned, and the Amalekites and all who had attacked it, so that traveling through the different "stopping places," namely those "many mansions" (cf. Jn 14:2) which are said to "be with the Father" (cf. Jn 1:9), it is more and more illumined, . . . until it becomes accustomed to bear the brilliance of the true majesty. . . . And before it comes to the perfect state it must dwell in the desert where it may gain experience in the commandments of the Lord and where its faith may be tested by temptation. And when it has conquered one temptation and its faith has been proven in it, it proceeds to another and passes on as it were from one stopping place to the next . . . and thereby fulfills what was written: "They will go from virtue to virtue" (Ps 84:7) until it comes to the final, indeed to the highest level of virtue and crosses over the river of God and comes into possession of the promised inheritance. . . .

And so the children of Israel withdraw from Egypt . . . and come first to Succoth (cf. Num 33:6), . . . but Succoth is translated tent. Thus the soul's first stage of progress is . . . to know that, like a wanderer and traveler, it must dwell in tents where, prepared for battle, so to speak, it has the means and the freedom to take quick action against attackers. From there, when it feels ready, it "moves from Succoth and encamps at Buthan" (cf. Num 33:6). Buthan means low-lying place. We have said that these things have to do with progress in virtue. But virtue is gained only by struggle and hard work, and it is not proven as much in prosperity as it is in adversity. And so the soul comes to the low-lying place. . . . And so our wayfarer goes down to those who are in the low places and in the depths, not to stay there but to gain a victory there. . . .

After this "they passed through the midst of the Red Sea and encamped at the Bitter Waters" (cf. Num 33:8). We have already said that the time of progress is a time of dangers. How difficult a temptation it is "to go through the middle of a sea," to see the waves rising into mountains, to hear the raging fury of the waters! And yet if you follow Moses, that is, the law of God, the waters will become a "wall on your right and left" and you will find a "dry path through the middle of the sea" (Exod 14:22). . . .

"And they set out from the Red Sea and encamped in the wilderness of Sin" (Num 33:11). "Sin" is translated thornbush or temptation. Already the hope of good things is beginning to smile on you. What is this hope of good things? It was from a thornbush that the Lord appeared (cf. Ex 3:2ff) and gave answers to Moses, and that was the beginning of the Lord's visitation to the children of Israel. But it is not by chance that "Sin" also means temptation, for temptations also are accustomed to come in visions. Not seldom does the angel of iniquity change itself into an angel of light (cf. 2 Cor 11:14). Thus you must take care and act cautiously in order to discern with knowledge the kind of vision. This is why among the spiritual gifts one of the gifts of the Holy Spirit is called "discernment of spirits."

"And they set out from the wilderness of Sin and encamped at Raphaca" (Num 33:12). Raphaca is translated health. You can see in this the order of the progress, how the soul, when it has already become spiritual and begins to have the discernment of heavenly things, comes to health so that it might worthily say: "Bless the Lord, O my soul; and all that is within me, bless his holy name!" (Ps 103:1). What Lord? "Who heals" it is written, "all your diseases, who redeems your life from the Pit" (Ps 103:3f). For there are many "diseases" of the soul: greed is one of its "diseases," indeed one of the worst; and there is pride, anger, boasting, fearfulness, inconstancy, weak-heartedness, and the like. When, O Lord Jesus, will you heal me from all these diseases? When will you make me so sound that I too can say: "Bless the Lord, O my soul, who heals all your diseases," so that I too can make my dwelling place "in Raphaca," which means "health." It would last too long if we wanted to go by each and every stopping place and at each one of them open up what is suggested by a contemplation of the names; but let us move through them quickly and briefly and give you not so much a full explanation, since there isn't time enough for that, as opportunities for understanding.

"They set out" therefore "from Raphaca and encamped at Alush" (Num 33:13). "Alush" means "hard work." Don't be surprised if hard work follows upon health. For the real reason why the soul receives health from God is that it might take up its labors with delight and not unwillingly; for it will be said to it: "You shall eat the fruit of the labor of your hands; you shall be happy, and it shall be well with you" (Ps 128:2). After this "they come to Rephidim" (Num 33:14). "Rephidim" means "praise of judgment." Quite justly does praise follow upon hard work. But what is praised? "Praise of judgment," it is written. Thus the soul becomes worthy of praise which judges rightly and discerns rightly, that is, which "judges all things spiritually, but is itself judged by no one" (1 Cor 2:15). From there it "proceeds to the wilderness of Sinai" (Num 33:15). Sinai is itself a certain place in the desert which previously has been mentioned as "Sin"; but here the name signifies a certain mountainous place in the desert. . . . Thus after the soul has become of praiseworthy judgment and has begun to have a right judgment, that is when it is given the law by God, when it has begun to be capable of the divine secrets and celestial visions. From there the soul "comes to the monuments of concupiscence" (Num 33:16 LXX).

What are the "monuments of concupiscence"? Doubtless the place where concupiscence is buried and consigned to oblivion, where all avidity is extinguished and the "flesh" no longer "desires against the spirit" (Gal 5:17), put to death by the death of Christ. Then "it comes to Hazeroth" (Num 33:17) which is translated "perfect courtyards" or "beatitude." Examine more carefully now, O my wayfarer, what the order of perfection is: after you have buried and handed over to death the concupiscences of the flesh, you will come to the spacious court-yards, you will come to beatitude. For blessed is the soul which is no longer driven on by the vices of the flesh.

After this a stop is made "in Ressa" (Num 33:21) which in our lan-guage can mean "visible or praiseworthy temptation." What is this, that even where the soul is making marvelous progress, its temptations are still not taken away from it? This reveals that temptations serve the soul as a kind of guard or protective wall. For just as meat, no matter how big and beautiful a piece, goes bad if it is not sprinkled with salt, so the soul, unless it is somehow salted by constant temptations, imme-diately goes soft and comes apart. This is the reason why it is written that "every sacrifice shall be seasoned with salt" (Lev 2:13). And this ultimately is the reason why Paul said: "And to keep me from being too elated by the abundance of revelations, a thorn was given me in the flesh, a messenger of Satan, to harass me" (2 Cor 12:7). . . .

After that the soul "comes to Terah" (Num 33:27), . . . which means "rapture" . . . when the soul is struck with astonishment in its admiration of great and marvelous things. Then the soul "comes to Mithkah" (Num 33:28) which, translated, means "new death." What is this new death? When "we die with Christ and are buried with Christ so that we might also live with him" (cf. 2 Tim 2:11). . . .

After this comes the stopping place in "Abarim before Nebo" (Num 33:47). The former means "passing through," while Nebo means "separation." For when the soul has made its way through all these virtues and risen to the height of perfection, it is already passing through and separating from this world, as it was written of Enoch: "And he was not to be found for God took him" (Gen 5:24). Because if someone like this seems to be still in this world and to live in the flesh, he is nevertheless "not found." In what way "not found"? In no worldly act, in no carnal thing, in no vain conversation is he found. For God has carried him across from these things and made him live in the land of virtues. The last stopping place is "in western Moab by the Jordan" (cf. Num 33:48). For this whole course is made for this reason, and run for this reason, to come to the river of God, that we might get very close to the flowing wisdom and be washed in the waters of divine knowledge so that, purified through all this, we might deserve to enter the promised land.

115   But for us to be able to get through to these things we need the divine mercy so that we might perhaps be able, once we have seen the beauty of the WORD of God, to be ignited with a salutary love for him, and that he himself might deign to love a soul of this kind whom he has seen to have a longing for him.

116   "I am the way" (Jn 14:6). . . . . Moses, therefore, because the place to which he had come and on which he was standing was holy ground, had to remove the shoes from his feet; Joshua, the son of Nun, had to do the same. But for the disciples of Jesus to walk along this life-filled and soul-filled way, it was not enough not to have shoes for the road, as Jesus himself had commanded the apostles (cf. Mt 10:10), but to go along this road it was also necessary for them to be washed by the Jesus who had laid aside his garments, perhaps to make their clean feet even cleaner, perhaps to take up the dirt on the feet of his disciples onto his own body by means of the towel which was all that he was girded with (cf. Jn 13:4). For he himself bears our weaknesses (Isa 53:4).

117   "I am the way" (Jn 14:6). On this way one must take nothing along, neither wallet nor coat; one must travel without even a staff, and not have shoes on one's feet. For this road has itself the power to supply for all the needs of the journey.

118   "Blessed are those whose way is blameless, who walk in the law of the Lord" (Ps 119:1). What does it mean to say that someone's way is blameless? It means this: to "walk in the law of the Lord" and not to go outside the law, and not to sin, but to strive forward, traveling towards virtue. But "blameless" will be the way of those who walk in the divine and in the spiritual law. For "the law of the Lord is blameless" (Ps 19:7). "Blamelessly" does that person walk who "forgets what lies behind and strains forward to what lies ahead" (Phil 3:13), who "does not look back" (Lk 9:62), who "does not turn aside to the right or to the left" (Deut 5:32; 28:14), who does not get lost, does not stand still, does not waste time, but travels on, straining toward the goal.

119   But to seek Jesus is to seek the Logos and wisdom and righteousness and truth and the power of God, all of which is Christ.

120   I put my soul in your hands forever; I make you its guardian, protector and guide.

21   The just person praises God constantly. Sinners, however, praise and confess God only when they receive something good from God.

22   "Every day I will bless thee," etc. (Ps 145:2). Even in dangers and temptations, he says, I will bless you; this means without ceasing. For we are indebted to him for many things; that he made us when we were nothing, that he made us as we are, that he maintains in being what has come to be, that he cares for us each day, both in general and in particular, both in secret and openly, even if we do not know it. But it is not for this reason alone that it is fitting to sing his praise without ceasing, but also because of the greatness of his glory, because of his incorruptible being. And that is why we owe him praise and blessing and never-ending thanksgiving [*eucharistia*] and adoration, and conscientious service.

II

WORD

WORD WITH GOD

THE WORD OF REVELATION

The Logos is the image of the Father from all eternity, the Father's intra-divine and, as such, not yet outward revelation (123). But because he is the Father's eternal revelation, he is also the one in whom the Father, to reveal himself, creates the world (124). He is the one and only simple, original idea, but whose wealth and fullness already contains in itself the rich diversity of the world's ideas (125–127). Thus he is the actuality [Eigentlichkeit] *of the world (128), he is its meaning, Word and life (129), its personal truth which gives as much truth to the world as it pleases him to give (130); but the multiplication of the primal truth into "many" different world truths is only the consequence of the very multiplicity of those sharing in it (131). These truths are a unity through the presence of the one primal truth in each created spirit (132–134). The richness of the primal idea can not be exhausted: the designation WORD (Logos) is only one among many (135). But the purposeful meaning of creation is that the objective and unconscious participation of creatures in the Logos be changed into a subjective, conscious participation (136), and this through a new possibility of the Logos: to be for creatures also the "way" (137). For he is the "all" of the world (138).*

23   If he is the invisible "image of the invisible God" (Col 1:15), I would like to venture the further affirmation that, as the likeness of the Father, there never was a time when he was not (cf. Jn 1:1–3). For when did God, who according to John is called "light" (1 Jn 1:5), not have the "radiance of his own glory" (cf. Heb 1:3), so that someone could dare to set the beginning of a Son who previously did not exist? When could the WORD whom "the Father knows" (cf. Mt 11:27; Jn 10:15), and who is the expression of the ineffable, unnamable and unutterable essence of the Father, not have existed? For they

77

who dare to say that there was a time when the Son was not, should consider that they will also have to say that there was a time when there was no Wisdom, a time when there was no Life. But it is not right nor, because of our weakness, without danger to take it upon ourselves to separate God from his only-begotten Son, the WORD, who is with him eternally, the Wisdom in whom he takes delight (cf. Prov 8:30). For in this way God is not even considered to be eternally happy.[1]

124   "In the beginning God created the heavens and the earth" (Gen 1:1). What is the beginning of all things if not our Lord and "Savior of all" (1 Tim 4:10) Jesus Christ, "the first-born of all creation" (Col 1:15)? In this beginning therefore, that is, in his WORD, "God created the heavens and the earth," as John the evangelist also said in the beginning of his gospel: "In the beginning was the WORD, and the WORD was with God, and the WORD was God. He was in the beginning with God; all things were made through him, and without him was not anything made that was made" (Jn 1:1-3). He is not talking here about some temporal beginning but "in the beginning," as he says, that is, in the Savior, "the heavens and the earth" were made and everything that was made.

125   The Savior has many designations which are distinguished from one another according to their spiritual content, since he is one in underlying [substance] but manifold in his powers.

126   "God by wisdom founded the earth; by understanding he established the heavens" (Prov 3:19). There is in God a prudent wisdom which is to be sought for only in Christ Jesus. For everything which is of God is Christ; he himself is the Wisdom of God, the Power of God, the Righteousness of God, Holiness and Redemption, and thus the Prudent Wisdom of God. Although he [Christ] is one in substance, the many names of his attributes refer to various things.

127   Christ is creator (demiurge) as "beginning" inasmuch as he is wisdom, for it is because of his wisdom that he is called beginning. For wisdom through Solomon says: "God created me the beginning of his ways for his works" (Prov 8:22) so that "in the beginning the WORD" (Jn 1:1) might be in wisdom. In relation to the structure of contemplation and thinking about the whole of things, he is regarded as wisdom; but in relation to sharing in the spiritual aspects of what is contemplated, he is understood as "word."

---

[1] This fragment probably comes, not from the lost commentary on Hebrews, but from the original Greek of PA 4, 1, 1. — R.J.D.

28   You will ask if "the first-born of all creation" (Col 1:15) could be "world" according to any of the meanings given, especially since "wisdom" is "manifold" (Eph 3:10). For since there are in him the inner principles of each and every thing, the principles by which was made all that was made by God in wisdom (as the Prophet says: "In wisdom hast thou made them all"), perhaps he would himself be a "world," as much more manifold than and superior to the sensible world as the bare principle of all matter in the material world is superior to the material world itself which is arranged not by matter but by participation in the WORD and the Wisdom which arranges matter.

29   There was, therefore, in this very existence of Wisdom, already every possibility and form of the future creation, of those things which have their own existence as well as of those things which have a derived existence,[1] . . . That is why Wisdom refers to itself in Solomon as "created at the beginning of the ways" of God (Prov 8:22), for it contains in itself the beginnings or forms or models of every creature. Now in the way in which we have understood Wisdom to be "the beginning of the ways" of God, and how it is said to be created (in that it pre-forms and contains in itself the models and forms of every creature), in that same way must Wisdom be understood to be the WORD of God because it opens up to everything else, that is, to every creature, the meaning of the mysteries and secrets which are, of course, contained within the divine wisdom. This is why Wisdom is said to be WORD, because it is the interpreter, so to speak, of the secrets of the mind. . . . This Son, therefore, is also the truth and life of all things which are. And rightly so. For how could created things have life except from LIFE? Or how could existing things exist in truth if they did not come down from the TRUTH? Or how could there be reason-endowed beings unless WORD and REASON preceded them?

30   The Holy, the True, the one who is this not by participation but in substance, he is the one who is God the WORD, and who "has the key of David" (Rev 3:7). For when the WORD became flesh, he opened up with this key the scriptures which were closed before his coming, and which no one can now close by claiming they have not been fulfilled. . . . He opens up as much as human beings can

---

[1] See above, Nos. 22–23.

understand, but keeps closed what they are unable to understand at the present time.

131   "I am the truth" (Jn 14:6). If Jesus says this, how does truth come about through Jesus Christ? For no one comes about through himself. But it is to be understood that truth itself or substantial truth and, so to speak, the archetype of the truth in rational souls — that truth whose images, so to speak, are imprinted on those who meditate on the truth — was not made by Jesus Christ or by anyone else, but by God. . . . But truth among human beings came about through Jesus Christ. For example the truth in Paul and the apostles came about through Jesus Christ. It is no wonder that, although the truth is one, many truths flow from it. In any case the prophet David knew many truths when he said: "The Lord searches out truths" (Ps 30:24 LXX). For the Father of truth does not search out the one truth but the many truths through which those who have them are saved. And things similar to what was said of truth and truths we find also said about righteousness and righteousnesses. . . . And thus it is written "that the Lord is righteous, and loves righteous deeds" (Ps 11:7). Consider if in a similar way the other things which are said of Christ in the singular can, when multiplied, be said analogously in the plural, such as: "Christ is our life," as the Savior himself says: "I am the way and the truth and the life" (Jn 14:6); and the Apostle: "When Christ who is our life appears, then you also will appear with him in glory." . . . For because Christ is the life in each one, life is multiplied. Is it perhaps here that we should seek the meaning of the text: "if you desire proof that Christ is speaking in me" (Col 3:4)? For in each saint, as it were, Christ is found, and through the one Christ there come about many Christs, imitators of him and transformed according to him who is the image of God.

132   But the Savior, who shines on beings with intellect and sovereign reason, that their mind might look upon their proper object of vision, is the light of the world of mind.

133   For whoever will keep the word will also keep the life which has been made within him and is inseparable from him, which is also the "light of men" (Jn 1:4).

134   The WORD of God is not like every other word: for no one's word is itself living, no one's word is God.

135   And so we insist that, just as in each of the titles already mentioned we must turn from the name to the concept of what is named and see how it applies, and explain how the Son of God is properly given this

title, the same must be done when he is called the WORD. How unreasonable it would be if, in each of these cases, we did not remain fixed upon the word but asked how and in what way he is called "door," and in what metaphorical sense he is called "vine," and why he is called "way," and then did not do this in the one case where he is called "WORD"!

136   But we must not pass over in silence that he does indeed happen to be the "wisdom of God" (1 Cor 1:24), and therefore is also called such. For the wisdom of the God and Father of all (cf. Eph 4:6) is not reducible in substance to mere fantasies, somewhat like the phantasms of human thought. Whoever is able to contemplate the bodiless reality of manifold speculations which include the rationale of all things, a reality which is living and, as it were, ensouled, will understand how rightly the wisdom of God which is above every creature speaks of itself: "God created me the beginning of his ways, for his works" (Prov 8:22). By this creating act all creation was enabled to exist, not being unreceptive of the wisdom of God by which it was made. For, according to the prophet David, God made all things in wisdom (cf. Ps 104:24). But many things are made by participation in wisdom, without attaining that by which they were created, and few indeed are the things which gain possession not only of the wisdom that concerns themselves but also of that which concerns many other things, while Christ is the wisdom of all things. But all wise persons, to the extent that they embrace wisdom, have a share in Christ, in that he is wisdom.

137   But then, since it was to come about that some of those who were created, unable to persevere unchangeably and with constancy in the good, for the good was in them not by nature or substantially but only contingently, turned away and fell . . . , the WORD of God and Wisdom also became the Way. For it is called the Way because it leads [back] to the Father those who enter upon it.

138   One good thing is life; but Jesus is the life. Another good thing is the "light of the world" when it is "true light" and the "light of men" (cf. Jn 8:12; 1:9; 1:4). The Son of God is called all these things. Another good thing which can be thought of besides life and light is truth; and a fourth in addition to these is the way which leads to it. Our Savior teaches that he is all these things when he says: "I am the way and the truth, and the life" (Jn 14:6). And would it not be good to receive from the Lord the gift of shaking off the dust and rising from mortality, since he is the resurrection, as he says: "I am the resurrection" (Jn 11:25)? The door too, through which one enters into the heights of

blessedness is a good; as Christ says: "I am the door" (Jn 10:9). And
what must one say of wisdom . . . in whom the Father rejoiced, de-
lighting in her manifold intellectual beauty which is seen by the eyes
of the mind alone and which invites the contemplator of divine beauty
to heavenly love? For good is the wisdom of God. . . .[1]

THE KNOWLEDGE OF GOD

*The doctrine of the knowledge of God is the subjective comple-
ment to the doctrine of the objective revelation of the WORD in creation. There is here below no immediate vision of the divine. But
because everything bodily is likeness, it is also veiled revelation of
the primordial WORD (139). In this veiled figure, therefore, God
is quite recognizable (140). But because the world as such is participation in the WORD, and thus in any essentially speaking being,
the knowledge of God can thus be real only as his revelation (141).
This revelation is sown across the length and breadth of the world:
the Logos is "logos spermatikos" (141–146). Yet, if Origen previously had to defend himself against a pagan agnosticism (140), he
must now reject again the general "spontaneous" knowledge of God
which Celsus seems to conceive according to the mode of scientific
deduction, since this too already presupposes a self-revelation of
God (147). Without God, God is not even sought (148); hence the
knowledge of God is made perfect not in the philosopher but in the
simple Christian who encounters the self-revealing God (149).*

139   After refuting every suggestion that there is something bodily
in God, we affirm, according to the truth, that God is beyond all

---

[1] That the relationship between Father and Son in Origen is like the relationship between one and mind (world of ideas) in Plotinus, is undeniable.
Above all the absolute unity of the Father and the potential multiplicity of the
Son is reminiscent of the Neoplatonic hierarchy of being. But this similarity is
by no means exclusively Origenistic. Through Augustine it becomes a fundamental trait of Christian trinitarian doctrine, to the extent that the Son is
always seen as the "place" of the world-ideas or "possibles." (If one wants to
avoid this "Platonism," one must, like Gregory of Nyssa, completely drop the
metaphysical existence of the ideas.) But in this relationship to Plotinus the
even greater difference is still very obvious. The Logos of Origen is a
supremely personal, free and sovereign being who is loved not like an objective sphere of value but as Creator and Redeemer.

comprehension and understanding. . . . Our eyes are incapable of gazing upon the nature itself of light, that is, the substance of the sun; but if we look at its brilliance or its rays through something like windows, . . . it becomes possible for us to examine how powerful the very forge and source of bodily light is. In the same way, the works of divine providence and the created beauty of this universe are like rays of God's nature in comparison with his very substance and nature itself. Thus, although our spirit cannot look upon God as he is in himself, it still understands him as the Father of all from the beauty of his works and the glory of his creatures.

140   When [Celsus] says that God is without name, we have to distinguish. For if he means that nothing in words or signs can represent the attributes of God, the statement is true; there are indeed many qualities which cannot be described in words. For who could express in words the qualitative difference between the sweetness of a palm and that of a fig? . . . But if you take the names we apply to God as meaning that it is possible to represent in words something about God in order to lead the hearer by the hand and make him understand something about God, as far as this is possible to human nature, then there is nothing out of place in saying that God can be described by name.

141   But when Celsus says that God cannot be reached with words, then we distinguish and say: if he means the word that is in us, whether conceived in the mind [*endiathetos*] or outwardly expressed [*prophorikos*], then we too say that it is not possible to reach God with words. But if we think about the words: "In the beginning was the WORD, and the WORD was with God, and the WORD was God" (Jn 1:1), then it seems to us that God is reachable by this WORD, and is comprehendible not only by it but also by each one to whom it reveals the Father.

142   [The pagans] deny providence even though it is manifest and almost palpable.

143   And not just the church, but every being endowed with reason is by nature a temple of God, created in order to receive in itself the glory of God.

144   ["The field is the world" (Mt 13:38).] The whole world, and not just the church of God, can be called "the field." For in the whole world has the Son of Man sowed good seed.

145   For how do "we live and move and have our being" (Acts 17:28) in God except by his encompassing the universe and holding in the world by his power . . . as if it were some huge and immense animal?

146   For not in inaccessible writings studied only by a few specialists, but in widely disseminated ones is it written that "ever since the creation of the world his invisible nature, namely, his eternal power and deity, has been clearly perceived in the things that have been made" (Rom 1:20). From this it can be seen that although human beings in this life must begin with the senses and sensible things, if they wish to rise to the nature of intellectual things, they must not stop with just sensible things.

147   Celsus supposes that by combination with other things, analogous to the method called synthesis by the mathematicians, or by separation from other things or by analogy, which is also employed by them, we can come to know God by being able to come at least to the entrance hall of the good. But when the WORD of God says: "No one knows the Father except the Son and anyone to whom the Son chooses to reveal him" (Mt 11:27), he is affirming that it is only by divine grace, and not without God coming to the soul by way of a certain divine inspiration, that one comes to know God. For it is obvious that knowledge of God exceeds the capacity of human nature (hence the many errors in the way humans think about God) and that it is due to the goodness and kindness of God and his marvelous divine grace that the knowledge of God is revealed to those of whom it was determined beforehand that they would live worthy of this knowledge and never do anything unworthy of the reverence due it.

148   Celsus then refers us to Plato, . . . quoting from the *Timaeus:* . . . "It is difficult to find the Creator and Father of the universe, and once found, impossible to communicate him to all." . . . Noble and admirable are these words of Plato. But see if sacred scripture does not give a greater instance of love for human beings in God the WORD who "was in the beginning with God" (Jn 1:2) becoming flesh so that the WORD (whom Plato says that, even when found, cannot be communicated to all) could come to all. Thus Plato could well say that "it is hard to find the Creator and Father of the universe," by which he indicates that it is not wholly impossible for human nature to find God in a way worthy of him, or, if not worthy of him, then at least more adequately than by the masses. If this were true, and God had been truly found by Plato or one of the Greeks, they would not have given reverence to some other thing and called it God and worshiped it; they would not have abandoned him or put in association with so sublime a God things which have nothing in common with him. But we proclaim that human nature of itself does not have the

wherewithal to search for God and attain clear knowledge of him without help from the object of its search who then lets himself be found by those who, after doing what they could, confess that they have need of him, who reveals himself to those whom he judges worthy to see him, in so far as it is possible for God to be known by a human being and for a human soul to know God while still in the body.

149   It seems to me that God—seeing the arrogance or contempt for others of those who have a lofty opinion of their knowledge of God and of their philosophical knowledge of things divine, but who, just as much as the uneducated, run after idols and their temples and the babbling mysteries—"chose what is foolish in the world," namely, the simplest of the Christians who live more moderately and purely than many philosophers, "in order to shame the wise" (1 Cor 1:27). . . . But even the unlettered Christians know for certain that every place in the world is part of the all, and that the whole universe is God's temple. Praying "in every place" (Mal 1:11; 1 Tim 2:8), shutting the eyes of the senses and elevating those of the soul, they transcend the whole world. Nor do they stop at the vault of heaven,[1] but, guided by the divine Spirit, they come in spirit to the super-heavenly place, and standing as it were outside the world, send their prayers up to God.

[1] Allusion to the sun cult of the Mithraic Mysteries which, in Origen's time, were consciously attempting to compete with Christianity.

WORD AS SCRIPTURE

THE SCRIPTURE AS BODY

*Later Fathers will see nature and holy scripture as two equally
ranked physical revelations of God's WORD. For Origen, however, there is a clear difference in level. Even if the whole bodily
world is a manifold likeness of the primordial WORD, scripture
still stands essentially higher. It is the personal manifestation of
God's WORD in the world, since the Logos is essentially WORD,
speech, discourse, proclamation. Origen determines the systematic locus
of scripture by placing it as word-discourse in the middle between
word-spirit and word-flesh (150). But that only intends to say that
this "incarnation" of the Word in the body of scripture is a both more
universal and more immaterial incarnation than the incarnation in the
fleshly body of Jesus Christ; it by no means intends to say that scripture is not a thoroughly worldly, created reality (151). In scripture the
foundation of the order of redemption is laid (152); in it a true "incarnation" is carried out (153). It is the body of truth (154–156).*

150   "The WORD is near you, on your lips and in your heart" (Rom
10:8). . . . The Lord himself says: "If I had not come and spoken to
them, they would not have sin; but now they have no excuse for their
sin" (Jn 15:22). The only thing that this can really mean is that the
Logos is saying that, on the one hand, those within whom he has not
yet come to fullness, have no sin, but that on the other hand, those
who after already having had part in him, act contrary to the ideas by
which he comes to fullness in us, are guilty of sin. And this alone is
the true meaning of "If I had not come and spoken to them, they
would not have sin." Now assuming, as most people do, that these
words apply to the visible Jesus, how is it true that they to whom he
did not come have no sin? For all who lived before the coming of the
Savior would be free of all sin if the physically visible Jesus did not
come. And also all those to whom he had not yet been preached would

have no sin, and it is clear that if they have no sin they are not liable to judgment. But the "logos" in human beings, in which, as we said, our race has a part, has two meanings: either the maturation of ideas, prescinding now from prodigies, which takes place in everyone who grows beyond childhood, or the highest perfection which is found only in the perfect. Therefore it is in relation to the first meaning that we are to understand the words: "If I had not come and spoken to them, they would not have sin; but now they have no excuse for their sin" (Jn 15:22). But to the second meaning we are to apply the words: "All who come before me are thieves and robbers; but the sheep did not heed them" (Jn 10:8). For before the consummation of the logos there are in human beings only blameworthy, imperfect and defective things which cannot command the full obedience of those irrational elements in us which are metaphorically called "sheep." Perhaps the former meaning is to be seen in the words: "The WORD became flesh" (Jn 1:14), and the latter meaning in the words: "The WORD was God" (Jn 1:1). Following this up one must ask if there is something to see in human affairs between "The WORD became flesh" and "The WORD was God." . . .

The Son could also be the Logos because he announces the hidden things of his Father who is intellect similar to the way in which the Son is called WORD. For just as in us logos is the messenger of what is seen by the intellect, so too the WORD of God who knows the Father, since no created being can approach him without a guide, reveals the Father whom he knows. For "no one knows the Father except the Son and any one to whom the Son chooses to reveal him" (Mt 11:27). And inasmuch as he is the WORD, he is the "messenger of great counsel upon whose shoulders will be the government" (Isa 9:6). For he reigned by his suffering the cross. In the apocalypse the faithful and true WORD is said to sit on a white horse (cf. Rev 19:11), indicating, I think, the clearness of the voice by which is borne the WORD of truth which dwells among us.

151   For "all things were made through him" (Jn 1:4), that is, not only creatures but also the law and the prophets.

152   For he who wants to give the world peace has come; he who reconciles heaven with earth and remakes earth into heaven by the teaching of the gospel.

153   Just as this spoken word cannot according to its own nature be touched or seen, but when written in a book and, so to speak, become bodily, then indeed is seen and touched, so too is it with the fleshless and bodiless WORD of God; according to its divinity it is neither

seen nor written, but when it becomes flesh, it is seen and written. Therefore, since it has become flesh, there is a book of its generation.

154   For [David] knew that the one perfect and harmonious [musical] instrument of God is the whole of scripture.

155   The one body of truth.

156   You are, therefore, to understand the scriptures in this way: as the one, perfect body of the WORD:

THE WORD WHICH COMES

In the totality of scripture takes place the one arrival into the world of the WORD of God. The letter, the "body," the external "voice" are the means, the effective signs and so to speak the sacrament of this ever new, irresistible, passionate arrival of the WORD into souls (157–160).

157   What is it that is abolished by the manifestation of Christ's coming — considering him as Wisdom and WORD — if not everything that is called wisdom but is really one of those things which God "catches in their craftiness" (1 Cor 3:19)? In fact John, describing the WORD riding a white horse, adds the most wondrous comment: "His eyes are like a flame of fire" (Rev 19:12).

158   For the other words of wisdom which are thought to be gold are only a bit of sand in view of the wisdom which God "created at the beginning of his ways, for his work" (cf. Prov. 8:22), and silver, i.e., the brilliant and persuasive discourse of many, shall be seen as rubbish before the pure and most excellent sayings of the Lord, seven times proven and purified (cf. Ps 12:6), which have come forth from the WORD which was in the beginning with God (cf. Jn 1:1).

159   "He sits on a white horse," he who is called "faithful" (Rev 19:11), and he rides more surely and, I would say, more regally on words [of scripture] which cannot be overthrown, which run more sharply and swiftly than any horse, overwhelming in their rushing course every opposing word pretending to be the Word and every truth seeming to be the truth.

160   Jesus is thus the WORD of God who enters into the soul, which is called Jerusalem, riding upon an ass loosed from its bonds by the disciples; riding, I say, upon the simple letters of the old covenant now made clear by the two disciples who loosed them, the one leading forth the writings and interpreting them allegorically for the health of the soul, the other pointing out from what lies in darkness the good

and true things to come. But he also rides on a young foal (cf. Zech 9:9), the new covenant; for in both of these is found the WORD of truth that purifies us and drives out from us all thoughts of buying and selling.

MYSTERY

Scripture, as the bodily expression of the divine, is the vessel of super-terrestrial mysteries (161–162). From the fact that God is the real author of scripture follows the manner in which it is to be regarded: nothing in it, right down to the last letter, is without meaning (163). It contains every spiritual medicine (164); like nature, it is an art work of the Creator which can be understood only through his grace (165–166). But it is not a kind of picture puzzle that can be solved once and for all, but becomes all the more mysterious the more one penetrates it (167). No human being can completely see through it (168); and in terms of its substance, it cannot even be translated into external speech (169).

161   But even though we cannot figure everything out, we still sense that all things are full of mysteries.

162   For the things that are described in the scriptures are the forms of certain mysteries and the images of divine things. There is only one position on this in the whole church, namely, that the whole law is spiritual.

163   I, believing in the words of my Lord Jesus Christ, think that even an "iota or dot" is full of mystery and do not think that any of these "will pass away until all is accomplished" (Mt 5:18).

164   There came the woman who was unclean from birth (cf. Mk 5:25 [Mt 9:20] and Lev 12:2ff); there came the leper who was kept apart "outside the camp" because of the uncleanness of the leprosy; they seek a cure from the physician, how to be healed, how to be made clean. And because Jesus, who is the physician, is himself the WORD of God, he prepares medicine for his patients not from the juices of herbs but from the mysteries [*sacramentis*] of words. Whoever, without knowing the power of the particular words, sees these word-medicines scattered through books like weeds in the field, will simply pass them by as worthless and uncultivated speech.

165   If the Law of Moses contained nothing written with a deeper meaning, the prophet would not have said in his prayer to God: "Open my eyes, that I may behold wondrous things out of thy law" (Ps 119:18).

166   For just as in the making of the world the divine skill is manifest
not only in the heavens and the sun and the moon and the stars . . .
but is also brought about on the earth and in the lowliest matter so
that not even the bodies of the tiniest animals are neglected by the
Maker (and how much more their souls, since each of them has
received a specific characteristic like self-preservation in animals),
nor did he neglect the plants of the earth since in each of them there
is something artistic in their roots and leaves, in the fruit they produce and in the varieties of their qualities, so is it our conviction,
regarding all that has been written by the inspiration of the Holy
Spirit, that sublime providence bestows super-human wisdom on the
human race by means of the letters, sowing, so to speak, saving
thoughts and traces of wisdom in each letter according to its capacity. For once one admits that these scriptures are from the Creator of
the world, one must also be convinced that whatever they discover,
who search for the meaning of creation, must also be true of the
meaning of scripture.

167   The more we read on, the higher rises the mountain of mysteries.
And as someone who sets out to sea in a small boat is less afraid as
long as the land is near, but when he has gradually moved out into the
deep and the waves get bigger, and he begins to be tossed up on the
crests and plunged down in the troughs, then indeed he is seized with
fear and terror for entrusting a slender craft to such great waves; the
same seems to happen to us who, with little merit and slight talent,
dare to enter into so vast a sea of mysteries. . . . For everything that
happens happens in mysteries.

168   And so we say to you, lest you read this with boredom, . . . that it
contains more inexpressible and greater mysteries than human
speech can utter or mortal ears can hear, mysteries which in my view
not only cannot be worthily and fully explained by one of "the least"
(cf. 1 Cor 15:9) like myself, but not even by those who are much better than me.

169   There are things whose meaning simply cannot be explained by
any words or human language (cf. 1 Cor 2:4), but is made clear more
by a simple act of understanding than by anything that comes from
the words. The understanding of the sacred scriptures also comes
under this rule, according to which the things that are said are to be
valued not according to the commonness of the words but according
to the divinity of the Holy Spirit which inspired them to be written.

IMAGE UPWARDLY OPEN

Scripture is mystery because it is, like every bodily thing, image which signifies beyond itself; except that here, the "body" consists of earthly histories, laws and sayings, but the "spirit" is the personal WORD of God himself. Hence the endlessly intensified tension between both poles. Paul is the best example of how the predominance of the spiritual, irresistibly breaking through, is a perspective that flashes through the letter (170). Everywhere a thousand mysteries break out from one point (171); and bodily expression is just simply too narrow for many a thought (172).

But talking in images is grounded in human nature itself (173); it is the means of showing the spirit the way from plurality to unity (174–175). That is why studying scripture is so sublime and so necessary (176–177).

In the understanding that every bodily thing in the scripture is only a sign towards what is above, which, as sign, does not itself contain the truth but points toward the truth, Origen wages his persistent battle against the literal exegesis of the Antiochean school (178–182). And all understanding of scripture grows, according to him, only from faith (183–185) and prayer (186).

170   Paul seems to be talking as if a trusted and prudent servant is being led by a great lord and king into the royal treasure chambers and there is shown various large rooms with such different and uncertain approaches that he is shown how to enter by one and leave by another, and sometimes by different entrances to come to the same chamber. . . . This faithful servant who is being led around is also shown the silver treasure of the king and another of gold. . . . And yet no one of these has its doors completely open to reveal all, but only partially open so that the servant might indeed recognize his lord's treasures and his royal wealth, but not have perfect knowledge of any of these. Now after this, that servant . . . is sent out to raise an army for the king, to levy a draft, to test the soldiers. And because he is loyal, in order to attract more to military service and gather a larger army for his king, he finds it necessary to recount in part what he has seen. And yet because he is prudent and knows that it is necessary to keep secret the mystery of the king, he makes use of certain indicators rather than precise accounts so that the power of the king is not exposed,

and the inner arrangement, the ornaments of the palace and the style of life remain secret. In the same way too, as I have said, does it seem to me that the apostle Paul is speaking here, not only because, as he himself says, his knowledge is imperfect and his understanding is imperfect (cf. 1 Cor 13:9, 12), but also because of us who are not able to get even some grasp of what he knows imperfectly; and so he carefully weighs his speech, and with but one or at most two words, touches on and lets us peek into the chamber of each mystery. Sometimes he goes in by one door and out by another, sometimes he goes in by a different door and from there into another chamber, so that if you look for him where he has gone in you won't see him go out.

171   And what must be said about the prophets whom we all know to be full of enigmatic and obscure words? And when we come to the gospels, their precise meaning, which is the meaning of Christ, requires the grace which was given to him who said: "We have the mind of Christ, that we might understand the gifts bestowed on us by God. And we impart this in words not taught by human wisdom but taught by the Spirit" (1 Cor 2:16, 12, 13). And who reads the revelations given to John without being struck by the obscurity of the indescribable mysteries being made known even to those who do not understand what is being written? And who, of those who know how to examine texts carefully, would find the letters of the apostles to be clear and easily understandable, since there too countless numbers of the most sublime thoughts are accessible only in a limited way, as if through a small opening.

172   In a general way we ought to think about every parable whose interpretation has not been recorded by the evangelists, although Jesus "explained everything privately to his own disciples" (Mk 4:34). And this is why the gospel writers concealed the clear meaning of the parables, because what was signified by them exceeded the capacity of the words to express, and every solution and exposition of such parables was such that "the world itself could not contain the books that would be written" (Jn 21:25) to explain such parables. But it might be that a fitting heart could be found, on which, because of its purity, the individual letters of the meaning of the parables could be "written with the Spirit of the living God" (2 Cor 3:3).

173   Is it for the Greeks alone to philosophize in interpretations, and for the Egyptians too, and for all the non-Greek peoples to pride themselves in their mysteries and secret truths, and only for the Jews . . . to have received no share in the divine power?

174   That is why [the prophet] has spoken in parables and riddles, so that our mind would be expanded or, better still, being gathered into one, might see the precise points that have been made, and, withdrawing from the vices of the body as it comes to understand the truth, direct the course of its life according to that truth.

175   "Lift up your eyes, and see how the fields are already white for harvest" (Jn 4:35). The WORD that is present to the disciples is encouraging the hearers to lift up their eyes towards the fields of the scriptures and to the fields of the WORD in each being in order to see the whiteness and the brilliance of the light of the truth which is everywhere.

176   [Knowledge of scripture] is the art of arts and the science of sciences.

177   To search after the meaning of the sacred scriptures is the injunction given us by Jesus who said: "Search the scriptures" (Jn 5:39), and is according to the wish of Paul who taught that we ought "to know" the answer which "must be given to everyone" (Col 4:6), and also to the wish of him who said: "Always be prepared to make a defense to any one who calls you to account for the faith that is in you" (1 Pet 3:15).

178   A person who carefully examines the gospels for the inconsistencies in their historical meaning . . . will be made dizzy by the results and will either cease to hold the gospels to be true and will make an arbitrary choice to prefer one of them, not daring to give up all faith in our Savior, or will hold the four to be true, but not in their bodily signs.

179   It was the intention of the evangelists as far as possible to speak the truth, both spiritual and bodily, but where this could not be done for both, to prefer the spiritual to the bodily, because the spiritual truth was often preserved in a, so to speak, bodily falsehood.

180   All bodily things are vanity, for it is the incorporeal nature that was made according to the image of God.

181   One must understand the divine scripture intellectually and spiritually; for the sensible or physical way of knowing that is according to the historical meaning is not true. If you try to draw the divine sense down to the purely external aspect of an expression, lacking any foundation there, it will go back to the home which is its proper object of contemplation; for, supplied for this by its guide, the Holy Spirit, it has wings, the spiritual graces. Therefore, high above the ether itself, so to speak, it flies away. Therefore not to rise above the letter, but to cling to it insatiably, is the sign of a life that is not true.

182   Knowledge is both a "cistern" and a "spring." To those just coming to virtue, it seems to be a deep "cistern"; but to those free of passion and purified, it is a "spring." . . . And just as a spring effortlessly

gives forth running water to the thirsty . . . and just as it flows constantly, so too does the sensible scripture flow in a ceaseless stream and readily dispense God to the thirsty.

183   When in reading the scriptures you come across a passage which . . . is a "stumbling stone" (Rom 9:32), put the blame on yourself . . . so that there may come about what was written: "He who believes will not be put to shame" (Rom 9:33). First believe, then you will find.

184   Many were the physicians who undertook to heal the pagans. If you consider the philosophers proclaiming truth, they are physicians attempting to heal. But she [i.e., humanity], after paying out all that she had, could not be healed by any of the physicians. But upon touching the fringe of Jesus' garment, who alone is the physician of souls and bodies, she was healed on the spot by the fire and warmth of faith. If we look to our faith in Jesus Christ and consider how great is the son of God and touch something of him, we will see that in comparison to the fringes in him we have touched but a fringe. But all the same the fringe heals us and enables us to hear Jesus say: "Daughter, your faith has saved you" (Lk 8:48).

185   The heretics are indeed on the pathways; not however on the ways made straight by the Lord but on those made crooked by the evil one. They deviate to the right and the left, not satisfied with mere faith; they indeed think more deeply, but not the truth.

186   Devote yourself above all to knowledge of the holy scripture . . . with faith and God-pleasing readiness. . . . And it is not enough to knock and seek, for what is most necessary for understanding the things of God is prayer.

FROM WORD-SCRIPTURE TO WORD-SPIRIT

The right direction for understanding the scriptures thus goes from the multiplicity of images to the unity of the inner event. By one single expression is ignited the passion of everything divine (187), by one word is the reader gradually caught by the whole net (188). But precisely this multiplicity is necessary in order to educate us from many sides unto the one Christ (189), and show us how the human way necessarily leads from the "lie" of the sensible to the truth of the spirit (190). The inner reality of the scripture is power (191), is holiness (192), is not just spiritual, but substantial spirit (193). Thus it is understood only by the Spirit or by those who share in the Spirit (194–195). Its self-witness however consists

*in the effectiveness of the scriptural word (196–197). But the
spirit-unity of scripture is Christ (198–199), as its personal sum-
mation (200–201). That is why each word of scripture is so
endlessly fruitful (202), and why the multiplicity of the letter is not
just poverty but an expression of spiritual richness (203).*

187   When something said by the Lord sets someone on fire so that he
becomes a lover of wisdom because of it, and burns with eagerness for
all that is beautiful, then one can say that the fire of the Lord has
come upon him.

188   The kingdom of heaven is likened to a net of varied texture because the scripture of the old and new testament is woven together
from all kinds of variegated thoughts. And just as with the fishes
that fall into the net, some are found in one part of the net and others
in another, and each in the part where it was caught, so too will you
find in the case of those who have come into the net of the scriptures
that some have been caught by the prophetic net (for example, of
Isaiah, because of this or that expression, or Jeremiah or Daniel),
others by the net of the law, and others by that of the gospel, and
some by the apostolic net. For when one is first caught by the WORD
or seems to be caught, one is held by a certain part of the whole net. It
is also quite possible that some of the fish, when caught, are surrounded by the whole texture of the net in the scriptures, are hemmed
in and bound on all sides, unable to escape from the net. Now this net
is cast into the sea, the tumultuous life of human beings who, everywhere in the world, swim in the bitter affairs of life. But before the
coming of our Savior Jesus Christ, this net was not completely filled;
for still lacking to the net of the law and the prophets was he who says:
"Think not that I have come to abolish the law and the prophets; I
have not come to abolish them but to fulfill them" (Mt 5:17). It is thus
in the gospels and the words of Christ, and through the working of the
apostles, that the texture of the net has been completed.

189   "The kingdom of heaven is like a merchant in search of fine pearls"
(Mt 13:45). He seeks pearls among all kinds of doctrines which profess to proclaim the truth, and among those who teach such. And let
the prophets stand so to speak for the mussels which conceive from
the dew of heaven, becoming pregnant with the heavenly WORD of
truth — the good pearls for which the merchant in this text is searching. But the leader of the pearls who, when found, all the rest are

found with him, the pearl of great value, is the Christ of God.[1] . . .
That is why Paul says: "I count everything as loss that I might gain
Christ" (Phil 3:8) . . . the one pearl of great price. Precious, then, is
a lamp to those in darkness, and a lamp is needed until the sun rises.
Precious too is the brightness on the face of Moses (and, I think, that
of the prophets) and a beautiful sight by which we are introduced to
the ability to see the glory of Christ. . . . And we have need of the
splendor which can pass away for the sake of "the splendor that surpasses it" (2 Cor 3:10), just as we need the "imperfect knowledge"
which "will pass away when the perfect comes" (1 Cor 13:9–10). Thus
every soul which is coming into childhood and making its way "to
maturity" (Heb 6:1) needs, until "the fullness of time" (Gal 4:4) has
come for it, a tutor. . . . But the multitude, ignorant of the beauty of
the many pearls of the law, and of all the knowledge, even though imperfect, of the prophets, think that they can, without a full explanation
or understanding of those things, find the one pearl of great price and
behold "the surpassing worth of the knowledge of Christ Jesus" (Phil
3:8), in comparison to which everything which preceded such tremendous knowledge, even though it may not be "refuse" in itself, still
appears to be "refuse" (Phil 3:8). Perhaps this refuse is the dung put
down under the fig tree by the vinedresser (cf. Lk 13:7–9) which is the
cause of its bearing fruit.

190   I will add that in the first period of its life, all kinds of false doctrines arise in the soul; for it is not possible for a human being to
grasp a true and purified view of things right from the beginning. But
God foreordained the stories of history and the words of scripture in
order to nourish the son born to Abraham according to the flesh first
of all with words according to the flesh, so that this son would be first
"the son of the slave girl" so that he could afterwards be born as "the
son of the free woman through promise" (Gal 4:23).

191   Just as among the herbs, each has a power either to heal bodies or to
do something else, but it is not the business of everyone to know what
each plant is good for, but . . . of those expert in plants . . . so

---

[1] Origen is here following the broadly disseminated ancient legends about
the life of the pearl mussels. They are thought, among other things, to open
their shells by night on the surface of the sea and receive a drop of dew which
they form into pearls. They swim very rapidly and, like the bees, have a king
which is distinguished by its size.

too is the holy and spiritual person a kind of botanist who reads every iota and every dash which happens to be in the sacred scripture, and finds out the power of the letter and what it is good for, and knows that nothing written down is superfluous. And if you also want to hear a second example of this, then consider that each member of our body has been made by God the Maker for a particular purpose; but it is not everyone's business to know what is the nature and purpose of the members right down to the smallest. For there are the anatomy experts among the doctors who can tell us to what purpose each part, even the smallest, was made by Providence. Understand the scriptures in this way too.

192   For just as all gold which is found outside the temple is not sanctified, so too every thought which is outside holy scripture (however admirable it may appear to some) is not holy because it is not contained in the meaning of scripture which, just as the temple makes holy only its own gold, sanctifies only the meaning it has in itself.

193   "The Lord said" (Lev 6:1). What is "the Lord"? Let the Apostle answer you. Learn from him that "the Lord is the Spirit" (2 Cor 3:17). And if the word of the Apostle is not enough for you, listen to the Lord himself in the gospel saying that "God is Spirit" (Jn 4:24). If therefore both the Lord and God are "Spirit," we must listen spiritually to what the Spirit says. And I will say more than this too: namely, that what the Lord says is to be believed not just to be spiritual, but to be Spirit itself. . . . Hear the Lord: "The words that I have spoken to you are spirit and life" (Jn 6:63).

194   No one can really understand the words of Daniel except the Holy Spirit which was in Daniel.

195   For just as "no one knows a man's thoughts except the spirit of the man which is in him," and "no one comprehends the thoughts of God except the Spirit of God" (1 Cor 2:11), so too, no one (except God) understands what has been spoken by Christ in similitudes and parables. No one, that is, except the Spirit of Christ and those who share it. This means that we are to share not only the Spirit of Christ as such, but also of Christ as Wisdom and as WORD, and in that way come to see what is being revealed to us in this passage.

196   If then it should be granted that in some cases the same doctrines are found in the Greeks and in the representatives of our faith, they still do not have the same power of winning souls. . . . And we do not say this in disparagement of Plato (for the great world of human beings has beneficially produced him too), but to demonstrate the

intention of those who spoke as follows: "And my speech and my message were not in plausible words of wisdom, but in demonstration of the Spirit and power, that your faith might not rest in the wisdom of men but in the power of God" (1 Cor 2:4–5). The divine WORD is saying that what is spoken, even if it is in itself true and trustworthy, is not of itself sufficient to penetrate into the human soul unless a certain power from God is given to the speaker and the words are filled with grace; and only from God does this come to those who speak efficaciously.

197   Notice now the difference between the beautiful words of Plato about the highest good and what was said in the prophets about the light of the blessed. And notice that the truth contained in Plato on this subject was of no help towards a purified worship of God, . . . but the simple language of the sacred scriptures has produced enthusiasm in those who read it sincerely. This light is nourished in them by the oil . . . which preserved the light of the lamps of the five wise virgins (cf. Mt 25:4).

198   "The kingdom of heaven is like treasure hidden in a field" (Mt 13:44). . . . That field, it seems to me, is the scripture, planted with what has become clear in the words and other thoughts of the histories, law and prophets (for the planting of these words in the whole of scripture is great and varied). But the treasure hidden in the field consists of the concealed thoughts (underlying what is manifest) of wisdom hidden "in mystery" (cf. 1 Cor 2:7) and in Christ, "in whom are hid all the treasures of wisdom and knowledge" (Col 2:3).

199   If truth is one, then it is clear that the preparation for it and its demonstration, which is wisdom, is rightly considered to be one; since nothing that is thought to be wisdom, but does not have the truth, can rightly be called wisdom. But if truth is one and wisdom is one, then reason [*logos*] too, which announces truth and makes wisdom simple and manifest to those who can receive it, will be one.

200   The Preacher (Ecclesiastes) says: "My son: beware of writing many books" (Eccl 12:12). I compare this with something from the Proverbs of the same Solomon which reads: "When you talk too much, you will not escape sin, but if you restrain your lips, you are prudent" (Prov 10:19). And I ask whether saying many things of whatever kind is "talking too much," even if the many things one speaks are holy and conducive to salvation. For if this is so, and the one who speaks many useful things is guilty of talking too much, Solomon himself did not escape this sin, for he uttered "three thousand proverbs and five thousand songs. And he spoke of trees from the cedar that is in Lebanon to the hyssop that grows out of the wall. He spoke also of beasts and of

birds and of reptiles and of fish" (1 Kgs 4:32–33). For how is it possible
to give instruction without, in the simpler sense of the word, talking
too much? Does not wisdom herself say to those who are perishing: "I
extended my discourse and you paid no heed" (Prov 1:24)? . . .

We have to ask what is this "much speaking," and then pass on to
see what are the "many books." Now all the WORD of God which was
in the beginning with God is not "much speaking," is not words; for
the one Word is composed of many doctrines [*theōrēma*], each of which
is part of the WORD in its entirety. . . . We can accordingly say
that whoever utters anything contrary to reverence for God is guilty
of much talk; but whoever says what is true, even if he says everything and leaves nothing out, is always speaking the one WORD: nor
are the saints guilty of much talk since they always have in view the
one word. If then "talking too much" is judged from the contents of
what is said and not from the multitude of words, let us see if we cannot say that all the sacred scriptures are one book, and that what is
outside of this are the "many books."

But since I need a proof of this from holy scripture, consider
whether I can prove this quite nicely by demonstrating that in our
view Christ is not written about in just one book (understanding
"book" in its usual sense). For he is written about in the Pentateuch,
he is spoken of in each of the Prophets and Psalms and, in a word, as
the Savior himself says, in all the scriptures to which he refers us
when he says: "You search the scriptures, because you think that in
them you have eternal life; and it is they that bear witness to me" (Jn
5:39). If then he refers us to "the scriptures" as giving witness of him,
he is not sending us to the one or the other, but to all the scriptures
which proclaim him, those which, in the Psalms, he calls the "head of
the book" when he says: "In the head of the book it is written of me"
(Ps 40:7). . . . He calls it all one "head," thus summing up in one the
word which has come to us about him.

201   "In the head of the book it is written of me" (Ps 40:7). He doesn't
refer us to one scripture text and not to another, but to the whole
God-inspired scripture announced by him. But he calls the whole of it
a "head of the book" because the WORD which came to us is summed
up there in one single point: "to do your will, O my God" (Ps 40:8).

202   It seems to me that each word of the divine scripture is like a seed
whose nature it is, once it has been thrown into the earth and regenera-
ted into an ear, or whatever happens to be the fruit of its species, to be
multiplied many times over. This happens all the more abundantly

the more effort the experienced farmer puts into it or the more largess is bestowed by the beneficial earth.

203   As long as the loaves remain whole, no one is fed or refreshed, nor do the loaves themselves seem to increase. Well then, consider how we break the few loaves: we take from the divine scriptures a few words, and how many thousand people are filled! But unless these loaves were broken, unless broken down into small pieces by the disciples, that is unless the letter was broken down into little pieces and discussed, its meaning would not be able to come to all. But when we have begun to work through and discuss every single part, then the crowds will take as much as they are able to. But what they cannot take is to be collected and saved "that nothing may be lost" (Jn 6:12). . . . We carefully collect these and preserve them in baskets until we see what the Lord wishes to be done with them as well.

ON INTERPRETING THE SCRIPTURE

From all that has been said it is clear that scripture is to be interpreted according to its spiritual unity of meaning. Paul provided a preliminary sketch of this method and it is a part of the tradition of the Church (204). The relationship of the image is twofold: first between the old and new covenant, and then between the whole bible and the "eternal gospel" in the hereafter (205). But "image" plays between open "sign" and veiled "seal" (206).

Following upon this come the four most common propositions about scriptural images: (a) the meaning is spiritual, (b) the expression is sensible, (c) the meaning appears veiled in the expression, (d) the expression, by means of its intended inadequacy, points beyond itself (207). Thus not everything has meaning in itself (208). Literal, moral and mystical meaning of scripture as body, soul, spirit (208–213).

But one can study the sensible without comprehending it as image (214). One must have one's own nose for this, like a hound in pursuit of a wild animal (215–216). And because the image is only a sign and must fail at a certain point, the decisive finding necessarily takes place precisely in this failure and quandary (217–219). But even this is not a natural technique, but simply closeness to Jesus (220).

204   Paul says somewhere in writing to the Corinthians: "For we know that our fathers were all under the cloud, and all were baptized into

Moses in the cloud and in the sea, and all ate the same supernatural food and all drank the same supernatural drink. For they drank from the supernatural Rock which followed them, and the Rock was Christ" (1 Cor 10:1-4). You can see how different Paul's tradition is from the historical reading: what the Jews think is a crossing of the sea, Paul calls baptism; where they see a cloud, Paul puts the Holy Spirit; and it is in this way that he wants us to understand what the Lord commanded in the gospels when he said: "Whoever is not born again of water and the Holy Spirit cannot enter into the kingdom of heaven" (cf. Jn 3:5). And the manna too, which the Jews think of as food for the stomach and satisfaction for hunger, Paul calls "spiritual food" (1 Cor 10:3). And not just Paul, but the Lord too, says in the same gospel: "Your fathers ate the manna in the wilderness, and they died. Whoever eats of the bread which I give him will not die for ever" (cf. Jn 6:49, 50). And right after that: "I am the bread which came down from heaven" (Jn 6:51). Hence Paul speaks quite openly about "the rock which followed them": "And the Rock was Christ" (1 Cor 10:4). How then are we to act, who have received such principles of interpretation from Paul, the teacher of the church? Does it not seem right that such a method coming to us from the tradition should serve as a model in all other instances? Or shall we, as some would like, abandon what so great and holy an apostle has given us and turn back to "Jewish myths" (Tit 1:14)? I at least, if I am interpreting this differently than Paul, think that in this I am extending my hands to the enemies of Christ, and that this is what the prophet says: "Woe to him who gives his neighbor to drink from the turmoil of confusion" (Hab 2:15).

05   With this we learn something of general import: if a sign signifies something, then each of the signs in scripture (whether in a historical or law text) is a sign indicative of something to be fulfilled later. Thus "the sign of Jonah" coming forth after three days from "the belly of the whale" was a sign of the resurrection of our Savior rising from the dead after "three days and three nights" (Mt 12:39-40). And what is called circumcision is a "sign" (Rom 4:11) of what Paul explained in the words: "We are the circumcision" (Phil 3:3). You too now should search out every sign in the old scriptures as a type of something in the new, and what is called sign in the new covenant as indicative of something either in the age to come or in the generations after that in which the sign took place.

06   Something is called a sign when, through something that is visible, something else is meant. So for example . . . the sign is Jonah, and

what is meant is Christ. . . . But something is called a seal when someone is given custody for a time over an object which no one may open but the one who gave it. By the seal [of circumcision] is signified the righteousness of faith which Abraham, still uncircumcised, merited to receive and become the father of many nations. It will be unsealed, we believe, when "the full number of the Gentiles has come in and all Israel will be saved" (Rom 11:25–26). That is when what the Apostle speaks of (Rom 4:12) will come about, namely, that Abraham will be the father not only of the nations but also, through faith, of circumcision. . . . Since one is talking about a sign, as we have explained, where something is indicated through what is visible, but one has a seal where something is closed for a time and is not visible, this can also be understood in such a way that the mysteries which are foreshadowed in the law and the patriarchs were this kind of reality. That is, they were to be both pointed to by signs and guarded by seals. When therefore they were to be pointed to with signs for the pagans who believed, then Abraham is said to have received a sign; but when they were to be kept concealed from the circumcised who were not to believe, he is said to have received a seal.

207   Since this is so, we now have to sketch out what seems to us to be the marks of the proper understanding of the scripture. First, it must be shown that the purpose of the Spirit, which by God's providence through the WORD who "was in the beginning with God" (Jn 1:2) illuminating the ministers of truth, the prophets and the apostles, was first of all to teach us something about the hidden mysteries regarding the fate of human beings. . . . A second purpose, because of those unable to bear the burden of investigating matters so important, was to conceal the doctrine concerning the things just mentioned in the revealed accounts which contained information about the physical work of creation, the creation of human beings and their growth through generation from the first pair to a great multitude. The Spirit also did this in other histories recounting both the deeds of the just and — since they were human — their occasional sins, and the wickedness, licentiousness and greed of the lawless and impious. And most remarkably, in the accounts about wars, the conquered and the conquerors, some mysteries are revealed to those able to examine them closely. And even more remarkably, the laws of truth are predicted through the written laws; and all this is written down in an order and with a power truly befitting the wisdom of God. For it was intended that the covering over of the spiritual

things — that is, the bodily part of the scriptures — should not be without profit in many things and that it should be able, as far as possible, to bring improvement to the multitude.

But since, if the usefulness of the law and the order and brilliance of the histories were perfectly clear, we might think that there was nothing else to be found in the scriptures but the obvious meaning, the WORD of God arranged it that some "scandals," so to speak, "stumbling blocks" and "impossibilities" (Rom 9:33; 14:13; 8:3) would be mixed in with the law and the writings so that we would not be totally swept away by the attractiveness of the reading and either, because we are learning nothing worthy of God, fall away from the true teaching, or, by not parting from the letter, learn nothing that is more divine.

08 There are some things which are in no way to be observed according to the letter of the law, and there are some things which allegory should not change at all but are to be observed in every way just as the scripture has them; [finally, there are also] some things which can also stand according to the letter, but in which it is also necessary for allegory to be sought.

09 We have often pointed out that there is a threefold mode of understanding in the holy scripture: a historical, a moral and a mystical. We understand from this that there is in scripture a body, a soul and a spirit.

10 The first glimpse of the letter is bitter enough: it prescribes the circumcision of the flesh; it gives the laws of sacrifice and all the rest that is designated by the letter that kills (cf. 2 Cor 3:6). Cast all this aside like the bitter rind of a nut. You then, secondly, come to the protective covering of the shell in which the moral doctrine or counsel of continence is designated. These are of course necessary to protect what is contained inside, but they too are doubtless to be smashed and broken through. We would say, for example, that abstinence from food and chastisement of the body is necessary as long as we are in this body, corruptible as it is and susceptible to passion. But when it is broken and dissolved and, in the time of its resurrection, gone over from corruption into incorruption and from animal to spiritual, then it will be dominated no longer by the labor of affliction or the punishment of abstinence, but rather by its own quality and not by any bodily corruption. This is why abstinence seems necessary now and afterwards will have no point. Thirdly you will find hidden and concealed in these the sense of the mysteries of the wisdom and knowledge of God (cf. Col 2:3) in which the souls of the saints are nourished and fed not only in the present life but also in the future. This then is

that priestly fruit about which the promise is given to those "who hunger and thirst for righteousness, for they shall be satisfied" (Mt 5:6). In this way, therefore, the gradation of this threefold mystery runs through all the scripture.

211   Because God commanded the ark to be built not just with two chambers but also with three chambers, let us get to work and, to this twofold interpretation which has gone before, also add a third as God commands. The first of these was the historical sense and is set at the bottom as a kind of foundation. The second, higher and more sublime, was the mystical. Let us try, if we can, to add a third, the moral sense, although this too — since it is called neither "two-chambered" with no addition nor "three-chambered" and nothing more, but when it is called "two-chambered" the "three-chambered" is also added — is not without mystery for this interpretation we are presenting. For three-chambered designates this threefold exposition. However, the literal sense in holy scripture cannot always stand but is often lacking, when for example it is written: "Thorns grow in the hand of the drunkard" (Prov 26:9 LXX), and when it is written of the temple built by Solomon: "The sound of the hammer and the axe was not heard in the house of God," and then in Leviticus when the leprosy of a wall and a skin and a warp are required to be inspected by the priests and purified (cf. Lev 14:34; 13:48).[1] It is therefore because of things like this that the ark was built not solely with three chambers but also with two chambers.

212   According to the teaching of the most wise Solomon, whoever "wishes to have wisdom" must begin with moral knowledge and understand the meaning of the words: "If you desire wisdom, keep the commandments, and the Lord will supply it for you" (Sir 1:26). This is the reason why this teacher, who was the first to teach people the divine philosophy, put the Book of Proverbs at the beginning of his work in which, as we said, the moral position is handed on so that, when progress has been made in understanding and morals, one may also come to the discipline of natural science and, distinguishing there

---

[1] It is essential to note that the "literal sense" of Origen does not have the broad connotations found in the modern use of this expression such as: "The primary meaning intended by the biblical author." The metaphorical meaning, even when it is primary, as in "I am the light of the world," is not, for Origen, part of the literal meaning. Such phrases, then, can have no literal meaning according to Origen's definition. — R.J.D.

the natural causes of things, may recognize that one must leave behind the "vanity of vanities" (Eccl 1:2) but hasten on to the eternal, lasting things. Thus, after Proverbs, one comes to the Preacher (Ecclesiastes) who teaches, as we said, that all things visible and corporeal are corruptible and fragile. When they who study wisdom come to see that this is so, they will doubtless scorn and despise them and, renouncing the whole world as it were, will turn towards the invisible and eternal things which are indeed taught in the Song of Songs, but clothed in certain images of love. . . . I think that this triple form of divine philosophy has been prefigured also in those holy and blessed men for the sake of whose holy instruction the most high God wished to be called "the God of Abraham, the God of Isaac and the God of Jacob" (Exod 3:6). For "Abraham" means moral philosophy through obedience. . . . "Isaac" stands for natural philosophy since he dug wells and searched into the depths of things. But "Jacob" stands for internal vision, for he is called "Israel" because of his contemplation of divine things and because he gazed upon the "gate of heaven" and the "house of God" and the routes of "the angels," the ladder extending from earth to "heaven" (cf. Gen 28:12, 17).

13 Therefore just as "the seen and the unseen" (cf. 2 Cor 4:18), earth and heaven, soul and flesh, body and spirit are related to each other, and this world is made up of these relationships, so too must it be believed that holy scripture is made up of seen and unseen things. It consists of a body, namely, the visible letter, and of a soul which is the meaning found within it, and of a spirit by which it also has something of the heavenly in it, as the Apostle says: "They serve as a copy and shadow of the heavenly sanctuary" (Heb 8:5). Since this is so, calling upon God who made the soul and the body and the spirit of scripture — the body for those who came before us, the soul for us, and the spirit for those who "in the age to come will receive the inheritance of eternal life" (Lk 18:18, 31) by which they will come to the heavenly things and the truth of the law — let us seek out not the letter but the soul. . . . If we can do this, we will also ascend to the spirit.

14 Not everyone who saw what the Savior did could, in "seeing," immediately "understand" (cf. Isa 6:9) why it was done. To take an example: "he washed the feet of the disciples" and they saw quite well how the master was washing the feet of the disciples (cf. Jn 13:5). Those who were present indeed "saw," but only what was done, not why it was done. For it was an image of that other washing of the feet in which the WORD of God washed the feet of the disciples. That is

why the Savior said to the reluctant Peter protesting: "You shall not wash my feet" (Jn 13:8) — what did he say? "What I am doing, you do not know now, but afterward you will understand" (Jn 13:7). What are you doing now? says Peter; I see you washing our feet; I see the basin there and you girded with a towel and serving us and drying our feet. But because this was not what was going on — but the Savior, stripped down, was pouring spiritual "water into the basin" according to the scriptures and was "washing the feet of the disciples" so that, when they were "clean," they could ascend to the one who said: "I am the way" (Jn 14:6) and not be full of the "dust" which he wanted to "shake off" on the unworthy who did not accept his peace (cf. Mt 10:14) and were not worthy of what was being said — and because this was what was being signified he said: "What I am doing you do not know now, but afterward you will understand" (Jn 13:7).

215   The parables and similitudes are not applied to all the circumstances to which they are likened or of which they are an image, but only to some.

216   When I consider the difficulties of investigating the meaning . . . of the words of scripture, something similar seems to be happening to me as happens to a hunter who goes out after his prey with the help of a dog's keen sense of smell. It sometimes happens that the hunter, intently following the trail, thinks he is close to the hidden lair, but suddenly loses track of the trail. He goes back and makes the dog sniff more carefully over the same tracks until he finds the place where the prey made a sharp turn onto another hidden trail which, when he has found it, he pursues more eagerly, more certain in his hope of gaining his prey and made more sure by the strength of the track. That is what happens to us when the traces of the explanation we have begun somehow disappear; we go back a bit and hope that the Lord our God will grant us our prey.

217   They who are making their way towards the vision of Christ's glory and the kingdom, that is, to the perfection of the WORD and to the kingdom which it reigns over and rules, making all enemy words their footstool and treading them underfoot (cf. Ps 110:1; Lk 20:43), they must often, in their search for truth, suffer a loss of that ability to perceive by which the soul is properly nourished in its search for what must be sought. And just as those who were making their way towards the promised land were afflicted at times and suffered hunger for physical food in order to receive the manna from heaven, so too must they who are to be nourished by the perfection of the WORD be frequently

tried by a failure of their ability to perceive, and not be downcast by this. And we see this daily in ourselves when we are seeking some understanding of the truth in the scriptures: before we find what we are seeking, we experience some inability to perceive, until that poverty of perception is lifted from us by God who "gives food in due season" (Ps 145:15) to those who are worthy.

18   Because such a WORD does not come to men and women stripped of matter and bodily signs, Jesus spits on the ground and makes a paste. Can you not interpret this as saying that all scripture and its mode of proclamation, as divine ideas, consists of the spittle of Christ but, as reporting of histories and human deeds, consists of the dust of the earth, such that the whole letter of the law and the prophets and the rest of the scriptures are of such clay with which the eyes of the unseeing must be anointed, and after this to be sent away by God to the pool of Siloam? By this is signified the "swimming" so to speak involved in the searching and groping for the truth.

19   Even if you do not know how you can give thanks to God in a worthy manner, you should still exult with the clear voice of a singing heart which soars above the signs of the doubtful letters and express the mysterious and inexpressible despite the confusion of the interpretations. If you soar above the sounds of the words, if you keep within you the proclamation made with the mouth, if you can sing praise to God with just the spirit, your spirit, which does not know how to express its movements in words, because the word in you cannot carry the inexpressible and divine meaning of the Spirit—then you are singing praise to God.

20   No one has revealed his divinity as John has. . . . One can even dare to say that the gospels are the first fruits of all the scriptures, but that John is the first fruits of the gospels. No one can grasp its meaning who has not lain on Jesus' breast and [like John] also received Mary from Jesus as one's own mother. So great must one be who is to become another John in order, like John, to be shown Jesus by Jesus. For if Mary has no other son but Jesus, . . . but Jesus says to his mother: "Behold your son" (Jn 19:26), and not: "Behold, this too is your son," it is the same as saying: "Behold, this is Jesus to whom you gave birth." For everyone who has come to perfection "lives no longer," but "Christ lives" in him. And because Christ lives in him, it is said of him to Mary: "Behold your son," Christ. How elevated a mind must we have in order to be able to perceive worthily this WORD lying hidden within the earthen treasures of the ordinary

word, while the letter can be read by all who come upon it and the audible sound of the WORD can be heard by all who turn their ear to it!

WATER AND WINE

Even the scripture of the Old Covenant is already an incarnation of the Word (221–223). But it is only in the New Covenant that the "letter" as such comes to life (224). The Old Covenant is thus a constantly increasing theophany (225) which, however, comes to its full life only in Jesus (226). Jesus changes the water of the Old Covenant into wine (227), yes, into his blood (228), to such an extent that the letter is now completely superseded and become impossible (229). The unity of the similitude has come out in the love-command (230), in the way that love supersedes fear (231). Thus, in its eternal essence, the Old Covenant is still "new" (232). But ultimately, every letter, even that of the New Covenant, points beyond itself to the living person of Jesus (233).

221   There is not just one coming in which my Lord Jesus Christ came down to earth; he also came to Isaiah, and he came to Moses, and he came to the people, and he came to each one of the prophets; and you should have no fear: even if he has already been received, he will come again. But that he has also come before his presence in the flesh, listen to his own lamenting words of testimony: "O Jerusalem, Jerusalem, killing the prophets and stoning those who are sent to you, how often would I have gathered your children together!" (Mt 23:37). "How often!" . . . He is not lying.

222   "The voice of my beloved" (Cant 2:8). Only from his voice is Christ at first recognized by the church. For he first sent his voice ahead by the prophets; even if he was not seen, he was still heard. But he was heard through the things that were proclaimed about him; and the bride, that is, the church, which was called together from the beginning of the world, continued to hear only his voice until the time when she would see him with her own eyes and say: "Behold, he comes, leaping upon the mountains, bounding over the hills" (Cant 2:8).

223   Just as "in the last days" the WORD of God, clothed with flesh from Mary, came into the world and there was one thing which was visible in him but quite another which was open to the understanding — for the sign of his flesh was open to all while only a few chosen ones were given a recognition of the divinity — so too when the WORD of God is spoken through the prophets and the lawgiver, it does not come forth

without appropriate clothing. For just as it is covered there with the veil of the flesh, so too here with the veil of the letter, so that the letter is seen as it were like flesh while the spiritual meaning, like the divinity, is perceived within. . . . But "blessed are the eyes" (Lk 10:23) which see within the divine Spirit covered by the veil of the letter.

24   Each and every letter of the gospel gives life to the scribes (if I may call them that) of the gospels. But the spirit which soars above the nature of the letters enlightens even more, with an action that is more divine, those from whom the gospel is not veiled. . . . For a certain benefit comes to those who believe in the scriptures; but they who see how the "curtain" of the scripture is torn "from top to bottom" (Mt 27:51), and who see what is within, are filled with a greater knowledge.

25   But when "the veil is taken away" from the spouse, namely, the church "turned to the Lord" (2 Cor 3:14, 16), she suddenly sees him "leaping over" those "mountains," namely, the books of the law, and not so much appearing as, because of his open and clear manifestation, "bounding over the hills" (Cant 2:8) of the prophetic books. It is as if she, paging through the sheets of the prophetic reading, finds Christ "bounding" out of them and in each passage in the readings, now that the "veil" which first covered them is "taken away," sees him emerge and spring forth and break out in an unmistakable appearance.

26   Isaac owns wells for which he must fight against the Philistines. Ishmael, however, drinks water from a skin; but this skin is leaky like all skins and thus he suffers thirst and finds no well. But you, who "like Isaac are a child of promise" (cf. Gal 4:28), "drink water from your own wells; and the water from your wells is not scattered abroad, but your waters flow in your streets" (cf. Prov 5:15–16). But the one who is born according to the flesh drinks water from a skin, and the water itself is insufficient and in many respects deficient. The skin of the law is the letter, . . . for the historical meaning is in many ways deficient. But the church drinks from the wells of the gospels and the apostles which never go dry but "flow in your streets" because they are ever full and flowing in the broad plain of spiritual interpretation.

27   For truly, before Jesus, the scripture was water, but after Jesus it has become wine for us.[1]

---

[1] This short text is only a brief reference back to the lost part of the commentary which deals with the Cana scene. That is where Origen must have extensively developed this comparison — the first one to do so — which later became so famous.

228 But I think that the man "carrying a jar of water" (Mk 14:13; Lk 22:10) who met the disciples as they entered the city, and whom Jesus wanted his disciples to follow as he entered a house . . . was one of the servants of the head of the household (i.e., of the spirit in a human being). He carried the purifying water in an "earthen vessel to show that the transcendent power belongs to God" (cf. 2 Cor 4:7). He served up drinkable water in that earthen vessel so that the Son of God might indeed provide the fruit of the vine (cf. Mt 26:29 par); for he is that servant of the spirit who serves up water from the law and the prophets which he mixes with the wine of the word of the gospel. We therefore, who want to belong to the church, who want to celebrate the passover with Jesus, let us follow that man who carries a jar filled with such water. That man, I think, is Moses the lawgiver who bears spiritual teaching in bodily histories. But those who come to the law and the prophets as if to the words of God himself, but do not spiritually follow him who carries the jug of "living water" (cf. Jn 4:10), they do not celebrate the Passover with Jesus nor drink the cup of the new testament.

229 [The Jews] indeed speak the commandments of the law, but they do not understand what they say nor what the words of the law mean "about which they make assertions" (1 Tim 1:7). Hence the Savior says of them: "For they tell you what to do and do not do it themselves" (cf. Mt 23:3). They tell you, for example, about circumcision, about the passover, about unleavened bread, about food and drink, about feasts, new moons, sabbaths and the other commandments of the law, but they do not do according to the will of the law. For they do not circumcise as the law wills (for the Apostle says: "For we are the circumcision, who worship God in spirit and put no confidence in the flesh" — Phil 3:3), nor do they sacrifice the paschal lamb (unaware that "Christ, our paschal lamb, has been sacrificed" — 1 Cor 5:7), nor do they eat the unleavened bread according to the intention of the law (" . . . let us celebrate the festival, not with the old leaven, the leaven of malice and evil, but with the unleavened bread of sincerity and truth" — 1 Cor 5:8). But they do not even celebrate the passover in a bodily way, since the law commands them to sacrifice the lamb in Jerusalem, "the place which the Lord has chosen" (Deut 16:6), and that "three times a year every male shall appear before the Lord" (cf. Deut 16:16). We, on the other hand, . . . do all that the law commands us and, since we understand the sense of the law, we do not do and observe it according to "what they do" (Mt 23:3). . . . For they bind heavy burdens and, as Luke says, "hard to bear" (Lk 11:46). . . . But the gospel is a light burden because it is the spiritual law.

30   You ask how it is that "all the law and the prophets depend on these two commandments" (Mt 22:40). For the text does seem to indicate that everything that was written in Exodus or Leviticus or Numbers or Deuteronomy depends "on these two commandments." . . . Whoever fulfills all that is written about the law of God and neighbor is worthy of receiving great graces from God, the foremost of which is "the utterance of wisdom through the Holy Spirit," and after that "the utterance of knowledge" which is according to "the same Spirit" (1 Cor 12:8). The one who is worthy, however, who is firmly grounded in all these gifts, rejoices in the wisdom of God, having a heart full of the love of God and a soul wholly enlightened by the light of knowledge and a spirit wholly enlightened by the WORD of God. And they who have received gifts of this kind from God do indeed understand that all the law and the prophets are a part of the whole wisdom and knowledge of God, and understand that all the law and the prophets depend on and are part of the principle and origin of the love of God and neighbor, and that the perfection of reverence consists of love.

31   There are two sons of Abraham, "one by a slave and one by a free woman" (Gal 4:22), but both are sons of Abraham although both are not sons of the free woman. Therefore the one born of the slave does not become an heir along with the son of the free woman, but he does receive gifts and is not sent away empty. He also receives a blessing, but the son of the free woman receives the promise. Ishmael also becomes "a great nation" (Gen 12:2), but Isaac becomes a people of adoption. Spiritually then, all who come by faith to a knowledge of God can be called sons of Abraham; but among these are some who cling to God out of love while others do so from fear of the judgment to come. This is why the apostle John says: "He who fears is not perfected in love; but perfect love casts out fear" (1 Jn 4:18). Whoever, then, "is perfected in love" is also born of Abraham and is a "son of the free woman." But whoever keeps the commandments not out of perfect love but out of fear of future punishment, is indeed a son of Abraham and does indeed receive gifts which are the reward of his work (because whoever gives even a cup of cold water in the name of a disciple will not lose his reward — Mt 10:42); nevertheless he is inferior to the one who has been made perfect in the freedom of love.

32   The law turns into an Old Testament only for those who insist on understanding it according to the flesh; and for them it has necessarily become old and feeble because it is separated from its sources of life. But for us, who understand and interpret it spiritually and according

to the gospel, it is always new; indeed both Testaments are new for us, not because of age but because of newness of understanding. In fact, isn't this what the apostle John was thinking of in his epistle when he said: "Children, I give you a new commandment, that you love one another" (cf. 1 Jn 2:8; 3:23), since he surely knew that the commandment of love was long ago given in the law? But because "love never ends" (1 Cor 13:8) nor does the commandment of love grow old in any way, what never grows old he pronounces to be ever new; for the commandment of love continually renews in the Spirit those who observe and keep it.

233   Whoever drinks from Jacob's well will thirst again, but whoever drinks from the water which Jesus gives has within him a fountain of water springing into eternal life. With this in mind let us examine further how much of a distinction can be made between the benefit obtained by those who have a direct and intimate relationship with the truth itself and the benefit we think comes to us from the scriptures, if they are exactly understood. For the more noble and divine mysteries of God are in part not contained in scripture and in part not attainable by human voice and human language. . . . Consider then, if it is not possible that the well of Jacob is the whole scripture, but that the water from Jesus is that which is above what is written. But it is not possible for all to search out the things which are above what is written, but only for the one who has become assimilated to them.

WORD AS FLESH

CHRIST

Old Covenant and New Covenant

Demolition of What Was Preliminary

All the embodiment of the WORD in scripture is only prepara-
tion for his incarnation in the flesh. Looked at this way, there is a
shift in perspective from the old to the new covenant. Christ is not
just fulfillment in the way that a simile supersedes, but fulfillment
in the sense of being a rejection of the people's servitude to the letter.
The law is a contrary to grace (234–236). It is thus dismantled
(237), gently at first (238), but violently in the end (239), unto
the external and internal desolation of Judaism (240–248).

234   If we want to know what righteousness is, we need to know what
unrighteousness is. When we have come to a full knowledge of unrighteousness, we will know from that what righteousness itself
is . . . and because righteousness is in God whose nature is inaccessible to human perception, but unrighteousness is at home in us
humans or even in every rational creature, from this unrighteousness
of ours which is known to us, that righteousness of God, which is so to
speak inaccessible to us and incomprehensible, is known and recom-
mended and springs, so to speak, as a contrary from its contrary.

235   "Through the law comes knowledge of sin. But now the righteousness of God has been manifested apart from law" (Rom 3:20-21).
Now this is not saying that the recognition of sin comes about through
the law, such that the manifestation of the righteousness of God also
comes about through the law; rather it is saying that "the righteousness of God has been manifested apart from the law." For the
law of nature could convict nature of sin and demonstrate the essence
of sin. But the righteousness of God far surpasses and transcends
whatever the human mind with only its natural powers can figure out.

236   Consider now what it might mean when it says in the law that the face of Moses was resplendent even though covered with a veil; but his hand, when "put into his bosom," was reported to have become "leprous, as white as snow" (Exod 4:6). Herein, it seems to me, is pointed out the whole essence of the law; for in his face the word of the law, but in his hand the works of the law are designated. Therefore, because no one was to be justified by works of the law (cf. Rom 3:20), nor could the law lead anyone to perfection, the hand of Moses was thus made "leprous" and is hidden in his bosom as something not destined to produce a work of perfection; but his face is made resplendent, though covered with a veil, because his word has the glory (but hidden) of knowledge.

237   The law and everything in the law is, according to the opinion of the Apostle, "imposed until the time of reformation" (Heb 9:10); and just as artists who make images from bronze and pour statues, before they make the final work out of bronze or silver or gold, first make a clay model in the likeness of the future image — which model is indeed necessary, but only until the principal work is completed; for as soon as the work is completed for the sake of which the clay model was made, there is no further need for the model — , in some such way should you also think of these things which were written or done in the law and the prophets as a type or figure of things to come. For the very artifex and creator of all comes and turns the "law which was but a shadow of the good things to come" into the "true form of these realities" (Heb 10:1).

238   "At that time Jesus went through the grainfields on the sabbath" (Mt 12:1). Because Christ the Lord knew in advance what the disciples would do, with this in mind he led them through the grainfields. He does this because it was his intention to dissolve the sabbath. And he never breaks it without cause, but gives good excuses for so doing, so that he would not only dissolve the law but also not hurt the Jews, if they were willing to understand.

239   "And cut off his right ear" (Jn 18:10; cf. Mt 26:51). What Peter did was perhaps a symbolic mystery, since the right "ear" of the Jewish people was to be cut off because of their wickedness towards Jesus. For although they seem to hear the law, they now hear with their left ear only the shadow of the tradition of the law, and not its truth; for they are servants of a word which professes slavery to God, not of that which serves in truth.

40 "I must be in my Father's house" (Lk 2:49). I presume that this is more the spiritual and living and true temple of God than the one which, in type, was built with earthly work. Hence that temple, built in type, has also been abandoned in type by Christ. For "Jesus left [the earthly] temple" (Mt 24:1) saying, "Behold your house is forsaken and desolate" (Mt 23:38), and leaving that house he came to the patrimony of God the Father, the churches spread out over the whole world, and said, "I must be in my Father's house."

41 It was for this reason that divine providence arranged for the city itself and the temple and everything to be destroyed, so that they who might still be "children in faith and living on milk" (cf. Heb 5:13; Rom 14:1), in seeing the temple standing and gaping in astonishment at the celebration of the sacrifices and the ranks of the ministers, might not be swept away by just looking at this multiplicity of forms.

42 "The kingdom of God will be taken away from you and given to a nation producing the fruits of it" (Mt 21:43). It is not that the scripture would be taken from them . . . for they have the books. But . . . the meaning of the scriptures is taken from them.

43 Just as, with the death of the prophets, their bodies were in their graves but their souls and spirits "in the land of the living" (Ps 116:9), so too with the words of the prophets: one must be aware that their simple historical narrative is the body, but the spiritual meaning and the very inner truth of the scriptures is the soul and spirit which lives in the simple historical accounts. And it does make good sense that we can think of the graves of the prophets as the very letters of scripture and as the books in which the historical narrative rests as a body in the grave. Thus, they who . . . do not grasp the spiritual realities of the scriptures and their truth . . . they do indeed . . . honor the bodies of the prophets which are placed in letters and books as if in graves . . . and they do indeed seem to be full of respect for the memories of the prophets . . . and do not want to be counted as the colleagues "of those who murdered the prophets" (Mt 23:31). But they are themselves condemned to surpass the sins "of those who killed the prophets" and to "fill up the measure" of their evil (cf. Mt 23:31–32), because they do not believe in Christ who is proclaimed not by the simple historical accounts of the prophets, but only by their spiritual sense.

44 "If her father had spit in her face . . . " (Num 12:14). To spit in the face is a sign of repudiation. . . . And truly, if you consider that earlier honor when the high-priestly order flourished among them,

when there were the insignia of the priests, the levitical services, the majesty of the temple and the prophetic splendor, and when heavenly figures consorted with them on earth — what an honor, what a glory that was! And if you look again now, in what terrible shame they tremble: without temple, without altar, without sacrifice, without prophet, without priesthood, without any visitation from heaven, scattered over the whole world and living as refugees! Could anyone miss the obvious fact that "her father has spit in her face"?

245   "And broken through the middle" (cf. Lev 2:14). The middle broke through when the letter was separated from the spirit.

246   "I was found by those who did not seek me" (Isa 65:1). It was of course the pagans who neither knew how to seek after Christ nor had learned how to inquire after him. And yet they found him whom they did not seek after because he himself first sought them out. For he is the good shepherd (Jn 10:14) and seeks out the sheep that was lost (Lk 15:4); for he is the wisdom which searches for the lost drachma and finds it (Lk 15:8). But the Jews to this day are seeking after Christ and they are searching the scriptures for him and do not find him because his cross is a stumbling block to the Jews (1 Cor 1:23), which is why the Lord says to them: "I spread out my hands all the day to an unbelieving and rebellious people" (Isa 65:2). That is, while he was hanging on the cross they not only did not find him but even went so far as to say: "If you are the Son of God, come down now from the cross and we will believe in you" (Mt 27:40, 42). But listen to what is also said in the Wisdom of Solomon: "He will not be found by those who put him to the test, but will manifest himself to those who do not distrust him" (Wis 1:2).

247   The whole scripture of the old testament, shaped by the structuring of significant words and built according to the historical sense, was a temple of God. Its builders, Moses and the prophets, constructed it by arranging the letters and putting the words in order, producing something that was the admiration of all. . . . This is what the disciples point out to Jesus, meaning the whole of scripture; Christ answers by saying that this first, bodily building must be destroyed by the WORD so that the more divine and mystical temple of another scripture can be built.

248   But thanks be to the coming of Christ who, tearing our souls away from gazing on this, guided them to the consideration and contempla-tion of heavenly and spiritual things; and he did indeed destroy what seemed great on earth, and transferred the worship of God from the

visible to the invisible and from the temporal to the eternal. But the Lord Jesus Christ demands, of course, ears that can hear and eyes that can see this.

The Definitive in What Was Preliminary

But in the very demolition, the eternal form of the law comes to the fore (249). This form is so much taken up with pointing to Christ (250) and educating to him (251), that the order of salvation encompasses and contains both in itself (252–253). Law is thus understood as in transition, but can be brought to completion only through Christ (254). In Christ, the dead letter has become thundering word (255), Moses and Elias taken up into him (256–257). Christ, in fulfilling the types, is only taking back what is his own: even the just ones of the old covenant are already members of his mystical body (258–265).

249   Now how can one call eternal what has clearly long since ceased to exist? One can only say that the law is called eternal in the sense that we say that the "law" is "spiritual," and that through it can be offered spiritual sacrifices which can never be interrupted or brought to an end.

250   "For the righteousness of God is revealed through faith for faith" (Rom 1:17). For that earlier people was also in faith because it believed in God and his servant Moses, from which faith it has now passed over to the faith of the gospel. This is what he [the Savior] is saying according to the testimony of the prophet Habakkuk, that "the just person lives from my faith" (Rom 1:17; Hab 2:4). This is true whether we are talking about someone in the law believing also in the gospels, or someone in the gospels believing also in the law and the prophets. For neither one has fullness of life without the other.

251   "For everything there is a season" (Eccl 3:1). For just as everyone who is to become wise in the words of truth must first be taught the rudiments, and then pass through the fundamentals and pay great attention to them, and yet not remain fixed on them—like one who has paid great respect to the fundamentals in the beginning, but then, passing on "to what is more perfect" (Heb 6:1), remains grateful for the introduction as something that was useful in the beginning—so too the perfect understanding of the law and the prophets is an elementary step towards the perfect understanding of the gospel and the whole meaning of the words and works of Jesus Christ.

252   For, since two things are to be understood with regard to the law,
the ministry "of death" which was engraved "in the letters" (2 Cor 3:7)
and has nothing in common with the spirit, and the ministry of life
which is understood in the spiritual law, those who with true sincerity
were able to say: "We know that the law is spiritual" (Rom 7:14) . . .
belong to the plant which the heavenly Father planted.

253   Thus the law contains both: the letter that kills and the Spirit that
gives life. One should perhaps consider whether an image of this is
contained in that tree which is called "of the knowledge of good and
evil" (Gen 2:9).

254   "Then he made the disciples get into the boat and go before him
to the other side, while he dismissed the crowds" (Mt 14:22). For the
crowd could not go across to the other side, . . . instead this was for
the disciples of Jesus to do: I mean to go across to the other side and
go beyond material things and "the things that are seen" as
"transient," and come to "the things that are unseen and eternal" (2
Cor 4:18). . . . Except that the disciples were unable to go before
Jesus to the other side; for when they had come as far as the middle of
the sea and the boat was in distress because "the wind was against
them," they were afraid; and then, "in the fourth watch of the night,
[Jesus] came to them" (Mt 14:24–25). . . . But what is the boat into
which Jesus forced the disciples to embark? Is it perhaps the conflict
of temptations and trials into which one is forced by the WORD, and
to which one goes unwillingly, as it were, all because the Savior
wishes his disciples to get some training in this boat as it gets buffeted
by the waves and the contrary wind? . . . For it is not possible to get
to the other side without enduring the temptations of waves and contrary wind.

255   That which before was in letters and was understood according to
the letter has now, because of the Lord's revelation, become speech in
the church of Christ, now that the holy apostles have begun to speak
about and apply it by removing the shell of the letter and revealing its
reality as spiritual speech.

256   Do you want to see that Moses is always with Jesus, that is, the law
with the gospel? Let the gospel teach you that when Jesus "was transfigured" into glory, "Moses and Elias" also "appeared" with him in
glory (Mk 9:2, 4), so that you might know that the law and the prophets
and the gospels always come together as one and stay together in one
glory. And finally Peter too, for wanting to make "three booths" for
them, is reprimanded for ignorance, as if he "did not know what to

say" (Mk 9:5, 6). For there are not for the law and the prophets and the gospel three booths but one; and that is the church of God.

257 But after the touch of the WORD, "lifting up their eyes, they saw no one but Jesus only" (Mt 17:8). For just one single thing is what Moses, the law, and Elias, prophecy, became with the gospel of Jesus. And they did not remain three as they were before, but the three became one. But you should understand this with me as relating to mystical matters, for according to the bare meaning of the letter, Moses and Elias "appeared in glory" (Mt 17:3; cf. Lk 9:31) and, after talking with Jesus, went away to the place from which they had come.

258 "Your father Abraham rejoiced that he was to see my day; he saw it and was glad" (Jn 8:56). . . . For he had believed, when ordered to sacrifice his only son, that God could raise him up even from the dead. He had also believed that this action concerned not only Isaac, but that the full truth of the sacrament was also being preserved for his progeny, Christ. That is why he ended up joyfully sacrificing his only son, because he could see therein not the destruction of his progeny but the salvation of the world and the renewal of every creature which was restored by the resurrection of the Lord.

259 It is written in the prophet, speaking for the Lord: "In the hands of the prophets I have become an example" (Hos 12:10). This means that, although our Lord Jesus Christ is one in substance and indeed the very Son of God, he still turns out to have quite different images and forms in the scriptures. For example, as I remember showing above, he himself was in the form of Isaac when he was offered as a burnt offering; but the ram too was a form of him. I will go further and say that in the angel who said to Abraham: "Do not lay your hand on the lad" (Gen 22:12), the Lord himself is present, because he later says to him: "Because you have done this . . . I will indeed bless you" (Gen 22:16–17).

260 The reason for saying this is to prevent the appearance of any division between ourselves and the just who lived before the coming of Christ, and to show that, even though they lived before the coming of Christ, they are still our brothers. For even though they then had an altar before the coming of the Savior, they still knew and sensed that it was not the true altar but the image and likeness of this true altar. They knew that true sacrificial offerings, those which can take away sins, were not being offered on that altar which the first-born people possessed, but that the heavenly offerings and the true sacrifices were being carried out on this altar where Jesus was. There is thus "one

flock and one shepherd" (cf. Jn 10:16), those who formerly were the just and who now are the Christians.

261   Whoever wishes to accept as coming from the mouth of the Savior what is written in the Acts of Paul: "I am about to be crucified again," could apply this just as well to the time after the coming of Christ . . . as to the time before, when there would be just as much reason for saying: "I am already about to be crucified." . . . Consider then whether "I have been crucified with Christ" (Gal 2:19) can have been spoken not only by the saints after the coming but also by those who came before in order to say that the saints after the coming are not different from Moses and the patriarchs. And the words "It is no longer I who live, but Christ who lives in me" (Gal 2:20) are to be said not only by those after the coming but also by those before. And consider, from the words of the Savior: "the God of Abraham, and the God of Isaac and the God of Jacob; he is not God of the dead, but of the living" (Mt 22:32), whether they do not imply that Abraham and Isaac and Jacob are living since they also have been buried with Christ and risen with him. . . . Thus, what we are teaching is that there never was a time when the spiritual order of salvation according to Jesus was not available to the saints.

262   Even those who are called Jews and glory in the letter of the law of Moses are convicted of transgressing the law for not believing in Christ. For if they believed Moses they would surely believe in him of whom Moses wrote (cf. Jn 5:46).

263   At the end of the ages the WORD has indeed become human, Jesus Christ; but before this visible coming in the flesh he was already, although not yet human, the mediator of human beings.

264   For in every generation he was always desirous [of gathering Jerusalem's children together] (cf. Mt 23:37), and he hastened to accomplish in them the will of his Father, even though he was not yet in the body as he is now at the end of the ages.

265   Therefore it was always so, that no matter who was coming to the faith or community of Israel, they were incorporated into Christ who was the true Israel.

The Life of Jesus as Parable

Incarnation

In the eternally impenetrable mystery of the incarnation (266) the invisible comes visibly and personally to the fore (267), not as a deus ex machina but as the inner fulfillment of the order of salvation (268). Incarnation is above all the becoming visible and presentation of God's "suffering" in the body: Origen speaks the, for a Greek, monstrous word about suffering in God (269). This presentation is the form of the very emptying of God (270–271), the victory of wisdom is victory over wisdom (272). And only in this "kenosis" does Christ fulfill and redeem the world (273–274) by continuing his redemption in his members (275–276). This salvation far transcends the Dionysus myth in sublimity (277). Through it a little piece of home has come into the alien world (278), a piece of earth can be worshiped (279). Summary in the parable of the Samaritan (280).

266   But of all his miracles and mighty acts, this far exceeds the limits of human wonder. It goes far beyond the weak power of the human mind to perceive or comprehend how it is supposed to believe that the divine majesty, that very WORD of the Father and Wisdom of God in which "all things were created, visible and invisible" (cf. Col 1:15), was held within the confines of that man who appeared in Judaea and, even more, that the Wisdom of God entered into the womb of a woman and was born a baby which cried and wailed like all little babies. And it is further reported that he suffered the anguish of death, as he himself admitted by saying: "My soul is very sorrowful, even to death" (Mt 26:38 par); and in the end he was led to that death which is reputed to be the most shameful among men, even though he did rise again on the third day. Thus, since we see in him some things so human that they seem to be no different from common mortal frailty, and some things so divine that they belong only to the primal and ineffable nature of God, the human mind is simply overwhelmed. It is so struck with awe that it does not know where to turn, what to hold, what way to go. If it perceives him as God, it sees him as human; if it thinks of him as man, it beholds him, triumphant over death's reign, returning from the dead with the spoils of victory (cf. Eph 4:8).

This must therefore be contemplated with reverential awe, so that the truth of each nature is proven to be in one and the same being in such a way that neither is anything improper or unworthy perceived in that divine and ineffable substance, nor are those things that were actually done taken as the illusory products of a false imagination. To present this to human ears and explain it in words far surpasses our poor merits. . . . It surpasses, I think, even the power of the holy apostles. Indeed the explanation of this mystery is probably beyond the grasp even of the whole creation of heavenly powers.

267   For him, "to come" does not mean to change place, but from being
invisible to become visible. For when he was invisible, because he was
the image of the invisible God, he took the form of a slave and became
visible as the WORD made flesh. He made his appearance this way
in order to lead us through this knowledge to the contemplation of his
very own glory, "the glory as of the only Son from the Father, full of
grace and truth" (Jn 1:14).

268   To this Celsus says . . . . : "God has no need to reform his works."
God has certainly never failed to do, nor will he ever fail to do, at
every moment what is fitting for him to do in this changing, variable
world. And just as the farmer, according to the different seasons of
the year, does different things to the earth and its plants, so too God
arranges all the ages like, so to speak, seasons of the year.

269   He came down to earth out of compassion for the human race, feeling our sufferings even before he suffered on the cross and decided to
assume our flesh. For if he had not suffered, he would not have come
to live on the level of human life. First he suffered, then descended
and became visible. What is this suffering which he suffered for us? It
is the suffering of love. And also the Father himself, the God of all
"slow to anger and abounding in mercy" (cf. Ps 103:8) and compas-
sionate, does he not in some way suffer? Don't you know when he
directs human affairs he suffers human suffering? For "the Lord your
God bore your ways as a man bears his son" (cf. Deut 1:31). Therefore God bears our ways just as the Son of God bears our sufferings.
The very Father is not without suffering. When he is prayed to, he
has pity and compassion; he suffers something of love and puts himself in the place of those with whom he, in view of the greatness of his
nature, cannot be.

270   We would like, now, to say something even more daring: what
came into this life emptied itself, so that through its emptiness the
world would be fulfilled. But if what came into this life emptied itself,
that very emptiness was Wisdom (cf. Phil 2:7).

271   The Son, "who was in the form of God, emptied himself," desiring
by this very self-emptying to show us the "fullness of the deity" (cf.
Phil 2:6–7; Col 2:9).

272   This is Christ's greatest victory: to have conquered and put to
shame the wise through the foolish, that is, through the simple. For
the greatest shame of the wise is to be vanquished by the simple.

273   Christ says these words; and he is the one who willingly begs for the
sake of human beings in order to make them rich.

274 But the WORD of God, after coming down to our level and, in view of his own dignity, humbling himself by his presence among human beings, is said to change over "from this world to the Father" (Jn 13:1) so that we might see him there in his perfection after he has returned from the emptiness into which he had "emptied himself" (Phil 2:7) to his own "fullness" (cf. Col 1:9; 2:9; Eph 1:23) where we also will, with him as our guide, be fulfilled and freed from all emptiness.

275 "Thou art near, O Lord, and all thy ways are true," etc. (Ps 119:151). This then is how he draws near to us. But unless we on our part make efforts to draw near to him as he approaches, we will not rejoice in his proximity.

276 Jesus and his disciples desired that his followers should not believe just in his divinity and miracles, as if he had not shared in human nature nor assumed that human flesh which lusts "against the Spirit" (Gal 5:17). For they saw that when the power which had come down into human nature and human vicissitudes and assumed a human soul and body was believed in, it contributed, along with the divine elements, to the salvation of the believers. They saw that with him the divine and human nature began to interpenetrate in such a way that the human nature, by its communion with the divine, would itself become divine, and not just in Jesus but in all who take up in faith the life which Jesus taught and which elevates to friendship and communion with God everyone who lives according to Jesus' commandments.

277 But do not these accounts, especially when understood as they should be, seem much more worthy of respect than that of Dionysus being deceived by the Titans and cast down from the throne of Zeus and split into pieces by them and then put back together again and come back to life, as it were, and ascended into heaven? . . . If Celsus but knew the destiny of the soul in the eternal life to come and what must be thought of its essence and origins, he would not have made such fun of the entrance of the immortal into the mortal body, expounded not according to the metempsychosis of Plato but according to another, higher theory.

278 We live now in a foreign land and pray that we might do the opposite of what the sons of Israel did in the holy land. For they [did foreign things and] worshiped foreign gods in the holy land. But we, in a foreign land, worship the God who is foreign to this land, foreign to the affairs of the earth; for here "the ruler of this world" (cf. Jn 12:31) holds sway, and God is foreign to the sons of that ruler. . . . We do not say: "How shall we sing the Lord's song in a foreign land?"

(Ps 137:4), but: How shall we sing the Lord's song in a non-foreign land? We are seeking a place to sing the song of this Lord, a place to worship the Lord our God in a foreign land. What (who) is this place? I have found him! He came to this earth bearing a body that saves, taking away "the body of sin" (Rom 6:6), "in the likeness of sinful flesh" (Rom 8:3), so that in this place (cf. Mal 1:11), through the coming of Jesus Christ who has overcome the ruler of this world and conquered sin (cf. Jn 12:31; 1 Cor 15:24–28), I will be able to worship God here. And after this I will worship in the holy land.

279   "We will worship in the place where his feet stand" (Ps 132:7 LXX). We worship the flesh of our Savior, not because of itself, but because Christ is in it. And this flesh is worthy because of the WORD which is God (cf. Jn 1:1) and lives in it.

280   "A man was going down from Jerusalem to Jericho" (Lk 10:30). The man is interpreted as Adam or as the reason of man and its previous life and fall by disobedience. Jerusalem is interpreted as paradise or the heavenly Jerusalem, Jericho as the world, the robbers as the hostile powers or the demons or the false teachers who came before Christ, the wounds as disobedience and sins, the stealing of the clothing as the stripping away of uncorruption and immortality and the taking away of all virtue. The man being left half dead shows how his nature has become half mortal — for the soul is immortal. The priest is interpreted as the law, the levite as the prophetic word, the Samaritan as Christ who took flesh from Mary, the beast of burden as the body of Christ, the wine as the teaching and evoking word, the oil as the word of friendship and merciful compassion, the inn as the church, the innkeeper as the apostles and their successors who are the bishops and teachers of the churches. . . . The return of the Samaritan is the second coming of Christ.

Childhood

If every body is a symbol, so too is the body of the God-man who fulfills the law. Thus Origen applies to his life and deeds the same methods of spiritual understanding as to the rest of scripture (we will give only a few examples of this below) (281).

Meaning of the childhood of Jesus (282). Appropriateness of his birth (283). The virginal mother (284–285). Symbolism of the census (286). Circumcision of Jesus and baptism of children (287). Necessity of the baptism of Jesus (288–289).

281   Our savior was himself the maker of the symbols of his own spiritual deeds.

282   "And Jesus increased in wisdom" (Lk 2:52). He learns and, as it were, acquires knowledge, not of great but of lesser and smaller things. And just as I, by forcing myself, learn to stammer when I talk to small children (since I, as an adult, do not, as it were, know baby talk, I force myself to talk as a child), so too the Savior, when he is "in the Father" and living in the greatness of God the Father (cf. Jn 14:10, 11), does not talk human talk and cannot speak to those below. But when he comes into his human body, he says at first: "I do not know how to talk because I am too young"; and young he is according to his human birth, but old in his being "the first-born of all creation" (Col 1:15); young because he has come "at the end of the age" (Heb 9:26) and only then entered into this life.

283   For he who took on human sufferings must first have taken birth upon himself. For he could not have taken upon himself human feelings, words, customs, the cross and death if he had not first had a human beginning. And it was logical for those who denied his birth to deny also his passion. . . . Indeed it is more of a scandal that Jesus was born than that he died.

284   And just as sin began with the woman and then spread to the man, so too what was good began with women.

285   And it seems to me to make sense that, among men, Jesus held the first place in being most pure in chastity, and that among women it was Mary.

286   Someone might say: Evangelist, what good to me is this story that the first census of the whole world took place under Caesar Augustus? . . . But if you look more closely a great mystery is being presented here, namely that Jesus had to be counted in this census of the whole world in order that, counted with all, he might sanctify all and be written down with them into "the book of the living" (cf. Rev 20:15), so that the names of those written down with him and who believe in him would be inscribed in heaven.

287   Every soul which has been clothed with a human body is stained. But that you might know that Jesus too of his own will has been stained in taking on a human body for our salvation, listen to the words of the prophet Zechariah: "Jesus [Joshua] was clothed with dirty garments" (Zech 3:3 Latin). This statement is useful against those who say that the Savior did not take human flesh but took a spiritual body from

heaven. . . . But when they are driven to the point of admitting that the dirty garment is to be understood as a spiritual body, they should logically conclude that, when the promise is fulfilled, namely, that what is "sown a physical body is raised a spiritual body" (1 Cor 15:44), we will rise up soiled. Even to think this is a sin. . . . It was thus fitting that also for our Lord and Savior, because clothed with dirty garments, a human earthly body, the offering prescribed by law for purification should be made.

Among the brethren, this passage frequently gives rise to a question. Infants are baptized "for the forgiveness of sins" (cf. Acts 2:38). But whose sins? Or, when did they sin? Or how can the logic of a purificatory bath for infants still stand except by recalling the word: "None are free of stain, even if they have lived only one day on earth" (cf. Job 14:4). It is because the stain of birth is removed by baptism that infants are baptized.

288   But because the Lord was baptized and the heavens were opened and "the Holy Spirit descended upon him . . . and a voice came from heaven saying, 'You are my beloved Son with whom I am well pleased'" (Lk 3:22), it must be said that at Jesus' baptism heaven opened, and that for meting out the forgiveness of sins—not of him "who committed no sin, nor was any guile found on his lips" (1 Pt 2:22) but of the whole world—the heavens were opened and the Holy Spirit came down so that, after the Lord "had ascended on high and led captivity captive" (Ps 68:18), he might give us the Spirit which had come down on him.

289   For the Spirit could not come to us unless it had first come down to someone like itself in nature.

Humility

Humility is the decisive characteristic of the teaching of Christ (290); in this Christ is our model (291, 293) and the highest revelation of the love of God (292).

290   It seems to me that if Jesus had chosen some who were wise in the eyes of the world and who could think and speak in crowd-pleasing ways, and used them as the ministers of his teaching, he would quite rightly have been suspected of preaching a doctrine like those philosophers who are leaders of certain sects. The divine character of his doctrine would never have been made manifest. His doctrine and

preaching would have consisted in persuasive words and fancy style, and the faith, like the faith one has in the opinions of the philosophers of the world, would have been "in the wisdom of men" and not "in the power of God" (1 Cor 2:5).

291   We learn from him that he is "gentle and lowly in heart" (Mt 11:29) and does not disdain to talk about such important things with a water-carrying woman who because of her great poverty has come out from the city to work at drawing water. The disciples, on their arrival, are astonished, since they had already seen the greatness of the divinity in him, and they wonder what manner of converse the great Lord can have with a woman. But we, led on by our boasting arrogance, look down on those who are lower, forgetting that to everyone is addressed the word: "Let us make man in our image and after our likeness" (Gen 1:26). And unmindful of the one who "forms in the womb" (cf. Jer 1:5) and "fashions the hearts of them all, and observes all their deeds" (Ps 33:15), we do not know that he is "God of the lowly, helper of the oppressed, upholder of the weak, protector of the forlorn and savior of those without hope" (Judith 9:11).

292   One must have the courage to say that the goodness of Christ appeared greater and more divine and truly conformed to the image of the Father when "he humbled himself and became obedient unto death, even death on a cross" (Phil 2:8) than would be the case if he did not will to become a slave for the salvation of the world.

293   For he is the one who will "clothe the heavens with blackness, and make sackcloth their covering," and receiving from the Father "the tongue of those who are taught" knew "how to sustain with a word" what God had entrusted to him; and the Lord "gave him an ear" to hear more than all who hear, and "the teaching" of the Father who sent him. With his own deeds he taught meekness and a praiseworthy humility to those eager to learn. But it was necessary for him to teach this in deeds, "giving his back to the smiters, and his cheeks to the blows, not hiding his face from shame and spitting," doing this, it seems to me, in order to save us who deserved to suffer all these indignities, by suffering them for us (cf. Isa 50:2–7). For he did not "die for us" (Rom 5:8 and elsewhere) so that we would not die, but so that we would not die for ourselves; and he was not struck in the face and spat upon for us so that we who were deserving of all this because of our sins would not suffer these things, but that, suffering them for justice's sake, we would accept them gladly.

Suffering

*The cross is the definitive form of salvation (294). It is as large
as the world itself (295). God, man and devil hand over Christ to
suffering (296). The agony of the Mount of Olives (297–298).
Vicarious suffering (299). The contradiction against Christ
(300–301) and the sword that is Christian (302). Grace and indeed all the words of revelation have their source in the wound in
Christ's side (303–304). The church itself began from there (305).
The conquering of death and hell (307). The crucifixion of hell in
the crucifixion of Christ and the meaning of the tree of paradise
(308). The whole passion taken up in the love of the Father (309).*

294   The Father's sign of salvation in the world is the Son; the Son's sign
of salvation in the world is the cross.

295   "That you may have power to comprehend with all the saints what
is the breadth and length and height and depth" (Eph 3:18). But all
this the cross of Christ possesses, through which he, "ascending on
high, led captivity captive" and "descended into the lower parts of the
earth"; for this cross had "height" and "depth" (Eph 4:8–9). And it
"went out through all the earth" (Ps 19:4) as it attained its "breadth"
and "length." And they who have been "crucified with Christ" (Gal
2:20) and stretched out with him, they comprehend "the breadth and
length and height and depth."

296   But not everyone handed him over with the same intention. For
God handed him over out of merciful love for the human race: "He did
not spare his own Son but gave him up for us all" (Rom 8:32). But the
rest handed him over with bad intentions . . . : Judas out of greed,
the priests out of envy, the devil out of fear that the human race would
be wrested from his grasp by his teaching. . . . And would that Jesus
had been "handed over" only "into the hands of [those] sinners"! But
now, it seems to me, Jesus is continually being "handed over into the
hands of sinners" (Mt 26:45), when they who appear to believe in
Jesus hold him in their hands,[1] even though they are sinners.

297   "Nevertheless, not as I will, but as you will" (Mt 26:39). For it is indeed typical of all the faithful to be, first of all, unwilling to suffer any
pain, especially when it leads to death, for the human being is of
flesh. But, if that is what God wants, it is also typical of them to be

[1] What is meant here is the reception of Holy Communion.

willing to give consent to it, lest their lack of hope in themselves seem
to be stronger than their hope in God.

298 "Nevertheless, not as I will, but as you will" (Mt 26:39). As the
"Son of the love" of God (cf. Col 1:13), he indeed loved in his foreknowledge those of the gentiles who were to believe; but the Jews,
as the seed of the holy fathers "to whom belong the sonship, the
glory, the covenants and the promises" (Rom 9:4), he loved like the
branches of the good olive tree (cf. Rom 11:16–24). But in loving
them he also foresaw what they were to suffer for demanding his
death and choosing life for Barabbas. That is why he said, suffering
for them: "Father, if it be possible, let this cup pass from me." But
again, revoking his own desires and seeing how much benefit would
come to the whole world from his passion, he said: "Nevertheless,
not as I will, but as you will" (Mt 26:39). And he also saw, because
of the cup of the passion, that Judas, who was one of the twelve,
would become "the son of perdition" (2 Thes 2:3); and he understood further, that through that cup of suffering the principalities
and powers would be triumphed over in his body (cf. Col 2:15). It
is thus on their account, whose loss he wanted to prevent by his
passion, that he said: "Father, if it be possible, let this cup pass
from me." But for the sake of the salvation of the whole human race
that was to be won for God by his death, he said, as if thinking it
over again: "Nevertheless, not as I will, but as you will." That is: if
it is possible that without my passion all those good things can come
about which are to come about by my passion, let this suffering
"pass from me" so that both the world will be saved and the Jews
not come to ruin through my passion. But if the salvation of the
many cannot be brought about but by the loss of some, as far as
your justice is concerned, let it "not" pass "as I will but as you will."
. . . Thus he is saying: I want your will to be done more than
my own.

299 The burnt offering should be a calf without blemish from the herd
(cf. Lev 1:2–3). But this calf without blemish, is it not perhaps that
"fatted calf" which the father, for the return and restoration of that son
who was lost and who had "squandered all his property," had slaughtered and made a great feast and was filled with joy (Lk 15:23–24), just
like the angels in heaven rejoicing in heaven at one sinner doing
penance (cf. Lk 15:10)? Therefore that man who "was lost and is
found," because he has nothing of his own substance to offer—for "he
had squandered away everything in loose living" (Lk 15:13)—finds

that calf sent indeed from heaven but coming from the line of patriarchs and the successions of generations from Abraham . . . and thus is called "from the herd" (Lev 1:2).

300   "And for a sign that is spoken against" (Lk 2:34). Everything which tells of the history of the Savior is spoken against. The virgin mother is a sign which is spoken against. The Marcionites speak against this sign and say that he is in no way born of a woman. The Ebionites speak against the sign saying that he was born of a man and a woman just as we all are born. . . . He rises from the dead and that too is "a sign that is spoken against." How did he rise? Was it just as he was when he died, or did he not rise into a body of better material? And it is a never-ending dispute. . . . All that history tells of him is a sign which is spoken against.

301   For the sign in which Christ had come was being spoken against, because one thing was seen in him and something else was understood. Flesh was being seen, but God was being believed.

302   For truly, before he came, the sword was not on the earth (cf. Mt 10:34–36; Lk 12:51–53) nor were "the desires of the flesh against the Spirit, and the desires of the Spirit against the flesh" (Gal 5:17). But when he came and we became aware of what is of the flesh and what of the Spirit, his teaching, coming like a sword over the earth, divided the flesh and the earth from the Spirit.

303   For Christ, in being beaten and nailed to the cross, revealed the fountains of the new covenant. This is why it is written of him: "I will strike the shepherd and the sheep will be scattered" (Zech 13:7). It was therefore necessary for him to be struck; for unless he had been struck and "water and blood come forth from his side" (Jn 19:34), we would all be suffering thirst for the WORD of God (cf. Am 8:11; below Nos. 716, 717, 718, 720).

304   For Christ has inundated the whole world with holy and divine streams. He waters the thirsty from the divine spring and makes the water flow from the wound which the sword had opened in his side.

305   For it is the church which has sprung from Christ's side and turns out to be his bride.

306   The Lord, in putting on the "scarlet robe," took the blood of the world on himself; and in that "crown of thorns" he received the thorns of our sins woven into his head (cf. Mt 27:28–29). Of the scarlet robe, it is written that "they stripped him of the robe" (Mt 27:31), but of the crown of thorns, the evangelists wrote no such thing because they wanted us to ask what happened with the crown of thorns which was

placed on him at one point and never removed. It is my opinion that that crown of thorns was consumed by the head of Jesus so that they are now no longer our old thorns, once Jesus has taken them from us and put them on his sacred head. But if something is also to be said about the "reed" which they put "in his right hand" (Mt 27:29), this is how we would explain it. That reed was the mystery of the vain and fragile scepter on which we all relied before we believed. . . . He accepted that scepter . . . and gave us in exchange the scepter of the kingdom of heaven.

307   "Death no longer has dominion over him" (Rom 6:9). . . . Death here is understood as the "final enemy" (1 Cor 15:26) whose prototype was the whale which swallowed Jonah and which was written about in Job: "Let him who cursed that day curse that [night], he who is about to kill the great whale" (Job 3:8 LXX). Just as Jonah into the belly of the whale, so Christ has entered into this death, into that place which the Savior himself has called "the heart of the earth" (Mt 12:40). . . . This is why he took on "the form of a servant" (Phil 2:7), to be able to enter into that place where death holds sway.

308   After all this, "the king of Ai was hung on a forked tree" (cf. Josh 8:29). There is a mystery hidden in this passage which is hidden from many; but supported by your prayers we will attempt to open it, not with our opinions but with the witness of sacred scripture. . . . The king of Ai can stand for the devil. But how he came to be crucified on a forked tree is worth investigating. The cross of our Lord Jesus Christ was a double cross. You might think it a strange and new idea when I say that the cross was double, but what I mean is that it can be considered as double, or from two sides. Because the Son of God was crucified visibly in the flesh, but invisibly on the same cross, the devil with "his principalities and powers was nailed to the cross" (cf. Col 2:14-15). Will not this seem true to you if I bring Paul forward as a witness to it? Hear then what he has to say: "That which stood against us," he says, "he set aside, nailing it to the cross. He disarmed the principalities and powers and made a public example of them, triumphing over them on the cross" (Col 2:14-15).

There is thus a twofold meaning in the cross of the Lord: the first is the one which causes the Apostle Peter to say that Christ crucified has left us an example (cf. 1 Pet 2:21), the second cross is this trophy of victory over the devil on which he was crucified and triumphed over. That is why the Apostle Paul says in the end: "But far be it from me to glory except in the cross of my Lord Jesus Christ, through whom the world has been crucified to me, and I to the world" (Gal 6:14). You can see that here too the Apostle is attributing a twofold meaning to the cross. He says that two contrary things are crucified — he as someone holy, and the sinful world — doubtless in the same way, as we said above, as with Christ and the devil. For we are "crucified to the world" when "the ruler of this world comes and has no power over us" (cf. Jn 14:30); and the world is "crucified to us" when we make no place for sinful desires.

But should any of my hearers be paying closer attention, he could say: the outline of what took place seems to be all right, but I'd still like to know how it is that in this symbolic history the devil and his forces are killed while we observe that, against the servants of God, the devil and his forces still have such power that the Apostle Peter also exhorts us to great caution and vigilance because "our adversary the devil prowls around like a roaring lion, seeking someone to devour" (1 Pet 5:8)? Let us see if we can also find here something worthy of the expressions of the Holy Spirit. One coming of Christ was accomplished in humility, but the second is hoped for in glory. And this first coming in the flesh is, in the holy scriptures, designated in a kind of mystical expression as "shadow," as Jeremiah proclaims: "the breath of our nostrils, Christ the Lord, he of whom we said: 'Under his shadow we shall live among the nations'" (Lam 4:20). But Gabriel too, when he announced to Mary the news of the birth, said: "The power of the Most High will overshadow you" (Lk 1:35). From this we understand that there are many things in this first coming of his which are indicated only in shadows, and whose fulfillment and perfection will take place in his second coming. And the Apostle Paul says that "He raised us up with him and made us sit with him in the heavenly places" (Eph 2:6). We do of course see that the faithful are not yet raised up or seated with him in the heavenly places, but these things are now foreshadowed by faith because our spirits and hopes are raised from earthly and dead works and our heart is lifted up to heavenly and eternal things. But the fulfillment of this will come about only in his second coming where what we now anticipate in faith and hope we will then also hold in our very hands. This then holds for the devil too: that he has indeed been conquered and crucified, but for those who have been crucified with Christ. But for all the faithful and for all nations too he will then be crucified, at which time will be fulfilled what the Apostle said: "For as in Adam all die, so also in Christ shall all be made alive" (1 Cor 15:22). . . .

And in order to extend the breadth of this mystery even more deeply, in this tree is understood to be the "knowledge of good and evil" (cf. Gen 2:9)[1] on which both the good Christ and the evil devil hung, the evil that it might perish but the good that it might live by power, as the apostle said of Christ: "Although he was crucified in weakness, he lives by the power of God" (2 Cor 13:4). And not just to live but also to give life because he is "the last Adam who became a life-giving spirit" (1 Cor 15:45). But this is to be understood symbolically; for Christ himself is called the "tree of life" (cf. Prov 3:18). But just as he on the one hand is simultaneously priest and victim and altar, and none of these understandings eliminates the other but each in its place is understood as applying symbolically to him, so here too in these images of the sacraments, the variety of roles does not prevent them from relating to one and the same person.

09   "He bowed his head," laying it, so to speak, in the bosom of his Father, who can protect and refresh it, "and gave up his spirit" (Jn 19:30; cf. Mt 27:50).

The Eternal Christ

Consumption of the Earthly

> As the old covenant was superseded in the new, so too was the image-life [i.e., bodily life] of Jesus brought by the consuming fire of death to its eternal spiritual truth. In the transfiguration of death there becomes visible for the first time the meaning of this life (310) which, from the viewpoint of eternity as a whole, was only an "as it were" (311). The sacrifice is consumed, the priest remains in eternity (312); the sacrifice has been swept away by the fire of God

---

[1] The image of the identity of the tree of life and the tree of the knowledge of good and evil contains, in its mystery-meaning, the idea of the "necessity" of the fall (cf. Text No. 940), or, more exactly, the idea of the *felix culpa* as the highest instance of the loving wisdom of providence. Gregory of Nyssa speaks of the identity of the two trees often and with the same understanding. Maximos the Confessor treats them like a secret doctrine since, in his time, the restoration could no longer be openly taught. Anastasius of Sinai does the same. Late medieval paintings still portray the tree of paradise with a crucifix on one side and a skull on the other side of its branches. It is understandable that Hegel returns to this identity in his philosophy of religion.

(313) which has transformed it into a divine-spiritual mode of being (314). But in this flesh-becoming-spirit, the flesh did not cease to be flesh (315–316), just as Christ as a whole did not cease to be human (317–318). Yet, in his sharing in the essential characteristics of the divine, this man is now freed from space and time (319–322). He is thus, seen from the point of view of earthly existence, only "as it were" a human being (323).

310   This WORD, speaking in human form and described as "flesh," calls to himself all those who are flesh that he might first cause them to be transformed according to the WORD made flesh and after that lead them up to see him as he was before he became "flesh," so that they, profiting therefrom and making progress beyond their initiation, would say: "Even though we once regarded Christ from a human point of view, we regard him thus no longer" (2 Cor 5:16). He has therefore "become flesh," and having become "flesh," "he pitched his tent among us" (Jn 1:14) and is not outside of us. And after tabernacling and dwelling in us, he did not remain in his first form, but bringing us up to the "high mountain" (Mk 9:2 parr), showed us his glorified form and the brilliance of his garments.

311   But if the immortal God, the WORD, by taking on a mortal body and a human soul, appears to Celsus to undergo change and transformation, let him learn that the WORD, remaining WORD in essence, suffers none of the things which the body and the soul suffer, but condescending occasionally to those unable to look upon the splendor and brilliance of his divinity, he becomes as it were flesh, and speaks in a bodily way until the one who has received him in this way, having been elevated after a while by the WORD, becomes able to gaze even, if I may so speak, upon his real form.

312   We have said that Isaac bore the likeness of Christ, but no less does the ram seem to bear the likeness of Christ. But how both apply to Christ, both Isaac who was not slaughtered and the ram which was, is worth investigating. Christ is the "WORD of God"; but "the WORD was made flesh" (Jn 1:14). One [thing] in Christ comes from on high, the other was taken from human nature and a virginal womb. Therefore Christ suffers, but in the flesh; and he undergoes death, but this is the flesh, whose image here is the ram, as John said: "Behold the lamb of God, who takes away the sin of the world" (Jn 1:29). But the WORD abides "in incorruption" (cf. 1 Cor 15:42), the WORD which is Christ according to the Spirit, the image of whom is Isaac. He himself

is thus both the offering and the priest. For according to the Spirit he sacrifices the offering to the Father, and according to the flesh he is sacrificed on the altar of the cross; for, just as was said of him: "Behold the lamb of God . . . " (Jn 1:29), so too was said: "You are a priest forever after the order of Melchizedek" (Ps 110:4; cf. Heb 5:7).

13   The heavenly fire quite fittingly, therefore, sweeps away all those things which were accomplished by the Savior in his body and restores them all to the nature of his divinity. Nevertheless it was with wood that that fire was lit; for the passion of Christ in the flesh extended all the way to the wood of the cross. But once hung on the wood, the dispensation of the flesh was ended; for rising from the dead he ascended to heaven with the fire showing the way by its nature. This is why the Apostle said: "Even though we once regarded Christ from a human point of view, we regard him thus no longer" (2 Cor 5:16). For the holocaust of his flesh offered through the wood of the cross has brought together the earthly with the heavenly and the human with the divine.

14   The goal of the sufferings of Christ is the resurrection, for after the resurrection, "he will never die again; death no longer has dominion over him" (Rom 6:9). . . . Through the indissoluble unity of WORD and flesh, everything that is of the flesh is attributed also to the WORD, just as what is of the WORD is predicated of the flesh.

15   He [Christ] took up with him his earthly body so that the heavenly powers were terrified and astonished to see flesh ascending into heaven. For it is written of Elijah that he was taken up as it were into heaven and of Enoch that he was taken away, but it is not said that he ascended into heaven . . . "in crimsoned garments from Bozrah" (Isa 63:1). For they saw the marks of the wounds in his body which he had received in "Bozrah," that is, in the flesh.[1]

16   "Now is the Son of man glorified" (Jn 13:35). . . . But the exaltation of the Son of Man given him because he glorified God in his death, consisted in this, that he is no longer anything different from the WORD but identical with it.[2] For if "he who is united with the Lord becomes one spirit with him" (1 Cor 6:17), so that it can no longer be said of him and the Spirit that they are two, how much more

---

[1] Origen is obviously playing on the meaning of the Hebrew word *basar* — "flesh." — R.J.D.

[2] For quite some time after Origen this overly simple manner of expression remained current, but without necessitating any implication of

should we not say that the human in Jesus has become one with the WORD, since he was exalted for not thinking "equality with God a thing to be clung to" (Phil 2:6),[1] while the WORD remained in its proper high state or was restored again to that which it once was with God: God-WORD — and still man?

317   As man he was installed through the order of salvation as heir of all things.

318   And it is fitting that the Father give such wondrous things to his Son who "humbled himself" and because of his love "did not count equality with God a thing to be grasped, but emptied himself, taking the form of a slave" (Phil 2:6-8), and became "the Lamb of God" in order to "take away the sins of the world" (Jn 1:29). "Therefore God has highly exalted him and bestowed on him the name which is above every name" (Phil 2:9). But he not only exalted him according to the spirit but also according to the body so that he would be exalted in every way.

319   For God is surpassing above every place and encompassing everything that is; and there is nothing that encompasses God.

320   But no one should think that we are affirming that only some part of the divinity of the Son of God was in Christ while the rest was somewhere else or everywhere. That could be thought by persons ignorant of the nature of incorporeal and invisible substances. For it is impossible for a part to be attributed to something incorporeal, or any division made; it is rather in all and through all and above all. . . . This excludes without doubt any kind of limitation of place.

321   "Among you stands one whom you do not know" (Jn 1:26). . . . [John] is describing the superior nature [*ousia*] of Christ: it has such power that, although it is invisible in its divinity, it is present to every human being and also extended to everything in the universe.

322   [Jesus] is everywhere and interpenetrates everything. We may no longer think of him in that smallness which he took on for our sakes,

---

Monophysitism. The following texts show that the human nature remains intact. Only after the resurrection of Christ does such a profound *communicatio idiomatum* come about that the human nature participates in the spatial and temporal transcendence of God. The consequences of this for the concept of the real eucharistic presence are already perceptible in Origen; they are expressly formulated in Gregory of Nyssa.

[1] Origen always relates this statement from the Letter to the Philippians to the (pre-existent) human soul of Jesus.

that is, in that limitation of space which he had in our body when he was with us on earth, and according to which he could be thought to be restricted, as it were, to one place.

23   "For it will be as if a man going on a journey called his servants together" (Mt 25:14). Let us see, first of all, why our Lord is compared to a man going on a journey, . . . especially since his going on a journey seems to contradict what he promised about himself when he said to his disciples: "Where two or three are gathered in my name, there I am in the midst of them" (Mt 18:20); and also when he said: "Lo, I am with you always, to the close of the age" (Mt 28:20); and also what the Baptist says of him, indicating his omnipresence: "Among you stands one whom you do not know" (Jn 1:26). . . . But in dealing with this subject we should also mention what Paul says of himself: "For though absent in the body I am present in the spirit" (1 Cor 5:3). . . .

Let us see if we can solve this problem in the following way. For he who said to his disciples: "Lo, I am with you always, to the close of the age" . . . is the only-begotten Son of God, God-WORD and Wisdom and Justice and Truth, who is not enclosed within any bodily limits. According to this divine nature of his he does not go off on any journey; but he does make journeys according to the economy of salvation in the body which he has assumed, and according to which he also became troubled and sad (cf. Jn 12:27; Mk 14:33–34). . . . But in saying this we do not separate the man of the assumed body [from the divinity], since it is written in John: "Every spirit which separates [variant: "does not confess"] Jesus is not of God" (1 Jn 4:3); rather we affirm for each substance its own properties. For if every faithful human being "who is united to the Lord becomes one spirit with him" (1 Cor 6:17), how much more is that man, whom Christ assumed according to the salvation economy of the flesh, not to be separated from him nor said to be something other than him? And notice too how he says: "as if a man going on a journey." For it was not: "a man," but "as if a man"; and the one who goes on a journey is, "as it were," a man, one who, according to the nature of the divinity, was everywhere. And note too that the wording here does not seem to say: "like a man going on a journey, so too Jesus," or: "so too I," or: "so too the Son of Man." Because it is he himself who in the parable is presented as going on a journey as a man. For it is not a man who is "wherever two or three are gathered in" his "name" (Mt 18:20); nor is a man "with" us "always, to the close of the age" (Mt 28:20); and when the faithful are gathered everywhere, what is present is not a man but the divine power which was in Jesus.[1]

Mystery of the Transitus

> *Christ's becoming spirit is the origin and enabling power of our becoming spirit (324). But this passing over into the spiritual is not accomplished in a "natural" way; it signifies rather a transformation into the dimension of the personal. That is why there is no direct expression of this (325). That is why Christ's miracles are signs (326). That is why neither can the resurrection be seen (327) nor the Risen One appear to those who have not been introduced to the mystery in faith (328–330). The hiddenness of Christ is an essential element (331), which in the face of unbelief becomes an absolute (332). The appearances of the WORD are now no longer that of a physical body which is seen in a natural way, but self-communication according to the free discretion (332–333) of him who in his omnipresence fulfills the church and the world (334).*

324   Had he not become man, no benefit would have come to us from the WORD. We would have received nothing had he remained God as he was in the beginning with the Father and not assumed the man who, as the first of all and the most worthy of all and by far the purest of all, was able to receive him. Because of that man we also will be able to receive him, each one in the measure and in the manner in which we make a fitting place for him in our soul.

325   "Blessed are you, Simon Bar-Jona! For flesh and blood has not revealed this to you, but my Father who is in heaven" (Mt 16:17). For if Christ in his bodily form had openly said to him: "I am Christ," flesh would seem to have revealed this to him and not the Father alone. . . . But observe that nowhere in the scriptures is the Lord found to be speaking this way and saying: "I am Christ," so that he would not be saying something similar to the many who would come in his name and say: "I am Christ." For the works of God were for him sufficient for the faith of the believers. . . . He said it through works.

---

[1] But figured in as part of this "divine power" is also the no-longer-human, super-human "humanity" of Christ which, in its new mode of existence, is totally divinized. On this, see the chapters "Human Being and Super-Human Being" (Nos. 351–359) and "Super-World" (Nos. 997–1008) and also No. 1018.

6   "This was now the second sign that Jesus did" (Jn 4:54). . . . Nowhere is there mention only of prodigies, for there is nothing marvelous in scripture that is not a sign and symbol of something other than a perceptible event. . . . Therefore, since we learn from the scripture that we must search for that of which the event is a sign, it is written: "This is now the second sign that Jesus did." But when the official is admonished for not believing unless he sees something extraordinary, scripture does not say: "Unless you see 'signs' you will not believe" (for the signs performed do not call to faith simply as signs without the sign also being a wonder), but: "Unless you see signs and wonders you will not believe" (Jn 4:48), whereby one believes because of the extraordinary deed; but we in addition bring that to completion of which it is a sign.

7   The beginning of his resurrection was not visible to any human being.

8   Great and wondrous and surpassing not only the capacity of the multitude of the faithful but also of those far advanced in the word are the reasons which lead me to suppose, according to the sense of this passage, why he who rose from the dead did not manifest himself in the same way as he did before.

9   Just as no one will lightly complain that Jesus did not take along all the apostles to the high mountain but only . . . three, since he was to be transfigured and show the splendor of his garments and the glory of Moses and Elias speaking with him, so too could no one reasonably object to the apostolic statements when they report that Jesus after his resurrection was not visible to all but only to those who he knew had received eyes capable of seeing his resurrection.

0   For he was sent not only to be known but also to remain hidden.

1   "For you will not see me again until you say, 'Blessed is he who comes in the name of the Lord'" (Mt 23:39). For although he appeared to some of the saints after the resurrection, he did not do so to the unbelieving Jews. And until they understand and repent of their dereliction and say: "Blessed is he who comes in the name of the Lord," they will not see the Son of God nor see his WORD nor contemplate the beauty of the wisdom of God. And even if one of us wants to be gathered "under the wings" of Christ (cf. Mt 23:37), but, because of the evil we do, refuses to be gathered under his wings, such a one will no longer see the WORD of God, especially from the time when, by actually consummated deed more than just by the body, we flee day by day from the one wishing to gather us in. Such a one will not see the beauty of the WORD, that is, Christ, until, converting

and repenting of his evil intentions, he says: "Blessed is he who comes in the name of the Lord." For the blessed WORD of God and the blessed Wisdom of God will then come into the human heart, in the name of God and of the Father, just as soon as anyone turns to him.

332 The WORD of God may well appear in different kinds of glory according to the ability and capacity which each individual soul has for seeing him. Thus, to those who are perfect and who, as far as their person is concerned,[1] have come to the end of the ages, the WORD appears in such a way that they who see him will say: "We have beheld his glory, glory as of the only Son from the Father, full of grace and truth" (Jn 1:14).

333 Bodily creatures which are not endowed with senses do nothing when they are seen by something else. Whether they like it or not, the eye of the one beholding them sees them merely by directing its gaze on them. For what could a man, or anything else which is circumscribed by a material body, do in order not to be seen when it is present to something else? On the other hand heavenly and divine things, even when present, are not seen, unless they themselves wish it; it depends on them whether they are seen or not. It was by grace that God appeared to Abraham and the other prophets, not just because the eye of Abraham's heart enabled him to see God but because God allowed himself by special favor to be seen by the just man. And this applies not just to God the Father but also to the Lord and Savior and to the Holy Spirit and, to move on to those lower down, to the Cherubim and Seraphim. . . . We say this not just about the present world but also about the future, for when we have migrated from this world God will not appear to all. . . . Something like this seems to me to have been the case with Christ: when he was visible in the body, not everyone who saw him was able to see him. For they saw only his body, but that which made him what he was as Christ they were unable to see. . . . Only those saw Jesus whom he thought worthy of such sight. Let us therefore work hard so that God will appear to us too; it is indeed promised by the holy word of scripture: "Because he is found by those who do not put him to the test, and manifests himself to those who do not distrust him" (Wis 1:2).

334 Behold the greatness of the Lord: "Their voice has gone out to all the earth, and their words to the ends of the world" (Rom 10:18;

---

[1] Cf. Text No. 887.

Ps 19:4). Jesus our Lord, because he is the power of God, is spread over the whole world and is now also with us as the apostle says: "when you are assembled, and my spirit is present, with the power of the Lord Jesus" (1 Cor 5:4). The power of our Lord and Savior is also with those who are widely separated from our world in Britannia and with those who live in Mauretania and with all under the sun who believe in his name. See then the greatness of the Savior and how he reaches out to the whole world, and I certainly have not done justice to his true greatness. Climb up to the sky and see him, how he fills the heavens (cf. Ps 139:8 LXX; Rom 10:6, 7), for "he was seen by the angels" (1 Tim 3:16). Climb down in thought into the abyss and you will find that he has gone down even there. For "he who descended is he who also ascended . . . , that he might fill all things" (Eph 4:10), "that at the name of Jesus every knee should bow, in heaven and on earth and under the earth" (Phil 2:10).

Body and Super-Body

The earthly body is a sinful body because it is the (freely chosen by God) expression of the sins of the soul: its spiritual darkening has brought on it the coarseness and heaviness of this body (335–338). Christ has this same sinful body on whose reality salvation depends (339–341). But this sinful flesh will not rise (342), even though the resurrection of the body is by all means to be affirmed (342–343). Origen explains this through the survival of the body's spiritual principle of form, its form (eidos) or actuality (entelecheia) (345–346), which is formed at the resurrection with a new body which, to be sure, is not substantially imperishable (only the spirit is that), but is de facto so by participation in the spirit (347–348). This spiritual body can be called in one sense "flesh" and in another sense "flesh-no-longer" (349). Faith in the resurrection however signifies freedom from any disordered dependency on the flesh (350).

35   The soul which has become flesh through sin will be changed and become spirit.

36   Every fire that needs fuel is perishable, and every spirit, if we take spirit in its more common meaning, is a body and is, as far as its nature is concerned, subject to change into something more gross.

37   This "body of sin" is thus our body; for it is written that Adam did not know Eve his wife and generate Cain except after sinning. . . .

This is also why the church received the tradition from the apostles to give baptism even to infants.

338   The Apostle himself says in another place: "Who will deliver me from this body of death?" (Rom 7:24). And again he calls our body "lowly body" (Phil 3:21). But he says of the Savior somewhere (Rom 8:3) that he has come "in the likeness of sinful flesh," . . . in which he shows that our flesh is really the flesh of sin but that Christ's flesh is only like the flesh of sin. For it is not conceived of the seed of man (cf. Jn 1:13) but "the power of the Most High came upon" Mary (Lk 1:35). . . . Paul too, through the inexpressible wisdom of God which was given to him, seeing something or other mysterious and hidden, called our body "sinful body" and "body of death" and "lowly body."

339   [But] the body of Christ, because he was the Son of David, was not of a substance other than earthly.

340   We do not classify his suffering as only apparent, lest the resurrection, which is true, also become a lie.

341   If it was only an apparent death, the resurrection would also not be true, and we will only appear to rise and not truly do so. And we will only appear to, and not truly, die to sin. And everything which was done and is being done only appeared to be done, but was not done. And thus we who have been saved would only appear to be, but not be truly saved.

342   The Sadducees, who deny the resurrection, reject not only what the more simple are accustomed to call the resurrection of the flesh, they also completely reject not only the immortality of the soul but even its continued existence. . . . [But Paul says:] "If for this life only we have hoped in Christ, we are of all men most to be pitied" (1 Cor 15:19). Now if one examines this more closely, it will be seen that someone who rejects the resurrection from the dead which the church believes, even when this rejection is unjustified, is not necessarily obliged to have hoped in Christ "for this life only" . . . since we say that the soul lives on and survives without putting on this same body again. . . . Nor are we, in saying this, showing lack of belief in this passage from Isaiah: "And all flesh shall see the salvation of God" (Isa 40:5 LXX), or in what was said by Job: "For eternal is he who is to save me on earth and resurrect my skin which is suffering these things" (Job 19:25–26 LXX). Nor are we showing disbelief in the voice of the Apostle which says: "He will give life to our mortal bodies" (Rom 8:11).

343   Let no one suppose that in saying this we are among those who call themselves Christian but deny the doctrine of the resurrection

according to the scriptures. . . . Thus we do not say that the corrupted body returns to its first condition, no more than the disintegrated grain of wheat returns to being a grain of wheat (cf. Jn 12:24; 1 Cor 15:37).

44   For man is a unity of both; and life is common to both and has need of both in order to set up again the life that comes from death.

45   We now turn our attention to some among us who, for want of understanding or lack of an explanation, give a very base and low interpretation of the resurrection of the body. . . . How do they understand it when the Apostle says that "we shall all be changed" (1 Cor 15:51)? Now this change is to be expected according to that rule we have already mentioned by which it is surely fitting for us to hope for something worthy of divine grace. This will take place, we believe, according to the rule described by the Apostle in which "a bare kernel of wheat or of some other grain" is planted in the earth, to which "God gives a body as he has chosen" after the grain of wheat itself has first died (1 Cor 15:37–38, 36). So too, must we realize, do our bodies fall to the earth like a grain of wheat; but in them is a principle which contains or holds together the bodily substance, and even though the body is dead, corrupted and dispersed, so at God's command that very principle, which survives in the bodily substance, can lift up the body from the earth and restore it, in the same way as that power which is in the grain of wheat, after its corruption and death restores the grain to a body of stalk and ear.

46   Artificially placed by God in each seed is a certain principle which contains the future material bodies as in the potency of marrow. And just as the whole size of a tree, its trunk, branches, fruit and leaves are not visible in the seed, they are still in the seed which the Greeks call *spermatismon*. In the grain of wheat there is, within, some marrow or a vein which, when dissolved in the earth, draws adjacent material to itself and raises it up to become stalk, leaves or ears. One part dies, another rises. . . . Similarly in the life-principle of human bodies, there are certain, already-existing principles of rising . . . but they are not restored to the same bodily flesh nor to the same forms which they had before. . . . "It is sown a physical body, it is raised a spiritual body" (1 Cor 15:44). Now we see with our eyes, hear with our ears, act with our hands, walk with our feet; but in that spiritual body we will see as a whole, act as a whole, walk as a whole; and "the Lord will change our lowly body to be like his glorious body" (Phil 3:21).

347   If the words: "The soul that sins shall die" (Ezek 18:4) mean that the soul is capable of sin, we agree that the soul is mortal. But if by death is meant its total dissolution and disappearance, we will not agree because it is impossible even to conceive of a mortal substance changing into an immortal one, or a corruptible nature into an incorruptible. For this would be like saying that something corporeal is changing into something incorporeal, as if there were something common underlying the nature of bodily and non-bodily things which remains the same, just as, say the experts, the material element remains while the qualities change into the incorruptible. It is not the same when a perishable nature puts on the imperishable (cf. 1 Cor 15:53) and when a perishable nature changes to the imperishable. And the same is true of its mortality; it is not changed into immortality, but only puts it on.

348   Indeed what "wisdom" has, as a relationship to "the wise," and "justice" to "the just," and "peace" to "the peaceable," the same relationship does "imperishable" hold to "the imperishable" and "immortality" to "the immortal." You see then to what the scripture encourages us in telling us to "put on the imperishable" and "immortality" (1 Cor 15:53); for these are like clothes, to those who put them on and cover themselves with them, which do not allow those who wear them to suffer corruption or death.

349   Just as the one circumcised loses a part of his flesh and keeps the rest safe, so, it seems to me, that which was lost signifies that flesh of which it was written: "All flesh is grass, and all its beauty is like the flower of the field" (Isa 40:6). The flesh, however, which remains and is kept safe, seems to me to be an image of that flesh of which it is said that "all flesh shall see the salvation of God" (Lk 3:6).

350   Since Celsus reproaches us for having a desire for the body, let him know that if the desire is bad, we desire nothing of it; but if it is indifferent, we desire all that God has promised to the righteous. It is in this sense, then, that we desire and hope for the resurrection of the just.

Human Being and Super-Human Being

"The human being," understood as this empirical, earthly existence, will be consumed just as will "the body," understood as this sensible body. "The human being" can not stand before God (351). But Christ has already prefigured the change into the super-human (352–355). This change signifies both the superseding of the

"Law" as something external and its transformation into pure freedom (356–358). The super-human is someone whose body and soul have been "superseded" in the Spirit (359).

351   "No one will see my face and live" (Exod 33:20). You must be changed in order to see the face of God which you are seeking.

352   "Cursed is the man who trusts in man . . ." (Jer 17:5). But I would like to say that I am not placing my trust in man when I hope in Christ Jesus. . . . Even when the Savior gives witness that what he took on was man—but even if it was man—he is man no longer. For "even though we once regarded Christ from a human point of view, we regard him thus no longer," says the Apostle (2 Cor 5:16). I am through him no longer man, if I follow his words. But he says: "I say, 'You are gods, sons of the Most High, all of you'" (Ps 82:6).

353   Jesus did indeed, according to physical appearances, go away to suffer on the cross. But according to what he truly was, he both went and remained in the world with his disciples, strengthening them in faith.

354   "Behold the Lamb of God who takes away the sin of the world" (Jn 1:29). It is not written that he will take away sin, nor that he is presently doing so, nor that he has taken away sin but is doing so no longer. For he is still working on this removal of sin in each individual in the world until sin be taken away from the whole world and the Savior delivers the kingdom thus prepared to the Father to reign over it when it no longer has place for sin (cf. 1 Cor 15:24).

355   If you are able to understand the WORD restored again after having become flesh and become so many things for creatures, becoming for them what each of them needed, in order to win them all (cf. 1 Cor 9:19); if you can see him restored again to the way he "was in the beginning with God" (for God was WORD—Jn 1:1-2), in his own glory, glory which is proper to such a WORD; you will see him sitting on his glorious throne (cf. Mt 19:28), and you will see that the Son of Man, the man perceived to be Jesus, is no other than he himself. For he is one with the WORD much more than those who become one spirit with him by being united with the Lord (cf. 1 Cor 6:17).

356   Christ thus comes to the judgment not like one who is under the law but like someone who is the law. And it seems to me that those who are already made perfect, and in union with the Lord "are one spirit with him" (1 Cor 6:17), are no longer under the law but instead are themselves law, as the Apostle says elsewhere: "The law is not laid down for the just" (1 Tim 1:9).

357   The saints whom God foreknew and predetermined and justified and glorified, they are themselves law and not under the law.

358   For if there are two laws, both the law "in our members" fighting against "the law of the mind," and "the law of the mind" (Rom 7:23), we must say that the law of the mind, that is, "the spiritual law" (Rom 7:14), is man to whom woman (the soul) is betrothed by God (cf. Rom 7:2) . . . but the other law [in our members] is an adulterer with the soul which is in subjection to it, . . . as long as the spiritual law lives (cf. Rom 7:1-2). . . . But the law dies for those who are ascending to the state of blessedness and no longer live under the law but are doing as Christ did. For Christ, although he came "under the law" for the sake of those who are subject to it that he might "win those under the law" (1 Cor 9:20), he nevertheless did not remain under the law nor allow those liberated by him to remain under it. For he led them up together with him to the divine citizenship which is above the law; which law contains, for those who are imperfect and still sinners, sacrifices for the forgiveness of sins (cf. Heb 5:1). Those, therefore, who are sinless and no longer in need of the sacrifices of the law, have, in their coming to perfection, surpassed perhaps even the spiritual law (cf. Rom 7:14) and attained even to the WORD which is above that law. For that WORD became "flesh" to those living in the flesh (cf. Gal 2:20; Phil 1:22; Jn 1:14); but to those no longer doing battle in the flesh, he became God the WORD just as he "was in the beginning with God" (Jn 1:2).

359   "The unspiritual man [*anthrōpos psychikos*] does not receive the gifts of the Spirit of God, for they are folly to him. . . . but the spiritual one [*pneumatikos*] judges all things" (1 Cor 2:14-15). We maintain that Paul deliberately did not add "man" after "spiritual." For the spiritual "man" is better than man when characterized as being in the soul or in the body or in both, but not when in the Spirit which is more divine than these two. It is when this Spirit becomes the dominating part that the human being is called spiritual.

And the soul, being lifted up and following the Spirit, is separated from the body; and not only does it follow the Spirit but enters into it. This is shown in the verse: "To you, O Lord, I lift up my soul" (Ps 25:1). Since its soul-existence has already been laid aside, how can it not become spiritual?

Universal Salvation

Christ is not only the Savior of the whole human race (360), he has also become incarnate on all levels of being (361-362). And because, according to Origen, no angel remained wholly without fault, he offered himself up also for all spiritual creatures (365). He even died on the cross for them (363), but not because the cross was a bloody sacrifice but only because of his spiritual offering (cf. 812–813), for the angels have no need of the passion (364). And because human beings and angels are essentially of the same nature (both spirit-bodily) and human beings rise through the eons into ever-higher realms, they will meet Christ on all levels. Christ is thus a ladder to heaven (366) and the ruler over the visible and invisible world (367).

60   For Christ, the only-begotten Son, is "everything to everyone" (1 Cor 15:28). He is the "beginning" in the human being as assumed, and the "end" in the perfection of the saints, and obviously everything in between. Or, he is the beginning in Adam and the end in his own coming, as it is said: "The last Adam became a life-giving spirit."

61   Thus I believe that just as he was "found in human form" (Phil 2:8) among us human beings, so among the angels will he also be found as an angel.

62   Now the God of all created a certain category of rational beings, which are, I think, called gods, as first in worthiness, and a second category which we will for the present call "thrones," and a third called, of course, "dominions." Thus we must go down the scale of rational beings to the last rational being, which is, of course, none other than the human being. Accordingly, in a much more divine way than Paul, the Savior became "all things to all" that he might either "gain all" (cf. 1 Cor 9:22) or make them perfect: he became a human being to the humans and an angel to the angels.

63   [Christ] is the great high priest (cf. Heb 5:14) who offered himself as a sacrifice once and for all (cf. Heb 9:7, 26–28) not just for human beings but for all rational creatures. "For he was to taste death for the sake of all except God," or, as in some of the manuscripts: "for the sake of all by the grace of God" (Heb 2:9). If one reads: "He was to taste death for the sake of all except God," then he died not just for human beings but also for all other reason-endowed beings. And if one reads "By the grace of God," he still died for all except God.

64   Jesus therefore, in completing the work of God—I mean every rational being and not just the human being—completes it in the same way. For the more blessed beings which are persuaded by the WORD and do not need suffering are made perfect by the WORD alone. But

the others, not persuaded by the WORD, need suffering so as to be able, after suffering and making progress, to be made perfect by these doctrines.

365 But he who is already so many things: "paraclete," "atonement," "expiation," who has sympathized with our weaknesses and been tempted in all human things as we are, but without sin (cf. Heb 4:15), is also the great high priest who has offered himself in sacrifice once and for all not only for human beings but for every rational being (cf. Heb 9:28).

366 And perhaps, just as in the temple there were certain steps by which one entered into the holy of holies, so too is the only-begotten Son of God all our steps; and just as there is the first step at the bottom, and the next highest, and so forth up to the highest, so too is the Savior all the steps. The first, at the bottom, is his humanity over which we proceed the whole way, step by step, so that one proceeds upward through him, who is also angel, and the rest of the powers.

367 See, then, if you can understand as sitting at Christ's right those creatures which are called unseen, and at his left the seen and the bodily; but Christ is king over them all.

CHURCH

The Church in the Old Covenant

Incarnation in the scripture and in an individual body were both an image and means to the third incarnation which was the meaning and purpose of the redemption: the incarnation of the Logos in his mystical body. In what follows we will see the church first in this character which it has: that of being body and appearance. Its inner mystical life will only later be made visible. But since the beginning of the world the church has existed as body, in all the just (368); the church is in the image of the ark (369), in Abraham, Sara, Jahel (370–372). Grown weary of talk in images, it longs for the coming of Christ in the flesh (373), and senses his coming incarnation (374). In the image of the meeting of Solomon with the Queen of Sheba is a prefiguring of the encounter of Christ with the church (375).

368 You are not to think that it is only since the coming of Christ in the flesh that it has been called bride or church, but from the beginning of

the human race and the very foundation of the world, or rather, to follow Paul's lead in seeking the origin of the mystery even earlier, even "before the foundation of the world." For his words are: "Even as he chose us in him before the foundation of the world, that we should be holy and blameless before him. He destined us in love to be his sons" (Eph 1:4–5). In the Psalms too it is written: "Remember your congregation which you have gathered from the beginning" (Ps 74:2). For the first foundations of the congregation of the church were laid right "from the beginning," which is why the Apostle says that the church "is built" not only "on the foundation of the apostles," but also on that of "the prophets" (Eph 2:20). But among the prophets is also counted Adam who prophesied a great mystery in Christ and in the church. This is found in the words: "Therefore a man leaves his father and his mother and cleaves to his wife, and they become one flesh" (Gen 2:24). For it is obviously about these words that the Apostle says that "this is a great mystery, and I take it to mean Christ and the church" (Eph 5:32). And when the same apostle says: "Christ loved the church and gave himself up for her, that he might sanctify her . . . by the washing of water" (Eph 5:25–26), he is by no means pointing out that the church did not exist before that. For how would he have loved her if she did not exist? . . . But she was in all the saints who have lived from the beginning of the world.

69   And so, just as that Noah at that time was told to build an ark and bring into it with him not only his sons and relatives but also animals of different kinds, so too was our Noah, the Lord Jesus Christ, who alone is truly just and who alone is perfect, told by the Father at the end of the ages to build for himself an ark . . . and fill it with heavenly mysteries.

70   If the natural law had been sufficient for faith, what was said to Abraham would seem superfluous: "Go from your country and your kindred and your father's house to the land that I will show you" (Gen 12:1).

71   According to the allegorical meaning of things, there was no way that Pharaoh, which is to say: the impure man who kills, could take to wife Sara, which is to say: virtue. But Abimelech, who lived purely and reasonably, could indeed have taken her to wife because he sought her "in the integrity of [his] heart" (Gen 20:5), but the time had not yet come (cf. Jn 7:6). Thus virtue remains with Abraham, remains with circumcision until the time comes that in Christ Jesus our Lord, in whom "the whole fullness of deity dwells bodily" (Col 2:9), full and perfect virtue would pass over to the church of the gentiles.

372   That foreign woman, Jahel, of whom the prophecy spoke when it said that victory will be "in the hand of a woman" (Jud 9:4) is a prefiguring of the church which has been gathered together from foreign nations. "Jahel" is interpreted ascension because there is in truth no other ascension by which to rise to heaven except "through the church of the manifold wisdom of God" (cf. Eph 3:10).

373   "That he would kiss me with the kisses of his mouth" (Cant 1:2). Let us see now if we can come to a proper inner understanding of this. It is the church which longs to be united with Christ; but under church is to be understood the gathering of all the saints. The church is therefore one person, made up as it were of all, which speaks the words: I have everything, I am showered with gifts which I received before marriage as wedding gifts or a dowry. For I have long been prepared for marriage with the son of the king and "first-born of every creature" (Col 1:15); his holy angels have served and ministered to me and brought me the law in place of a wedding gift, for the "law" is said to be "ordained by angels through an intermediary" (Gal 3:19). The prophets also served me. For they not only said everything needed in order to tell me about the Son of God to whom they wished to wed me by the offering of these, as it were "pledges" (cf. Gen 38:17) and wedding gifts, but also, in order to arouse me to love and desire for him, they prophesied to me about his coming and, filled with the Holy Spirit, preached about his countless virtues and tremendous deeds. They also described the beauty of his appearance and his gentleness so that from all these things I was unbearably inflamed with love for him. But because the world has now almost come to an end, and his presence is still not given me, and I see only his servants ascending and descending to me, for this reason I turn my prayer to you, the Father of my Bridegroom, and beseech you to take pity at last on my love and send him, so that he will no longer speak to me through his servants, whether angels or prophets, but will himself come in season and "kiss me with the kisses of his mouth," which is to say, that he would pour his words into my mouth and I would hear him speaking and see him teaching.

374   "The fragrance of your ointments is above all sweetness" (Cant 1:3 LXX). . . . The bride therefore already had experience and knowledge of fragrances, that is, of the words of "the law and the prophets" (cf. Mt 7:12). . . . "But when the time had fully come" (Gal 4:4) and she had grown up and the Father "sent his only-begotten Son into the world" (1 Jn 4:9) "anointed with the Holy Spirit" (Acts 10:38), the

bride smelled the fragrance of the divine ointment, and perceiving that all those ointments which she had previously made use of were far inferior in comparison with the sweetness of this new and divine ointment, said: "The fragrance of your ointments is above all sweetness" (Cant 1:3 LXX). And because the same Christ is called "bridegroom" and "priest" — "priest" insofar as he is "mediator of God and humans" (1 Tim 2:5) and of every creature, . . . but "bridegroom" insofar as he is united with the church which is "without spot or wrinkle or any such thing" (Eph 5:27) — consider whether that priestly "anointing oil," whose formula of composition is laid down in the book of Exodus (cf. Exod 30:22–33), might not perhaps have the same meaning as that ointment which the bride now smells and marvels at.

375   There came the queen of Sheba. Indeed, prefigured by her, it was the church of the gentiles coming to hear the wisdom of the true Solomon and the true prince of peace, our Lord Jesus Christ. She came first of all to "test him with hard questions" (1 Kgs 10:2) which until then seemed insoluble. But these questions about the knowledge of the true God and the creatures of the world or the immortality of the soul and the judgment to come, these questions which for her and her doctors, the pagan philosophers, always remained fraught with uncertainty, were answered by him. She came therefore to Jerusalem, i.e., to the vision of peace, "with a very great retinue" (1 Kgs 10:2). Nor did she come with just one nation, like the synagogue which used to be made up only of Hebrews, she came with the nations of the whole world, also bearing gifts worthy of Christ, the sweetnesses of good odors which are the good works which rise up to God with the "odor of sweetness" (cf. Lev 1:9, 13, 17 and passim). She came also "with very much gold," doubtless the experimental and intellectual disciplines which, before coming to faith, she had put together from the common sources of erudition. She also brought precious stones which we can understand as the ornaments of morality. Together with all this, she thus enters in to the peaceful prince, Christ, and opens to him her heart, in confession that is, and with repentance for her previous sins, and "she told him all that was on her mind" (1 Kgs 10:2). Therefore Christ, who "is our peace" (Eph 2:14), "answered all her questions; there was nothing hidden from the king which he could not explain to her" (1 Kgs 10:2-3). . . . She saw too "the house that he had built" (1 Kgs 10:4), doubtless the mysteries of his incarnation, for that is the house which wisdom has built (cf. Prov 9:1). She saw also the food of Solomon which, I think, refers to the Lord's words:

"My food is to do the will of him who sent me, and to accomplish his work" (Jn 4:34). She saw also the "seating of his officials" (1 Kgs 10:5) which is, I think, the ecclesiastical order found in the seats of bishops and presbyters. And she saw the "place of his servants" (1 Kgs 10:5), the rows of deacons, it seems to me, who serve at the divine office. But she also saw his "clothing" (1 Kgs 10:5), the clothing I mean with which he clothes those to whom is said: "As many of you as were baptized into Christ have put on Christ" (Gal 3:27). She also saw "his cupbearers" (1 Kgs 10:5), the teachers I presume who mix for the people the WORD of God and his doctrine like a wine which "gladdens the hearts" (cf. Ps 104:15) of the hearers. She saw also "his burnt offerings" (1 Kgs 10:5), certainly the mysteries of prayer and impetration. All this thus did she see in the palace of the king of peace, who is Christ, and this "very dark, but comely" one (Cant 1:5) was astonished and said to him: "The report was true which I heard in my own land of your affairs and of your wisdom" (1 Kgs 10:6). For because of your word, which I have recognized as the true WORD, I have come to you. For all the words which were said to me and which I heard when I was in my own land from the scholars and philosophers of this world were not true. This alone which is in you is the true WORD. But perhaps it will seem necessary to ask how the queen can say to the king "I did not believe those who were telling me" about you, since she would not have come to Christ if she had not believed. Let us see if we can solve this as follows. "I did not," she says, "believe those who were telling me." For I have directed my belief not to those "who have spoken" about you, but to you. That is, "I have believed" not in human beings but in you, my God. I did indeed hear through them, but it was to you I came.

The Church in the New Covenant

If the church already existed even in the Old Testament, it was still only in relation to the incarnation. With this arrival it comes into existence in the full sense for the first time because its life, its soul is Christ. It is the new paradise (376), indeed the new, spiritual world-creation (377–378). It radiates the light of Christ into the world (379), in its preaching the still-living Christ speaks (380–382), it continues in the spiritual realm the miracle of Christ (383). Thus the church must be listened to (384), for its word has the power of interior grace (385), and it also has the obligation to

speak in order not to become liable to the punishment of God (386).
Christ's presence in the community (387). Promise of faithfulness
to the church (388–390). It alone has the entire truth and protects
it (391), it alone is the entire incarnation of God (392).

376   Those who are born anew through divine baptism are placed in paradise, that is, the church, in order to carry out spiritual works therein.

377   Those who are in the church are the ones who inhabit the globe.[1]

378   Just as in this firmament, by now called heaven, God commanded
two lights to be made "to separate the day from the night" (Gen 1:14),
so can it also happen to us (if we but exert ourselves both to be called
and to become "heaven") that we will have lights, namely, Christ and
his church, within us to illuminate us. For he is the "light of the world"
(cf. Jn 8:12) who also illuminates the church with his light. For just as
the moon is said to receive its light from the sun so that through the
moon the night also can be illuminated, so too the church, having
received the light of Christ, illumines all who dwell in the night
of ignorance.

379   Christ is the light of the apostles, but the apostles are "the light of
the world" (Mt 5:14).

380   When you read: "He taught in their synagogues, being glorified by
all" (Lk 4:15), beware of judging them [in the synagogues] to be blessed
and thinking of yourself as deprived of instruction. If what is written is
true, the Lord spoke not only then in the congregations of the Jews,
but is also speaking today in this congregation; and not only in this
congregation but also in every other gathering and in the whole world
Jesus is teaching, and searching for organs through which to teach.
Pray, that he will find me also prepared and qualified to sing.

381   The teachers are the lips of Christ.

382   Jesus, then, because of the power he had given to his disciples even
to nourish others, said: "You give them something to eat" (Mt 14:16).
They however, while not denying their power to give out loaves of
bread, thought that the loaves were far too few and insufficient to feed
those who were following Jesus; for they did not realize that Jesus can
take each loaf (or word) and stretch it as far as he wishes and make it
sufficient for all whom he wishes to nourish with it.

---

[1] The globe (*oikoumenē*) means in Greek "the inhabited world."

383   "He who believes in me will also do the works that I do; and greater works than these will he do" (Jn 14:12). . . . I have made people rise bodily from the dead, you will make people rise spiritually from the dead. I gave this sensible light to the blind, you will give spiritual light to those who do not see.

384   "How are they to believe in him of whom they have never heard?" (Rom 10:14). That they did not hear we can understand as their unwillingness to hear either him in the flesh or the apostles preaching about him. As the Lord himself says: "He who hears you hears me, and he who rejects you rejects me" (Lk 10:16). Now this too can be understood as saying that both now and at all times Christ as WORD and as reason speaks in the heart of each individual and teaches what one should do, and encourages to justice, . . . as he himself says: "My sheep hear my voice"[1] (Jn 10:27).

385   Do you want to know that it is not just Jesus alone in his speaking who transmits the Holy Spirit to his hearers, but that everyone who speaks God's word in his name actually hands on the Spirit of God to those who listen? See then how, in the Acts of the Apostles, when Peter is speaking to Cornelius, Cornelius himself and those with him were filled with the Holy Spirit (Acts 10:44). Hence, if you speak God's word and do so faithfully with a pure conscience, it can come about that while you are speaking the fire of the Holy Spirit will inflame the hearts of your hearers and immediately make them warm and eager to carry out all you are teaching in order to implement what they have learned.

386   Let us therefore examine the prophecy itself and, first of all, let us consider how it really came to the prophet whether to "speak" or not. "The WORD of the Lord came to him and said: Son of man, make known to Jerusalem her abominations; and you shall say: Thus says the Lord . . ." (Ezek 16:2-3). The Lord did not force him but left it to the free decision of the speaker to "make known to Jerusalem her abominations." "You shall say," he says. . . . It was left to the prophet who heard this "you shall say" whether he would say it or not, just as it was with Jonah. It was indeed up to him who heard: Say: "Yet three

---

[1] In the mind of Origen both meanings apparently form a unity similar to the working together of Christ and the apostles at the resurrection of Lazarus: Christ gives the inner life, the sacramental action of the apostles "loosens" the external "bonds." (This symbolism discovered by Origen for the effectiveness of confession was later taken over by Ambrose and Augustine.)

days, and Nineveh shall be overthrown"[1] (Jon 3:4), to speak or to keep silent. And because it was left to his free choice, and he did not want to speak, see how many things happened to him as a result. "The ship threatened to break up" because of him, through the casting of lots he was discovered in his hiding place, and the great fish swallowed him up when he was thrown into the sea (cf. Jon 1:4–17). Now then, the prophets who came after Jonah, considering perhaps what happened to him or to other prophets, saw how they were hemmed in from all sides: persecution from the world if they spoke the truth, punishment from God if, for fear of man, they said what was false instead of the truth.

87   "And the eyes of all in the synagogue were fixed on him" (Lk 4:20). . . . O blessed gathering! . . . How I wish that the same could be said of this congregation here! That the eyes of all, of the catechumens and the faithful and the women and the men and the children, not the eyes of the body but those of the soul would be fixed on Jesus! For if you were looking towards him, your faces would become more illuminated from his light and countenance, and you would be able to say: "Sealed over us, O Lord, is the light of your countenance" (Ps 4:7 LXX).

88   "But for me it is good to be near God" (Ps 73:28), and just as "to God" so also to our Lord Jesus Christ and the apostles, and to draw understanding from the sacred scriptures according to the tradition that has come from them.

89   I want to be a man of the church. I do not want to be called by the name of some founder of a heresy but by the name of Christ, and to bear that name which is blessed on the earth. It is my desire, in deed as in Spirit, both to be and to be called a Christian.

90   Does it not happen that the hand of our body is a scandal to us, or is it of this bodily hand that the gospel says: "Cut it off and throw it away" (Mt 5:30)? However, this is what it really says: if I, who seem to be your right hand and am called presbyter and seem to preach the WORD of God, if I do something against the discipline of the church and the rule of the gospel so that I become a scandal to you, the church, then may the whole church, in unanimous resolve, cut me, its

---

[1] Jonah 3:4 reads "yet *forty* days . . . ." This seems to be an instance which shows how Origen, in quoting scripture from memory (or the scribe in transcribing), is occasionally inaccurate in details.

right hand, off, and throw me away. For it is better for you the church
to enter into the kingdom of heaven without me, your hand which in
doing wrong has given scandal, than with me to "go into hell"
(Mt 5:30).

391   "As the lightning comes from the east and shines as far as the west,
so will be the coming of the Son of man" (Mt 24:27). We must,
however, be aware that this lightning, because it is the brilliance of
truth, is not just something that shows up in one scripture text but
cannot be proven from another text; it can be found in the whole
scripture, whether of the law or the prophets or the gospels or the
apostles. This "lightning" of truth, "coming from the east," i.e., from
its origins in Christ, shines as far as the economy of his passion which
is its evening. And like to this lightning is "the coming of the Son of
Man," that is, of the WORD of truth. . . . Not even the church
takes away any word or meaning from this lightning, nor adds anything else to it by way of prophecy.

392   Hence we should pay no attention to those who say: "Look, here is
Christ" (cf. Mt 24:26), but do not indicate his presence in the church
which is full of lightning "from the east as far as the west" (cf. Mt
24:27), which is full of the "true light" (Jn 1:9), which is "the pillar and
bulwark of truth" (1 Tim 3:15), in which fullness (cf. Jn 1:16) is also
the fullness of the coming of the Son of Man who says to everyone
everywhere: "Lo, I am with you always, to the close of the age"
(Mt 28:20).

Harlot and Holy

*Origen is the first to break from the early Christian dream of a
sinless church (that bride "without spot or wrinkle"—Eph 5:27—of
which Paul spoke) not only in his exhortatory sermons but also in
his theology.*

*The axiom "outside the church is no salvation" is inseparably
connected in Origen to the image of Rahab the whore (Jos 2:1–24;
6:22–25) who received the spies of Joshua and was thus spared by
the victors together with all who could flee into her house (393–
397). But this image, like that of the converted Magdalen, still
continues to leave open the idea that the church was indeed once a
sinner but is now only holy. In this sense Origen too hesitates to
count sinners in the "real" church (398), and only the human im-
possibility of separating the just and the sinners would then be the*

reason why these "dead members" of the church still appear as members at all (399). But he has a still deeper knowledge of the dark mystery of the church: Sin does not stop in the outer court of the church (400). Hence the sorrow of Christ over the spiritual city of Jerusalem (401–403), hence the failure of the church (404). This church is both the bride without spot, and one constantly being cleansed of sin (405); she is also the wonder-working mother of humanity (406). The whore of Jerusalem as mirror and warning for Christians and the church (406a).

393   One could thus say that the WORD of God, abandoning the synagogue of the Jews as adulterous, left it and took on "a wife of harlotry" (Hos 1:2), namely, the gentiles, . . . who, like Rahab the harlot (cf. Isa 1:21; Josh 2.1–24; 6:17–25) had received the spies of Jesus . . . continuing her harlotry no longer but coming to the feet of Jesus and drenching them with the tears of repentance (cf. Lk 7:38).

394   Thus the church on earth, still at the beginning of its service of God and knowledge of Christ, is a stool for his feet (cf. Mt 22:44; Ps 110:1; Acts 2:35; Heb 1:13; 10:13), just like that woman who was a sinner doing penance at the feet of Jesus (cf. Lk 7:37–38); for she was not yet able to pour the fragrant ointment of her good works over the head of Christ. For even to stand by the feet of Jesus and anoint them was desirable for her.

395   Meanwhile spies were sent by Jesus [Joshua] into Jericho and were received by the "harlot" Rahab (Jos 2:1). . . . Let us see then who this harlot is. She is called Rahab. Rahab signifies breadth. What then is this breadth if not this church of Christ which is made up of sinners as if gathered in from harlotry? And she says: "The place is too narrow for me; make room for me to dwell in. . . . Who has borne me these?" (Isa 49:20–21). And again she is told: "Enlarge the place of your tent, and let the curtains of your habitations be stretched out" (Isa 54:2). That is therefore the breadth which took in the spies of Jesus. Those thus accepted she leads up to the roof and establishes them in the exalted mysteries of the faith. For no one sent by Jesus is found below lying on the ground, but remains in the higher places, and not only he remains among the higher places and peaks, but also the harlot who took them in and is turned from a harlot into a prophet. For she says: "I know that the Lord has given you this land" (Jos 2:9). Do you see, then, how she who once was a harlot, evil and unclean, is now filled with the Holy Spirit and confesses the past, believes in the

present and prophesies and foretells the future? Thus it is that Rahab, which means breadth, expands and makes progress until her "voice has gone out to all the earth" (Rom 10:18; cf. Ps 19:4). . . . For this mandate was given her who once was a harlot: "And whoever shall be found in your house will be spared. But if anyone leaves the house, we shall be guiltless in regard to this oath to you" (cf. Jos 2:18–20). Whoever therefore wishes to be saved should come into this house of the former harlot.[1] . . . Let no one be persuaded otherwise, let no one be deceived: outside this house, that is, outside the church, no one is saved. Any who go outside are responsible for their own death.

396   If someone is found who is in no hurry to come back into the walled cities (cf. Zech 2:4–5), and is not "in the churches of God" (2 Thes 1:4) but is standing outside, that person will be captured and carried away by the enemies.

397   Not only are there battles outside the church, but there are also dissensions within the church.

398   "I appeal to you, brethren, by the name of our Lord Jesus Christ, that all of you agree and that there be no dissensions among you" (1 Cor 1:10). The church, then, was mixed, if one can indeed give the name "church" to this whole mixture of just and unjust.

399   Therefore, just as in the gospel the weeds are permitted to grow along with the wheat (Mt 13:29–30), so also here in Jerusalem, that is, in the church, are certain Jebusites, those who lead a low and

---

[1] Cf. what Irenaeus (*Adv. Haer.* IV 20, 12) has already written on this: "For this reason did Hosea the prophet take 'a wife of harlotry' (Hos 1:2), prophesying by means of the action 'that in committing fornication the earth should fornicate from the Lord' (Hos 1:2–3), that is, the men who are upon the earth; and from men of this stamp it will be God's good pleasure to select out (Acts 15:14) a church which shall be sanctified by fellowship with his Son, just as that woman was sanctified by intercourse with the prophet . . . . That which had been done typically through his actions by the prophet, the apostle proves to have been done truly by Christ in the Church . . . . Thus also did Rahab the harlot, while condemning herself, inasmuch as she was a Gentile, guilty of all sins, nevertheless receive the three spies [Irenaeus has "three" instead of "two," apparently due to a lapse of memory] who were spying out all the land, and hid them at her home; [which three were] doubtless [a type of] the Father and the Son, together with the Holy Spirit. And when the entire city in which she lived fell to ruins at the sounding of the seven trumpets, only Rahab the harlot was preserved . . . together with all her house . . . . Hence the Lord said: 'The publicans and the harlots go into the kingdom of God before you' (Mt 21:31)"—*ANF*, Vol. I, 492.

degenerate life, and who are wrong in faith and deeds and in all their activity. For it is not possible to purify the church with certainty while it is on earth so that no evildoer or sinner would remain in it. . . . For where the sin is not perfectly obvious, we could not expel anyone from the church, lest in pulling out the weeds we pull out the wheat with it.

400 "How many wicked things the enemy has done in the sanctuary!" (Ps 74:3). . . . And the enemy is even now doing wicked things in the sanctuary, that is, in the church.

401 Since there are many transgressions among the gentiles, but also among us who are counted as members of the church, he grieves and groans about our sins, saying: "Woe is me! For I have become like one who gathered straw" (Mic 7:1).[1]

402 "When" our Lord and Savior "drew near" to Jerusalem," "seeing it he wept and said: Would that even today you knew the things that make for peace! But now they are hid from your eyes. For the days shall come upon you, when your enemies will cast up a bank about you" (Lk 20:41–43). These are mysteries [*sacramenta*] which are spoken here. . . . For we are the Jerusalem which is wept over, we who think of ourselves as having more insight! Because if, after the mysteries of truth, after the preaching of the gospel, after the teaching of the church and after the vision of the mysteries [*sacramentorum*] of God, one of us should sin, he will indeed be mourned and wept over!

403 If he had reason to weep over Jerusalem, he will have much more reason to weep over the church, built to be a house of prayer but become, through the shameful greed and luxury of some (and are not leaders of the people among them?!) a den of thieves . . . , so that, over those sinning in the living temple which he built, Jesus can pronounce the words of the psalm which say: "What profit is there in my blood, if I go down to the Pit?" (Ps 30:9).

404 He comes, he seeks for something to harvest; he finds a few little grapes and small clusters, but nothing flourishing and not much in

---

[1] We are here translating *nomizomenoi* with "are counted as . . . "; but it could just as well have the meaning "presumably" or "supposedly." Between both meanings sways the theology of Origen: he still cannot come to the full decision of considering the "dead" members on the body of the church as "true" members. Augustine is like this too in his theory of the wheat and of the straw and of the two intermingled states "Jerusalem" and "Babylon" whose true boundaries will be unveiled only eschatologically.

quantity. Who of us has grapes of virtue? Who of us has fruits from God? "O Lord, our God, how majestic is thy name in all the earth!" (Ps 8:1).

405   But it can happen that someone who sinned before, but has stopped sinning, is said to be without sin. And so it was that our Lord Jesus Christ "presented to himself a glorious church without stain" (Eph 5:27), not because some in the church have never been stained but because they no longer stain themselves. "Having no wrinkle" (cf. Eph 5:27) does not mean that there never was a wrinkle of the old man on them (cf. Eph 4:22; Col 3:9), but that they no longer have it.

406   And when, in the congregation of what is ordinarily called the church, you see the catechumens cast down behind those who are at the outer edge of it, at the feet, so to speak, of the body of Jesus, the church, and coming forward with their own deafness and blindness, lameness and crookedness, and in time being healed by the WORD, you would not be wrong in saying that such people, going up with the crowds of the church to the mountain where Jesus was, are cast at his feet and healed, so that the multitude of the church is astonished to see these improvements from such great evils.

406a   What is it then that I admire in Ezekiel? It is that when he was commanded to give witness and to "make known to Jerusalem her abominations" (Ezek 16:2), he did not put before his eyes the danger that could come from this preaching but, mindful only of fulfilling God's command, he spoke all that he was told to speak. Certainly it is a mystery, it is the revelation of a sanctified understanding about Jerusalem and about all the things said of her. And yet he prophetically accuses her of "fornication" because "she spread her legs to everyone who passed by" (Ezek 16:15, 25). He attests this with condemnatory voice, he excoriates the city for its wickedness. But because he was confident of doing the will of God and was ready to die as well as to live, he spoke boldly . . . "Thus says the Lord: Your origin and your birth are of the land of the Canaanites; your father was an Amorite, and your mother a Hittite" (Ezek 16:3). What city was raised so high or carried its head so high as this "city of God"? And yet this very city which thought of itself so highly, as very close to God and as "his city," is, because it sinned, convicted by the Holy Spirit as degenerate and foreign. For her father is the Amorite, no longer God. As long as she did not sin, God was her father; but when she sinned, the Amorite became her father. As long as she did not sin the Holy Spirit was her father; but when she sinned, the Hittite woman became her mother. . . . But if in relation to Jerusalem, about which such great and marvelous things are written, such things are said and promised, what will happen to some poor wretch like me if I should sin? Who will be father or mother to me? . . . If I, who believe in Jesus Christ and have entrusted myself to so great a master, should sin, who will be father to me? Certainly not the Amorite, but a worse father. Who is he? "Everyone who commits sin is born of the devil" (1 Jn 3:8). And again: "You are of your father the devil" (Jn 8:44). . . . Thus if I have become a sinner, the devil who begets me in sin, assuming that voice with which God the Father spoke to the Savior, says to me: "You are my son, today I have begotten you" (Ps 2:7). . . .

"On the day you were born your navel string was not cut" (Ezek 16:4). . . . Allegorically, this presents Jerusalem under the image of a newborn baby girl. But we should know that everything said about Jerusalem applies to all people in the church. Its first time is as described here; but far be it from us to have as a third time what is said to Jerusalem. For all of us who at first were sinners are called "Jerusalem" by God, and our beginning was as described here. But the second time, if after God's coming and taking note of us we persist in sin, also applies to us. The third time, which we so deeply abhor, we will take up later. . . . Just as in a man the foreskin is circumcised, so in a woman the umbilical cord is cut off. . . . But if she sins her umbilical cord is not cut off. . . .

"You were not washed with water unto salvation" (cf. Ezek 16:4). Let us see what happens to Jerusalem lest the same fate befall us. . . . We, who have received baptism in the name of Christ, have been washed; but I do not know who has been "washed unto salvation." Simon [the magician] was washed, "and after being baptized he continued with Philip" (Acts 8:13), but because he "was not washed unto salvation," he was condemned by him who said to him in the Holy Spirit: "Your silver perish with you!" (Acts 8:20). It is very difficult for someone who "is washed" to be "washed unto salvation." Pay attention, you catechumens, to what is being said here; prepare yourselves well, . . . lest you be washed like some who "are washed" but "not unto salvation," who receive the water but do not "receive the Holy Spirit" (Acts 8:17). . . . To every sinful soul which seems to believe, these things are said which we now read as being said to Jerusalem — to say nothing of climbing to higher levels to search out meanings which are beyond my power and ability.

"Nor rubbed with salt" (Ezek 16:4). And the fault for this lies with
Jerusalem because it was not worthy of the "salt" of God. If I believe
in my Lord Jesus Christ, he will make *me* to be salt and will say to me:
"You are the salt of the earth" (Mt 5:13). If I believe in the Spirit who
has spoken in the Apostle, I am seasoned with salt and become able to
carry out the command which says: "Let your speech always be
gracious, seasoned with salt" (Col 4:6). . . .

"You were cast out on the open field because of the depravity of
your soul on the day you were born" (Ezek 16:5). Can anyone already
have a depraved soul on the very day of birth? He is really describing
our passions and human vices and customary depravities. . . . If,
after the rebirth of baptism, after receiving the word of God, we sin
again, on that day on which we are born, we are cast out (cf. Ezek
16:5). All too often we find people who have been washed in the baptism of the second birth and do not "bear fruits that befit repentance"
(Lk 3:8) nor rejoice in the mystery of baptism with a greater fear of
God than they had when they were catechumens, nor with a fuller
love than they practiced when they were only hearers of the word, nor
with holier deeds than they did before. These will suffer the kind of
fate spoken of here: "You were cast out on the open field because of
the depravity of your soul on the day you were born" (Ezek 16:5). But
see the mercy of God; see his extraordinary mercy! Although Jerusalem
was "cast out on the open field," he did not despise it to the extent of
casting it out forever, nor did he abandon it to its depravity so as to
forget it totally or never lift it up again. Note what follows: "And . . .
I passed by you" (Ezek 16:6). You were cast out but I came back to
you; you were not deprived of my coming even after your fall.

"And I saw you weltering in your blood" (Ezek 16:6). It is as if he
said: I saw you guilty of murder, guilty of bloodshed and mortal sins
. . . and still I made you "grow up like a plant of the field" (Ezek
16:7), and you were multiplied. Because I came to you and visited
you in your abjectness, I became the cause of your being multiplied.
"Your breasts were formed and your hair had grown; yet you were
naked and bare" (Ezek 16:7). Whoever has not "put on Jesus Christ"
(Rom 13:14) is naked; whoever has not put on the sentiments of "compassion, kindness, lowliness, meekness, patience and forbearance of
one's neighbor" (Col 3:12–13), is disgraced. "You were naked and
bare, and I passed by you" (Ezek 16:7–8). A second time he comes to
her, sees her sinning, goes away again because of the sins, and still
comes back; again the merciful and benevolent God comes to visit

her. "And I came to you and looked on you and behold, it was your time and the time of those who lead astray"[1] (cf. Ezek 16:8). What is the meaning of "your time"? It signifies puberty at which time one has become old enough to commit fornication. . . . Who are "those who lead astray"? While we are children, those who want to "turn aside" to us and are trying to destroy us, namely, the bad Christians, the unclean demons, the angels of the devil, do not have the means by which they can "turn aside" to us. But when we have come of age and are able to sin, they try to get to us to turn us aside. . . . because this time had come, our Lord and God Jesus Christ this poor Jerusalem, that is, our sinful soul. . . .

"I spread my wings over you, and covered your nakedness" (Ezek 16:8). Blessed indeed whose shame God covers with his wings, but only if one perseveres in the blessedness in which Jerusalem did not wish to persevere! . . . After so much, returning again, and turning away yet again, after such frequent visitation, he now for the first time "enters into a covenant" with her (Ezek 16:8).

"And you became mine. Then I bathed you with water and washed off your blood from you . . . and anointed you with oil . . . and clothed you in bright clothes" (Ezek 16:8–10). . . . "You ate fine flour and honey and oil" (16:13). . . . But this wretched Jerusalem is again reviled as a whore. And so we must really be on our guard lest we too, after the clean words "of fine flour," after the sweet words of the prophets, after "the oil" that makes faces happy and with which we wish to "anoint our head" to make our fast acceptable, fall away again. But we do not merely anoint ourselves with this oil, we eat it too.

"And you grew exceedingly beautiful" (Ezek 16:13). He praises her beauty, he praises her appearance and beautiful figure. "And you came to regal estate" (Ezek 16:13). What an ascent, that she came even to the royal state! "And your renown went forth among the nations" (Ezek 16:14). This applies to one who, after beginning to be free from the world, and whose manner of life is in progress towards a blessed life, also gains a famous name in the world. But don't let happen what now takes place; it is written to strike fear into the hearers.

---

[1] Origen apparently does not (presuming the accuracy of Jerome's Latin translation which is all we have to go by) translate the Greek *kataluontōn* with, as we would expect here, "living together" or "loving" but according to its alternate meaning of "turning aside; leading astray; dissolving; destroying."—R.J.D.

After the beauty given her, after the great renown, Jerusalem, the wretched, fell into harlotry. Therefore, "Do not boast about tomorrow, for you do not know what a day may bring forth" (Prov 27:1), . . . and again: "Look to yourself, lest you too be tempted" (Gal 6:1).

"And your renown went forth among the nations because of your beauty, for it was perfect through the splendor which I had bestowed upon you, says the Lord God; but you trusted in your beauty" (Ezek 16:14–15). The beautiful Jerusalem grew haughty and proud in the consciousness of her beauty. And because she became proud and did not humble herself and glorify God, listen to what is said to her: "You played the harlot because of your renown, and lavished your harlotries on any passer-by. You took your garments, and sewed them into idols for yourself" (Ezek 16:15–16). You took the things I gave you to adorn yourself and make yourself beautiful, and you made them into idols. . . . These clothes are the divine scriptures and the meaning which lies in them. The heretics tore up these clothes and sewed together expression to expression and word to word, but without the right connection. And in sewing together impious things, they made idols for themselves with which they led some astray to believe and agree to their cult and to accept an artificial church order.

Let us then be especially on our guard against those heretics who lead a blameless life, but who have perhaps been brought to this more by the devil than by God. For just as bird-catchers put out tasty bits of food as bait so as to capture birds more easily by pleasing their appetite, so too, if I may speak so boldly, the devil has a certain chastity or deception for the human soul to enable him to capture it more easily by a chastity and meekness and justice of this kind, and lead it astray with false words. The devil fights with different kinds of snares to bring a poor human being to ruin; he gives a good life to evil people to deceive observers, and stirs up a bad conscience in good people. He is always setting traps for me, because I preach in the church, that I might confuse the whole church by my action. Thus, those who are in the middle of things are subject to special attack by the enemy so that, by the fall of one man which cannot be hidden, a scandal is committed before all and the faith is hurt by the very bad activity of the clerics. . . . Hence, whoever is concerned for his own life is neither taken in by the meekness of the heretics to agree to their doctrine, nor will he be scandalized by my sins which I seem to preach in the church, but, weighing the doctrine itself and holding fast to the faith of the church, will indeed turn away from me but accept the teaching which, according to the Lord's command, says: "The scribes and the Pharisees sit on Moses' seat; so practice and observe whatever they tell you, but not what they do; for they preach, but do not practice" (Mt 23:2–3). This word is about me who teach what is good but do the opposite and am sitting on Moses' seat like a scribe and a Pharisee. . . . Let us imitate no one; or if we wish to imitate someone, Jesus Christ is put before us to imitate. The Acts of the Apostles have been described and we know the deeds of the prophets from the sacred books; that is a safe model. . . . But if we seek out blameworthy people for us to imitate, as if to say: he teaches, and he himself acts contrary to what he teaches, we are acting contrary to the Lord's command. . . .

Much indeed did wretched Jerusalem sin in this way! How often indeed did God wish through the prophets to lead her back to a better life! But because she did not wish to hear the counsel of God nor wish to accept God's commandments, God hesitates and says he does not know what to do: "How shall I restore your heart? says the Lord God" (Ezek 16:30).[1] What shall I do? How shall I restore you? You are bound by many chains of sins, your crimes prevent your life from being restored by my words. I often tried to restore you by speaking through my saints, and you did not listen. I don't know any longer what to do, and thus I say to you: "How shall I restore your heart, says the Lord God, seeing you are doing all these things, the deeds of a brazen harlot?" (Ezek 16:30). . . . Those who have not wholly fallen away from practicing the faith but are conquered by sin and want to remain undetected in their sin, they are acting like a whore who gets embarrassed. But those who are wholly turned away from the faith and don't care about the bishop, priests, deacons or brethren, but sin in all audacity, are like the shamelessly public whore. . . .

"You are the sister of your sisters who loathed their husbands and their children. . . . your elder sister is Samaria who lived with her daughters to the north of you. Your younger sister, who lived to the south of you, is Sodom with her daughters" (Ezek 16:45–46). . . . At first there was no talk about Jerusalem having sisters. Here it is added. . . . Virtue causes me even to have Christ as a brother who, if I am good and persevere well, will say to his Father: "I will tell of thy name to my brethren; in the midst of the congregation I will praise thee" (Ps 22:22). . . . And so just as virtue makes the Lord Jesus to be my

---

[1] Origen is apparently following a variant reading of Ezek 16:30. — R.J.D.

brother, so evil wins for me many brothers, sinners; and this evil, the more it grows, continues to generate "brothers" for me. Indeed when sinful Jerusalem was at her beginning, she had no sister Samaria and no sister Sodom; but as she grew in wickedness, as we have seen, she took up the middle place between the two sisters. . . . Who are these two? . . . Schism and division brought forth Samaria. . . . Therefore if we as people of the church sin, we are not far from the heretics and the wickedness of their doctrines. For a sinner is a poor believer. If we live badly, Sodom is our sister; for the gentiles are Sodom. Thus we are brothers of the heretics and gentiles when we sin. . . .

"Behold, this was the guilt of your sister Sodom: . . . pride, surfeit of food and prosperous ease" (Ezek 16:49). . . . What sin then is greater than all the others? . . . Haughtiness, pride, arrogance are the sin of the devil. . . . The material of pride is wealth, rank and worldly glory. Very often priesthood and the Levitical rank is a cause of pride in someone who forgets he has an ecclesiastical position. How many who have been raised to the priesthood have forgotten humility! As if the purpose of their ordination was to stop being humble. How much more should they not have pursued humility precisely because they had been raised to high office, as scripture says: "The greater you are the more you must humble yourself" (Sir 3:18). Think of the gospel: with what severity the pride and arrogance of the Pharisee is condemned! "The Pharisee stood and prayed thus with himself: 'God, I thank thee that I am not like other men, extortioners, unjust, adulterers, or even like this tax collector. I fast twice a week.' But the tax collector," humbly and meekly "standing far off, would not even lift up his eyes and said: 'God, be merciful to me a sinner!' And the tax collector went down to his house justified" (Lk 18:11–14); not justified in an absolute sense, but justified in comparison with the Pharisee. . . . For it is one thing to be justified, and another thing to be justified by another. Just as the tax collector was justified by comparison with that Pharisee, so were Sodom and Samaria justified by comparison with a sinful Jerusalem. For we must know that each one of us on the day of judgment will be condemned by one and justified by another. Even when we are justified by another, that justification is less an object of praise than of blame. If, for example, I am found guilty of Sodomitic sins and someone else is brought forward who has committed twice as many serious sins, I am indeed justified; but I am not justified as a just man, but in comparison with him who has committed more I am judged to be just, although I am a long way from justice. . . . I most certainly do not wish to be justified by evil people, because such justice is still full of guilt.

I have jumped ahead of myself in saying this because in the reading we hear: "Even your sister Sodom and her daughters have not done as you and your daughters have done. . . . Samaria has not committed half your sins; you have committed more abominations than they, and have made your sisters appear righteous by all the abominations which you have committed" (Ezek 16:48–51). . . . Sodom has sinned and Samaria too, Jerusalem is buried in misdeeds. . . . There is only one who is justified by all and who himself justifies no one. Hence, "no man living is righteous before thee" (Ps 143:2). Although Abraham may have been just and Moses just, and each one of the famous men just, compared with Christ they are not just; their light compared with his light turns out to be darkness. And just as the light of a lamp becomes dark before the rays of the sun, and becomes dark like any other blind matter, so too the light of all the just: it may be bright before men, but it is not bright before Christ. . . . As the splendor of the moon and the glittering stars of the heaven sparkle in their places before the sun rises, but as soon as the sun rises go into hiding, so too before the true light of the sun of justice rises, the light of the church, like the light of the moon, is bright and clear before men; but when Christ comes it fades before him. As it is written: "The light will shine in the darkness" (Jn 1:5). . . . Whoever gives this long and diligent consideration will hardly be able to get puffed up at seeing his own light considered as darkness in comparison with that greater light. . . . "The sin of your sister Sodom is pride" (Ezek 16:49).

As often as we read the description of the destruction of the Sodomites, let us not say: Oh, the poor Sodomites, whose progeny the earth no longer bears; how unfortunate and much to be mourned, who suffered such sad and fearsome things! We should rather apply this word to our own hearts, examine our inmost being and thoughts, and then we will see that what we are mourning is contained within us, and that the Sodomitic and Egyptian and Assyrian and all the other sins which scripture excoriatingly lists are found in ourselves. . . . For it must simply be said that nothing leads one up to arrogance more than wealth and overabundance and the eating of many good things, and also position and power. There is also sin to be seen at a higher level, because I frequently am nourishing pride if I understand the divine word, if I am wiser than the rest. "Knowledge puffs up" (1 Cor 8:1) is not from me but the Apostle. . . . So great a man as the apostle Paul needed the blows of "a messenger of Satan, to harass him, to keep him from being too elated" (2 Cor 12:7). . . . Before Uriah no sin is found in David; he was a blessed man and without blame in the sight of God. But because he became conscious of his blameless life and said what he should not say: "Listen, O Lord, to my righteousness. . . . If thou triest my heart, if thou visitest me by night, if thou testest me, thou wilt find no wickedness in me" (Ps 17:1–3). Therefore he was tempted and deprived of help that he might see what human weakness can do. And he was caught in the very sin from which he prided himself on being free.

Now the first thing is to perform no shameful deed but only such as can look upon God with an open face. But because, as human beings, we often sin, we should know that the second plank so to speak after a shameful deed is to be ashamed and have downcast eyes because of one's misdeeds instead of walking around with a bold look as if not having sinned at all. It is good, after a shameful deed, to be ashamed. . . . Thus a great grace is saved for Jerusalem, if she would only believe the Lord's word: "So be ashamed, you also, and bear your disgrace, for you have made your sisters appear righteous" (Ezek 16:52). . . . Let us take an example from life in the church. It is a disgrace to be separated from the people of God and from the church; it is a disgrace in the church to leave the priesthood or be expelled from the rank of deacon. And of those who are thrown out, some cause dissensions while others accept with all humility the judgment made on them. Thus those who rebel and in reaction to their deposition gather people around them to make a schism, . . . do not bear their disgrace (cf. Ezek 16:15). . . . But those who in all humility, whether they have been rightly or wrongly deposed, leave the judgment to God and patiently bear the judgment made about them, they gain mercy from God and are frequently called back even by men to their earlier office and to the honor which they had lost. . . .

Hence, if someone has carried out this directive of scripture: "Be ashamed," if someone has carried out this sentence of God: "Bear your disgrace, for you have made your sisters appear righteous" (Ezek 16:52), let him also see the grace, how clemency is returned to him for his shame. . . . What then is promised? "I will restore their fortunes, . . . the fortunes of Sodom and her daughters, . . . for you have made your sisters Sodom and Samaria appear righteous" (Ezek 16:53, 52). First I will restore the fortune of the Sodomites, second that of Samaria, and third that of Jerusalem. And if I restore the fortunes of the Sodomites and Samaria and Jerusalem, they will then be restored to their former estate, first Sodom, . . . second Samaria, . . . third Jerusalem. The healing or restoration is granted later to those who are more loved by God. Sodom, justified by Jerusalem, is the first to receive mercy; these are the gentiles. Samaria, that is, the heretics, receive their healing second. But third, as if unworthy of a more rapid healing, those who were in Jerusalem are restored to their former estate. The gentiles first, and then the heretics, will be granted mercy before us, if we have offended God, and if sins have overwhelmed us. For the nearer we have been to God and the closer we have been to beatitude, the farther we put ourselves from it when we have sinned, and the closer to the most terrible and greatest punishments. For God's judgment is just and "the powerful will suffer powerful torments" (cf. Wis 6:5, 6). But whoever is very small will earn mercy more quickly. Sodom is the smallest, and after her, in comparison with Jerusalem, Samaria is the smallest, but not as small as Sodom. . . .

But when will he restore my fortune if I have been found to be a "Jerusalem" and a sinner in the midst of my sisters? It will be when I hear: "that you may bear your torment" (cf. Ezek 16:54). . . . And see now the end of the promise: "I will remember my covenant with you in the days of your youth, and I will establish with you an everlasting covenant. Then you will remember your ways and be ashamed . . . and never open your mouth again because of your shame, when I forgive you all that you have done" (Ezek 16:60–63). And not even then when my many sins are forgiven me can I open my mouth, and even then, when he forgives my wrongdoings, I do not escape from shame.

Heresy

The church is not only internally sinful, but also torn by heresy and schism. This is nothing other than the passion of Christ continued in the mystical body (407–410). But this "application" of the crucifixion to the WORD makes it at first sweet and palatable (411). And heresy is necessary in order to keep doctrine alert (412).

Indeed heresy seems to be a relative concept, since no one takes up and understands the whole message of Jesus (413). Further, heresy is an "analysis" of the contents of faith (414) and, in the opposition of opinions, the concrete form of human knowledge (415); Christ is a sign of contradiction (416).

But this necessity makes no inroads on the sole validity of the catholic church (417). Heresy is only one form of sin against the Spirit (418–420). But the church does not yet possess Christ without veil, she is a widow (421). Her mystery is within and not visible to all (422–423). But that is precisely why it escapes the grasp of the heretics, while the church herself can pass judgment on them (424–426). The beauty of the church is a spiritual one (427), and one must have the Spirit in order to see it (428). Her theology is the garment of the glorified Christ, but which shines illuminatingly only on those whom Christ takes with him into his mystery (429).

407   I see Jesus every day "giving his back to the smiters" (Isa 50:6). Go into the Jewish synagogues and see Jesus being beaten by them with blasphemous tongue. Look at the pagan assemblies, plotting against Christians and how to capture Jesus. And he "gives his back to the smiters". . . . So many beat and strike him, and he is silent and says not a word. . . . And to this day, Jesus "has not hid his face from shame and spitting" (Isa 50:6).

408   Thus the accusation: "You dishonor me" (Jn 8:49) can be made against everyone who scorns wisdom, since Christ is wisdom.

409   Even now the new chief priests . . . crucify with false interpretations and kill with lies the WORD of truth which is in the scripture. But the WORD of truth, although it is killed by them, lives on in its own nature; it is constantly finding and choosing vessels in which it is rising again and living and constantly putting its murderers to shame.

410   They want to kill the WORD and break it up into pieces, as it were, because they do not have room within them for its great size. Again and again one can see people who want to kill the unity of the majesty of the WORD because their own vessels are too small to contain it, as if they would have more room for it after it was broken up into pieces and its members separated.

411   "Come, let us mix wood in his bread" (Jer 11:19 LXX). The bread of Jesus is the WORD by which we are nourished (cf. Jn 6:48–58). But since some, while he was teaching among the people, wanted to oppose his teaching, they delivered him up to crucifixion saying: "Come, let us mix wood in his bread." For when the crucifixion of the teacher is applied to the WORD of Jesus' teaching, wood is indeed mixed in his bread; and their intention in this really was to plot against him. . . . But I want to point out something quite wondrous here: the wood mixed in his bread actually made the bread better. To

take an example from the law of Moses: the wood cast into the water made the water sweet (cf. Exod 15:25). So too, the "wood" of the suffering of Christ, when it came into the WORD, made his "bread" sweeter.

2   For if the teaching of the church were only simple and not surrounded from without by the assertions of heretical doctrines, our faith could not be as clear and as thoroughly examined as it is. That is why catholic teaching undergoes attacks from its opponents; it is so that our faith will not grow sluggish from inactivity but be made shining by activity. This, ultimately, is why the Apostle said: "There must be factions among you in order that those who are genuine among you may be recognized" (1 Cor 11:19). . . . Who would know that the light is good if we did not experience the darkness of night? Would anyone who had not first tasted bitterness recognize the sweetness of honey?

3   "And no one accepts his testimony" (Jn 3:32). How can it be true, since some do accept his testimony, that "no one accepts his testimony"? The problem is to be solved this way: Jesus, having come from above telling what he has heard and seen, gives a most sublime and powerful witness about the Father and himself; but no one accepts this witness as Jesus gives it. . . . For no one is capable of receiving his witness as it is; one has to accept it in the manner that is possible for those just coming to the faith.

4   Apparently someone will not understand why the blessings of Moses took place on Mount Gerizim. The answer to this is that the word Gerizim means division or separation. The meaning "division" applies, e.g., to the time when the people were divided under Jeroboam and the king lived in Samaria; while the meaning "separation" is to be taken in a favorable sense as when wise men, making proper use of analysis, apply it to each of the problems which must be solved for the understanding of truth.

5   There is no matter, which has been founded seriously and is useful for life, in which various heresies have not arisen. For since the science of medicine is useful and necessary to the human race, and there are many questions in it on the manner of healing bodies, there are as a consequence several schools of medicine among the Greeks, as is well known. . . . And no one would act rationally in avoiding medicine because of its different schools . . . or want to hate philosophy under the pretext that there are different schools. . . . Now if these arguments hold, should we not similarly also defend the fact of heresies in Christianity? Paul seems to me to speak of this in a most

remarkable way: "For there must be factions among you in order that those who are genuine among you may be recognized" (1 Cor 11:19). For just as a renowned doctor is someone who, from his experience of the various medical heresies and his careful examination of most of them, has selected the preferable system, and an eminent philosopher is someone who has tried out the various views and has given his adherence to the best, so too would I say that the one who has taken a careful look into the heresies of Judaism and Christianity is the wisest Christian.

416   "Thou didst deliver me from strife with the peoples; thou didst make me the head of the nations" (Ps 18:43). He who has become a sign that is spoken against (Lk 2:44) says this, Christ, whom God made to be head of the nations. For the head of the church is Christ (cf. Eph 5:23).

417   We must watch out for ourselves lest we be caught up by the specious arguments of heretical doctrine and fall away from the mystery of the church.

418   If you ask why heresies also are listed among the works of the flesh, you will find that they come from the senses of the flesh. For, as the Apostle says of someone: "puffed up without reason by his sensuous mind" (Col 2:18).

419   Whoever causes the understanding, which was made to contemplate wisdom, to sin, sins against wisdom itself.

420   We frequently observe it happening among the heresies and the churches of the evildoers (cf. Ps 22:16 LXX), that the nation of one heresy rises up against the nation of another heresy, and thus the kingdom of one mistaken word will rise up against the kingdom of another mistaken word (cf. Mt 24:6–7). For Satan, and every lie, is constantly divided against himself, and hence cannot stand (cf. Mt 12:25–26).

421   The church is a widow because she has not yet received Christ, her spouse.

422   The cause of the glory which the church possesses lies in the hidden reaches of the heart, and its glory is within, under true garments which are according to God's wisdom, and in a conscience full of confidence.

423   "Everyone who curses his father or his mother shall be put to death" (Lev 20:9). The name of father is a great mystery and the name of mother a hidden reality to be reverenced. Your Father, according to the Spirit, is God; your mother, the heavenly Jerusalem (cf. Gal 4:26; Heb 12:22). Learn this from the prophetic and apostolic witnesses. Moses himself writes this in his hymn: "Has not this, your father,

acquired you and possessed you?" (cf. Deut 32:6). But of the heavenly
Jerusalem the apostle says that "she is free, the mother of us all" (cf.
Gal 4:26).

24   "And they tried to arrest him" (Mt 21:46). All those who insidiously
try to capture the WORD so that, once captured, they can get rid of
him, will never be able to lay their hands on him. . . . But in order
to understand who these chief priests and pharisees are who are trying
to lay hands on him, but are unable to catch him, you should consider
the fact that, with the exception of the WORD of Christ, it is possible
to "capture" every other teaching. It is possible to grasp the spirit of
each and every system, gain control of it and, as scripture says, come
to terms with it. Thus it is that the one who is wise according to the
gospel, as a "spiritual person judges all things, but is in turn judged
by no one" (cf. 1 Cor 2:15–16). The spiritual person judges and tests
and refutes the other teachings, whether they be from the philosophers of this world or from the leaders of heresies. But the mind of
Christ which is in that person is not judged or captured or overcome
by those who try to oppose it. "For who has known the mind of the
Lord so as to instruct him?" (1 Cor 2:16).

25   "The spiritual person judges all things" (1 Cor 2:15). For the one
who sees all things sees also the things of those who do not see, but
none of them see the things of the spiritual person.

26   "They divide my garments among them, and for my raiment they
cast lots" (Ps 22:18). The Jews, in observing the written law, also
divide up the physical garments of the WORD; but we, guardians of
the Spirit of the WORD, baptized in Christ and clothed with him as
with wisdom and truth and justice, share among ourselves the spiritual
garments of our savior.

27   The body [of the church] will seem to be beautiful and attractive if
the souls from which this body is made persevere in every ornament
of perfection. For just as when the soul is angry it makes the countenance of the body confused and wild, but when it perseveres in gentleness and peace it makes for a peaceful and mild appearance, so too
will the countenance of the church, according to the virtues and actions of the faithful, be judged as beautiful or ugly, as we read in the
scripture: "The mark of a good heart is a cheerful face" (cf. Sir 14:26).

28   "For your voice is sweet" (Cant 2:14). And who would not confess that
sweet indeed is the voice of the catholic church professing the true faith,
but not sweet and unpleasant is the voice of heretics who do not utter
doctrines of truth but blasphemies against God and iniquity against

the Most High (cf. Ps 73:9). So too is the countenance of the church attractive, but that of the heretics shameful and repulsive, provided of course there is someone who knows well how to judge the beauty of a face, I mean someone who is spiritual and knows how to "judge all things" (cf. 1 Cor 2:15, 14). For among inexperienced and unspiritual or natural persons (1 Cor 2:14), the deceptions of a lie seem more beautiful than the doctrines of truth.

429   One can ask, concerning the occasion when "he was transfigured before those" whom he had led "up a high mountain" (Mt 17:1-2), whether he was seen "in the form of God" which he previously possessed, while for those below he had the "form of a servant" (cf. Phil 2:6-8). . . . But listen to this spiritually, if you can, and observe that it is not said simply that he was transfigured; there is in addition a vitally important observation recorded by Matthew and Mark who both say that "he was transfigured *before them*" (Mt 17:2; Mk 9:2). From this one can ask if it is possible whether Jesus was transfigured with this transfiguration before some people, while before others, who were there at exactly the same time, he was not transfigured.[1] If you want to see the transfiguration of Jesus which took place before those who climbed "up a high mountain apart" with him, consider how, on the one hand, Jesus is understood in a simple way and known so to speak "from a human point of view" (*kata sarka* — 2 Cor 5:16) by those who do not go up the high mountain of wisdom with ascending works and thoughts, and how, on the other hand, he is, by those who are ascending, known no longer "from a human point of view," but contemplated from the divine point of view — as he is in all the gospels and according to their knowledge — in the form of God. . . .

And not only was he transfigured before these disciples, . . . but also, to those whom he "led up the high mountain apart," "his garments became white as light" (Mt 17:2). The garments of Jesus are the words and letters of the scripture which he had put on. But I think that the things said by the apostles about him are also the garments of Jesus, and they too become white for those climbing up the high mountain with Jesus. . . . Thus, when you see someone who is expert not only in the theology of Jesus but also in interpreting the

---

[1] This theory has nothing to do with docetism, which is sharply rejected by Origen (cf. Nos. 338–341). But it must be compared with No. 333. The whole passage is the clearest expression of a *theologia gloriae* (theology of glory) over against a *theologia crucis* (theology of the cross).

phrasing of all the gospels, do not hesitate to say of such a person that for him "the garments of Jesus have become white as light."

THE LAW OF SUBLATION

The whole objective salvation-historical event: the "incarnation" of the WORD in scripture, in Christ and in his mystical body, the church, stands under the same formal basic law which is set forth here (in the Hegelian double meaning) as "sublation" ['Aufhebung']. In the creaturely bipolarity of image and truth, the fundamental movement goes from the first to the second, from body to spirit. But this takes place in such a way that the bodily image is both broken off and preserved. Origen consistently expresses this event in the image of shining upon and being shone upon.

Old and new covenant, above all Moses and Christ, John and Christ stand in this relationship; but also the earthly Christ and the eternal Christ, indeed the earthly Christ and the church (to the extent that its fate is symbolically represented in the life of Christ), and finally the whole earthly salvation event (Moses-Christ-Church) and the eschatological, otherworldly, fulfilling event (430–438).

30   "And behold, the curtain of the temple was torn in two, from top to bottom" (Mt 27:51). As long as Jesus had not yet accepted death for the sake of us men, he remained "the expectation of the nations" (Gen 49:10 LXX) and the veil of the temple concealed the interior of the temple. That had to remain concealed until he, who alone was able to reveal it, made it manifest to those who desired to see it, so that through the death of Christ who destroyed the death of the believers, those who had been liberated from death could look upon what was within the temple. . . .

But someone who reads the scriptures carefully might, in searching further, notice that there are two veils, one inside which conceals the Holy of Holies, and the other outside of the tent or temple which were images of the holy tabernacle which the Father prepared from the beginning. One of these veils of the temple "was torn in two from top to bottom" when "Jesus, crying out with a loud voice, yielded up his spirit" (Mt 27:50–51), demonstrating, it seems to me, the mystery of how, in the passion of our Lord and Savior, the outside veil "was rent from the top to the bottom" so that "from the top" (that is, from the beginning of the world) "to the bottom" (that is, to its end) by means of the torn veil those mysteries might be made public which had properly been hidden until the coming of Christ. And if we did not now see only "imperfectly" (1 Cor 13:10) but instead everything had already been made fully clear to the beloved disciples of Christ in the flesh, both veils, the outer and the inner, would have been torn. But now, since we are moving forward to the knowledge of new things, the outer veil is for now torn "from the top to the bottom" so that "when the perfect comes" (1 Cor 13:10) and everything else is revealed, then the second veil will also be removed so that we can see also what is hidden inside the second veil, namely, the true ark of the covenant and the way it looks in reality, and so that we can see the cherubim and the true mercy-seat [*propitiatorium*] and place of the manna in its golden urn (cf. Heb 9:1–5).

431   And this too must be kept in mind, that as "the law contains but a shadow of the good things to come" (cf. Heb 10:1) which are made known by the law proclaimed according to truth, so the gospel, which is thought to be understandable by everyone, also teaches a shadow of the mysteries of Christ. But what John calls the "eternal gospel" (Rev 14:6), which might rightly be called the spiritual gospel, presents clearly to those who understand, everything about the Son of God in himself, both the mysteries contained in his words and also the realities of which his deeds were the symbols.

432   "For the law has but a shadow of the good things to come" (Heb 10:1). In regard to this there is indeed doubt whether the food and drink and feast days and new moons and sabbaths contain the shadow of the future things in such a way that in the coming of Christ the truth of this shadow is fulfilled, or whether instead it is to be fulfilled in the world to come . . . because in another place too it is written about these things which are under the law, that "they serve as copy and shadow of things heavenly" (Heb 8:5).

433   But we should in no way seem to be bypassing the objection . . . that the Apostle seems to be writing contradictory things when he says here that the law is not overthrown but upheld (Rom 3:31), but then in the Second Letter to the Corinthians writes: "Now if the dispensation of death carved in letters on stone came with such splendor that the Israelites could not look at Moses' face because of its brightness, fading as this was, will not the dispensation of the Spirit be attended with greater splendor?" (2 Cor 3:7–8). . . . But see now if we can solve this as follows: It is not the same thing to say: "Do we overthrow the law?" (Rom 3:31) and: The law is overthrown. Paul therefore

proclaims in this place that he does not overthrow the law. For if the law is overthrown by that glory which surpasses it, it is not overthrown by Paul nor by any other of the saints. Hence the Lord himself said: "I have not come to abolish the law but to fulfil it" (Mt 5:17). Therefore no one of the saints nor the Lord himself destroys the law; rather its temporal and transient glory is destroyed and superseded by the eternal and perduring glory. . . . Thus, what is of Christ, he says, remains; what is of Moses is destroyed; but not destroyed by men but, as we explained, by comparison with the new glory taking its place. . . . But what the Apostle here calls "to be overthrown" needs to be understood according to his custom of using this word in other places too, as when he says: "Our knowledge is imperfect and our prophecy is imperfect; but when the perfect comes, the imperfect will be overthrown" (1 Cor 9:10). . . . We understand this to mean that in comparison with what is perfect, the imperfect is but vain and empty.

434   Therefore Christ does not turn aside his face "from the shame of being spat upon" (Isa 50:6), that his face might be glorified more than the face of Moses was glorified, and with such tremendous glory that Moses' glory, in comparison with it, is simply overwhelmed, just as in the light of the sun the light of a lamp is overwhelmed.

435   From the standpoint of the bodily meaning, a somewhat more divine revelation took place in the tent of meeting and in the completion of the temple and on the face of Moses when he spoke with the nature of God. But from the standpoint of the higher meaning one would say that seeing the glory of God requires a careful knowledge of the things of God seen by an intellect made ready for this by a very high degree of purity. For the purified spirit, which has risen above all material things in order to enjoy with clarity the contemplation of God, is divinized by what it contemplates. Such is to be understood as taking place in the glorification of the face of the one who saw God and spoke with him . . . that the glorified face of Moses was the symbolic expression of his spirit being divinized. This is what the Apostle meant in saying: "And we all, with unveiled face, beholding the glory of the Lord, are being changed into his likeness" (2 Cor 3:18).

436   "Therefore this joy of mine is now full" (Jn 3:29) [says the Baptist] because all are going over to Jesus. For I came to give witness to him, that all might believe in him through me. Hence, "he must increase, but I must decrease" (Jn 3:30). Now this too must be examined carefully, for the Savior does not increase by taking on something, nor

does John decrease by losing something, for each remains as he was. The real meaning is this: the morning star, rising before the sun in order to accustom the sight to look upon an even greater light, has a limited brightness. At first sight it seems greater than the sun. But soon, when the sun rises, the morning star diminishes, not by losing anything of its own greatness but in comparison with the brilliance of the rising sun. Thus it is that John is great in the fullness of his sanctity. Jesus came after him, as was said before (Jn 1:15), was baptized and given John's testimony. And with the divinity of Jesus manifested by these salvation-historical events, the one is revealed as the servant, the other as the master.

437   But just as no one can believe or grasp this glory which the apostles in the gospels say they saw, "the glory as of the only son from the Father, full of grace and truth" (Jn 1:14), except by following the way of understanding through that glory which was given through Moses in the law (as affirmed by him who said to Nathaniel: "We have found him of whom Moses and the prophets wrote, Jesus of Nazareth" [Jn 1:45], clearly showing that it was as illuminated by the law and the prophets that they gazed upon the light of this glory which was as of the only Son from the Father), so too what the Apostle said: "And we all, with unveiled face, beholding the glory of the Lord, are being changed into his likeness from one degree of glory to another; for this comes from the Lord who is the Spirit" (2 Cor 3:18), this must also be understood in the same way, namely, that whoever contemplates this glory of the only-begotten with uncovered face, that is, with the full understanding of faith, that person is illuminated by the internal gaze of faith and by that same image by which he came from the law to the gospels and to the bodily coming of the Savior. As a result, that person turns his mind's eye also to Christ's second coming in glory and is transformed from the present to the future glory for which we hope.

438   To the extent that the Son was not known to the world (for "he was in the world, and the world was made through him, yet the world knew him not"—Jn 1:10), he was not yet glorified in the world. . . . This was no loss to Christ for not being glorified, but it was a loss to the world for not glorifying Christ. But when the heavenly Father had revealed the knowledge of Jesus to those who were of this world, the Son of Man was then glorified in those who knew him; and by the same glory with which he was glorified among those who knew him, he gave glory to those who knew him. For those who behold the glory of the Lord with unveiled face are changed into his likeness (cf. 2 Cor 3:18).

Look at where he says this glory is coming from and where it is going: from the glory of the one being glorified, to the glory of the one glorifying. Thus, when he came to that moment in the economy of salvation when he was to appear to the world and, in being known, be glorified for the sake of the glory of those glorifying him, he said: "Now is the Son of man glorified" (Jn 13:31). And since "no one knew the Son except the Father and those to whom the Son revealed him" (cf. Mt 11:27; Lk 10:22) it was according to the economy of salvation for the Son to reveal the Father, because "in him God is glorified" (Jn 13:31).

III

SPIRIT

LIFE IN THE SPIRIT

THE SPIRITUAL GOD

Jesus said, if I do not go away, the Holy Spirit will not come to you (cf. Jn 16:7). If the whole sense-perceivable and "sacramental" salvation-event does not get "sublated," it has failed to fulfill its purpose, namely, to be internalized as life within souls. This internal appropriating of the revelation of the WORD as SPIRIT is the re-forming of a sinful, fleshly human being into a temple of God the Father. The following section depicts this new forming in its process and its stages; the concluding section ("God") will describe the entering of the soul into the kingdom of GOD the Father.

Only in Christianity did it become clear what it really means to say God is a Spirit (439). The Holy Spirit is the heart of the mystery of the Christian idea of God (440): Spirit as person (441). The Holy Spirit is a co-agent in the salvation-event and dispenses grace (442–443).

This is a straightening up of the warped human being (444), entrance into God's intimacy (445), inner life (446), prayer (447), divine wisdom (448–449), that union with God whose first fruit was Christ (450), guaranty of beatitude (451).

Everywhere then, as in Paul, Irenaeus, Justin and most of the theologians before Origen, as a result of the theory of the triple division of the human being, the Holy Spirit and the human spirit overlap without sharp boundaries. Now Origen did expressly emphasize their difference (51). However, the idea of grace as a participation of the human spirit in the divine and as a living indwelling of the divine in the human spirit makes this border so to speak fluid. That is why Origen and the majority of the great Greek Fathers speak so often of "divinization."

439   Now Celsus, like one with no understanding of the Spirit of God —
"the unspiritual [*psychikos*] man does not receive the gifts of the Spirit

of God, for they are folly to him, and he is not able to understand them because they are spiritually [*pneumatikōs*] discerned" (1 Cor 2:14) — contradicts himself in that we, when we say that God is a spirit, are no different from the Greek Stoics who say that God is a spirit which interpenetrates and encompasses all things. Now God's overseeing and providence does indeed interpenetrate all things, but not like the spirit of the Stoics. And indeed providence encompasses and includes everything it sees in advance; but it does not encompass it like an encompassing body, even when the encompassed is body, but like a divine power.

440   Indeed all who in any way sense that there is a providence will profess that God is not born, and that he has created and ordains all things. . . . But that he has a Son we are not alone in proclaiming . . . but even among some of the Greeks and barbarians there seems to have been some idea of him when they confess that everything was created by the WORD of God. . . . But of the existence of the Holy Spirit, no one could have had even a suspicion.

441   "The Spirit blows where it wills" (Jn 3:8). This shows that the Spirit is also a reality [*ousia*]. For the Spirit is not, as some think, a mere power of God which, according to them, has no being of its own.[1] And also the Apostle, when enumerating the charisms of the Spirit, immediately added: "All these are inspired by one and the same Spirit who apportions to each one individually as he wills" (1 Cor 12:11). If then he wills and works and disposes, he is a being [*ousia*] which acts and not just energy [*energeia*].

442   For although the only-begotten Son of God became man and suffered for the salvation of the human race, and by his death destroyed life, and by his resurrection restored life, just as marvelous, apart from the incarnation, were the things brought about by the Holy Spirit.

443   I am convinced that the Holy Spirit gives the "material" so to speak of the gifts of God to those who through him and through participation in him are called saints.

444   It is written in the gospel that a certain "woman was bent over and could not fully straighten herself" (Lk 13:11). . . . And how many others are there, still bound by Satan, who are bent over, unable to

---

[1] "Being of its own" — *idiotēs hyparxeōs* — only later becomes the technical term for personhood in God. But the rest of the fragment is so like Origen that there is no doubt of Origen's authorship of it.

straighten up fully because he wants us to be looking downwards? And no one can straighten them up except the WORD dwelling in Jesus.

45　For God makes no display before us with a view to recognition and understanding of his preeminence. But, wanting only the blessedness that grows in our souls from knowing him to be implanted in us, he brings it about through Christ and the continual indwelling of his WORD that we ascend to intimacy with him.

46　Spirit is called, according to the scripture, "what gives life," obviously not with the ordinary or neutral but with the more divine meaning of "life-giving." For the letter kills and brings death, not as the separation of soul from the body but as the separation of the soul from God and from its Lord and from the Holy Spirit.

47　For our mind is not even able to pray unless the Spirit, as if obeying it, prays for it; nor could it with proper rhythm, melody, measure and harmony sing songs and hymns to the Father in Christ unless "the Spirit" which "searches everything, even the depths of God" (1 Cor 2:10) first praised and sung hymns to him.

48　"For the Spirit searches everything, even the depths of God" (1 Cor 2:10). It is the Spirit which can search everything. But the Spirit must enter into us more strongly so that it can take its place in us and search all things, even the depths of God. And when it has become mingled with us and we with it, we too will search all things, even the depths of God.

49　All the wisdoms of this world are human words which can be learned according to each of the systems of thought; but this does not teach what is taught by the Spirit. Nor can one say that they who teach in the Spirit have been instructed in what they teach, for the Spirit in them illuminates them as they seek out[1] and investigate the truth. In this way they are constantly discovering in the renewal of their minds what they learn from human beings (cf. 1 Cor 2:15–16; Rom 12:2).

50　"Give the king thy justice, O God, and thy righteousness to the son of the king" (Ps 72:1). . . . I therefore think that the name "king" is here given to the preeminent nature of the firstborn of all creation (cf. Col 1:15); to it, because of its superiority, is given the judgment. The humanity which it assumed, formed and molded by it unto righteousness, is called "son of the king." I am led to this conclusion by the way

---

[1] Read *ereunōnti* instead of *eneurōnti*.

in which both are drawn together into one concept and the statement is made not as if of two things but as if of one. For the Savior made both one (cf. Eph 2:14), for he made them according to the prototype of the two which had been made in himself before all things. I refer this "of the two" also to human beings since the soul of each one is mixed with the Holy Spirit and each of those who are saved is made spiritual [*pneumatikos*].

451   "Let us serve not under the oldness of the letter," as before, but "in the newness of the Spirit" (Rom 7:6), which Spirit we have received from our bridegroom as a wedding guarantee, as it is written in another place: "who has given us the Spirit as a guarantee" (2 Cor 5:5).

AWAKENING

"What good is it to me?"— With this fright the soul awakens in order to enter into the mystery of the threefold "incarnation" spread out before it (452–459).

452   "The WORD became flesh" (Jn 1:14). This is what is of benefit to the faithful: that the WORD comes to be in each one. For what good is it to me if the WORD comes to dwell in the world, but I have no part in him?

453   Therefore, since the first "rulers of this world" (cf. Jn 16:11) had broken into the inheritance of the Lord, it was necessary for "the good shepherd" (Jn 10:11) to leave the ninety-nine in the upper regions and come down to earth to look for the one sheep that was lost, and on finding it and lifting it to his shoulder, to bring it back to the upper sheepfold of perfection (cf. Mt 18:12; Lk 15:4f). But what good is it to me if the seed of Abraham "which is Christ" (Gal 3:6) "possesses the cities of its enemies" (Gen 22:17 LXX), but does not possess my city? — if in my city, that is in my soul, which is "the city of the great king" (cf. Mt 5:35), neither his laws nor his statutes are observed? What good is it to me that he brings the whole world into subjection and possesses the cities of his enemies if he does not also conquer his enemies who are within me, if he does not destroy "the law which is at war in my members with the law of my mind, and making me captive to the law of sin" (Rom 7:23)?

454   God renews his promises in order to show you that you also ought to renew yourself. He does not remain with the things that are old, nor should you remain an "old man" (cf. Rom 6:6). He says this "from heaven" so that you also might accept "the image of the man of

heaven" (1 Cor 15:49). For what good is it to you if God renews his promises and you are not renewed? — if he speaks "from heaven" and you listen from the earth? What good is it to you if God binds himself with an oath and you let it go as if you were listening to a common fable? Why do you not take note that, because of you, God is doing even some things which do not seem at all suited to his nature?

-55   "The Lord knows that the thoughts of the wise are futile" (1 Cor 3:20). It is not surprising if "the Lord" in himself "knows that the thoughts of the wise are futile." But I wish that it would be the Lord who has come to be in me who "knows that the thoughts of the wise are futile." For if Christ is in me, he can show me how "the thoughts of the wise" of this world "are futile," and how it is only the illuminating wisdom of God that conquers and tramples under foot all apparent wisdom.

-56   "Ask for a sign," he is commanded, and not just simply, but to "ask for himself"; for the scripture says: "Ask for yourself a sign of the Lord your God; let it be as deep as Sheol or high as heaven" (Isa 7:11 LXX). The sign proposed is my Lord, Jesus Christ, . . . "as deep as Sheol" because he is the one who comes down (cf., e.g., Jn 6:33), but "as high as heaven" because he is the one who "ascended far above all the heavens" (Eph 4:10). But this proposed sign, my Lord, Jesus Christ "as deep as Sheol and as high as heaven" is of no good to me unless the mystery of his "depth" and "height" is taking place within me. For when I have received the mystery of Christ Jesus from its "depth" and "height," then will I receive the "sign" according to the command of the Lord, and then will there be said to me as having within me this "as deep as Sheol" and "as high as heaven": "Do not say in your heart, 'Who will ascend into heaven?' (that is, to bring Christ down) or 'Who will descend into the abyss?' (that is, to bring Christ up from the dead). . . . For your powerful WORD is near, on your lips and in your heart" (cf. Rom 10:6–8).

57   God said to Abraham: By circumcision "shall my covenant be in your flesh" (Gen 17:13). I want to show how we too can have the covenant of our Lord Jesus Christ "in" our "flesh." . . . If "I put to death my earthly members" (Col 3:15), I bear the covenant of Christ in my flesh. If I am "always carrying in my body the death of Jesus Christ" (2 Cor 4:10), the covenant of Christ is in my body because "if we endure, we shall also reign with him" (2 Tim 2:12). If I am implanted into the likeness of his death (cf. Rom 6:5), I am showing that his covenant is "in my flesh." For what good is it to me if I say that Jesus has come only in that flesh which he took from Mary and do not show that he has also come in this flesh of mine? . . . I am showing that

the covenant with God is in my flesh if I can say with Paul that "I have been crucified with Christ; it is no longer I who live but Christ who lives in me" (Gal 2:20), and if I can say as he said: "I bear on my body the marks [*stigmata*] of my Lord Jesus Christ" (Gal 6:17).

458   For what good is it to you if Christ once came in the flesh if he does not also come to your soul? Let us pray that his coming take place in us daily so that we can say: "It is no longer I who live but Christ who lives in me" (Gal 2:20). For if Christ lives in Paul and not in me, what good is that to me?

459   "The blossoming vines gave forth their fragrance" (cf. Cant 2:13). It is not without reason, I think, that it does not say "gave forth fragrance," but "gave forth their fragrance," in order to show that every soul has the possibility of choice and the freedom of the will by which it can do everything good. But while this good of nature, deceived by the occasion of sin, had been diverted to cowardice or wickedness, still when it is repaired by grace and restored by the teaching of the word of God, it gives forth once again that fragrance with which God the Creator had endowed it in the beginning, but which the guilt of sin had taken away.

VOICE

But even in its adoption, the fundamental structure of the created nature perdures: only through bodily, direction-giving image does the way lead to the living content. Before meaning comes the voice, before the "experience" its external manifestation. John the precursor is an eternally valid figure of church history (460–468).

460   Speech is one thing, voice is something else.

461   Just as some are men of God [*homines Dei*], so others are sheep of God. . . . The sheep hear his voice, but the men hear his WORD.

462   For the voice comes to the ears first; then after the voice but still with the voice, the word is heard.

463   Thunder comes before the lightning, but the lightning is seen first.

464   In the gospel it is not the voice that is perceived, but the speech, which is of greater excellence than the voice.

465   We make a distinction between voice and speech. For voice can be produced without meaning and without a word being spoken, and speech can also be reported to the mind without voice, as when we make internal mental excursions. And thus John is different from the Savior who, according to one aspect, is WORD. . . . Thus John is

by birth a little older than Christ, for we hear the voice before the word. But John also points to Christ, for the word is signified by the voice. . . . In a word, when John points out Christ, it is a man pointing out God.

466   "I am the voice of one crying in the wilderness" (Jn 1:23). This is not the "crying voice in the wilderness" but "the voice of one crying in the wilderness," the voice of one who stood up and proclaimed: "If any one thirst, let him come to me and drink" (Jn 7:37). . . . There is need of this voice crying in the wilderness so that the soul which is bereft of God and deserted by truth (for what could be a more desolate wilderness than a soul bereft of God and all virtue?) and in need of instruction because it is still following crooked ways can be exhorted to "make straight the way of the Lord" (Jn 1:23).

467   I think that the mystery of John is being fulfilled to this day in the world. Whoever are to believe in Jesus Christ, the spirit and power of John first comes to their souls and "makes ready for the Lord a perfect people" (cf. Lk 1:17). . . . Not just at that time were the "ways prepared" and the "paths made straight." . . . What wondrous mysteries of the Lord and his plan of salvation! Angels go before Jesus, angels daily ascend and descend over the salvation of humankind in Christ Jesus!

468   The precursor of Christ and "the voice of one crying in the wilderness" (Lk 3:4) preaches "in the wilderness" to the soul which does not have peace. And not just then, but now too, the "burning and shining lamp" (Jn 5:35) comes first and "preaches a baptism of repentance for the forgiveness of sins" (Lk 3:3); then the "true light" (Jn 1:9) follows.

INITIATION

At the threshold of the church. In being cast out by the world the soul encounters salvation (469). The voice of the church is also heard outside the church (470). Indeed, even before entrance into the church through baptism, there is grace, spiritual gifts and encounter with the bridegroom (471), when the true sanctification comes about first through baptism (472). Dead to the world, the baptized person begins a new life (473).

469   "Jesus heard that they had cast him out, and having found him he said, 'Do you believe in the Son of Man?'" (Jn 9:35). Because the Jews had expelled him from their community because of his outspokenness

about the Savior, Jesus for this reason "found him." For if the Savior "came to seek and to save the lost" (Lk 19:10), the goal of the seeker is the finding of what is being sought. It is clear, then, that the words "he found him" are not to be understood in a merely ordinary way. For it was particularly necessary for him to be found when he was cast out by those who did not accept the witness about Jesus. For once cast out by them, he was ready to be found.

470   "As we have heard, so have we seen in the city of the Lord of hosts, in the city of our God" (Ps 48:8 RSV). Outside the city we indeed heard; but inside the city we saw what before we only heard.

471   "Then the kingdom of heaven shall be compared to ten maidens who took their lamps and went to meet the bridegroom and the bride. Five of them were foolish, and five were wise" (Mt 25:1-2). . . . Not without reason do we say that the powers of perception of all who have come to know divine things, no matter how they have received the WORD of God, "whether by chance or by truth" (cf. Phil 2:18), are "virgins" — made virgins by the WORD of God in which they have believed or wish to believe. For such is the WORD of God that it shares of its purity with all who through its teaching have withdrawn from the service of idols or from the service of the elements of God's creation (cf. 1 Cor 10:14; Gal 4:3), and have come to the service of God through Jesus Christ even if they have not carried out good works nor prepared themselves for beatitude. But just as, according to the WORD of truth, the individual virtues — which are, in substance, Christ — go together, so that whoever has one has all (for Christ cannot be separated from himself), so too do all the powers of perception go together; and wherever one of these senses has too little of the right teaching of the WORD, there will all the other senses be deceived, as it were, and turned into fools. By powers of perception or senses I mean both those ordinarily understood as such: seeing, hearing, smelling, tasting, touching, and those which the Book of Proverbs calls divine with the words: "You will find the knowledge of God" (cf. Prov 2:5). But again, the WORD of God is the cause of the right use of the senses, and it is not possible that, . . . someone use certain activities of the senses and neglect others. Thus if the Word has made one of the senses wise, so as to constitute it a virgin, it is necessary for it to pour out its wisdom into the other senses as well. Thus it is not possible that, of the five senses one has, some should be foolish and others prudent; they must rather all be prudent or all wise.

All these senses now take their "lamps" . . . when they accept that the Word of God and the Son of God is the bridegroom of the church; "they go out" from the world and from the errors of many gods and come to meet the Savior who is always ready to come to these virgins so that, with the worthy among them, he might go in to his blessed bride, the church. And after the reception of the WORD, as long as the light of the faithful "shines before men, that they may see their good works and give glory to their Father who is in heaven" (Mt 5:16), they are prudent [maidens], the kind who take along the oil which nourishes the light which is always poured forth in good works, i.e., the WORD of doctrine. They fill the vessels of their souls from this WORD, buying it from the teachers and keepers of the tradition who sell it, as much as is needed, even if their end is late and the WORD coming to their fulfillment is delayed; for they hasten to him to be fulfilled and to be set outside the world. But those who, after becoming Christian, were concerned to receive only enough teaching to last them to the end, . . . these are "foolish." They accepted their lamps, which of course were lit at first, but they did not take oil along for such a long journey to go meet the spouse.

"As the bridegroom was delayed, all the maidens slumbered and slept" (Mt 25:5). When the bridegroom delays this way and the WORD does not come quickly to make perfect their life, the senses suffer somewhat while they remain and sleep, so to speak, in the night of the world. For they sleep in that they lose something of their alert vigilance; but those prudent maidens did not lose their lamps nor give up hope of saving their oil. . . .

"But at midnight," that is, at the high point of that remissness, and at the midpoint between the spent light of evening and the still-awaited light of day, "there was a cry" (Mt 25:6), the cry of angels, I think, wishing to awaken all the slumbering senses and call them to go to meet the bridegroom. Inside the senses of those sleeping they cry out: "Behold the bridegroom! Come out to meet him!" (Mt 25:6). . . . All indeed heard and got up, but not all dressed their lamps in the proper way . . . and at an inopportune time "the foolish said to the wise, 'Give us some of your oil'" (Mt 25:8). For although they were foolish, they still understood that they needed to go meet the bridegroom with light, with all the lamps of their senses illuminated.

And since this parable was spoken for everyone to hear, Christ added for his disciples the words: "Watch therefore, for you know neither the day nor the hour" (Mt 25:13).

472   When the Apostle in the letter to the Corinthians first says: "To the church of God which is at Corinth, to those sanctified in Christ Jesus, called to be saints," and then adds some others as if of another degree or order, and says of them: "with all those who in every place call on the name of our Lord Jesus Christ, both their Lord and ours" (1 Cor 1:2), he will seem perhaps to be making a distinction between those whom he calls "church of God" and those who only "call upon the name of our Lord Jesus Christ." Consider now whether that difference is somewhat like what is contained in the present chapter of Romans in which he teaches that it is not possible to call upon the name of the Lord unless one first believes in Christ (cf. Rom 10:14). But when someone has believed in Christ, even if he is not yet sanctified and not yet incorporated into the body of the church, it is still necessary for that person to call upon the name of him in whom he has believed. For Christ came to reconcile the world to God and make an offering to the Father of those who believe in him [Christ]. Those whom he offers to the Father, the Holy Spirit takes in order to sanctify them and give them life as members of the heavenly church of the first-born (cf. Heb 12:23).

473   Those fish [in the parable] which are taken up into the nets, die. . . . But those who are caught by the fishers of Jesus and brought up out of the sea, indeed die, but they die to the world and to sin, and after this dying to the world and to sin, are given life by the WORD of God. . . . If you then have come up out of the sea and been caught in the nets of the disciples of Jesus, turn away from the sea; forget it; go to the mountains—the prophets, and to the hills—the just, and lead your life there, so that afterwards, when the time for your departure has come, many hunters may be sent forth who are different from the fishers . . . : "Behold, I am sending forth many fishers, says the Lord, and they shall catch them; and afterwards I will send forth many hunters and they shall hunt them down on every mountain and every hill" (Jer 16:16).

GRACE

Faith as Grace

While Augustine at a later time in his battle against the Pelagians embedded human freedom so completely in divine grace that (true) freedom actually becomes an effect of grace, Origen, in his battle against a naturalistic gnosis (which transferred good and evil into the nature created by God) had to emphasize human freedom. His specific solution is as follows: that on the one hand all natural powers are given and preserved by God, but the human being is free in using them for good or ill; and that on the other hand, in the area of the virtues, there is for each virtue a human, "natural" virtue to be gained by one's own activity, and a corresponding divine, "supernatural" virtue given only as grace. God gives these gifts of grace to whoever works for the natural virtue, but he is in no way obliged to do so.

Thus Origen certainly emphasizes more strongly than Augustine the human being's freedom of choice and his own activity as distinct from grace. But in no way is he to be for that reason suspected of Pelagian tendencies. God's grace and human cooperation interpenetrate, but in such a way that grace always remains strictly undeserved and free, and no human work can make the slightest claim to it. Everything in the type of spirit that Origen is and the whole system of his thought exclude the possibility that the impulse to conversion (initium fidei) comes from the human being (474–488).

474   "Even if one is perfect among the sons of men, yet without the wisdom that comes from thee he will be regarded as nothing" (Wis 9:6). In the same way, we could say: Even if someone is perfect in faith among the sons of men, if he is lacking in the faith which comes from your grace, he will be regarded as nothing. . . . And so it is in everything. . . . There is a certain perfection among the sons of men which is gained by one's own work and diligence, whether it be in wisdom or in teaching or in other offices. But if they do not have the grace that is given by God, they will be nothing; for if the grace of the Spirit is not there, they cannot be members of the body of Christ.

475   "Why do you not understand what I say? It is because you are unable to hear my word" (Jn 8:43). The reason, he says, that you do not understand what I say is that you are unable to hear my word. First of all, therefore, the capacity to hear the divine WORD must be brought about so that we might then become able to hear everything Jesus says. . . . for as long as someone's hearing is not healed, he is unable to hear the WORD speaking to the deaf: "Be opened!" (cf. Mk 7:34).

476   As for the meaning of "hearing," I think it signifies the perception of what is said; but "knowing" or "understanding" refers to the one

understanding giving his assent, illuminated by the light of the knowledge of what is said.

477 "And behold, a Canaanite woman from that region came out and cried, 'Have mercy on me, O Lord, Son of David; my daughter is severely possessed by a demon'" (Mt 15:22). I should think that if she had not departed from that region, she would not have been able to cry out to Jesus with the great faith that is reported of her. For it is "in proportion to our faith" (Rom 12:16) that one comes out of the territory of the gentiles.

478 "But, because I tell the truth, you do not believe me" (Jn 8:45). Consider now whether it is possible to believe under one aspect the same thing which under another aspect one does not believe: for example, . . . those who believe in the Jesus who performed the wonders and signs described in Judaea, but do not believe in him as the Son of him who created heaven and earth: they believe and do not believe in the same person. . . . But also those who believe in the maker of heaven and earth, but do not believe in the Father of Jesus who was crucified under Pontius Pilate, they believe in God and do not believe in him. Therefore, to avoid the toils of an obvious contradiction which the gospel writer supposedly did not notice, one can say that when Jesus said to the Jews who believed in him: "Because I tell the truth, you do not believe in me," he was speaking to those who under one aspect believed, but under another aspect did not. This was apparently because they believed in him from what they saw of the miracles, but did not believe in the deeper meaning of what he said. The words: "Because I tell the truth, you do not believe me" are like the words: "You will know the truth" (Jn 8:32) spoken to those who did not know the truth, as if he were saying: "You believe in me for the miracles I perform, but do not believe in me for the truth I speak." You can see this in many people of today as well, people who marvel at Jesus when they examine his history, but no longer believe when the deeper meaning which is beyond their capacity is explained to them; they suspect that it is false.

479 "He did not do many mighty works there because of their unbelief" (Mt 13:58). . . . Or, as Mark wrote: "He could do no mighty work . . . " (Mk 6:5); not "He did not want to" but "He could not," as if from the faith of the one on whom the power was working, assistance came for the working of the power, but from lack of faith came hindrance to this working. . . . And perhaps, just as with bodies there is a physical attraction of some things to others, like the magnetic stone

to iron and what is called naphtha to fire, there is this kind of attraction of faith to the divine power.

But it seems to me that, just as with bodily things, agriculture alone does not bring about the harvest of fruits without the cooperation of the environment (or better, of him who gave the environment the qualities he wished it to have), nor does the environment do this without agriculture (or better, without him who exercises providence and does not let the plants of the earth grow without agriculture) . . . so too the exercise of power without the faith of the one to be healed cannot by itself bring about a work of healing, nor can faith, however great, without the power of God. What is written about wisdom you can apply both to the faith and the individual virtues so as to be able to say: "Even if one is perfect" in faith "among the sons of men," yet without the power "that comes from you, he will be regarded as nothing" (Wis 9:6); or "perfect" in moderation as far as this is possible "among the sons of men, yet without the" moderation "that comes from you, he will be regarded as nothing." . . . So then: "let not the wise man glory in his wisdom, nor the mighty man glory in his might" (Jer 9:23). For what is worthy of glorying is not ours but is the gift of God; wisdom is from him and strength is from him and everything else as well.

480   What is it that God plants? Moses says that "God planted paradise" (Gen 2:8). But God is planting now as well, and he is planting daily in the souls of the faithful. For in the soul from which he removes anger he plants gentleness, and in the soul from which he removes pride, he plants humility.

481   If one asks what God has given to human beings and what human beings have done with what they receive from God . . . one will find that God has given human beings all the desires and all the impulses with which they can work towards virtue and make progress, and also planted in them the power of reason with which they can recognize what they ought to do and what to avoid. But if human beings, who have all that is needed from God, fail to tread the path of virtue after receiving these gifts, they themselves turn out to be failures in what is given them by God.

482   God is more pleased with those who with their whole strength do something that is lesser than he is with those who accomplish more from a potential that is able to do a great deal more. . . . As Jesus . . . saw the poor widow tossing in two small coins . . . a person who perhaps thought quite simply about divine things, and lived

accordingly, he said: "Truly I tell you, this poor widow has put in more than all of them" (Lk 21:3).

483 Let us look now at what is said here: "It depends not upon man's will or exertion, but upon God's mercy" (Rom 9:16). Our opponents say: If it does not "depend upon man's will or exertion," but on God's mercy, then our salvation does not depend on our own free will, but on our nature which depends on him who made human beings as they are, or on the intention of him who shows mercy when he pleases. To these opponents we must put the following questions: Is it good or bad to desire what is good? And to run in the desire of reaching the goal in the pursuit of the good, is this worthy of praise or blame? If they say that it is worthy of blame their answer makes no sense. . . . Should they give a third answer, that willing the good and striving after the good is something indifferent . . . one would have to say that if willing the good and striving after the good is indifferent, then so is its opposite, namely, willing evil and striving after evil. But willing evil and striving after it is by no means indifferent.

Solomon says in the Book of the Psalms: "Unless the Lord builds the house, those who build it labor in vain. Unless the Lord watches over the city, the watchman stays awake in vain" (Ps 127:1). He doesn't say this to warn us away from housebuilding nor to teach us not to be on watch to guard the city in our soul, but to show that what is built without God and does not have his protection is built in vain and guarded to no purpose. Thus, since human willing does not suffice to reach the goal, nor the striving of those who are like athletes enable them to take "the prize of the upward call of God in Christ Jesus" (Phil 3:14)—for these things are accomplished with the help of God—it is thus well said that "it is not a matter of our willing or striving but of God's mercy" (Rom 9:16). . . . Thus, our perfection does not come about without us doing anything, but it is not completed by us; God does most of the work. . . . What God does is infinitely more than what we do.

There are, in addition, the words: "The willing and the doing is from God" (cf. Phil 2:13). Now some say that if the willing is from God and the doing is from God, if we wish and do evil this is from God; and if this is the case we have no free will. In other words, if we will the better and do what is excellent, since willing and doing is from God, it is not we who have done the excellent thing—we only seem to have; it was all given by God. We have therefore, as this shows, no free will. To this we must answer that the words of the Apostle do not say that willing evil or willing good (and the same with doing the better and the worse) is from God, but the willing as such and the doing as such. For just as we have from God our reality as living beings and human beings, so too, as it were, our ability to will and to be moved. Although we have as living beings the capacity to be moved and, for example, to move certain members — hands and feet, one could not rightly say that we have from God the specific action of moving to strike or to kill or to steal from someone. Rather we have received from God the generic power of motivation which we employ for the worse or the better. Thus the power of action by which we are living beings we have received from God, and our willing we have received from the Creator; but we employ this power of willing, as well as that of doing, either for the best or its opposite.

84   When [the Apostle] says: "To one who works, his wages are not reckoned as a gift but as his due; and to one who does not work but trusts him who justifies the ungodly, his faith is reckoned as righteousness" (Rom 4:4-5), he seems to be indicating that the grace of the one justifying is as it were in the faith, but that the justice of the one making retribution is in the work. But when I consider the exalted status of this WORD, I can barely persuade myself that there can be any work which would require payment from God as something owed, because even our ability to do anything at all, or to think, or to talk, we can do only as a result of his gift and generosity.[1]

85   Nothing which God gives to a created nature is given by way of obligation; instead he gives everything as grace. [Sin, on the other hand, bears a binding relationship to death: "Death is the payment of sin."] In no way is eternal life a payment or any kind of debt on the part of God; it is instead his grace. . . . One must not think, therefore, that it is because of our good works that the gospel says: "The measure you give will be the measure you get" (Mt 7:2). "For by grace [we] have been saved; and this is not [our] own doing, it is the gift of God, lest any man should boast" (Eph 2:8-9). It must be assumed that it is the punishment which is meted out to us according to our sins.

---

[1] That this strongly Augustinian passage must not necessarily have been added by Rufinus is proven by the following fragment which has been preserved in Greek. No. 487 has also been preserved in Greek. Nos. 484-488 come from the Commentary on Romans, the last and most mature work of Origen. The apologetics of freedom against a naturalistic Gnosticism here recedes into the background and gives way to a genuinely Pauline theology of faith.

486   But if it should seem that what is given because of faith is not given gratis, because human beings must first offer their faith and thus earn grace from God, then listen to what the Apostle teaches about this elsewhere. For where he lists the gifts of the Spirit (cf. 1 Cor 12:8–11) which he says are given to the faithful according to the measure of their faith, he then mentions among others also the gift of faith as given by the Holy Spirit.

487   But that the law of faith suffices for righteousness, even if we have done nothing, can be demonstrated from the robber crucified with Jesus and the sinful woman in Luke. . . . For it was not from any work but from her faith that her sins were forgiven her; and she heard the words: "Your faith has saved you; go in peace" (Lk 7:50). But that unrighteousness committed after coming to true knowledge destroys the faith of the one justified, Paul will show quite clearly. I also think that the works done before faith, even if they seem to be correct, do not justify the one doing them because they are not built upon the proper foundation of faith.

488   In writing to the Romans and the Corinthians, Paul seems to me to be teaching three ways of receiving grace in order to show that we have something to do with it, but that it consists mostly in God's gift. He holds therefore that there is a "measure of faith" (Rom 12:3) through which one receives grace, that it is given for what is necessary, and that the Spirit gives it out as he wills. Therefore, that such faith be found in us by which we can merit to receive a higher grace, seems to be due to our work and our efforts. But that it be given for what is necessary, and that it be useful to the receiver, is for God to decide; whether he wishes to give it at all is entirely up to him. . . . But when Paul says that grace is given "for the common good" (1 Cor 12:7), this can mean that even though the measure of faith in someone is so great as to merit receiving a higher grace, if the Holy Spirit in looking into the future judges that this is not helpful to the one receiving it, he will necessarily divide it up "as he wills" and "as it is needed" (1 Cor 12:7, 11).

Work from Nature and Work from God

The doctrine of the positive value of works is already grounded in what has gone before. It is clear that the only works which have "supernatural" value are those which are built on the foundation of "supernatural" faith (489–492). But what then is the value of the "good" works of the unbelievers? Origen here occupies a prudent and delicate middle position between the indiscriminate identification of pagan and Christian moral values and the strict Augustinian rejection of the pagan virtues as veiled vices (because true moral sentiment grows only out of the love of God). Doubtless this "humane" spirit of reconciliation in Origen is required by his doctrine of recapitulation (see Part IV below). Thus faith often seems to fall back to a level with the other moral virtues (493). But Origen never forgets that no natural and human good can possibly stand up to the measure of the supernatural good (494–496). It is only "common oil" in contrast with the "fragrant ointment" of the church (497). Actually, this assessment comes quite close even to the Augustinian (498–502). And ultimately, the human being can offer to God only God's own gifts (503).

89 One must be aware that the works which Paul rejects and often vilifies are not the works of righteousness which are commanded in the law, but those in which they glory who observe the law according to the flesh. . . . But whoever is justified by grace, of that person these works are no longer required; but that person must take care lest the grace received remain empty in him, as Paul says: "His grace toward me was not in vain; on the contrary I worked harder than any of them." And then he added, thinking of grace: "though it was not I, but the grace of God which is with me" (1 Cor 15:10). Thus, whoever brings about works worthy of it and does not prove to be ungrateful to the grace of God, does not allow this grace to be "in vain." . . . If you do not allow this to be "in vain," your grace will be multiplied and you will receive, as payment so to speak for your good works, a multitude of graces.

90 The observance of the law only releases from punishment, but the merit of faith brings hope for what is promised. A commandment is laid upon servants; faith is expected of friends.

91 But where the faith which justifies the believer is lacking, and even though one may have the works of the law, and even though they may seem to be good, they still cannot justify their doer. This is so because they are not built on the foundation of faith, because they do not have faith.

92 Could someone by natural means sense something of that righteousness which says: "Beware of practicing your righteousness before men," and "Let not your left hand know what your right hand is doing" (Mt 6:1, 3)? The natural law is unable to command these things

and things like them. This is why the Apostle says: "But now the righteousness of God has been manifested apart from law [i.e., of nature]" (Rom 3:21), having the witness of the law of Moses and the prophets in whom the Holy Spirit wrote many things in images and mysteries about God's righteousness. . . . For the natural law can offer help and provide insight, as we have said, for example with regard to equity between people, or even for getting a sense of God's existence. But who could sense by natural means that Christ is the Son of God?

493   But how can the Apostle leave open so much hope to the gentiles who do not yet believe, since this seems to be against the rule of the church which states that "unless one is born anew of water and the Holy Spirit, he cannot enter into the kingdom of God" (Jn 3:3, 5)? And Peter too in the Acts of the Apostles says of Christ: "There is no other name under heaven given among men by which we must be saved" (Acts 3:12). How is it that he makes the gentiles sharers in glory and honor and peace in second place after the Jews (cf. Rom 2:10)? . . . It can happen that a person who lives under the law, even though he does not, because of the common belief [of his people], believe in Christ, nevertheless does what is good, practices justice, loves mercy, observes chastity and continence, acts modestly and gently and practices every good work — such a person, even if he does not have eternal life, . . . cannot be lost. Or when he is a Greek, that is, a gentile, . . . and is moved by natural reason, as we observe among some of the gentiles, practicing justice and observing chastity, and living according to prudence, temperance and modesty, even though he seems to be a stranger to eternal life because he does not believe in Christ and would not be able to enter the kingdom of heaven because he has not been born of water and the Spirit (cf. Jn 3:5), it still seems, according to what is said by the Apostle, that he can hardly lose the glory, honor and peace of his good works. . . . Just as the believer who has committed some other sin must, despite his faith, face judgment, so too the nonbeliever who has done a good work will, despite his lack of faith, not be deprived of his reward. Unless perchance someone wants to raise a hard and unbearable objection: to claim, namely, that a sinner is not to be reckoned among the believers; because a believer would not sin: but if he does sin, this very fact proves that he does not believe.

494   Now the Apostle calls matrimony a gift because, as it is written: "Woman is joined to man by God" (Prov 19:14 LXX); but this gift is not a spiritual one. Many other things too can be called gifts of God

such as wealth and bodily strength, a pretty figure or an earthly kingdom. For these also are given by God, as Daniel says: "He removes kings and sets up kings" (Dan 2:21). But these are not spiritual gifts.

5   "When you have done all that is commanded you, you must say, 'we are useless servants'" (Lk 17:10). . . . I think that when someone does what is commanded in the words: "Depart from evil and do good" (Ps 34:14), he indeed does good in comparison with what other men do. But in comparison with the truly good, just as "no one alive is righteous before God" (cf. Ps 143:2), and all human righteousness proves to be unrighteousness in the sight of God's righteousness, so too can no one be found good before the good God, even though in comparison to lower things someone might be called good.

6   Whenever someone has something by natural gift and then makes use of it, he then receives the same by God's grace so that he will have it in abundance and be in firmer possession of what he has. For the words of Solomon are to be understood as referring not just to wisdom but to every virtue: "For even if one is perfect among the sons of men, yet without the wisdom that comes from thee, he will be regarded as nothing" (Wis 9:6). Thus if someone is perfect in chastity or in justice or in strength or devotion that comes from the grace of God, such a person is "regarded as nothing." Therefore if we want the more perfect virtue to be given to us and to abound in us, let us make every effort to acquire what is perfect among men, and when we have acquired it, understanding that all this without God's grace is to be thought of as nothing, we should humble ourselves "under the mighty hand of God" (1 Pet 5:6) so that the perfection of all the good things that are in us might be a gift from God that he might make us perfect and acceptable to God as children of God.

7   If someone does good to another, motivated by natural reasons rather than by God (as the pagans sometimes did and as many people still do), that work is like an oil of common value that has no great fragrance; but it is still acceptable to God, as Daniel had in mind when he said to Nebuchadnezzar who did not know God: "Hear my advice, O king, and free yourself from your sins by works of mercy" (Dan 4:27). Peter says something similar in the Clementines:[1] that the good works of the unbelieving help them in this world, but not in the next world or for attaining eternal life. And that makes sense

---

[1] Pseudo-Clement, *Recognitions* 10.2.

because they are not doing them because of God but because of their own human nature. But those who do good because of God, namely, the faithful, they benefit not only in this world but also in the next, and much more in the next. What the faithful do for God's sake is indeed the ointment of sweet fragrance. Of this work of the faithful for God, this sweet-smelling ointment, part is done for the benefit of human beings: almsgiving for example, or visiting the sick, taking in travelers, humility, gentleness, forbearance and other such things which help others. Whoever does these things for Christians is anointing the feet of the Lord with ointment, for they are the feet of the Lord with which he continually walks. . . . But those who cultivate chastity, devote themselves to "fasting and prayer" (cf. Lk 2:37), have patience in adversity like Job, and in temptations are not afraid to confess the truth of God—all of which are of no benefit to others but only to the glory of God—: these are what constitute the ointment which anoints the head of the Lord Christ and from there flows over the whole body of Christ, that is, over the whole church. This is the very precious ointment whose fragrance fills the whole house, the church of Christ.

498   God wills to accept good deeds from those whose spirit sees God and who are consecrated to God by faith. But the pagan, even if he seems to be moral and upright in deed, his uprightness is not holy because he boastingly does not attribute his soul's virtue to God but to himself.

499   "Love without pretense" (Rom 12:9). I consider that all love that is not from God is with "pretense" and is not true. For the reason why God, the creator of the soul, implanted it with the other virtues and also the inclination to love, was that it might love God and what God wills. Therefore, since God put this mandate of love in the soul, whoever loves anything other than God and what God wills is said to have a love that is false and with pretense.

500   Those who love Christ necessarily love their neighbor also.

501   For the words: "Let him deny himself" (Mt 16:24), it seems to me that what Paul said about denying himself is helpful: "It is no longer I who live, but Christ who lives in me" (Gal 2:29). . . . This was the voice of one denying himself, of one who was, as it were, laying down his life and taking on Christ so that Christ might live in him as "righteousness," and as "wisdom," and as "sanctification," and as "our peace" and as the "power of God"—all these things working in him.

502   For there is a great difference between someone who speaks from grace and one who speaks from human wisdom. For it has often come

about that some eloquent and learned men, outstanding not only in speech but also in insight, even though they spoke a great deal in the church and drew great praise to themselves, still did not by their words move any of their hearers to contrition of heart or progress in faith . . . but sent them away only with something pleasant in their ears. And on the other hand it often happens that men of no great eloquence, with little care for fancy speech, with simple, uncomplicated words convert many of the faithful to faith, bend the proud to humility, plant in sinners the impulse to conversion. . . . And that is certainly a sign . . . that they are talking from grace.

03   What is it that the human being offers to God? Nothing other than what stands written in the law: "My gifts are what I give" (Num 28:2 LXX). It is therefore from what God has given that human beings nonetheless make offering to God. What did God give them? Knowledge of himself. What does the human being offer God? His faith and love.

Human Wisdom and Divine Wisdom

The interrelationship of human and divine wisdom naturally plays a great role in the thought of Origen; it has already been basically laid out in the previous passages. The analogy between a natural and a supernatural work is reflected here in the grounding of the supernatural act of faith in a natural act of faith which is at the basis of all knowing and doing (504), yet in such a way that the latter is indifferent while the former is good and intelligent in itself (505).

But as a consequence of sin, there slips in between human wisdom (which remains wholly a matter of this world) and revealed divine wisdom a hybrid or in-between reality: the realm of demonic-occult knowledge that was quite extensively cultivated in late antiquity but was exposed and overcome by Christ (506). The inadequacy of human wisdom (507–510) and its danger of deception (511) does not prevent the Christian from making use of it (512). For philosophy and faith can overlap quite extensively (513). But philosophy has to be purified of human error (514–515); then it can become a resource for faith (516).

Nevertheless, "every person is a liar," and the whole level of the human pro and con can be properly seen only when one has transcended the human (517–518).

504   Isn't it true, when people go into philosophy and throw themselves
into some sect of the philosophers by chance, or because they happen
to have found a teacher there, that they do this because they believe
that sect to be better than the others? For, not waiting to hear the
arguments of all the philosophers and various sects, and the reasons
for rejecting the one and supporting the other, they thus choose to be
Stoics or Platonists or Peripatetics or Epicureans, or the followers of
some other school of philosophy. Thus, following a certain non-
rational impulse, even if they do not want to admit it, they come to
practice Stoicism, let us say, and disregard the others.

Since therefore, as reason shows, one must believe in some one of
those who have introduced sects among the Greeks or barbarians,
should it not rather be in the God who is above all things, and in him
who teaches us that we must worship only this God? Is it not more
reasonable, since all human beings are dependent on faith, to believe
God rather than them? For who goes to sea, or marries, or begets
children, or sows seed on the earth without believing that better
things will come of this, even if the opposite can and sometimes does
happen? And yet the belief that the better things, according to their
desires, will come about makes everyone dare to undertake things
which are uncertain and could go wrong. If, then, hope and belief in
a better future supports life in every uncertain enterprise, why should
not this faith be accepted more reasonably by one who believes in
something more than the sea being sailed on, the ground being sown,
the wife being married, and the other things that human beings do? I
mean belief in the God who made all these things and who with surpassing grandeur of spirit and divine wisdom dared to proclaim this
doctrine to everyone on the earth at the cost of great dangers and a
death considered to be shameful.

505   For truly, it is faith which brings about such a [natural and, hence,
apparently indifferent] assent in us. But isn't it possible that this faith
is itself worthy of praise when we entrust ourselves to the God who is
over all, giving thanks to him [i.e., Christ] who has led us to such
faith, and affirming that he could not have undertaken or succeeded
in such an enterprise apart from God? We also put faith in the intentions of the gospel writers when we encounter the devotion and conscientiousness manifest in their writings where there is no trace of
anything false, deceptive, fictitious or cunning. For it is clear to us
that souls untutored in the kinds of cunning sophistry taught by the
Greeks, characterized as it is by great plausibility and cleverness,

would not have had the ability to invent events capable in themselves of leading to faith and a life conformed to faith.

06   I am of the opinion that the "wisdom of this world" (cf. 1 Cor 2:6–8) has for its object the things which are of this world. But there is nothing in it which enables it to come to know anything about the divinity or the cause of the world or any of the other more important things, or about the leading of a good and holy life. Instead it has to do with such things as, for example, poetry or grammar or rhetoric or geometry or music, and among these perhaps medicine should also be mentioned. In all these things the "wisdom of this world" is to be seen. However, we understand the "wisdom of this world" to refer to such things as the secret and occult philosophy of the Egyptians, as it is called, and the astrology of the Chaldaeans and Indians who profess knowledge of elevated things, but also the many various opinions the Greeks have about the divinity. In sacred scripture we find that each nation has its princes. We read in Daniel, for example, that a certain person is "prince of the realm of the Persians" and someone else is "prince of the realm of the Greeks" (cf. Dan 10:13, 20); but from the context it is clear that human beings are not meant but certain powers. And in the prophet Ezekiel, the words "prince of Tyre" (cf. Ezek 28:1) quite obviously signify a spiritual power. Now when these and the other "princes of this world" like them, each with its own wisdom and with its own different kind of teaching, saw our Lord and Savior professing and proclaiming that he had come into this world to destroy all those teachings which falsely claim to be science, they immediately, not knowing what was within him, plotted against him: "The kings of the earth set themselves, and the rulers take counsel together, against the Lord and his Christ" (Ps 2:2). But with their snares uncovered, the Apostle says that "we speak wisdom among the mature, although it is not a wisdom of this age or of the rulers of this age who are doomed to pass away, but we impart a secret and hidden wisdom of God . . . which none of the princes of this world knows."

07   "Let him who boasts, boast of the Lord" (1 Cor 1:31). Not in one's own wisdom, nor in strength or wealth, but only in God is it right to boast. But perhaps you might say: Doesn't wisdom belong to the virtues of the soul? Why then is it considered wrong to boast in wisdom? See how carefully the word of scripture, which is thought to be unpolished and rough, expresses itself; not: "Let not the wise man boast in wisdom," and then nothing more, but: "Let not the wise man boast in his wisdom."

508 While the acquisition of that wisdom in which all things were made (for according to David, "God made all things in wisdom"—Ps 104:24) is impossible for human nature, the impossible has become possible through our Lord Jesus Christ "whom God made our wisdom, our righteousness and sanctification and redemption" (1 Cor 1:30).

509 "I kept my faith, . . . I said in my consternation: All men are liars" (cf. Ps 116:10–11). . . . Since there are many opinions among human beings and many have philosophized about the search for truth, and since the Son of God should have the first place in all these things, some have indeed sought without first believing, and found nothing. But I, because I believed before I sought, found what I was looking for; and not only did I find it, I have also spoken it and proclaimed to the nations the truth I have found. Nevertheless, even though I had found the truth, I did not become proud in wisdom nor puffed up in my knowledge; instead I was all the more humbled when I came to know and understand that it is the Lord who teaches all knowledge (cf. Ps 94:10–11). Then, reflecting on what has been said by human beings and how many things have been said by philosophers and even by barbarians on the subject of truth, and that for all their efforts and words they found nothing because they did not believe before they sought; considering all that they said and wrote, and filled with consternation or struck with astonishment that all this . . . was so far from the truth, I said: "Every human being is a liar" (Ps 116:11).

510 "The promises of the Lord are promises that are pure, silver refined in a furnace" (Ps 12:6). Even though the words of those who do not belong to Christ may be beautiful, they are still not "pure" because they are filled with innumerable lies. Only the words of the Lord are pure; there is no falsehood mixed in with them. They are thus pure and proven like silver purified in the furnace.

511 There is much elegance and great beauty in the words of the philosophers and rhetoricians who are all from the city of Jericho, that is to say, they belong to this world. If then you find among the philosophers false teachings clothed in beautiful words, that would be the "bar of gold" (Jos 7:21). Make sure that the brilliance of the work does not deceive you, and that the beauty of golden speech does not possess you. Remember that Jesus [Joshua] ordered a "ban" to be placed on all the gold which was found in Jericho. . . . If you take it and put it in your tent, if you take it in to your heart (as they did in the Book of Joshua), you will befoul the whole church of the Lord.

12   If we sometimes come across something which has been said wisely by the pagans, we should not immediately spurn what was said just because of the author's name; nor is it right for us, because we observe God's law, to spurn the words of prudent people. We should do as the Apostle says: "Test everything; hold fast what is good" (1 Thess 5:21).

13   For philosophy is neither contrary in all things to the law of God nor consonant with it in all things. For many of the philosophers write that God is one and that he created all things. In this they agree with God's law. Some even add that God made and governs all things through his WORD, and that it is the WORD of God through which all things are directed. In this they agree not only with the law but also with the gospels. Indeed, what is called moral philosophy and natural philosophy agrees in almost every point with ours. But it differs from us when it says that matter is co-eternal with God. It differs when it denies that God has a concern for mortal things and when it restricts providence to the space that is under the influence of the moon. They differ from us in making the lives of those born in this world dependent on the stars. They differ when they say that this world is eternal and will have no end.

14   Whatever we find expressed well and reasonably by our enemies, . . . that we must purify, . . . for they have no wisdom which is not mixed with some impurity.

15   Human teaching is, for example, the art of grammar or rhetoric or even dialectic. Nothing should be taken from this teaching for sacrifice, that is, for what is to be thought about God. But it is commanded that clarity in speech and the glory of eloquence and the skill of argumentation be fittingly admitted to the ministry of God's word.

16   We sometimes take over teachings from the pagans with the intention of leading them to the faith; and if we see that they are quite opposed to Christianity and feel a loathing for its name and hate to hear that this is a doctrine of the Christians, it does not help to say from the beginning that this is a Christian teaching. But when that doctrine has been firmly grounded to the best of our ability, and it seems to us that the hearer is becoming warmly interested in what is being said, then we profess that this praiseworthy doctrine is a doctrine of the Christians.

17   "Every human being is a liar" (Ps 116:11 LXX). To the extent that one is "human," one is a "liar"; but if one stops being[1] "human," then

---

[1] I read *apostētai* instead of *apistētai*. Cf. PG 12, 1576D.

one is no longer "liar" but truthful. When David is "human," he is a "liar"; but when he, as "liar," calls himself a "liar," then he is no longer "liar" but truthful. But if he is truthful, he also speaks truly when he calls himself a "man who lies," and thus is indeed a "liar." It is in this way, then, that the statement is sublated: not only in that he, as "human," is truthful, but also that he is a "liar."

518   "Every human being is a liar" (Ps 116:11 LXX 115:2). We must set ourselves to the task of fleeing with all our might from our human existence and strive to become "gods," for as long as we are human beings, we are "liars," just as the "Father of Lies" is a liar. For it is the same thing for us to have one and the same name and to have the reality signified by that name — I am referring to ourselves, as long as we remain human beings, and the devil who is characterized as liar.

THE INNER HUMAN BEING

Doubly Human

The anthropology given above (cf. Part I) will be applied here: the formation of Christian life is the strengthening of the inner human being, according to the model of the growth of Christ himself (519–521).

519   "Human being human being from the house of Israel" (cf. Ezek 14:4 LXX). All of us human beings are born as human beings, but not all of us are "human being human being". . . . When this "human being" who is "external" (cf. 2 Cor 4:16) is a human being while that which is the "internal human being" is a serpent, there is not in us the "human being human being," but just the human being. But when the "interior human being" has persevered in the image of its Maker, then a [new] human being is born and becomes thus, according to the "external and internal human being," a double "human being human being."

520   Therefore, since the Apostle frequently writes in a way that indicates that in each one there are two human beings, one of whom he calls the external, the other the internal, calling one of them according to the flesh and the other according to the Spirit (following, I think, what is written in Genesis where one was created in God's image and the other formed from the dust of the earth) . . . it must be observed that each of these is set up so as to be in some things different and in others similar. For some things begin with the internal

human being and move on to the external, and others which have their beginning in the external human being move on to the internal. What I mean is this: If chastity begins with the internal human being, it obviously moves on to the external. . . . But if someone begins with the chastity of an external human being, one does not always arrive at internal continence.

521   The expression "grow" is used two ways in the scripture: in a bodily way, with which the human will has nothing to do, and in a spiritual way, in which the cause of the growth depends on human effort. Of this second way, the spiritual, the evangelist now relates: "The child grew and became strong in spirit" (Lk 2:40). . . . he did not remain at the same level where he began, but the Spirit was continually growing in him, and while the Spirit was growing hour by hour and minute by minute, his soul was also receiving its increase. And not just his soul but also his mind and senses were following along with the increase of the Spirit. Those who take what God commanded: "Increase and multiply" (Gen 1:28) in a simple and literal way — I don't know how they can explain it. . . . For what human being would not like to add to his stature and become taller? . . . Do you want to know how one should understand "increase"? Listen to what Isaac did; it is said of him: "Isaac became rich, and gained more and more until he became very wealthy" (cf. Gen 26:13). For his will, striving for the better, was always making progress.

Fall of the Idols

The building up of the inner human being must begin with the cleansing of the temple from which the hidden idols of the spirit are to be driven out (522–527), and in their place the statues of the virtues must be set up (528). In this tearing down and setting up, the great rhythm of the Christian life is announced: death and resurrection (529–530). For the WORD of God wills war and sword (531–532), but only to liberate the soul (533). Thus confession of sin and praise of God are, in their unity, the one Christian "confession" (534).

522   The first commandment is: "You shall have no other gods before me." And after that: "You shall not make for yourself a graven image, or any likeness of anything that is in heaven above, or that is in the earth beneath, or that is in the water under the earth; you shall not

bow down to them or serve them; for I, the Lord your God, am a jealous God, visiting the iniquity of the fathers upon the children to the third and the fourth generation of those who hate me, but showing steadfast love to thousands of those who love me and keep my commandments" (Exod 20:3-6). Some think that all this is only one single commandment. But if one counts them this way, the full number of the ten commandments is not arrived at, and where then would be the truth of the decalogue?[1]

523   That which someone cherishes above all else, admires and loves above all, this is that person's God. . . . Did not the error of the whole pagan world have its beginning here, in that what human beings love very much they want to be gods, and ascribe divine names to all human vices and desires?

524   Everyone who makes some thing into a god is serving alien gods. Do you worship food and drink? Your God is your "belly" (Phil 3:19). Do you hold silver and earthly wealth in great reverence? Your lord and god is Mammon.

525   "Cry aloud, ye graven images" (Isa 10:10 LXX). Should someone, even now, consider the great number of sinners, he will not hesitate to say that everyone who makes a god of what pleases him and is a servant to sin is someone accursed who makes a graven image and pours a statue and sets it up in secret; for if we sin we are making many idols in the secret of our heart. This is why the Word teaches us to do penance and cry aloud over the graven images and idols which are "in Jerusalem and Samaria" (Isa 10:11). And if we who want to be in the church commit sin, we are making "graven images in Jerusalem." But if those who are outside the church like the heretics commit sin, they are making "idols in Samaria." Nevertheless, God in his goodness calls all to repentance with the words: "Cry aloud, ye graven images."

526   Take, for example, those among the Greeks who invent teachings, whether in this philosophy or that, or those who are the originators of heresies: they make for themselves idols and images of their soul, and

---

[1] Only with Augustine are these two first commandments combined into one, while the coveting of one's neighbor's wife and one's neighbor's goods are separated into two commandments. But even in Origen's day there must have been tendencies to leave out the prohibition against idols and images. Flavius Josephus, Philo, Theophilus of Antioch, Tertullian and Gregory of Nazianzen, among others, count them as Origen did.

turning to them have worshiped the works of their hands, taking their own images as the truth.

527 "For you are the Lord our God." For we confess nothing as God; neither the belly, like the gluttonous whose "god is the belly" (Phil 3:19); nor gold, like the avaricious, and greed, which is idolatry; nor do we idolize or make a god of anything else as so many do. But our God is he who in everything is "over all and through all and in all" (cf. Eph 4:6; Rom 9:5), and being attached to the love of God (for love binds us together with God) we say: "Behold we are yours, because you, Lord, are our God."

528 Then Celsus says that we shrink from raising up altars, images and temples . . . not seeing that for us the spirit of every good person is an altar from which arises a truly and spiritually sweet-smelling "incense," the "prayers" of a pure conscience (cf. Rev 5:8; Ps 141:2). . . . But the statues and gifts which are fit offerings to God, not made by ordinary artisans but traced and shaped in us by the WORD of God, are the virtues: our imitation of the firstborn "of all creation" (Col 1:15) who is the model of justice, prudence, courage, wisdom, piety and the other virtues. Thus, in all those who, according to the divine Word, build up in themselves prudence and justice, wisdom and piety and the structures of the other virtues, there are images in which we believe it is fitting to honor the prototype of all images, "the image of the invisible God" (Col 1:15), God the Only-begotten. . . . And in general all Christians make efforts to raise up such altars as we have here described, not soulless or senseless ones, . . . but such as are open to receive the Spirit of God. . . . This is what the Word of God intended in making this promise to the just: "I will live in them and move among them, and I will be their God, and they shall be my people" (2 Cor 6:6)—and when the Savior said: "Whoever listens to my words and does them, I and my Father will come to him and make our home with him" (Mt 7:24 [Lk 6:47]; Jn 14:23). So then, let anyone who wishes compare the altars which I have described with those spoken of by Celsus, and the images in the soul of those who worship the God of all with the images of Pheidias and Polycleitus and the like; it will be obvious that the latter are lifeless things subject to the ravages of time, while the former dwell in the immortal soul and remain there as long as the spiritual soul wishes to keep them.

529 "Behold, this child is set for the fall and rising of many" (Lk 2:34). . . . God says: "I kill" (Deut 32:39). I am glad that God is killing.

For when the old man is in me and I am still living like a man, I want God to kill the old man in me and raise me up from the dead. For it is written: "The first man was from the earth, . . . the second man is from heaven. . . . Just as we have borne the image of the man of dust, we shall also bear the image of the man of heaven" (1 Cor 15:47–49). It is in this sense that we are also to understand the words: "For judgment I came into this world, that those who do not see may see, and that those who see may become blind" (Jn 9:39). . . . Let us consider, then, that the Savior has not come for the fall of some and the resurrection of others, but for their fall and resurrection.

530   It was necessary for me first to fall and, when I had fallen, then to rise up, lest the Savior occasion for me a very bad fall. But he made me fall so that I might rise up, and so that the fall might become much more useful to me than I thought at that time.

531   For we can be sure of this: before the WORD of God is heard . . . there is no tribulation or temptation, because unless the trumpet sounds the war does not begin. But when the trumpet gives the signal for war, then comes affliction and all the battles of temptations. It was when Moses and Aaron began to talk to Pharaoh that the people of God were afflicted (cf. Exod 5:23). When the WORD of God comes into your soul, the battle of virtue against vice is necessarily joined within you . . . and a ruthless war begins.

532   "They left part of the manna till the morning, and it bred worms and became foul" (Exod 16:20). . . . But if you say that this is the WORD of God, where do the worms come from? And yet, worms do develop in us out of nothing other than the WORD of God. For, as he himself says: "If I had not come and spoken to them, they would not have sin" (Jn 15:22). Therefore, should someone sin after receiving the WORD of God, the WORD itself becomes for him a worm which continually bores into his conscience and gnaws at the secrets of his breast.

533   It is thus necessary to die first to the letter so that the soul, finally free, can wed the Spirit and enter into the matrimony of the new covenant.

534   "We will confess you, O God; we will confess and call upon your name!" (Ps 75:1 LXX). Because confessing is twofold, it is mentioned twice. The first signifies the confession of sins, the second signifies thanksgiving for favors received. But because no one can call upon the name of the Lord in the way meant by the text: "Whoever calls on the name of the Lord shall be saved" (Acts 2:21; cf. Rom 10:13; Joel 2:32) unless he has first renounced sin and confessed the sins he has committed, the church accordingly perseveres in confessing. Thus if

we wish to be numbered among the elect and be saved with them, we must first become accusers of our own guilt, and in so doing, give it up completely.

Law of Love

Once the idols have been driven out, there remains but one law and one guide for Christians, the law of love. Plato spoke sublimely of love; the love of Christ, however, is from the outset in no danger of being led astray into the external and sensual because the God which it proclaims is wholly spirit and wholly love. This is the new element which Plato did not know about: that there is not just the rising eros of the creature, but also, preceding all created love, a mystery of love in God himself, and that all love of the creature towards God always presupposes an invitation from God to enter into the mystery of the Trinity (535).

535   Many of the learned Greeks, wishing to investigate the nature of truth, have written various things, some even in dialogue style, about the nature of love. They have tried to show that the power of love is the same as that which leads the soul from earth to the lofty heights of heaven, and that one cannot arrive at full beatitude without the inspiring call of love. Moreover, questions on this subject are reported as being brought up in so-called banquets. This was, I think, among those for whom the banquet was not a matter of food but of words. But others too have left written descriptions of techniques by which this love can apparently be conceived or increased in the soul. But people of the flesh have misused these arts to satisfy foul desires and to serve the mysteries of a false love . . . using the writings of the ancients to disguise their incontinence.

Therefore, lest we too offend in some way against what the ancients have written about in a competent and spiritual manner, perverting it in a foul or fleshly way, let us open up the palms of our body as well as of our soul to God in prayer, that the Lord who "gives his WORD with great power to those who preach it" (Ps 67:12 LXX) might also give us his WORD in power, and that we . . . might be able to explain the nature of love.

At the beginning of Moses' writing, where he was describing the creation of the world, we find mention of the creation of two men: the first "made in the image and likeness of God" (Gen 1:26), the second "formed from the dust of the earth" (Gen 2:7). Knowing this well and being quite well informed in these matters, Paul the Apostle wrote quite clearly and openly in his letters that there are two men in each human being. Thus he says: "Though our outer man is wasting away, our inner man is being renewed every day" (2 Cor 4:16), and also: "For I delight in the law of God in my inner man" (Rom 7:22). And he writes this way in other places as well. . . .

Let us see now why we have mentioned the inner and outer man. What we want to point out is that in sacred scripture, both the members of the outer man and his internal parts and affections are designated by the same names and even by the same words, and that they are compared with one another not only in name but also in reality itself. For example, someone who is a boy in age according to the inner man can grow and come to the age of a young man, and then by successive increases arrive at "mature manhood" (Eph 4:13) and become a father. . . . But "babes in Christ" (1 Cor 3:1) is clearly said in relation to the soul and not in relation to the age of the body, for Paul says the same thing again in another place: . . . "until we all attain . . . to mature manhood, to the measure of the age of the fullness of Christ" (Eph 4:13). . . . Just as these designations of age we have mentioned are ascribed with the same words both to the outer and the inner man, so too will you find the names of bodily members being transferred to the members of the soul, or rather, they are used to refer to the powers and desires of the soul. Thus the word of Ecclesiastes: "The wise man has his eyes in his head" (Eccl 2:14); likewise in the gospel: "He who has ears, let him hear" (Mt 13:43); and also in the prophets: "The WORD of the Lord which was put into the hands of Jeremiah the prophet" (cf. Jer 50:1), or of any other prophet. . . . It is thus quite obvious that these names for members simply cannot apply to the visible body but have to be referred to the parts and powers of the invisible soul. . . . There is therefore for this material man, who is also called the outer man, bodily and earthly food and drink which is suited to its nature. And so too for the spiritual man, who is also called interior, there is a proper food in that "living bread which came down from heaven" (cf. Jn 6:33, 41, 51). And his drink is from that water which Jesus promised when he said: "Whoever drinks of the water that I shall give him will never thirst" (Jn 4:14). . . . Thus it happens that some of the more simple souls, not knowing how to distinguish or keep apart which things in sacred scripture are to be ascribed to the inner man and which to the outer, and deceived by the verbal similarities, are taken in by certain foolish fables and senseless fictions so as to believe that even after the resurrection bodily food is to be eaten and drink is to be taken which does not come exclusively from that "true vine" which lives forever. . . .

If then this is true, just as there is said to be a carnal love which the poets call Cupid or Eros, . . . so too is there a spiritual love according to which that inner man, in his love, "sows in the Spirit" (cf. Gal 6:8). . . . But the soul is moved by a divine love and ardor when, on seeing the beauty and glory of the WORD of God, it falls in love with his splendor and is thereby struck with a kind of arrow and suffers a wound of love. For this WORD is the "image" and glory "of the invisible God, the first-born of all creation, in whom all things were created, in heaven and on earth, visible and invisible" (Col 1:15). Whoever then has a spirit capable of bringing together and considering the glory and splendor of all these things which have been created in him, struck by their brilliance and pierced by the magnificence of their beauty as if, as the prophet says, "by a select arrow" (Isa 49:2), he will receive from it a saving wound and will burn with the blessed fire of its love. But we must also be aware: just as the outer man can get caught in forbidden and unlawful love and, for example, not love his wedded wife but a prostitute or an adulteress, so too can the inner man, or the soul, fall in love not with its legitimate spouse which we have pointed out is the WORD of God, but with some seducer. . . . Sometimes this spiritual love of the soul also becomes inflamed towards certain spirits of evil. . . .

But one should also be aware that it is impossible for human nature not to be always in love with something. For everyone who comes to the age called puberty loves something, whether incorrectly when loving something improper, or correctly and usefully when loving something proper. . . . This then is the love spoken of in this Song of Songs in which the blessed soul becomes inflamed with love towards the WORD of God and sings in the Spirit that wedding song of love in which the church is united to her heavenly spouse, Christ, desiring to become one with him through the WORD so as to conceive by him and become able "to be saved by this chaste bearing of children — if they continue in faith and holiness with modesty" (1 Tim 2:15). These children are conceived from the seed of the WORD and carried and brought to term by the spotless church, the soul. . . . And one should know that there is as much that should be said about this love as there is about God, who of course is himself love. . . . "Let us love one another, for love is of God"; and a few words later: "God is love" (1 Jn 4:7–8). This is affirming that God himself is love and, further, that whoever is "of God" is love. But who would be "from God" if not he who says: "I have come from God and have come into this world" (cf. Jn 16:27–28)? But if God the Father is love and the Son is love, and this "love" and "love" are one and in no way different, it follows that the Father and the Son are one and in no way different. . . . And because "God is love," and the Son, who is "of God," is "love" (1 Jn 4:7–8), he looks for something like this in us so that through this love which is in Christ Jesus, we might become related to God, who is love, through the name of love as if through a family relationship — as can be inferred from the words of one already bound to God: "Who shall separate us from the love of God which is in Christ Jesus our Lord?" (Rom 8:35, 39).

Now this love leads every human being to his neighbor. For this reason the Savior reproved someone who thought that a just soul does not have obligations of love towards one who is involved in sin. This is why he invented the parable which tells that "a certain man fell among robbers" while "he was going down from Jerusalem to Jericho"; he reproves the "priest" and the "levite" who "seeing him half dead, passed by," but he embraces the "samaritan who had compassion." Jesus' answer confirmed that this was the neighbor for the one who asked the question; and he added: "Go and do likewise" (Lk 10:30–37). For by nature we are all neighbors to each other; but by works of charity, a neighbor becomes the person who can do good to someone who is helpless. Hence our Savior became our neighbor and did not pass us by when we were lying half-dead from the wounds of robbers. One must therefore be aware that the love of God always tends towards God from whom it takes its origin, and it also looks to the neighbor with whom it has in common that it is likewise created in incorruption.

Thus it is that the name of love belongs first of all to God, which is why we are commanded "to love God with our whole heart, and with our whole soul, and with our whole strength" (cf. Lk 10:27) as the one from whom we have our very capacity to love. Doubtless contained in this is our obligation to love also wisdom and justice and piety and truth and all the other virtues as well; for it is one and the same thing to love God and to love the good. Secondly, by way of a transferred and derived title, we are commanded to "love our neighbor as ourself" (cf. Lk 10:27). . . .

God thus is love. For just as "no one knows the Father except the Son and any one to whom the Son chooses to reveal him" (Mt 11:27), so too "no one knows" love "except the Son." And so too, "no one knows the Son," since he "is love" itself, "except the Father." But also, in view of the fact that he is called love, it is the Holy Spirit alone who "proceeds from the Father" (Jn 15:26) and thus knows what is in God just as "the spirit of a man knows that man's thoughts" (cf. 1 Cor 2:11). Therefore this "Counselor, the Spirit of truth who proceeds from the Father," goes about looking for worthy and capable souls to whom to reveal the greatness of this "love" which "is of God" (cf. 1 Jn 4:7).

THE INNER SENSES

SPIRITUAL SENSE AND SPIRIT-DISCERNMENT

Senses for God

Working from scattered words in scripture and from his own doctrine of the "double" human being, Origen was the first to build up the doctrine of the spiritual senses which has remained a core element of all later mystical theology. This inner "divine" faculty of perception and the great variety of its realizations is, so to speak, the form in which the numerous aspects of the law (for Christians now superseded) still live on in Christian life. For through grace Christians have received a sensory capacity for the divine which, in its delicacy and precision, can be refined endlessly, and which indicates to them ever more correctly what God wants from them in all of life's situations. One can call these senses "mystical" in the broad sense, but they are, at least initially, given along with grace itself and as such are not really mystical phenomena, still less an unveiled experience of God. In many things they coincide with the "gifts of the Holy Spirit."

Scripture uses expressions of sentient activities even of God. This shows the possibility of a spiritual "super-sensibility" ['Übersinnlichkeit'] (536). The spiritual differences among human beings show from their side that abstract laws can never regulate these spiritual individualities in all their richness; inner life must have instead the bright variety of a higher sensibility (537). Even though in the last analysis these senses are always reaching out towards God, the sole inner teacher (538), the divine WORD still encounters the soul in such a variety of ways that it satisfies each "sense" in a different way (539–540). The great variety of the inner sensibility (541–544). Just as God can be felt with inner senses, so too can God's contrary, spiritual death (545). The withering away of these senses as a sign of this death (546). The necessity and sublimity of the spiritual senses (547–548).

36 But we repeat: we do not say in accord with the error of the Jews, or even of some of our own people who make the same mistake, namely, that since human weakness is unable to hear anything about God except through things and words that are known to it, to think, therefore, that God acts in a human manner and with members like ours. This is contrary to the faith of the church. What we do say is this: whether he breathes in the heart of each saint or makes the sound of a voice come to his ears, God is said to have spoken to human beings. And so when he indicates that it is known to him what each one says or does, he says that he "hears"; and when he indicates that something unjust is being done by us, he says he is "angry," and when he complains we are ungrateful for his gifts, he says he "repents," making his point by means of these feelings which are customary among human beings, but not actually using these members which are those of a corporeal nature.

37 Now all of us human beings are alike, but each of us has his own distinguishing characteristics, in our face or height or carriage, or in the way we act. . . . And the same diversity that there is in facial characteristics is found also in souls. . . . Everyone who can read knows the twenty-four letters . . . and with them writes all that can be written. And yet the letter *A*, for example, which Paul writes is different from what Peter writes; and thus you will find in every person who writes different ways of writing each individual letter. Thus the handwriting of each individual is recognized by certain characteristic signs and traits. Even though the basic signs are the same, there are still in the very similarity of the letters great differences in the way they are written. . . . We pass on now to the movements of the spirit and of souls, by which movements they are stirred to do something. Examine the "handwriting" and see how, for example, the soul of Paul presents its chastity, and how the soul of Peter does this as well; there is a certain chastity that is uniquely Peter's and another that is Paul's. . . . It is the same way with wisdom and all the other virtues. Now if even in these cases we have mentioned as examples it is possible for there to be some difference in the particular way they possess the virtues, even though they are one through the Spirit of God, how much more will the souls of the rest of us have unique characteristics in their actions and virtues.

38 It is sound doctrine that the true teacher of virtue cannot be a human being. "He who teaches men wisdom," as it says in the Psalms (94:10), is none other than God. God teaches by pouring light into

the soul of the learner and illuminating the mind with the true light, his own WORD. And even though we are taught by just men who have received the grace of teaching, it is still the Lord who teaches us through them; the very insight we gain and the opening of our hearts to receive the divine teaching is brought about through the grace of God.

539   Although Christ is one in substance, he gives himself in a different way to each, in accord with the need of each one in whom he works.

540   Since Christ is a "fountain" and "rivers of living water flow from him" (cf. Jn 7:38), and since he is "bread" and gives "life," it should not seem strange that he is also "nard" and "gives forth fragrance" and is the "ointment" (cf. Cant 1:12) by which those who are anointed themselves become Christ, as it says in the Psalm: "Touch not my anointed ones" [literally: "my Christs"] (Ps 105:15). And perhaps, according to what the Apostle says, in those "who have their faculties trained by practice to distinguish good from evil" (cf. Heb 5:14), each one of the senses of the soul becomes Christ. For that is why he is called the "true light" (cf. 1 Jn 2:8) so that the souls might have eyes with which to be illuminated; and why he is called the "Word" (cf. Jn 1:1), that they might have ears with which to hear; and why he is called "bread of life" (Jn 6:35), that the souls might have a sense of taste with which to taste. So too is he called "ointment" or "nard" so that the soul's sense of smell might receive the fragrance of the WORD. And so too is he called perceivable, and touchable by hand, and the "WORD became flesh" (cf. Jn 1:14), so that the inner hand of the soul might be able to make contact with the Word of life. But all this is one and the same WORD of God which, in each of these, is adapted to the movements of prayer and leaves no sense of the soul untouched by his grace.

541   "We hurry after you, after the fragrance of your ointments" (cf. Cant 1:3, 4). And this happens, as we said, only when his fragrance has been perceived. What do you think they will do when the WORD of God takes over their hearing and sight and touch and taste? — and when he gives to each of their senses the powers of which they are naturally capable? — so that the eye, once able to see "his glory, glory as of the only Son from the Father" (Jn 1:14), no longer wants to see anything else, nor the hearing want to hear anything other than the "WORD of life" (1 Jn 1:1) and "salvation" (Acts 13:26). And the "hand" which "has touched something of the Word of life" (1 Jn 1:1) will not touch anything else which is material, fragile, and subject to decay, nor will the taste, once it has "tasted the goodness of the WORD

of God" (Heb 6:5) and his flesh and the "bread which has come down from heaven" (Jn 6:33, 52–58), be willing to taste anything else after this.

542   There are the more divine senses which Solomon calls divine (cf. Prov 2:3, 5) and which Jeremiah says are the "senses of the heart" (cf. Jer 4:19) and which are called by Paul writing to the Hebrews: "faculties trained by practice to distinguish good from evil" (Heb 5:14).

543   The holy prophets discovered this divine faculty of sensing and seeing and hearing in a divine manner, and of tasting and smelling in the same way they touched the Word with faith in a way that was, so to speak, simultaneously sensing and non-sensing, so that it poured over them like a healing rain.

544   For just as in the body there are the different senses of tasting and seeing, so are there, as Solomon says, divine faculties of perception. One of them is the seeing and contemplating power of the soul, the other, a faculty of taste for receiving spiritual food. And since the Lord, as the bread come down from heaven (cf. Jn 6:51), can be tasted and is food for the soul, and since, as wisdom, he is visible, of whose beauty Solomon confesses to be a lover when he says: "I became a lover of her beauty" (cf. Wis 8:2), . . . the Psalm accordingly says: "O taste and see that the Lord is good" (Ps 34:8).

545   And just as the Lord can be tasted and seen, so too can his adversary, death, be tasted and seen. That death can be tasted is established in the words: "There are some standing here who will not taste death . . ." (Mt 16:28); . . . that he can be seen, in the words: "If any one keeps my word, he will never see death" (Jn 8:51). . . . Consider too whether there is not also an odor of death in the wounds of sin, of which the scripture says: "My wounds grow foul and fester" (Ps 38:5), and the odor of death which was in Lazarus. . . .

546   For just as in bodily death the senses decay so that no one receives anything further through the body, neither hearing nor smelling nor tasting, or through the touch, so too with the person who loses the spiritual senses in the soul so as not to see God nor hear the WORD nor smell the sweet fragrance of Christ nor taste the goodness of the WORD of God (cf. Heb 6:5): such persons are rightly called dead. This was the way the coming of Christ found us, but he has given us life through his grace.

547   For one should not pay just casual or arbitrary attention to what the apostle says about the "perfect," namely, that they "have their faculties trained by practice to distinguish good from evil" (Heb 5:14). To clarify this, let us first take an example from these bodily

senses, and then come to those divine senses which the scripture calls
the senses of the "inner man." If therefore the bodily eye is to exercise
the faculty of seeing, it should, without obstruction and error, perceive
the colors of bodies and their sizes and qualities. For if the sight is
hindered by darkness or some infirmity, and sees red where there is
white, or green where there is black, or thinks something is straight
when it is curved and winding, the judgment of the mind will doubtless be confused and one course of action taken instead of another. So
too the inner sense: if it is not "trained" by practice and diligence,
. . . but the darkness of ignorance and inexperience covers its eyes,
or the eyes themselves are infected by some disease, it becomes wholly
incapable of distinguishing good from evil (cf. Heb 5:14). As a consequence, it does evil instead of good and misjudges the good as something evil.

548   As long as Moses was in Egypt and was being "instructed in all the
wisdom of the Egyptians," he was not weak in voice nor slow in
tongue, nor did he claim to be without eloquence. For he was, compared to the Egyptians, of powerful voice and incomparable eloquence. But when he began to hear the voice of God and take on
divine eloquence, then he understood that his voice was thin and
weak, that his tongue was slow and obstructed (cf. Exod 4:10); then
he confessed himself to be dumb when he began to recognize that true
WORD which "was in the beginning with God" (Jn 1:1-2). . . . The
rational human being, when compared with the dumb animals, will
seem eloquent. . . . But if we consider the divine WORD itself and
gaze upon the divine wisdom, we will prove to be far more of a dumb
animal in relation to God than the animals are in relation to us. This
indeed was what the blessed David saw when, weighing himself in
comparison with divine wisdom, he said: "I was like a beast toward
thee" (Ps 73:22). It was therefore in this sense that the greatest of the
prophets, Moses, tells God in this passage that he is "weak of voice
and slow of tongue" (Exod 4:10). Blessed are they whose mouth God
opens for them to speak. I fear, however, that there are some whose
mouth is opened by the devil. . . . See what is written of Judas, how
it is told that "Satan entered into him" and how "the devil had put it
into his heart to betray him" (Jn 13:2, 27). And it was the same Satan
that opened his mouth to "confer with the chief priests and Pharisees
how he might betray him to them" (cf. Lk 22:4) when he had received
the money. . . . Without the grace of the Holy Spirit it is not possible
to distinguish between mouths and words of this kind. Thus, in the

classification of spiritual graces it is also added that some are given the gift of the discernment of spirits (cf. 1 Cor 12:10). It is therefore a spiritual grace by which the spirit is discerned, as the Apostle says in another place: "Test the spirits to see whether they are of God" (1 Jn 4:1). But just as God opens the mouth of the saints, so, I think, does God open the ears of the saints to hear the divine words. For this is what the prophet Isaiah says: "May the Lord open my ear that I may know when the word should be spoken" (Isa 50:4, 5).

The Spiritual Battle

The senses do not merely bring about the communication of the spirit with God, they are also senses for the discernment of good and evil. For the interior life is a battle which the soul wages for God against the devil. This concept of the "spiritual battle" also comes, for the most part, from Origen. We owe to him even the particular formulations which, by way of Basil, have stayed alive right up to the [Ignatian] book of the Exercises.

Origen does not, of course, as do some later Fathers, see the devil in every temptation and disorder of nature (549). It is only when one has given in to the natural beginnings of disorder that the Evil One gets involved in the act (550–551). Thus, temptation brings to light an already existing inner disorder (552) which is only driven further by the enemy power (553). If this battle is about the growth of the image of God in the soul (554), it is a growth that by its very nature takes place in battle (555). For if this growth consists in the following of Christ, the soul is thereby drawn into the great, cosmic battle which Christ our field marshal wages against the kingdom of darkness (556–559).

549   The more simple among those who believe in Christ the Lord think that all the sins which human beings commit are caused by enemy powers attacking the mind of the sinners. . . . They think, for example, that if there were no devil, no one would ever sin. But we, examining the matter more carefully, do not agree, especially in view of what obviously comes about from bodily necessity. Or is one supposed to think that the devil concerns himself with our eating and drinking? . . . I for one do not think that human beings could practice such moderation, even if there were no allurements from the devil. No one, I think, could fully observe moderation and control

without having learned this by long practice and experience. . . .
And don't you think that, in the longing for sexual satisfaction, or in
moderating natural desires, something similar would happen to us?

550   Within you is the battle you are to fight; the evil structure which
must be torn down is within; your enemy comes from your own heart.

551   The enemy would not grow strong against us, nor would the devil
himself be able to do anything in us, unless we gave him strength by
our vices. Our enemy would be quite weak against us if we did not
make him strong by sinning, and if he did not find through our sins a
place to enter and take over.

552   Now the usefulness of temptation is something like this: what has
come into our soul and is hidden from everyone except God, and
even from ourselves, is brought to light by temptations.

553   Thus the obvious reason for this is that, just as in good things the
human will is in itself insufficient for bringing the good to completion
(for whatever comes to perfection does so only with God's help), so
too with the bad: the beginning and, so to speak, the seeds of sins we
receive from the things that have their natural place in our lives. But
when we indulge ourselves more than what is sufficient and do not
resist the first inclination of intemperance, then the enemy force, taking possession of the place of this first sin, pushes and drives in every
way possible to try to increase the sins as much as possible.

554   "My soul magnifies the Lord" (Lk 1:46). Just as the soul of the just
person magnifies the Lord through the greatness of its life and spirit,
so does another person lessen him through the evil that is within him.
But the Lord is certainly neither lessened nor decreased; what happens is that, in place of the image of the Savior, we put on other images, and in place of the image of the WORD, the image of wisdom,
justice and the other virtues, we take on the form of the devil.

555   When a human soul has united itself with the WORD of God, it
should have no doubt that it will immediately have enemies, and that
the friends it used to have will be turned into enemies; and it should
not expect to suffer this only from men, but it should also know for
sure that it will be threatened by the contrary powers and the spirits
of evil.

556   Just as there are many orders under God, so too in the opposing
camps there are not only powers but also "world rulers of this present
darkness" and "spiritual hosts of wickedness in the heavenly places"
(Eph 6:12), and perhaps also principalities. For I think that everything that is on God's side also has its corresponding opposite.

557   "Many are my persecutors and my adversaries" (Ps 119:157). The multitude refers to visible and invisible enemies whose persecutions and tribulations take many forms. For some, pretending friendship, suggest pleasures; but others reveal their enmity and apply all kinds of temptations.

558   The Apostle says that there is not just one principality among the "contrary powers," but several, against which he and all of us have to do battle. But I think that all these have a prince, one so to speak more prominent in evil and more accomplished in vice who, as the sole leader of all the princes, and as master of all this wicked warfare, makes war on the whole world. Meanwhile, each of them in his own way tries to entice us to particular individual sins.

559   Does not the leader of our army, the Lord and savior Jesus Christ call out now to his soldiers and say: Whoever is "fearful and anxious of heart" (cf. Judg 7:3), let him not come to war with me? For this is also what he says in the gospels in other words but with the same meaning: "Whoever does not take his own cross and come after me is not worthy of me" (Mt 10:38; Lk 14:27), and again: "Whoever does not renounce all that he has cannot be my disciple" (Lk 14:33). Is not Christ thus culling out the fearful and anxious and sending them from his camp? . . . But don't let such a life of warfare turn you away; there really is nothing difficult, nothing arduous or impossible in it.

The Nature and Discernment of Spirits

The following "rules for the discernment of spirits" which antici- pate to an astonishing extent the Ignatian discernment rules derive from the activity of the spiritual senses. They provide massive confirma- tion of the extent to which Origen's theological thought has an ascetic- mystical, inner, dramatic life. As in their later forms, these rules of discernment are related to two "spirits" which (in the transitional element which we have already discovered in the concept of spirit) simultaneously signify both two human "spiritualities" and two ac- companying "spirits" (guardian angel and personal devil), and finally the highest opposition of God-"Spirit" and satanic "spirit." Only in this multiplicity can the perspectival situation covered by the rules be somehow described. But in the end, the various "spirits" clearly converge in the Spirit of God of which they are the many mani- festations. The immediate vitality and liveliness of these insights is so self-evident that no further analysis is needed (560–603).

560   It is not possible for composite human beings, as long as "the desires of the flesh are" still "against the Spirit and the desires of the Spirit are against the flesh" (Gal 5:7), to celebrate a feast with their whole being. For whoever celebrates in the spirit lets the body suffer . . . or celebrating according to the flesh leaves no room for the spirit to celebrate.

561   For each person there are two angels, one good and one bad. If there are good thoughts in our heart and the spirit of justice is flourishing, there is no doubt that the good angel is speaking to us. But if evil thoughts are harbored in our heart, it is the devil's angel who is speaking to us.

562   Our soul is either "enlightened with" Christ, "the true light" (Jn 1:9) which never goes out, or, if it does not have that light which is eternal, it is doubtless illumined by a temporal and extinguishable light, i.e., by him who "disguises himself as an angel of light" (2 Cor 11:14) and fills the hearts of the sinners with a false light so that what is really passing and subject to decay might seem good and valuable.

563   When we see that a soul is confused by sins, vices, sadness, anger, desires and greed, then we know that she is the one whom the devil is leading off into Babylon (cf. Ezek 17:12). But if in the depth of the heart calmness, serenity and peace bring forth their fruit, then we know that Jerusalem dwells within; that is, the vision of peace is within her.

564   We have it in our power, when the evil force begins to entice us to evil, to drive away the base suggestions and resist the wicked enticements and commit no guilty act whatsoever.

565   The adversary is always walking with us. He never leaves us alone in his search for an opportunity to trap us and bring us down.

566   It is obvious, then, and demonstrable in many ways that the human soul, while in the body, is subject to the influence of various good and evil spirits. . . . One is subject to the influence of the good spirit when being moved and called to good things and inspired to heavenly or divine things . . . in such a way, of course, that it remains up to the person's free will and judgment whether to follow or not to follow. Hence, from this obvious discernment, it can be seen when the soul is moved by the presence of the better spirit. That would be when it suffers not the least disturbance or sadness of spirit from what is being breathed into it.

567   "We went through fire and through water" (Ps 66:12). "Water" and "fire" are opposites. Unpurified human beings suffer the same [contradictions] to this day: they are fearful and bold, they practice

polytheism and are godless, they love without modesty and hate immediately afterwards.

568 "You will hear of wars . . .; see that you are not alarmed; for this must take place"; for it is not unusual for such spiritual battles to be waged with all kinds of arguments against the just to confuse them and to drive their souls to doubt . . . "but the end" which we seek "is not yet" (Mt 24:6), for we must get ourselves settled down and established in peace so that we can be without fear and not be upset by upheavals so that we can move to the peaceful end that lies beyond all this.

569 "My soul has gone through a torrent" (cf. Ps 124:5 LXX). Temptations are called a "torrent" because they are not lasting: they attack the spirit suddenly, and then dry up again and go away.

570 "Listlessness" [*akēdia*] is a simultaneously existing feeling of irritation and desire, a dissatisfaction with the present and a longing for what is not there. Drowsiness is the spiritual soul's neglect of the virtues and of the knowledge of God. Sleep is the voluntary separation of the spiritual soul from real life.

571 Consolation [*paraklēsis*] is the repose of the soul after labors.

572 Consolation is the recreation of the soul after labors.

573 "The delight [of the just] will be in the fullness of peace" (Ps 37:11; cf. LXX). But the "fullness of peace" is the quiet of the soul together with its vision into the true nature of things.

574 When the Spirit of God sees our spirit struggling in its battle against the flesh, and clinging to Him, He stretches forth his hand and helps its weakness. And just as a teacher with an uneducated, totally illiterate student must, to be able to teach him, come down to the starting level of the student, and must himself first pronounce the names of the letters so that the student can learn by repeating, and just as the teacher himself becomes somewhat like the beginning student, speaking and reflecting the way the beginner would speak and reflect, so too does the Holy Spirit: when he sees our spirit become upset by the attacks of the flesh and not know how or what to pray, he himself begins the prayer which our spirit, if it still desires to be a disciple of the Holy Spirit, will continue: he himself utters groans which will teach our spirit to groan in order to reconcile itself with God. However, if the Spirit teaches, but our spirit . . . does not follow, the teaching of the master becomes, through our own fault, sterile in us.

575 It is Christ who commands the wind and the sea and creates the great calm so that the sailors can reach the shore toward which they are pressing (cf. Mk 6:45–51 parr; Jn 6:16–21 parr).

576   When you are sailing on a ship, you see the land and the hills and the mountains passing by. However, it is not because they are being moved that they seem to recede, but because you are passing by on a favorable wind. It is the same here: when the Holy Spirit breathes through and inspires your mind, you sail along successfully on a favorable wind; you pass by in the senses all these visible things because they are temporal, and you gaze upon those which are eternal; and you say, doubtless, that all these visible things even now do not exist, because in the future, they will not.

577   At all times we need the memory of God's words (cf. Ps 119:55) but especially when darkness surrounds me and the walls hide me, when impure desire enters in and disturbs the higher part of the soul.

578   Those who suffer tribulation and are still not reduced, let them know that they are to be freed from their tribulation and led to the holy spaciousness of God . . . as it is written: "You have given me room" (Ps 4:1).

579   I think that just as our sun makes days for our world, so too does "the sun of righteousness" (Mal 4:2) produce some spiritual days which are illumined by the brilliance of truth and the lamp of wisdom.

580   In two ways is God said to give, either by permitting or by actually doing. One can say, in the same way, that it is the sun that makes the day and the night; however it makes the day by shining, but the night by going away.

581   If "the way that leads to life is narrow and hard" (cf. Mt 7:14), then you must have much bitterness in this life and be separated from all sweetness. Or do you not know that your festival is to be celebrated with bitter herbs?

582   If examples be necessary, take the case of the man in the First Epistle to the Corinthians who "lived with his father's wife" (1 Cor 5:1). For evil of this kind cannot come about without the devil having something to do with it. But he repented of that evil, as the scripture attests, and grieved for it "with a godly grief," such a grief as "produces a repentance that leads to salvation" (2 Cor 7:9–10). But after he had become sad in this way, the devil once again approached to try to exaggerate this sadness beyond measure so that the sadness itself would no longer be "godly," . . . and Satan could overwhelm him in "excessive sorrow" (cf. 2 Cor 2:7). Knowing this in advance, the Apostle advises the Corinthians to reaffirm their love for him (cf. 2 Cor 2:8), giving as his reason: lest someone in such a situation be overwhelmed

by excessive sorrow, "for we are not ignorant of his [Satan's] designs" (2 Cor 2:11).

83   Not only does the suffering of the saints have no narrowness, it even has breadth; for it is the just person who says: "You have given me room when I was in distress" (Ps 4:1). . . . Therefore God does not merely dwell in this breadth of heart in the saints, he also walks therein. But into the hearts of the sinners which is all narrowness, the devil, because they have made room for him, indeed enters, but not to dwell or to walk, because there is no room there: instead he slinks around therein as if in a cave — for he is a serpent.

84   Evil works constrict the evil one in himself. The love of God makes room in our souls.

85   "Jesus lifted up his eyes and said" (Jn 11:41). . . . From this we learn that Jesus separated his spirit from intercourse with those here below and lifted it up on high, directing it in prayer to his Father who is above all. But someone might wish to contrast this with the tax collector who did not dare to lift up his eyes and who struck his breast saying: "O God, be merciful to me a sinner" (Lk 18:13). The answer to this would be that, just as it is not desirable that the grief of repentance towards God be active in everyone at all times, . . . and it must be practiced with moderation and not excessively, . . . so too it may not be desirable for all to stand far off and not dare to raise their eyes (Lk 18:13).

86   There is a certain spirit within the human beings; far be it from me that I should walk after it! Instead, understanding the Holy Spirit of God, I will walk after the Lord my God. These prophets, then, who prophesy out of their own hearts and walk after the spirit — not so much God's as their own . . . they see nothing (cf. Ezek 13:2–3).

87   Let us consider whether the following makes sense: Just as it is good for the soul to follow the spirit, which happens when the spirit conquers the flesh, so too does it seem to be bad for it to follow the "flesh which struggles against the spirit" (cf. Gal 5:17) and wants to bring the soul under its influence. Yet, it might still turn out to be more helpful in the long run for the soul to be dominated by the flesh than to remain in the control of its own will. For while it is in that condition, it is said to be "neither hot nor cold" (Rev 3:15) but to be stuck in a kind of tepid middle state in which it could find conversion to be a slow and quite difficult process. But if it clings to the flesh, then from the very evils which it suffers from its carnal vices it sometimes

becomes as it were so surfeited and satiated and wearied by the awful burdens of luxury and lust that it can more easily and quickly be converted from material filth to spiritual grace and a desire for heavenly things.

588   A "hard heart" (cf. Rom 2:5) seems to be spoken of in scripture when the human mind, like wax, hardened by the ice of iniquity, no longer accepts the seal of the divine image.

589   The very strength and the very foundation of the saints is the Lord. None of them is strong or firmly founded outside of the Lord. But "firm" is not the same as "hard," nor is "strong" the same as the strength of a madman.

590   The arrogance [of pride] is the hypocrisy of greatness.

591   When our heart is not hardened, it is made to rise like incense before the Lord.

592   For, left to itself, I do not think that human nature could do battle against "angels" and "heights and depths" and "anything else in all creation" (Rom 8:38–39). But when it senses the Lord present and dwelling within it, confident of God's help, it will say: "The Lord is my light and my salvation; whom shall I fear?" (Ps 27:1).

593   I know that a soul can be dwelled in; I know that a soul can be empty. If it does not have God, it does not have Christ either, for he said: "I and my Father will come to him and make our home with him" (cf. Jn 14:23).

594   "And Jesus left the temple" (Mt 24:1). Since therefore all are holy temples of God because of the Spirit of God dwelling within them, if they sin they become responsible for their own emptiness, responsible for Christ leaving them, and responsible for what was once a temple of the Son of God turning into an abandoned house.

595   If in passing judgment, for example, you give preference to a person of power or suppress the truth for the sake of a friend, you are not paying due honor to justice and truth; you are instead dishonoring justice and making a mockery of truth. And since Christ is justice and sanctification and truth (cf. 1 Cor 1:30), you are like those who struck Christ and spat in his face and struck his head with a reed and put a crown of thorns around his brow.

596   Just as with physical light which enables those with healthy eyes to see both the light itself and other sensible objects, so too does God come with a certain power to the mind of each one. As long as those to whom he comes are not all closed off and their ability to see clearly not impeded by their passions, God makes himself known and leads

those illumined by him to a knowledge of other spiritual things. But it is no wonder if some, who are expert in the arts or sciences or very advanced in a knowledge of some ethical and logical problems, are nevertheless ignorant of God. Their understanding is like the eye that examines everything except the sun.

97 "The spirit rested upon them and they all prophesied" (cf. Num 11:25). We do not read that the Spirit rested on anyone, but only on the saints and blessed ones. For the Spirit of God rests upon those who are "pure in heart" (cf. Mt 5:8) and upon those who purify their souls from sin. But on the other hand, he does not dwell in a body subject to sin even though he may have once dwelled therein; for the Holy Spirit cannot bear the company and community of the spirit of evil. For it is certain that in the time of sin the spirit of evil is present in the heart of each one, wreaking his havoc. When the evil spirit is given room and is accepted by us through bad thoughts and evil desires, the Holy Spirit, feeling grieved and crowded out so to speak, flees from us. . . . But when in the end, because of their purity of heart and integrity of mind . . . the Holy Spirit rests on them, he is immediately at work in them, wasting no time wherever he finds material he can work with. For the scripture says: "The spirit rested upon them and they prophesied" (Num 11:25).

98 The Apostle talks about the particular fruits of good works: . . . "The fruit of the Spirit is love, joy, peace" (Gal 5:22). But "the works of the flesh" which he reproves are listed in great number (cf. Gal 5:19-21). But should it be objected that what is written in the Psalms: "You shall eat the fruit of the labor of your hands" (Ps 128:2) both has a positive meaning and signifies a great number, it should also be recognized that, just as the merchant dealing with many pearls, upon finding one precious pearl, sold everything in order to buy that one (Mt 13:45-46), so too must one start from many fruits in order to strive for the one fruit of perfection.

99 "He led forth the winds from his treasure house." There are indeed certain treasures of the winds, treasures of the spirits: "the spirit of wisdom and understanding, the spirit of counsel and might, the spirit of knowledge and piety, the spirit of the fear of God, the spirit of power and love" (cf. Isa 11:2-3; 2 Tim 1:7). . . . What are these treasures? "In whom are the treasures of wisdom and knowledge" (Col 2:3)? These treasures are in Christ. . . . All these treasures have one single treasure in which they dwell. That is why Paul says: "in whom are hid the treasures of wisdom and knowledge" (Col 2:3). And as I

sell the many others in order to buy "the one pearl of great value" (cf. Mt 13:46), I thus come to the treasure of treasures, to the Lord of Lords, to the king of kings (cf. Rev 17:19; 14:16), when I become worthy of the spirits which live with the treasures of God.

600   The different gifts of the Spirit are thus called many spirits by Paul.

601   God "delivers us from evil" (cf. Mt 6:13) not when the enemy against whom we are struggling in no way attacks us with any of his tricks or helpers, but when, courageously resisting his attacks, we are victorious. . . . . God delivered Job not because the devil did not receive permission to subject him to such and such temptations (he did receive this permission), but because in all that befell him Job did not sin before the Lord, but was proven to be just (cf. Job 1:9-12, 22).

602   For Christ wins over no one against his will, but only by persuasion, for he is the WORD of God.

603   God forces no one to come along against his will. For if he were forcing him he would not say: "Come to me all who labor and are heavy laden, and I will give you rest" (Mt 11:28), and: "If you are willing and obedient, you shall eat the good of the land" (Isa 1:19). Paul "was caught up to the third heaven" (2 Cor 12:2), but only after he had given himself to God.

HEARING

> *The tremendous significance of the doctrine of the inner senses is revealed fully only by looking into the activity of the individual senses. Each sense contains a different mode of spiritual contact with the divine. "Hearing" is the inner readiness and "listening attitude" of the soul towards God for the inner dialogue which takes place without sound from the soul to God (604–606) and from God to the soul (607–609). Sin causes deafness in the soul and silence from God (610–612); but quiet readiness brings about an ever more mysterious and close union with God (613–618). Nevertheless, this "hearing" can be kept up only when it is simultaneously action (619).*

604   For one must be aware that human beings have in the depth of their heart a bodiless voice which they, after recollecting themselves and after entering their chamber and closing the door of their senses, and being wholly outside the body, send up to him who alone can hear such a voice.

5   But meanwhile, Moses is crying out to the Lord. How does he cry
out? No sound of his voice is audible, and yet God says to him: "Why
do you cry to me?" (Exod 14:15). I would like to know how the saints
cry voicelessly to the Lord. The Apostle teaches that "God has sent the
Spirit of his Son into our hearts, crying, 'Abba! Father!'" and he
adds: "The Spirit himself intercedes for us with sighs too deep for
words." And further: "He who searches the hearts of men knows what
is the mind of the Spirit, because the Spirit intercedes for the saints
according to the will of God" (Gal 4:16; Rom 8:26-27). This is how,
through the Holy Spirit's intercession with God, the cry of the saints
is heard through the silence.

6   Believe in God and consecrate yourself to him. Though you be
weak of voice and slow of tongue (cf. Exod 4:10), entrust yourself to
the WORD of God. Afterwards you will say: "I opened my mouth
and drew in the spirit" (Ps 118:131 LXX).

7   If the human voice is defined as air which has been beaten or moved
by the tongue, so too can the voice of God be called air which has
been moved by the divine power or will. And that is why, when a voice
comes from God, it doesn't come to the ears of everyone but only to
those who are supposed to hear it. You can see from this that the
sound is not made by the action of a tongue — otherwise it would be
heard by all — but is controlled by the divine will. That is why we hear
that the WORD of God often came to the prophets and patriarchs
and other saints without the sound of a voice, . . . whereby, to be
brief, the illuminated mind is formed into words by the Spirit of God.
In both ways then . . . one can say that God speaks.

8   "And all were amazed." At what were they amazed? Not at his
questions, although they too were marvelous, but "at his answers" (Lk
2:47). . . . He was asking questions of the teachers and, because
they sometimes could not answer, he himself was giving the answers
to his own questions. . . . Sometimes Jesus asks, sometimes he
answers; and, as we have said, marvelous as his questioning is, his
answering is much more marvelous. Therefore, that we too might
hear him and that he might ask us questions which he would answer
himself, let us beseech him and seek him with intense effort and sorrow so that we might then be able to find him whom we seek. For not
for nothing was it written: "Your father and I have been looking for
you anxiously" (Lk 2:48). Those who are searching for Jesus should
not do so negligently, casually, or just now and then as some do, and
are consequently unable to find him.

609   "'Have you understood all this?' They said to him, 'Yes'" (Mt 13:51). . . . Jesus Christ asks not out of ignorance but because, once having assumed humanity, he makes use of all things that are human, one of which is to ask questions.

610   But how is God supposed to listen to us when we do not listen to him? How is he supposed to do what we want when we do not do what he wants? Yet God wants us to be such that, like Gods, we talk to God. He wants us to be sons of God, to become co-sharers and co-heirs of the Son of God, and say as he said: "Father, I know that you hear me always" (Jn 11:41–42).

611   There is a certain hardness of hearing which is harmful to the human soul. What is this "hardness" or "heaviness"? . . . Sin is, according to scripture, "serious" or "heavy." This is why the Psalmist who sensed his own sins said: "My iniquities . . . weigh like a burden too heavy for me" (Ps 38:4). . . . What is it that makes hearing not hard or heavy but light and easy? The wings of the Word, the wings of virtue (cf. Ps 55:6).

612   But if the Logos who is present and revealing himself is not accepted he threatens to go away, and says: "I go away"; and if we seek him after he has gone away, we will not find him but will die in our sin (cf. Jn 8:21).

613   We do not think that God speaks to us from outside. For those holy thoughts that arise in our heart, they are the way God speaks to us. This is what it means when you hear that God has spoken to such and such a person. That it actually happens this way, scripture is our witness: "Happy the man whose help is from you, Lord; he has prepared steps toward you in his heart" (cf. Ps 83:6 LXX).

614   He does not wish that you remain in the deeds of the flesh and darkness, but that you go out to the desert and come to the place that is free from the storms and waves of the world, to the place of silence and repose. For "the words of the wise are heard in silence and repose" (cf. Qoh 9:17).

615   For how can it be formulated, what the Spirit of God says to God, when at times even our own spirit cannot express in words what it senses and understands?

616   "If you do not hear in secret, your soul will weep" (cf. Jer 17:13). . . . I can hear the law in secret or in the open: . . . Whoever hears in secret the prescriptions of the law concerning the Passover, eats of Christ the Lamb, "for Christ, our paschal lamb, has been sacrificed" (1 Cor 5:7). Knowing what is the flesh of the WORD and knowing

that it is "true food" (cf. Jn 6:55), he receives it; he has heard [or observed] the passover in secret.

7   The more one hears God's words, the more that person will be from God.

8   Those to whom God is silent are "like those who go down to the Pit" (Ps 28:1). . . . Those who go down to the Pit are those who worriedly concern themselves with these cold material things. . . . All sin is cold; but the things of God, as is fitting, are warm.

9   But we beg the mercy of almighty God who makes us "not only hearers" but also "doers of the Word" (Jas 1:22), that he send over us the flood of his water, and wipe out in us what he knows should be wiped out, and vivify what he judges worthy to be vivified, through Christ our Lord and his Holy Spirit.

SIGHT

Inner Sight

There are two different ways of seeing: one according to the flesh and one according to the Spirit; neither is compatible with the other (620–623). By the former we do not mean the outer seeing of the senses, but the sinful seeing-of-oneself in sensible things instead of looking through them to see God (624–625). Not everyone who physically saw Christ also saw him spiritually (626–628). How Jesus can reveal himself simultaneously at various spiritual "stages" (629). Through a spiritual laying on of Christ's hands, we too come to see (630–631), if at the same time we also turn our spiritual countenance toward him and renounce sin (632–634). Still, our view from here below remains scant and dim (635) unless ecstasy snatch us out of the body (636).

0   As human beings, all of us have within us both sight and blindness. Adam could both see and not see. Eve too, before "their eyes were opened," is said to have seen: "The woman saw that the tree was good for food, and that it was a delight to the eyes, . . . and she took of its fruit and ate; and she also gave some to her husband and they ate" (Gen 3:6). They were, therefore, not blind, but could see. Then come the words: "And their eyes were opened" (Gen 3:7). Thus they were still blind and unable to see since their eyes were opened only afterwards. They who before this could see well, after they had disobeyed

the Lord's command, began to see poorly; and after sin had slipped in, they lost the sight of obedience. This is how I understand what God said: "Who makes him dumb or deaf, or seeing or blind? Is it not I, the Lord?" (Exod 4:11). There is an eye of the body with which we view these earthly things, an eye according to the sense of the flesh, of which scripture says: "coming in puffed up without reason by his sensuous mind" (Col 2:18). Over against this we have another, better eye which perceives the things of God. Because it had become blind, Jesus came to make it see.

621 "Their eyes were opened" (Gen 3:7). Opened were those eyes of the senses which had been properly closed in order not to be hindered by distraction from seeing with the eyes of the soul. These eyes which, until then, had been seeing and enjoying God and his paradise, were now, I think, closed by sin.

622 In the same order in which some eyes are closed and others are opened, are also some ears to be closed and others to be opened. . . . Unless the sight of evil things is first shut off, the view of good things will not be opened up.

623 That there is another "face" besides this bodily face of ours is clear from many sources, but it is also noted by the Apostle: "We all with unveiled face, beholding the glory of the Lord, are being changed into his likeness from one degree of glory to another, as from the Lord who is the Spirit" (2 Cor 3:18). All of us human beings have our bodily face unveiled unless we happen to be threatened with danger and difficulty. But the face of which the Apostle speaks is covered in most people and unveiled in only a few. Only the person who has confidence in a blameless, healthy faculty of sense and true faith does not have the veil of misleading confusion and sin, but, because of a pure conscience, contemplates the glory of the Lord with unveiled face.

624 Truly, those who make idols and put confidence in them are like their gods: without senses, without reason, turned into stones and wood. For even when they see great order, beauty and function in creation and this world, they refuse to see the Creator in his creatures. . . . They are blind, seeing the world only with those eyes with which it is seen by dumb animals and wild beasts. For they do not even see that there is reason in the things which they see are governed by reason.

625 "Look, you blind, that you may see!" (Isa 42:18). The blind see when, "seeing the world from the greatness and beauty of created things" (Wis 13:5), they see their Creator.

26   The sight with which God is seen is not that of the body but of the
      mind and spirit. The Savior himself, making this distinction in the
      gospel with just the right words, did not say: "No one" sees "the Father
      except the Son," but: "No one knows the Father except the Son" (Mt
      11:27). And finally, to those whom he allows to see God, he gives the
      "spirit of knowledge" and the "spirit of wisdom" (Isa 11:2; cf. Wis 7:7,
      22), that they might see God through the same spirit. That is why he
      said to his disciples: "He who has seen me has seen the Father" (Jn
      14:9). And surely we will not be so stupid as to think that whoever
      sees Jesus in his body sees also the Father. Otherwise one would have
      to conclude that the "scribes and Pharisees, hypocrites" (cf. Mt 23:13)
      and Pilate who had him scourged (cf. Jn 19:1) and the whole crowd
      which cried out "Crucify, crucify him!" (cf. Lk 23:21), in seeing Jesus
      in the flesh also saw God the Father—which seems not only absurd
      but also blasphemous. For just as, when the crowd was pressing
      around him as he went along with the disciples, none of those pressing
      in and crushing him are said to have "touched" him except she alone
      who, suffering from a "flow of blood . . . came up behind him and
      touched the fringe of his garment." Jesus is speaking of her alone
      when he says: "Some one touched me; for I perceive that power has
      gone forth from me" (Lk 8:42-48 parr). So too, although there were
      many who saw him, of none of them is it written that they "saw" him
      unless they recognized that he is the WORD of God and Son of God
      in whom the Father is said to be simultaneously recognized and seen.

27   The apostles therefore saw the WORD not only because they saw
      Jesus in the flesh, but because they saw the WORD of God.

28   "Now the chief priests and the Pharisees had given orders that if
      any one knew where he was, he should let them know, so that they
      might arrest him" (Jn 11:57). Those who plot against Jesus do not
      know where he is. . . . And also, whoever gets involved with Chris-
      tianity to oppose or attack it, is a Pharisee.

29   It is no great wonder that matter, which is by nature subject to
      modification and change and can be turned into anything the Creator
      wishes, and is capable of taking on any quality the Artificer chooses,
      has at one time the quality of which it is said that "he had no form or
      comeliness" (Isa 53:2), and at another time a quality so glorious, ma-
      jestic and wondrous that the three disciples who went up the moun-
      tain with Jesus "fell on their faces" (cf. Mt 17:6 parr).

30   "And Joseph will lay his hands on your eyes" (Gen 46:4). Just as the
      true Joseph, our Lord and Savior, placed his bodily hand on the eyes

of the blind man and restored him to his lost sight, he also placed his spiritual hands on the eyes of the law (the eyes that were blinded by the bodily understanding of the scribes and Pharisees) and restored their sight so that the spiritual view of and insight into the law would be manifest to those to whom the Lord opens the scriptures.

631   Would that we too, understanding from this that we are blind and do not see, as we sit by the road of the scriptures and hear that Jesus is passing by, might by our prayers make him stop and tell him we want our eyes to be opened (cf. Mt 20:29–34). If we make this request with the desire of seeing what one is given to see when Jesus touches the eyes of the soul, our Savior will be struck with compassion and will touch our eyes which did not see before he came. For he is power and Word and wisdom and everything like this which has been written of him. And at his touch, darkness and ignorance will immediately flee and we will not only see but will also follow him who gave us our sight back for no other reason than that we might always follow him and be led by him to God and that, with the eyes he has opened and with those blessed because of their clean heart, we might see our God (cf. Mt 5:8).

632   "When someone turns to the Lord, this veil is removed; for where the Spirit of the Lord is, there is freedom" (2 Cor 3:16–17). Therefore we must beseech the Lord himself, the Holy Spirit himself, to take away all the fog and darkness which, heaped up by the filth of sin, darkens the vision of our heart, so that we might be able to gaze on the marvelous spiritual meaning of his law, just like the Psalmist who said: "Open my eyes that I may behold wondrous things out of your law" (Ps 119:18).

633   "We slept in our shame, and our dishonor covered us" (Jer 3:25 LXX). We have often spoken of the veil which covers the face of those who do not turn to the Lord. Because of this veil, "whenever Moses is read" (2 Cor 3:15) the sinner does not understand him. . . . For as long as we do "the works of shame" (cf. 2 Cor 4:2), it is clear that we have the veil spoken of in the forty-third Psalm: "And the disgrace of my face covered me" (Ps 43:16 LXX). But those who do no works of shame also do not have this veil. Paul was like that. He said: "We all with unveiled face behold the glory of the Lord" (2 Cor 3:18). . . . If our soul harbors anger against someone, a veil lies over our face. If then we want to say the prayer: "May the light of your countenance be stamped on us, O Lord" (Ps 4:7 LXX), we must first take away the veil. . . . For it is not God who hides his glory from us, but we

ourselves who pull the veil of iniquity over the spirit. . . . For "whenever Moses went in before the Lord . . . the veil was removed" (cf. Exod 34:34–35; 2 Cor 3:1). He is the model of those who turn back to the Lord.

34   "And all flesh shall see the salvation of God" (Lk 3:6; cf. Isa 40:5). You were once flesh, or rather, to say something quite astonishing, while you are still in the flesh, you see the salvation of God.

35   "God blessed Isaac, and he lived at the well of vision" (Gen 25:11 LXX). This is the whole blessing the Lord bestowed on Isaac: that he live at the well of vision. For those who understand, this is a great blessing. May the Lord grant to me too this blessing of being worthy of dwelling at the well of vision. . . . But when will we be able to gain enough merit to be able to pass by the well of vision? Isaac deserved to remain and live in vision; but we, illuminated by God's mercy, can barely sense or suspect even a small part of any vision.

36   The person therefore who is sitting down at midday (cf. Gen 18:1) in contemplation is the one who takes the time to see God. That is why Abraham is said to be waiting not inside the tent but outside, "sitting at the door of his tent" (Gen 18:1). For the mind which keeps itself outside the body and is far from bodily thoughts and the desires of the flesh, and thus set apart from all these things, this is whom God comes to visit.

Faith, Deed and Vision

But vision is the unfolding of a faith that is already there (just as inner hearing is the unfolding of an outer hearing which is the proclamation of doctrine). Faith, however, becomes vision only when it is appropriated as deed. First, there are the stages of faith (637–638), and also its dark side (639). But these stages are, as such, already stages of action, because progress on the "way" of knowledge is necessarily also a walking on the way which is Christ, that is, on "holy ground" (640). Thus knowledge and action mutually affect each other (641); God's light stands equally over both (642). Of course there is also a "truth" which is bare and lifeless; but the truth of God is life (649). Sin kills the capacity to see the essential truth (650). The superiority of the Christian truth is its foundation in action (651–652). The true light is founded in the true life (653). Gradualness of the development (654–655) from faith through hope to love (656–658).

637   For apart from the Word [*logos*], and I mean the perfect Word,[1] it
is impossible for the human being to become sinless.

638   "We will make you images of gold studded with silver" (Cant 1:11).
As long as the soul is still small and undeveloped and "under guardians and trustees" (Gal 4:2) — whether they be doctors of the church or
angels of the "little ones" who are said to "behold always the face of my
Father who is in heaven" (Mt 18:10) — "images of gold" are made for
it. For it is not nourished by the "solid" and strong "foods" (cf. Heb
5:12) of the WORD of God, but is fed on "images." We could say that
it is taught by parables and examples in the way in which Christ himself was said to "increase in wisdom and stature and favor with God
and man" (Lk 2:52). It is thus nourished with "images," and little "or-
namentations of silver" (Cant 1:11) are made for her. For sometimes
even those who are grown up are shown some slight glimpses of the
more hidden mysteries so that they might get a taste of greater things;
for something cannot be desired if it is not even known.

639   Although we are not under that shadow which the letter of the law
was casting (cf. Rom 6:15), we are under a better shadow. For "we
live" in the shadow of Christ "among the nations" (cf. Lam 4:20). And
it is indeed a step forward to come from the "shadow of the law" to the
shadow of Christ so that, since Christ is "the way, and the truth, and
the life" (Jn 14:6), we might be placed first in the shadow of the way
and in the shadow of the life and in the shadow of the truth, and that
we might first "understand in part and in a mirror dimly," so that
afterwards, if we have entered on this "way" which is Christ, we might
come to "understand face to face" what at first we saw only in a
shadow and dimly (cf. 1 Cor 13:12). For no one can come to what is
true and perfect unless he has first had the desire and longing to live
in this shadow (cf. also 1 Chr 29:15).

640   "Make straight the way of the Lord" (Jn 1:23). The way of the Lord
is made straight in two ways: on the theoretical level, clarified with
the truth without any admixture of falsehood, and on the practical
level after the sound contemplation of what should be done to produce an action consistent with a sound theory of conduct. To see
more precisely the meaning of "Make straight the way of the Lord," it
will help to compare it with Proverbs: "Do not swerve to the right or

---

[1] *chōris gar logou. kai tauta teleiou.* It would take a paragraph to begin to
translate these six words. — R.J.D.

to the left" (Prov 4:27). For they who go off in either direction have given up making their path straight; and when they have deviated from the straightness of the path they are no longer worthy of regard. "For the Lord is righteous, he loves righteous deeds, and his face has regard for what is straight" (Ps 11:7 LXX). But he illuminates what he looks upon; hence, those who are the objects of this regard, upon receiving its benefits, say: "The light of your countenance has been stamped upon us, O Lord" (Ps 4:6 LXX). Let us then, as Jeremiah exhorts, stand by the roadside and look and ask for the ancient paths of the Lord; let us see where the good path is and walk in it (cf. Jer 6:16), just as the apostles stood and searched for the ancient paths of the Lord, i.e., the patriarchs and prophets. The apostles searched in their writings and, when they had understood them, they saw the good way, Jesus Christ, who said "I am the way" (Jn 14:6), and they walked in it. For he is the good way which leads the good and faithful servant to the good Father (cf. Mt 25:21). This way is indeed narrow; neither the multitude nor those who are fat can walk on it. It is also trampled on by those who use force to enter it (cf. Mt 11:12; Lk 16:16). . . . For they who fail to take off their shoes and recognize truly that the place on which they are standing and treading is holy ground (cf. Exod 3:5), they are trampling down the living way which is sensitive to the qualities of the people who walk on it. It leads to him who is life and who says: "I am the life" (Jn 14:6). . . . Those who travel on this way are taught to take nothing with them, since the way itself has bread and all that is necessary for life.

641   Therefore, the clean and pure of heart seem to me to be those who have a heart that is purified of all false doctrine. So too, those with guiltless hands pure of sin I consider to be those who lead an irreproachable life. But one must know that just as consistency with the truth makes it impossible for someone with guiltless and sinless hands not to be also of pure and clean heart in relation to false doctrines, so too is it impossible for someone of sound and pure doctrine not to be also of guiltless hands and free of sin (cf. Ps 24:4–5; Prov 20:9; Mt 5:8). For these things go together inseparably: the pure word in the soul and an irreproachable life.

642   Perhaps "the light of men" (Jn 1:4) is a generic concept that covers two different things. . . . For they who possess "the light of men" and share in its rays will both perform and recognize the "works of light," since they have been illuminated by the "light of knowledge" (Hos 10:12).

643   They who, among other things, have learned from the divine WORD and put into practice the following: to bless when "reviled," to endure when "persecuted," to conciliate when "slandered" (cf. 1 Cor 4:12–13), these would be the ones who have set themselves on the right path and are purifying and preparing their soul. They do this in order to distinguish, not just in words, being from becoming and the intellectual from the sensible, and in order to connect the truth with being and avoid in every way the errors connected with becoming. They do this by looking, as they have been taught, not at what is becoming . . . but to the higher things.

644   We live as household sharers in his blessedness because of the sublime spirit of "sonship" which, in the sons of the heavenly Father, cries not with words but with deeds that speak with a loud voice from the inmost heart: "Abba, Father!" (Rom 8:14–16; Gal 4:6).

645   For one cries out "Lord!" in a perfect way when one's works are crying out and saying, "Lord, Lord!" (cf. Mt 7:21).

646   They can be said to "know the works of the Lord" (cf. Judg 2:7) who actually do them. They are ignorant of God's work who do not do it.

647   The fruit of works is the vision of being.

648   To know righteousness means to practice righteousness. Therefore, whoever preaches righteousness and does not practice it does not know righteousness.

649   There is also a truth in unrighteousness. Take for example that spirit of divination which in the Acts of the Apostles (Acts 16:16–18) is reported to have lived in a certain slave girl and to have cried out after the apostles that "these men are servants of the Most High God, who proclaim to us the ways of God." There was truth in these words, for what was said was true. But that truth was not in Christ. Consequently, Paul turned to her and said: "Be quiet, and come out of her." . . . Thus, one must believe that the truth of Christ is there where the other virtues which are described as Christ are also found. That is, where there is justice, peace and the Word of God, there too is the truth of Christ.

650   Just as, if I may so express myself, darkness looked at for a long time destroys the sight of those looking at it, so too death, when seen by those who do not keep the WORD, kills the sight and blinds those who look upon it.

651   Just as we are ahead of the pagans in faith, let us make sure that we also excel them in deeds and works.

652   "His hands shall offer sacrifice to the Lord" (cf. Lev 7:20). Is not the lawgiver clearly proclaiming that it is not the man who is offering the sacrifice, but his hands, that is, his works? For works are what commend a sacrifice to God.

653   Let us not neglect to note that while John might have written: "What came to be in him was the light of men, and the light of men was the life," he wrote just the opposite (cf. Jn 1:4). For he puts "life" ahead of "light of men," even though the "life" and the "light of men" are the same. The reason is that among those who share the life, which is also the light of men, the first thing one comes upon when being illuminated is the divine life we have mentioned. For life must be there first if the living person is to be illuminated.

654   But we must also be aware that this mortification of the deeds of the flesh is accomplished through patience; not suddenly, but gradually.

655   For the will is a quick-acting thing which can easily change. An action, however, is slow, for it requires the practice, the art and the effort of work.

656   Deservedly, however, and as he usually does when he treats of faith, the Apostle also joins hope with it, knowing that hope is inseparably connected with faith, as he says in making this same point in the Epistle to the Hebrews: "Now faith is the assurance of things hoped for" (Heb 11:1). . . . And it seems to me that the first beginning and the very foundation of salvation is faith, the development and expansion of the building is hope, but the perfection and summit of the whole work is love.

657   Would you not say that, just as Abraham "in hope believed against hope" (Rom 4:18), so too do all the sons of the Faith of Abraham believe in all things "in hope against hope," whether it concerns the resurrection of the dead or inheriting the kingdom of heaven or kingdom of God? For to the extent that these things are "against hope" as far as human nature is concerned, to that extent are they "in hope" for those whose hope is from faith, as far as God's power and his faithful promises are concerned. And because the believer believes in hope, faith and hope abide; and from these is born the third and greatest of these: love (cf. 1 Cor 13:13). And I think that faith has the meaning of foundation, hope that of progress, and love that of perfection.

658   For the spiritual knowledge of God is love.

Faith as Seeing

Now that the way from faith to seeing through its living and active appropriation has been described, the "analogy of faith" as such can now be brought out. All Christian understanding rests on the foundation of faith (659) and is only the unfolding of the seed of faith to fully developed, understanding faith (the Augustinian credo ut intelligam). From a merely abstract "in something," faith moves along to a concrete, self-giving believing "in someone" (660). That alone is already something salutary and positive (661). Yet the outer proclamation of the Word is only a means to lead the soul to immediate faith in Christ (662). Faith is not superseded in understanding, but only there does it become fully itself; eschatological faith in the vision of God is the fulfillment of non-understanding faith (663). Yet this way does not mean a leaving behind of the incarnate Christ: rather, union with Christ is made perfect precisely through his flesh (666–667). Faith is grace (668), and understanding is the reward of this grace (669). Perfect faith "includes everything" (670). But even the highest understanding trembles before the awesome power of God (671), nor does it know God here below as he is (672). Faith as the hidden way to God the beloved (673). All-grace (674).

659   Every time we understand, we owe it to our faith that we understand.

660   There is a difference between believing in him and believing in his name. . . . Jesus did not trust himself to those who only believed in his name (cf. Jn 2:23–25). We must, therefore, have belief more in him than in his name so that we will not have to hear what was said to those who worked miracles in his name (cf. Mt 7:22). . . . Those who believe in him are those who tread the narrow and hard path that leads to life and which is found by the very few (cf. Mt 7:14).

661   We ask now, in relation to the great crowds of the faithful who have rid themselves of the great mire of wickedness in which they formerly wallowed, is it better for them to believe without deeper understanding and thus put their morals in order and draw profit from the belief that sins will be punished and good works praised, or is it better to put off their conversion on the basis of a simple faith until they can give themselves a thorough analysis of the reasons? For it is clear that, with few exceptions, all would not draw this profit which comes from a simple faith, but would remain in their life of evil. Thus, whatever

other evidence there is of the fact that the love of the Logos for human beings has not come into their life against God's will, this should be added to the list.

262 Therefore, that believing without knowledge is something less than knowing is clear from the words John records: "If you continue in my word, . . . you will know the truth, and the truth will make you free" (Jn 8:31–32). . . . The twelve first believed, but did not understand; afterward, through faith, they had the beginning of knowledge . . . and finally they made progress in knowledge.

263 "They said to the woman, 'It is no longer because of your words that we believe, for we have heard for ourselves, and we know that this is indeed the Savior of the world'" (Jn 4:42). The Samaritans reject the faith based on the words of the woman, because in hearing the Savior himself they had found something better which enabled them to know "that this is indeed the Savior of the world." And it is certainly better to see the WORD with one's own eyes and hear him teaching and, without using other teachers, impressing images on our mind which then discovers the forms of truth in a most clear manner. That is certainly better than it is not to see him and, not illuminated by his power, only to hear about him through others who see him. For it is impossible for the same affection which comes about in the mind of one who sees, to be experienced by one who has not seen but is only taught by one who has. For it is better to walk by sight than by faith (cf. 2 Cor 5:7).

263a "When he was raised from the dead, his disciples remembered that he had said this; and they believed the scripture and the word which Jesus had spoken" (Jn 2:22). Faith in its full sense is accepting with one's whole soul what is professed at baptism. Now as for the higher sense, since we have already spoken of the resurrection from the dead of the whole body of the Lord, it must be noted that the disciples were "reminded" of the fulfillment of the scriptures which were incomprehensible to them when they were in this life, but which now lay before their eyes showing them of what heavenly things they were copies and shadows (cf. Heb 8:5). They believed in what they formerly did not believe; and they believed in the word of Jesus which, before the resurrection, as the speaker intended to show, they did not understand. For how can one be said in the true sense to believe the scripture when one does not see in it the mind of the Holy Spirit which God wishes us to believe much more than what the letter commands? From this it must be said that none of those who live according to the flesh believe in the spiritual content of the law of whose origin they have no idea. But, they say, more blessed are they who do not see and believe than those who do see and believe, quoting what was said by the Lord to Thomas at the end of the Gospel of John: "Blessed are those who have not seen and yet believe" (Jn 20:29). But he does not call them more blessed . . . for in that view those who come after the apostles are more blessed than the apostles, which is the height of foolishness. But they who are to be blessed must, like the apostles, see in their spirit what they believe, and be able to hear the words: "Blessed are your eyes, for they see, and your ears, for they hear"; and: "Many prophets and many of the just longed to see what you see, and did not see it" (Mt 13:16-17). . . . Now I have said this about the text: "They believed the scripture and the word which Jesus had spoken" (Jn 2:22) that we might grasp, after this examination of faith, that the perfection of faith will be given us at the great resurrection from the dead of the whole body of Jesus, his holy church.[1] . . . For now I believe "in part"; but when the perfection of faith comes, what is "in part" will be abolished, and faith in its own fullness will be something quite different, if I may say so, from faith as we now know it, which is "through a mirror, dimly" (1 Cor 13:10-13).

664   But all who see are not illuminated by Christ in the same way, but every individual is illuminated to the extent that each one is capable of receiving the power of light. And just as the eyes of our body are not illuminated in the same way, but the higher one climbs and the better the viewpoint from which the sun's rising is watched, the more one perceives its brilliance and warmth, so too is it with our mind: the higher it climbs in approaching Christ and the closer it comes to the glory of his light, so much the more magnificently and brightly does it shine in his light, as he himself says through the prophet: "Turn to me and I will turn to you, says the Lord" (Zech 1:3). And further: "I am a God at hand and not a God afar off" (Jer 23:23). But we do not all come to him in the same way, but "each according to his ability" (Mt 25:15). For we either come to him with the crowds and he nourishes us with parables just enough to keep us from fainting with hunger along the way, or else we sit constantly and without interruption at

---

[1] The meaning of this comparison, briefly, is this: The mutual relationship of the faith of the disciples before, and their (understanding, perfect) faith after, the resurrection of Christ provides us with a comparison of the relationship of earthly faith as such and transcendent (seeing, post-resurrection) faith.

his feet, interested solely in hearing his word without being "anxious about many things" but choosing the "best part which shall not be taken away" from us (cf. Lk 10:41–42). Indeed, those who come to him in this way will receive much more of his light. But if, like the apostles, we never move away from him but remain with him in all his trials, he will then privately explain and interpret for us what he had said to the multitudes (cf. Mk 4:34), and illuminate us much more brightly. But if there is someone who is able to climb the mountain with him like Peter, James and John, that person will be illuminated not only by the light of Christ but also by the voice of the Father himself (cf. Mk 9:2–8 parr).

665   It is one thing to know God, and something quite different to know him only by faith. . . . And should any think we are doing violence [to the words] by saying that believing and knowing are not the same, let them hear what Jesus said to the Jews who believed in him: "If you continue in my word . . . you will know the truth and the truth will make you free" (Jn 8:31–32). Note well . . . that before this stand the words: "Jesus then said to the Jews who had believed in him." . . . There is a great difference between knowing by faith and faith alone. For "to one is given through the Spirit the utterance of wisdom, and to another the utterance of knowledge according to the same Spirit, to another faith by the same Spirit" (1 Cor 12:8–9). . . . But see now whether the scripture is not talking about a different situation than one in which they who are merged with something know what they are merged and united with, but before such a union and communion, even though they have conceptual knowledge of it, really do not know it. So it was with Adam: when he said of Eve: "This at last is bone of my bones and flesh of my flesh" (Gen 2:23), he did not yet know his wife. For when he was joined with her it then says: "Now Adam knew Eve his wife" (Gen 4:1). And should any be scandalized that we have taken the words "Adam knew Eve his wife" as an example of the knowledge of God, let them recall first the words: "This is a great mystery" (Eph 5:32), and second, let them consider what is said by the apostle about male and female; the same words are used both for human beings and God: "He who joins himself to a prostitute becomes one body with her . . . and he who is united to the Lord becomes one Spirit with him" (1 Cor 6:16–17). Thus, whoever is united to a prostitute knows the prostitute, and whoever is united to his wife knows his wife; but far more than this, and also in a holy way, whoever is united to the Lord knows the Lord. But if we do not take knowing

in this sense of being merged and united, how can one explain the words: "now that you have come to know God, or rather to be known by God" (Gal 4:9), and: "The Lord knows those who are his" (2 Tim 2:19; cf. Num 16:15)? For it is in relation to us that the Lord knows those who are his own in that he merges himself with them and shares with them his own divinity and takes them up in his hand (cf. Jn 10:28–29).

666   "For mine eyes have seen thy salvation" (Lk 2:30). For before, said [Simeon], I believed by way of understanding, I knew through reasoning; but now I have seen with the eyes of my flesh and am thus brought to fulfillment.

667   "Our God will visibly come" (cf. Ps 50:2–3 LXX). Now if our God will visibly come, but this God is Christ, and Christ came in the flesh, this "visibly" thus means the flesh. For the flesh of Christ was endowed with bodily senses so that he could give himself with passion to those become worthy through devotion.

668   He will hear us when we confess the reasons why we do not yet believe; he will help those of us who are sick and need a physician, and will work with us that we may gain the grace to believe which Paul lists in third place in his list of charisms (cf. 1 Cor 12:9).

669   For each virtue of understanding, certain mysteries of wisdom, corresponding to the type of virtue in question, are opened up to those living a life of virtue. For to those not overcome by the gates of hell, the Savior gives as many keys (which open up an equal number of gates) as there are virtues.

670   We call faith sound when it is perfect and lacks nothing. That is the faith which believes it can eat everything (i.e., understand everything).

671   It is written that, upon hearing the voice from the cloud bearing witness to the Son, the three apostles, unable to bear the glory of the voice and its power, "fell on their faces" beseeching God; for they were "filled with awe" at the brilliance of the vision and the words which came from it (cf. Mt 17:1–8 parr). Consider now whether one might not make the following interpretation of this passage: namely, that the disciples, thinking that it was the Son of God who had spoken to Moses, and that he himself was the one who had said: "For man shall not see my face and live" (Exod 33:20), and hearing now God's witness about him, . . . humbled themselves "under the mighty hand of God" (1 Pet 5:6).

672   For even though we may be made worthy to see God in spirit and heart, we do not "see him as he is" (1 Jn 3:2) but according to the

order of salvation given to us; however, at the end of the world and "the restoration of all things" (Acts 3:21) . . . we will see him not as we do now, the way he is not, but, as will then be fitting, as he is.

673 But I [says the bride] who want to be seen by you alone, I want to know by what way I can come to you so that it can be secret, so that no one will be between us, so that no strange onlooker will meet me on the way.

674 "I will have regard for you and will make you fruitful and multiply you" (Lev 26:9). Just as the sun shines on the grain field and it bears fruit—and if it didn't shine on it, the field would surely remain unfruitful—so too does God, looking on the grain field of our heart, and illuminating us with the rays of his WORD, make us fruitful and multiply us.

TOUCH

Just as faith progresses from an objective holding-something-to-be-true to subjective appropriation and insight, so does the spiritual sense of touch progress from an objective, sacramental to a subjective, personal "contact" with God. Far more than other Platonizing Fathers, more even than Augustine, Origen has a thoroughly realistic concept of the sacramental opus operatum. A real divine power dwells in the baptismal water (P 4, 142–43); it is "no longer just water" (P 4, 512). The same is true, in a greater degree, of the Eucharist. But this effectiveness of the outer element is grounded in the special effectiveness of the body of Christ which, as body of the WORD, itself possesses divine powers.

Contact with Jesus is salutary also for children (675), although this contact (being only objective) is not as effective as that which, in adults, is accepted with subjective dispositions (676). Bodily healings are "sacraments" of spiritual healings (677). The spiritual sense of touch and spiritual contact with Christ (678–679). In this contact with Christ exists the only access to contact with God (680). The presence of the WORD in each soul (681) must be more and more transformed from an objective and virtual into a subjective and actual contact (682–685). The kiss as symbol of the highest spiritual contact (686). Simeon as parable (687).

675 The wish of those who brought children to Jesus was, according to Matthew, that he "should lay his hands on them and pray" (Mt 19:13),

and according to Mark, "that he might touch them" (Mk 10:13). . . . For by the prayer and touch of Jesus, the children and babies who are unable to hear what those who are already spiritual were hearing, could receive the help and assistance of which they were capable, for the power of Jesus clung to them. . . . Because many evil spirits concern themselves with the human soul and make plots against it right from its birth, . . . these people, apparently aware of this, were bringing their children to the Savior so that through his laying on of hands and prayer . . . the evil would be driven away. They believed that the power bestowed would suffice also for the future, since it can prevent contamination from the enemy powers. Now the savior, who did not think this to be trivial or unimportant, but salutary for those whom he touched by the laying on of his hands, said to his disciples who were reproaching the people and thereby trying to prevent the children from being brought to him: "Let the children come to me and do not hinder them" (Mt 19:14).

676 But don't forget that even though children, as children, cannot follow all that is said, Jesus still laid his hands on them and then went away (cf. Mt 19:13–15). After he had put his power on them by his touch, he withdrew from them who were unable to follow him the way the disciples did.

677 And similar to this, but in a manner more spiritual than physical, Jesus "touched" the leper in order to heal him, it seems to me, in two ways: not only to free him, as most thought was happening, from physical leprosy by physical touch, but also from that other leprosy by his truly divine touch.

678 Let us first see what touching is, and what the touching is that makes one unclean, and then what the touching is that makes one clean. The Apostle says: "It is well for a man not to touch a woman" (1 Cor 7:1). This touching is unclean; for this is what the Lord spoke of in the gospel: "Every one who looks at a woman lustfully has already committed adultery with her in his heart" (Mt 5:28). For his heart has touched the vice of concupiscence and his soul has become impure. Whoever then touches something in this way, that is, by lusting after a woman or by being greedy for money or by any other sin of desire, he has touched something unclean and become defiled. . . . Do you want me to show you a soul which has "touched an unclean thing" and "become unclean" (cf. Lev 5:2), and then touched something clean and become clean? The woman who had a flow of blood and spent all that she had on doctors and was no better: it was by the uncleanness

of sin that she was brought to this state. For she had touched sin and for that received a scourge of the flesh. But as soon as she, in full faith, touched Jesus' hem, the hemorrhage ceased and she was immediately clean (cf. Mk 5:25–29).

579   "Whoever touches these things shall become holy" (cf. Lev 5:18). Christ has been sacrificed (cf. 1 Cor 5:7), the one and perfect sacrifice which all these sacrifices preceded in type and image. They who touch the flesh of this sacrifice are immediately made holy if they are unclean, cured if they are wounded. This is what that woman we have just mentioned understood, the one who "had a flow of blood" (Mk 5:25). She understood that he is the flesh of sacrifice and the "most holy" flesh (cf. Lev 6:17) . . . and thus she approached him. Now she didn't dare to touch the holy flesh itself . . . but touched the hem of the garment with which the holy flesh was covered; and by this touch of faith she drew power from the flesh which purified her from her uncleanness and healed her wound. . . . All those who have come from paganism and believed, they have touched this flesh. It was also touched by the one who said: "For we ourselves were once foolish, unbelieving, led astray, slaves to various passions and pleasures. . . . But when the goodness and loving kindness of God our Savior appeared, he saved us . . . by the washing of regeneration and renewal in the Holy Spirit" (Tit 3:3–5). And in another place he says: "And such indeed were you . . . but you were sanctified, you were justified in the name of the Lord Jesus Christ and in the Spirit of our God" (1 Cor 6:11). For if, as we said, someone touches the flesh of Jesus in the way we have just described, and with complete faith and full obedience comes to Jesus, to the WORD made flesh, that person has touched the flesh of sacrifice and has been sanctified.

580   God is not in a place, but is indescribable, ineffable and invisible. But if God is not in a place and it is possible at times to approach God, then we obviously approach him by something invisible in us. And what is invisible in us if not the human being hidden in the heart which scripture calls the "inner human being" (cf. Rom 7:22)? This is what can come near to God. We too can come near through Jesus Christ, especially if we understand that Jesus Christ is justice and truth and wisdom and resurrection and the true light. For without these it is not possible to come near to God, nor is it possible without the peace which watches over the heart and its thoughts—which peace is Christ. And the more any of these is missing, justice and wisdom I mean, the more is one distant from God.

681   "Among you stands one whom you do not know" (Jn 1:26). These
        things are to be understood of the Son of God, the Logos, through
        whom all things were made, who exists substantially throughout the
        underlying nature of things, since he himself is wisdom. He per-
        meates the whole of creation, so that what comes to be always comes
        to be through him, and that of any and every thing it is always true
        that "all things were made through him and without him was not any-
        thing made" (Jn 1:3), and that "all things you have made in wisdom"
        (Ps 104:24). If then he permeates all creation, it is clear that he also
        permeates those who asked: "What then is your baptism if you are not
        the Christ nor Elijah nor the prophet?" (cf. Jn 1:19–21). In the midst,
        and standing firm, stood the WORD himself, established everywhere
        through the Father. Or the words "among you stands" can be under-
        stood as saying that there stands among you human beings, because
        you are rational beings, the rational Word. . . . They therefore who
        have the Logos in their midst but pay no attention to his nature, nor
        from what source and principle he has come, nor how he came to be
        in them, they are the ones who have him in their midst but know him
        not. . . . The WORD stands constantly there in his saving activity,
        even when he becomes flesh and is in the midst of human beings not
        comprehended and not even seen (cf. Jn 1:11). He stands there teach-
        ing and inviting all to drink from his abundant spring (cf. Jn 7:37).

681a   In giving his testimony, John [the Baptist] knew that God was
        Logos, for this is known to everyone with reason. The intellectual fac-
        ulty, also called rational faculty [*hēgemonikon*], is in our midst. For
        there is found the immanent reason [*endiathetos logos*] which makes us
        rational beings and which the Christ and Logos, as God, examines
        when he comes to be baptized. He stands unrecognized in your
        midst, penetrating the hearts and minds of all (cf. Heb 4:12).

682   Consider whether these do not mean the same thing: to be "with"
        someone, . . . and: to stand in the midst of those who do not recog-
        nize you.

683   This is the way in which Christ, who is the WORD of God, is next
        to us in possibility. That is to say, one must believe that he is next to
        every human being the way reason is to little children. But in reality,
        he is said to be in me when I have openly confessed the Lord Jesus
        and have believed in my heart that God has raised him from the dead.
        . . . He is therefore also in the midst of those who do not know him;
        he is there in their midst by way of possibility, not reality, that is, not
        in actual fact and activity.

684   If we should be asked the reason why the Logos is not called the "light of men" but the life that has come to be in the WORD, we would answer as follows. The life spoken of here is not that which is common to rational and non-rational beings, but the life which comes to be in us when our reason comes to maturity by sharing in the primordial Logos. And it is when we turn away from the life that only appears to be and is not the true life, and yearn to gain the true life, that we first gain a share of it; and once there, it becomes in us the foundation of the light of knowledge. With some, perhaps, this light is there only in possibility and not actually . . . but with others it is there actually.

685   "I am with you until the end of the world" (Mt 28:20). "I am with you" does not say the same as "I am in you." So, perhaps we would be more correct to say that the Savior is not "in" his disciples, but "with" them as long as they have not arrived in spirit at the "end of the world." But when they see, as far as their efforts are concerned, that the end of the world which is crucified to them (cf. Gal 6:14) is at hand, then, since Jesus is no longer with them but in them, they say: "It is no longer I who live but Christ who lives in me" (Gal 2:20).[1]

686   "O that he would kiss me with the kisses of his mouth" (Cant 1:2). Just as the church was given for its dowry the books of the law and the prophets, so too were the law of nature, reason, and free will given [to the soul] as gifts. Endowed with these gifts it is ready to take its first lessons from instructors and teachers. But because the soul does not find the perfect fulfillment of its desire and love in these things, it prays that its pure and virginal mind be enlightened by the illuminations and visitations of the WORD of God himself. For when the mind is filled with divine perceptions and understandings which do not come from any human or angelic ministration, it then believes that it has received the "kisses" of the very WORD of God. . . . This, perhaps, is what the perfect mind of the prophet meant when he said: "I opened my mouth and drew in the Spirit" (Ps 119:31 LXX). The "mouth" of the bridegroom is to be understood as that power which illuminates the mind and comes to it as a kind of love-talk, provided it deserves to grasp the presence of such great power, and reveals to the mind what is unknown and concealed from it; this is the more true and proper and holy "kiss" which is said to be given by the

[1] Cf. No. 887.

bridegroom who is the WORD of God, to the spouse which is the pure and perfect soul. The image of this is that "kiss" which we give to each other in the church when we celebrate the divine mysteries.

687   What good did it do [Simeon] to see Christ? Was he only promised to see Christ and draw no further benefit from it, or does there lie hidden here some gift worthy of God which the blessed Simeon merited and received? "The woman touched the hem of Jesus' garment and was healed" (cf. Mk 5:25–34 parr). Now if she drew so much benefit from the outermost part of his clothing, what must we think of Simeon who "took him up in his arms" (Lk 2:28), and holding him in his hands was filled with joy? For he saw the child he himself was holding, the one who had come to set free those in chains and to free him too from the bonds of the body; for he knew that no one can release anyone from the prison of the body with hope for future life except he whom he held in his arms. So he said to him: "Now, Lord, you may dismiss your servant in peace [Lk 2:29]. For as long as I did not hold Christ, as long as I did not cradle him in my arms, I was locked in and could not escape my chains." But this applies not just to Simeon but to the whole human race. When someone leaves the world, when someone is released from prison and from the house of bondage in order to come into his own, let him take Jesus in his hands and cradle him in his arms; let him hold Jesus completely to his breast, and he will then be able to go rejoicing wherever he wishes. . . . Therefore, that we too, standing in the temple and holding and embracing the Son of God, might be worthy of forgiveness and progressing to better things, for this let us pray to almighty God; let us also pray to the infant Jesus himself whom we long to hold in our arms and talk to.

SMELL

The spiritual sense of smell is what is popularly called "having a nose for," but in relation to the things of God. Those who have this sense can, from the things of this world, smell out what is Christian (688). But just as, according to Origen, the word of God flows out into the world only because spiritual blood has flowed from the wound in the side of the Crucified, so does the fragrance of God flow out into the world only because, in the self-emptying (kenōsis) of God, the jar of nard (his body) broke open. Souls pursue this fragrance with longing (689) until, in the mystical body, the fragrance of the creature and the Creator mysteriously mingle (690).

688 Whoever has a pure sense of smell and through understanding of the divine WORD can run after the fragrance of his ointments (cf. Cant 1:4 LXX), that person has a "nose" which is sensitive to spiritual fragrances and thus able to find out what seems to be of value in pagan teaching.

88a "We are the aroma of Christ to God in every place" (2 Cor 2:15). It is my opinion that each virtue has its own proper fragrance which is the complement of the virtues. On the other side, the vices stink, as it is written: "My wounds grow foul and fester" (Ps 38:5).

689 "Your name is perfume poured out; therefore the maidens love you, they draw you on, we run after you in pursuit of your perfume" (Cant 1:3-4 LXX). Unless he had "poured out the perfume," that is, the fullness of the divine Spirit, and unless he had "emptied himself, taking the form of a servant" (Phil 2:7), no one would have been able to grasp him in the fullness of his deity, except perhaps the bride alone because she seems to indicate that he gave that poured-out perfume not for herself but for the maidens, to make them fall in love. . . . For the sake, therefore, of these maiden-souls, and for their growth and progress, "he who was in the form of God emptied himself" (Phil 2:6–7) so that his "name" might be a "poured-out perfume" and he no longer would "dwell in inapproachable light" (1 Tim 6:16) and stay "in the form of God," but that "the WORD would become flesh" (Jn 1:14) so that these maiden-souls in their growth and progress would be able not only to love him but also to draw him to themselves. For each and every soul attracts and takes to itself the WORD of God according to the measure of its capacity and faith. But once souls have drawn the WORD of God to themselves and brought him into their minds and senses and taken in the pleasantness of his sweetness and fragrance . . . and when they have recognized the reason for his coming and the causes of the redemption and passion, namely, his love by which he, the immortal one, went to his death on the cross for the salvation of all, then these maiden-souls, filled by this with new strength and youthfulness, and spurred onwards as if by some divine and indescribable fragrance, "run after him," pursuing his sweet fragrance not with measured and grave steps but running just as fast as they can, as did he who said: "I run so as to win the prize" (cf. 1 Cor 9:24). . . . But I ask: If his name alone, just because it became "poured-out perfume," could do so much and so excite the maidens . . . what will his actual presence do? . . . I think that when they finally do come to this, they will no longer walk or run,

but, bound by the chains of his love, will cling to him. They will have no more room to move but will have become "one Spirit" with him (cf. 1 Cor 6:17). There will be fulfilled what was written: "Even as you, Father, in me and I in you are one, that they also may be one in us" (cf. Jn 17:21).

690   "My nard gave forth its fragrance" (Cant 1:12). In the course of this dramatic action, this is what seems to be happening: after these words the bride went in to the bridegroom and anointed him with her ointments. She did this in such a marvelous way that the nard, which at first had no fragrance when she still had it, gave forth its fragrance when it touched the body of the bridegroom. Thus, it seemed not so much that he received fragrance from the nard as the nard received fragrance from him. However, if we read the text according to the variant found in other manuscripts: "My nard gave forth his fragrance," we find something even more divine, namely, that this ointment of nard with which the bridegroom is anointed took not so much its own natural fragrance which it usually has, but that of the bridegroom, and carried that back to the bride . . . who then said something like the following: "my nard" with which I anointed the bridegroom has brought back to me the fragrance of the bridegroom and, with its natural fragrance apparently overwhelmed by the fragrance of the bridegroom, has brought me his sweetness. This is the explanation of the plot of the drama; let us now come to its spiritual understanding. Let us see in this the spouse as the church in the person of the Mary who "took a pound of costly ointment of pure nard and anointed the feet of Jesus and wiped his feet with her hair" (Jn 12:3). Through the hair of her head, as it were, she received the ointment back imbued with the fragrance and power of his body; and through her hair with which she dried his feet, she drew to herself the fragrance not so much of the ointment of nard as of the WORD of God himself. . . . What is the difference when in the Canticle of Canticles the bride anoints the bridegroom with ointment or when in the gospel the disciple Mary anoints Christ her Master hoping, as we have said, that the fragrance of the WORD and the sweet odor of Christ would return to her from this ointment, so that she too could say: "We are the aroma of Christ to God" (2 Cor 2:15)? And because this ointment was full of faith and precious dispositions, Jesus also gives testimony of it: "She has done a beautiful thing to me" (Mk 14:6). Back in the Canticle, a bit farther on, he praises the "emissions" of the bride, just as he here praises the work of Mary, for he says:

"What you send forth are a paradise of pomegranates, henna with nard, nard and saffron" (Cant 4:13–14).

TASTE

The spiritual soul tastes God's spiritual sweetness, while sin makes this sweetness bitter (691–693). The spiritual sense of taste will, however, only become completely clear from the following passage.

691   "Say to the embittered house" (Ezek 17:12). If we want to see what kind of sin "embitterment" is, let us hear how sweet are God's words to him who understands, for he says: "How sweet are thy words to my taste!" (Ps 119:103). When the faithful take in these naturally "sweet" things, they are either living as they should or doing the contrary. If they are living according to God's law, the words of God retain the sweetness with which they were first uttered. Indeed it seems to me that through the goodness of their life they even increase the sweetness of the WORD. But if someone sins and perversely walks contrary to the precepts of God (cf. Lev 26:23), such a one takes the most sweet words of God and, through the most bitter nature of sin . . . turns all the sweetness into a bitter taste.

692   Therefore, whoever sins makes bitter and reviles and dishonors as well the words of God he receives as well as him who taught them.

693   Whoever hears the words of God and does not obey them, "rebels against" his words (cf. Ps 105:28).

FOOD

SPIRITUAL NOURISHMENT

Origen had found the spiritual senses through his general law of sense-spirit analogy. The same law now reveals to him the spiritual foods as well. In both of these instances, as also in the allegorical interpretation of scripture, it would be completely wrong to interpret spiritual reality (senses, food, scriptural meaning) as only a shadowy, metaphorical reality. On the contrary, the spiritual is the fundamental reality (analogatum princeps). Thus the spiritual nourishment of the soul through the substantial WORD of God is very much the highest reality, even more real than bodily nourishment. It is one of the basic functions of the inner human being in his life of unity with God.

There is therefore spiritual nourishment (694). The realm of the bodily-perceptual already offers such to the spirit (695). There is revulsion and hunger even in divine food (696–698). And there is progress in this food (699). The essential bread of the soul is the WORD (700–706) which makes the bread immortal (707) and, in its being eaten, makes it become richer and richer (708). No creature can live without this bread (709–710). It is the nourishment of the whole world (711–712), to which it constantly brings life (713).

694   Just as sheep are nourished by grass and water, so are human beings kept alive by action and knowledge.

695   "And God said, 'Behold, I have given you every plant yielding seed, . . . it shall be food for you and every beast of the earth'" (Gen 1:29–30). . . . According to the allegorical sense, the "grass" of the earth and its fruit, which is given to human beings for food, can be understood as referring to the passions of the body. Anger and concupiscence are, for example, bodily seed. The fruit of this "seed," that is, the deed itself, is common to us rational beings and to the beasts of

the earth. For when we become angry for justice' sake, that is, for the correction of the evildoer and his improvement for salvation, we are being nourished by this fruit of the earth and bodily anger becomes our food through which we beat back sin and restore justice. . . . Thus, this earthly food of anger becomes our food, when we use it reasonably for justice. . . . The same holds true also of concupiscence and each of the other passions of this kind. For when "our soul longs and faints for the living God" (cf. Ps 84:2), then concupiscence has become our food.

696   Just as the sick feel revulsion for all food, so do the impure reject all knowledge. . . .

697   "Their soul loathed all food" (Ps 107:18 LXX). The soul of those who died the death of sin feels, because of its sickness, loathing for the spiritual nourishment which would be suited to its nature. It spits out all spiritual nourishment.

698   "The hungry soul" (Ps 107:9 LXX). Empty is the soul which is full of evil and distraction. . . . Consider now whether a soul which is so full that it can't feel its hunger [for God] can not be led to feel this hunger. The good things with which God feeds the hungering soul are our true good things.

699   "I have food to eat of which you do not know" (Jn 4:32). The one who makes more progress than the stragglers, who cannot see the same things, will always say: "I have food to eat of which you do not know." . . . Therefore, the more progress we make, the better we eat and the more we eat, until perhaps we come to eat the same food as the Son of God, the food which the disciples here do not yet know.

700   "Give us this day our essential bread" (Mt 6:11; cf. Lk 11:3). Because some suppose that we are being told here to pray for physical bread, it will be helpful, after exposing their error, to present the true understanding of this "essential bread." . . . "God sent forth his WORD and healed them" (Ps 107:20) as is written in the Psalms, obviously referring to those perishing from hunger. They who believe in the WORD do "the works of God" (Jn 6:28) which are "food that endures to eternal life." And "my Father," he says, "gives you the true bread from heaven; for the bread of God is that which comes down from heaven and gives life to the world" (Jn 6:32–33). True bread is that which feeds the true human being, the one made in God's image who, upon eating this bread, also comes to be in the likeness of the Creator (cf. Gen 1:26–27; Col 3:9–10). . . . The expression "essential" is used to show that the bread goes over into the being of the one eating it.

701   No one who "bears the image of the man of dust" (1 Cor 15:49) can eat the "bread from heaven," for the soul-man [*psychikos anthrōpos*] cannot comprehend the things of the spirit. It is for this bread that you were taught to pray, "the essential bread" which is not excreted [from the body] but is taken up into the being of the soul.[1]

702   The human being who lives in the secret of the heart and is created in God's image, becomes a table-companion with the angels and sharer of the true manna and the food from heaven, but not of the accursed earth which the sinners eat in tears.

703   . . . Since the bread which we seek is spiritual, we must consider the essence of the soul as being related to the bread, so that just as corporeal bread, when taken up in the body of the one being nourished, turns into his being, so too the "living bread" which has "come down from heaven" (cf. Jn 6:31–33), when taken up in the spirit and soul, gives a share of its own power to the person being nourished by it.

704   But the true food of the spirit is the WORD of God.

705   Only the words of God constitute for the spiritual soul its own proper life.

706   What is more nourishing for the soul than the WORD, or what is more noble for the mind that makes room for it than the wisdom of God? What is more suited to a rational nature than truth?

707   The essential bread then, which is most suited to a rational nature and is related to being itself, gives health, vigor and strength to the soul and (since the WORD of God is immortal) shares its own immortality with those who eat it. . . . . We must pray for this, that we may be made worthy of it, and, nourished by the WORD that is God and was in the beginning with God (cf. Jn 1:1), we may be made divine.

708   For this is the bread which, the more it is eaten, the more it remains, indeed, the more it increases. It is, as the Apostle says, the "spiritual food" (1 Cor 10:3) which, the more it is consumed, the more it increases. For the more you accept the WORD of God, the more assiduously you eat this food, the more richly will it abound in you.

---

[1] This assimilation of the essence of the food through the spirit is to be compared with the doctrine, common in the first centuries, that the eucharistic species are not excreted from the body but are taken up as a whole into the organism, and hence with the idea of a kind of preparation of the mortal body for the resurrection through the eucharist. Origen completely rejects this view (Mt Co 11, 14). The eucharistic species have no prerogative here; only the WORD spoken over them sanctifies the soul and nourishes it substantially.

709 One must rise in spirit above the level of animals and human beings up to that of the angels. For they too take nourishment and are not wholly without need.

710 The angels too are not without their Well of Jacob from which they drink; each of them has in himself a "spring of water welling up to eternal life" (Jn 4:14) which has been opened by the WORD himself and by Wisdom herself.

711 "You prepared their food" (Ps 65:9). The psalmist means spiritual food, and he says that it was prepared. For before the foundation of the world, the mystery of Christ, who is the bread come down from heaven (cf. Jn 6:31–33), was established.

712 "Man ate the bread of angels" (Ps 78:25). At first, then, angels ate this bread, but now human beings do too. Here, "to eat" means "to know." For the spirit (mind) eats what it knows and does not eat what it does not know.

713 "Give us our essential bread" (cf. Mt 6:11). The words "each day" are necessarily added. For the true life is our restorative, as it were, so that the interior human being might live according to God.

WORD AS FLESH AND BLOOD

The WORD comes to us only by means of the death of Christ. All revelation is rooted in the bloody event of salvation. Consequently, the substantial "bread" from heaven is at the same time flesh and blood. In saying this, Origen does not by any means wish to "spiritualize" the eucharist, even if the spiritual, inner mystery of the eating of the WORD seemed to him to be the fulfillment of the ritual, sacramental (but in itself obviously effective) consumption of the eucharistic species (just as understanding was abiding but also fulfilled faith). Eucharist and Holy Spirit of course thus come very close to each other: but both, in different ways, are "sacraments" of the senses, effective signs of the presence of the divine WORD in the world (714–718). From the sacrificial character of revelation follows also the necessity of the sacrificing of Christ the preacher (718–720), the mystery-character of the church's proclamation (721–726). The true vine (722–724). Satan as dead bread (725). The outer and the inner of the Word (727).

714 Every day Christians eat the flesh of the Lamb; that is, they receive daily the flesh of the WORD.

715 "This is my body" (Mt 26:26). The bread which God the WORD professes to be his *body* is the WORD which is the nourishment of souls; it is the word which proceeds from the heavenly WORD and the bread which comes from the heavenly bread. . . . And the drink which God the WORD professes to be his *blood* is the WORD which marvelously waters and inebriates the hearts of those who drink it. He is the cup of which is written: "And your inebriating cup, how marvelous it is." That drink is also the product of the true vine which says: "I am the true vine" (Jn 15:1); and it is the blood of that grape which, thrown into the wine press of the passion, has produced this drink, just as the bread is the word of Christ made from that grain of wheat which, "falling into the earth . . . bears much fruit" (Jn 12:24). . . . For what else could the *body* or the *blood* of the WORD of God be but the WORD which nourishes and the WORD which gives joy to the heart (cf. Ps 103:15; Wis 16:26)?

716 "He fed them with the essence of wheat and satisfied them with honey from the rock" (Ps 81:16; cf. LXX). This is the "wheat" spoken of in the words: "Unless a grain of wheat falls into the earth and dies, it remains alone; but if it dies it bears much fruit" (Jn 12:24). From the "essence" of this "grain of wheat" God feeds us; he gives us the "bread of life" (Jn 6:35) which the Father generates. And the "wheat" is also the "rock . . . and the rock was Christ" (1 Cor 10:4). From this "rock" flows not just "water" to slake the thirst of the people, but "honey" also satisfies the blessedly hungering. This was formerly said of the water of circumcision, but it is now said of the "water of life" (cf. Rev 21:6; 22:1) which flowed from the wound in Jesus' side (Jn 19:34).

717 For Christ has covered the earth with holy and divine rivers. He who pours forth the divine water for the thirsty and makes water flow from his lance-pierced side (Jn 19:34), he is also the one who changed the bitterness of Marah (that is, of the cruel law) into the sweetness of the wood of the cross and his mystery (cf. Exod 15:22–25).[1]

718 Who then are the people who have the custom of drinking blood? . . . We drink the blood of Christ not only in the sacramental rite, but also when we receive his words in which are life, as he himself says: "The words that I have spoken are spirit and life" (Jn 6:63). Thus, he himself is the wounded one whose blood we drink. . . . But there are also wounded ones who have preached his word to us; for

[1] Cf. No. 411.

when we read the words of his apostles and gain life from them, we are "drinking the blood of the wounded" (cf. Num 23:24).

a   "Wisdom has slaughtered her sacrificial animals, she has mixed her wine" (Prov 9:2). Here he applies the name "sacrificial animal" to all those prophets who were sealed with Christ's instruction and killed because, in the mixing bowl of knowledge, for those who understand, they mixed like wine the sweet knowledge of Christ, who said: "Do not fear those who kill the body but cannot kill the soul" (Mt 10:28); for he himself has offered them in sacrifice and continues to do so in that he exhorts those who believe in him to die for him as he himself died for you (cf. Rom 5:8; 1 Thes 5:10).

9   "To be a minister . . . in the priestly service of the gospel of God" (Rom 15:16). Just as the priests, when offering sacrifice, had to make sure there was no blemish in the victim . . . so too the one who offers the priestly service of the gospel and proclaims the WORD of God must make every effort to ensure that no falsehood in preaching, no error in teaching and no fault in instruction creep in. But, as I have said, he should if possible first offer himself and mortify his members because of sin, so that not only by teaching but also by living example he might make his offering acceptable to God for the salvation of the disciples.

20   So then let the preparation of the Word glow with fire so as to be able to gain a hearing and show the blood-filled and life-giving quality of the words which come from the lips which are bathed as it were in the true drink of the blood of Christ.

21   Accustomed as you are to attend the divine mysteries, you know how carefully you receive the body of the Lord and reverently make sure that no particle drops to the ground, lest anything of the consecrated gift be lost. . . . But if you exercise such concern in taking care of his body—and indeed with every right—how can you think it a lesser crime to neglect the WORD of God than his body?

22   To what has been said must be added how the Son is "the true vine" (cf. Jn 15:1). This will be clear to those who understand the words: "Wine gladdens the heart of man" (Ps 104:15) in a manner worthy of prophetic grace. For if the heart is the intellectual faculty and what gladdens it is the most drinkable WORD which draws one away from human things and makes one feel inspired and intoxicates with an intoxication which is not irrational but divine, . . . then he who brings wine which gladdens the heart of man is indeed the true vine.

23   But if the "blood of the covenant" was poured into our hearts "for the forgiveness of" our "sins" (cf. Mt 26:28), then once that drinkable

blood is poured out into our hearts, all the sins we have previously committed are forgiven and removed.

724   Thus, there "will come upon" them "all the righteous blood" (cf. Mt 23:35) which they shed because they wish to subvert the truth of the scriptures, which truth is rightly called the blood and life of the scriptures because all scripture, unless it is understood according to the truth, is dead. Therefore they pour out the truth of the scriptures, like its blood, just as the blood of Abel was shed. Nor was it only at that time that the voice of the blood of Abel cried out to God (cf. Gen 4:10); but the truth of the scriptures . . . —beginning from the blood of Christ, that is, from the truth of the gospel—constantly makes representation through all the scriptures before God against those who seek to overthrow it.

725   Just as Christ is the living bread, so is his enemy, death, the dead bread. Every rational soul is nourished by one or the other of these.

726   Let us not take what is given for our nourishment and turn it into food for swine or dogs; rather let us prepare in ourselves food fitting for those who receive in the guest chamber of our heart the Word and Son of God coming with his Father to make in us a dwelling place in the Holy Spirit.

727   Thus, every word through which we receive spiritual drink, or every story through which we are nourished, is a vessel of food and drink. We are admonished therefore not to worry about words and stories which come from the outside but only about those which come from within so that our heart will be filled with pure, drinkable and eatable senses, and not with mere words or fancy speeches; for "the kingdom of God does not consist in talk but in power" (1 Cor 4:20). Whoever, then, is more concerned to produce a carefully crafted speech rather than one filled with salutary meaning, the cup of his narration is clean on the outside, but on the inside is filled with the filth of vanity. Hence Paul, who was not in the habit of cleaning the cup and the bowl from the outside but from the inside, professed to be "unskilled in speaking but not in knowledge" (2 Cor 11:6; cf. 10:10). . . . Moving now to a similar series of thoughts, we can say that the letters of the law and the prophets are the cups of the soul's spiritual drink, and the bowls of the foods necessary for the faithful, or the vats of wisely stored nourishment. . . . The scribes and Pharisees search after the external and common meaning and try to show that this is pure and holy; but the disciples of Christ try to purify the internal and spiritual meaning and to sanctify it with understanding and convincing

proof. This enables them to eat and drink the law and the prophets which have been purified from within, and makes them eager to hear and accept the internal and mystical sense and go beyond the external senses of the words. It is good then to clean the cup and the bowl or vat carefully from within, for they who first clean the inside of the cup also find the outside to have been truly cleaned. For the vessels of speech are truly clean when their true and spiritual senses have been made more manifest.

TRANSFORMATION OF THE NOURISHING WORD

Just as in the tradition the manna took on every taste, so too Christ becomes all to all (728). Every level has its own kind of nourishment, for every human being has his own truth (cf. 131). Despite these changes in truth, no lie is involved (729). The levels of foods (730–734) culminate in the true heavenly banquet (734–738) where the whole mystical body will be trod in the wine press (735), and where also endless progress is to be expected (736) in the midst of full satiety (737–738).

28   Now then let us hurry to receive the heavenly manna, for in the mouth, that manna takes on the taste each one wants. For listen to what the Lord says to those who come to him: "Be it done for you as you have believed" (Mt 8:13). And you too, if you accept with full faith and devotion the WORD of God which is preached in the church, the WORD itself will become for you whatever you desire. For example, if you are troubled, he comforts you saying: "A broken and contrite heart, O God, you will not despise" (Ps 51:17). If you are rejoicing in hope for the future, he heaps up your joys saying: "Be glad in the Lord, and rejoice, O righteous" (Ps 32:11). If you are angry, he calms you saying: "Refrain from anger, and forsake wrath" (Ps 37:8). If you are in pain, he heals you saying: "The Lord heals all your diseases" (cf. Ps 103:3). If you are being eaten up with poverty, he comforts you saying: "He raises the poor from the dust and lifts the needy from the ash heap" (Ps 113:7). This is how the manna of the WORD of God puts in your mouth the taste you want.

29   Now as regards the nature of the WORD, just as the quality of food in the nursing mother changes into milk according to the nature of the infant, or is modified by the physician according to what is

beneficial for a sick person, or is prepared for a stronger person of greater vigor, so too does God change, according to each one's needs, the power of the WORD which has the function of nourishing the human soul. . . . And the WORD is by no means false to its own nature when it becomes food for each according to the capacity of each. It neither misleads nor deceives in so doing.

730   God did indeed once "give his people bread from heaven which, without their toil, provided for every pleasure; for it changed to suit every one's liking" (cf. Wis 16:20–21). The same nature of the WORD which is nourishing the soul is adapted to the capacity of the one being nourished. If, as law, it nourishes the infant, it becomes milk; if a weak soul, it becomes vegetables; if someone perfect, then solid food.

731   If someone is a child and "weak in faith" (cf. Rom 14:1), he needs rain, but the "rain" of "milk" (cf. 1 Cor 3:2). . . . But there is another earth which can receive strong floods, even support "rivers" (cf. Jn 7:38) and bear up under the strong torrents of the WORD of God. For this is what the prophet is talking about in the Psalms: "You give them drink from the river of your delights" (Ps 36:8).

732   If this happens, our "dry land" will not remain dry.

733   "Whoever drinks of the water that I shall give him . . . it will become in him a spring of water welling up to eternal life" (Jn 4:14). But will any, if they have this well in them, be able to thirst again? The principal meaning, however, might well be something like this: when we have to do with words which seem to be profound, we will be satisfied for a while, but only as long as we accept as most profound the ideas we seem to have dug up and discovered. But upon further reflection we will again become doubtful concerning what we had been sure about, because the profundity we thought was there cannot provide a clear and distinct concept of the object of our investigations. And even if we had been fully convinced by the persuasiveness of what has been said, we will later find arising in ourselves the same uncertainty which we had before we learned this. But, as it is, I possess the kind of WORD that turns into a fountain of living drink in those who accept my preaching. And such a benefit accrues to those who accept my water that it becomes in them a fountain of up-ward-springing water which can find everything they are looking for; and with their spirit riding and coursing along at top speed, because

of the mobility of this water, it becomes possible for them to spring upwards into eternal life.

34   Just as for those in whom wisdom and knowledge is coming to be [the WORD] confers wisdom and knowledge, not suddenly, but by gradually progressing steps according to their efforts and desire and faith . . . so too for those in whom the "true vine" is growing (cf. Jn 15:1): he does not immediately produce mature and sweet grapes and suddenly become the sweet "wine to gladden the heart of man" (Ps 104:15), but at first brings them sweetness only in the fragrance of a blossom so that the souls, attracted at first by the grace of his fragrance, might afterwards be able to bear the bitterness of troubles and trials . . . and only then does he give them the sweetness of maturity so as to lead them at last to the wine presses where the "blood of grapes" is poured out (Gen 49:11), the "blood of the New Covenant" which may be drunk at the heavenly festival where a great feast has been prepared (cf. Mk 14:24–25; Mt 26:29).

35   This is the "wine" harvested from that "vine" which said: "I am the true vine," the wine which the heavenly "Father, the vinedresser" is pressing (Jn 15:1). It is the "wine" brought forth by those "branches" which have abided in Jesus (cf. Jn 15:2–4).

36   But that "wine" which comes from the "true vine" is always "new" (cf. Jn 15:1); for through the progress of those who are learning, recognition of the divine knowledge and wisdom is being always renewed. Hence Jesus said to his disciples: "I will drink it new with you in my Father's kingdom" (Mt 26:29). For the knowledge of secret things and the revelation of what lies hidden is constantly being renewed, not just for human beings but also for the angels and heavenly powers.

37   There will be a blessed satisfaction in the appearance and clear vision of the glory of God. For this is the food which fills the whole table of the soul, the food with which they will be filled who hunger for and desire it in a way conducive to salvation.

38   Why then do we hesitate and hold back from putting off the obstacle of a "perishable body" which "weighs down the soul," and this "earthly tent which burdens the thoughtful mind" (Wis 9:15)? Why do we hesitate to be freed of our bonds and leave behind the stormy waves of flesh and blood (cf. Phil 1:23; 1 Cor 15:50), in order to enjoy with Christ Jesus the repose of blessedness, contemplate the living WORD who is all in all, be nourished by him, comprehending his manifold wisdom, and be molded by the Truth itself?

GENERATION

GENERATION BY GOD

The parallelism of the inner and outer human being reveals one final mystery of spiritual union with God, the mystery of marriage and of spiritual fruitfulness. Origen wrote the first mystical commentary on the Song of Songs and at least touched on all the subsequent fundamental themes of bridal mysticism.

Between God and the soul exists the relationship of bridegroom and bride (739–742). From its union with the WORD, the soul conceives and gives birth to spiritual children: the virtues and good works (743–745). But its spiritual fruitfulness extends even farther: it can generate souls for Christ (746–747), and do that in the real bride of Christ, the church (748). But ultimately, this fruitfulness is a co-generation of the mystical body of Christ and hence, in each instance, a new coming-to-birth of Christ himself: the soul comes to be with Mary its mother (749–754).

739   "Whoever seeks to gain his life will lose it, but whoever loses his life will gain it" (Lk 17:33). The martyrs wanted to save their souls; hence they lost them in order to gain them. . . . Further: "He who is united to the Lord becomes one spirit with him" (1 Cor 6:17). Thus when someone who is still a rational animal is paired with God, he is turned by that into a spiritual being and becomes "one spirit." Let us too lose our sense-soul so that, clinging to the Lord, we might be transformed into one spirit.

740   If we refer the tent of the testimony to the human being, we would interpret the interior of the veil where the inaccessible things are hidden as the very "heart" of the soul which alone can receive the mysteries of truth and is receptive to the hidden mysteries of God.

741   God can come to be in the soul, and the soul emigrates to God.

742   The soul becomes sterile when God abandons it; but becomes a mother when he is at work in it.

43   Just as there is no begetting of children without a woman and without receiving the power needed for begetting children, so too will no one be able to receive this or that without having prayed for it with the right disposition and faith, or without having led the right kind of life before prayer. . . .

44   In spiritual nuptials, however, consider the union of the WORD as bridegroom with the soul as bride. She is not hurt or harmed by him, but with each embrace receives incorruption and fertility; and the children born of such nuptials are spiritual offspring.

45   Just as the seed is formed and shaped in those with child, so is it in the soul which accepts the WORD: the conception of the WORD is gradually formed and shaped in it. . . . In his Epistle to Timothy Paul says that "woman will be saved through bearing children, with modesty" (1 Tim 2:15). But who is this woman, if not the soul which conceives the divine Word of truth and brings forth good works which are like Christ?

46   "God said to Abraham: . . . whatever Sarah says to you, do as she tells you" (Gen 21:12). . . . I think that Sarah, which is translated "prince" or "leader," stands for virtue. . . . Therefore, if someone is betrothed to virtue, let him listen to her voice in all things in which she gives him counsel. Abraham thus no longer wants to call virtue his wife. For as long as virtue is called wife, it belongs to someone in particular and cannot be shared with anyone else. It is fitting that, while we are on the way to perfection, the virtue of our soul be within us and proper to us; but when we have come to perfection so that we can also teach others, then we should no longer hold virtue in our lap like a wife, but should marry her off like a sister to others who also want her. To those, finally, who are perfect, the WORD of God says: "Say to wisdom, 'You are my sister'" (Prov 7:4). It was in this sense, then, that Abraham called Sarah his sister.

47   Seventy-five souls went down into Egypt with Jacob. They are the souls which Jacob begot. But I do not believe that anyone can generate a soul unless he happens to be someone like the one who said: "For though you have countless guides in Christ, you do not have many fathers. For I became your father in Christ Jesus through the gospel" (1 Cor 4:15). It is persons like that who generate souls and bring them forth, as he said in another place: "My little children, with whom I am again in travail until Christ be formed in you!" (Gal 4:19). For others do not want to be burdened with this kind of generation, or they are incapable of it.

748   Rational substance, of which the human soul is also a part, cannot of itself bring forth any good, although it is capable of receiving good. It must therefore, like a woman, generate from another what it can bring forth in the way of practical and theoretical virtues. Hence, I call it "bride." . . . It is in this sense that one must take what Paul wrote to the Corinthians when he said: "I betrothed you to Christ to present you as a pure bride to her one husband" (2 Cor 11:2), in which he gives the name "bride" to the whole church which is a pure virgin because of the correctness of her doctrine and practice. And writing to another church, the same apostle, after mentioning Adam and Eve, continues: "This is a great mystery, and I take it to mean Christ and the church" (Eph 5:32): that just as they were the parents of all human beings, so are Christ and the church the generators of all good deeds, thoughts and words.

749   Who are they "who sow" (cf. Mk 4:14)? Those who proclaim God's WORD in the church. . . . To souls . . . they should entrust the secret mysteries, to them speak the WORD of God and the mysteries of faith, so that "Christ might be formed" in them through faith. Or don't you know that from this sowing of the seed of the WORD of God Christ is born in the hearts of the hearers? As the Apostle expresses it: "until Christ be formed in you" (Gal 4:19). . . . This is the child-bearing of saintly souls, this the conceiving and these the holy embraces which are right and fitting for the great high priest, Christ Jesus our Lord.

750   A pregnant woman is what the soul is called which has recently conceived the WORD of God. . . . The "formed infant" (cf. Exod 21:23 LXX) can be taken as the WORD of God in the heart of that soul which has received the grace of baptism.

751   Not just in Mary did his birth begin with an "overshadowing" (cf. Lk 1:35); but in you too, if you are worthy, is the WORD of God born.

752   If you are so pure in mind, so holy in body and so blameless in deed, you can give birth to Christ himself, according to him who said: "my little children, with whom I am again in labor until Christ be formed in you" (Gal 4:19). The Lord himself also said of himself: "Whoever does the will of my Father in heaven is my brother and sister and mother" (Mt 12:50).

753   They who do not know the mystery of the virgin say to Jesus: "your brothers" (Mk 3:32; Lk 8:20), for if they had known they would have believed in him. It is from doing the will of his Father in heaven that one becomes the brother or sister or mother of Jesus. When the wholly

virginal and uncorrupted soul, although not by nature a brother, etc., to Jesus, conceives of the Holy Spirit in order to give birth to the will of the Father, it becomes the "mother" of Jesus.

754 "Blessed are they who do righteousness always." To do righteousness always is what the perfect do who are formed after the image of their creator. Those who do righteousness do Christ who is justice. Their souls become, in bringing him forth, the mother of Christ. For Christ — righteousness — is formed in them.

FIDELITY

But not just the fleshly aspect of marriage is transferred to the inner level, but also the spiritual relationship of fidelity. Every sin is personal infidelity, is fornication and adultery (756–760). The more intimate was the relationship to God, the more serious is the break (761). The holy fear of the soul (762).

755 The human soul is a comely work and has a marvelous beauty. For when its Maker first created it, he said, "Let us make man in our image and likeness" (Gen 1:26). What is more beautiful than this beauty and "likeness"? Some adulterous and dissolute lovers, attracted by its beauty, want to corrupt it and play the harlot with it (cf. Ezek 16:25). Thus Paul in his wisdom says: "I am afraid that as the serpent deceived Eve by his cunning, your thoughts will be led astray" (2 Cor 11:3). In the fornication of the flesh, bodies are corrupted; but in spiritual impurity, the spirit-sense is corrupted and the soul itself is wounded.

756 The contrary powers love the beauty of the human soul, and when the human soul accepts the seeds of their lovers, it so to speak commits adultery with them.

757 The marriage of our soul was first with the evil man and worst of husbands, the devil. But when he was destroyed and eliminated, our soul was "freed from the law" (cf. Rom 7:3) of that earlier and worst of men and united to our good and legitimate husband.

758 Every woman is either under a man and subject to the laws of a man or is a whore and makes use of liberty to sin. Whoever visits a whore knows that he has gone in to a woman who is a prostitute and lays down for anyone who wants; thus he cannot be angry if he sees other lovers with her. But whoever makes a legitimate use of marriage does not allow his wife any opportunity to sin but is full of zeal to

protect the chastity of his marriage by which he can become a legitimate father. This example shows us that every soul is either prostitute
to the demons and has many lovers (so that at one time the spirit of
fornication enters into it, and when he departs the spirit of greed
enters, and after him comes the spirit of pride, then of wrath and envy
and vainglory too, and many many others), . . . or if the soul is
betrothed to an upright spouse (to that spouse to whom Paul betroths
and unites souls when he says: "for I betrothed you to Christ to present you as a pure bride to her one husband" [2 Cor 11:2]), . . . that
spouse simply doesn't allow the soul which has taken him as husband
to have anything to do with adulterers; his jealousy over her is aroused
and he defends the chastity of his marriage. God is called a "jealous
God" (Exod 20:5) because he does not allow the soul which is bound to
him to have anything to do with demons. But if she still does, . . . he
gives her a "bill of divorce" (Isa 50:1) and sends her away.

759   "Rebecca was a virgin, she was a virgin whom no man had known"
(Gen 24:16). . . . But is there such a thing as a virgin whom a man
has known? Now I have often said that it is not history being narrated
here, but mysteries being woven. I think that something like the following is meant here. Just as Christ is called the man of the soul
whom the soul marries when it comes to faith, so too is that other,
contrary man whom the soul marries when it falls away from the
faith; he is the one called the "enemy" who "sowed weeds among the
wheat" (Mt 13:25). Therefore it is not enough for a soul to be chaste
in body; it is also necessary that this worst of men "not know her." For
it can happen that someone who has bodily virginity also knows that
worst of men, the devil, and, receiving the darts of concupiscence in
her heart, loses her chastity of soul. Therefore, because Rebecca was
a virgin holy in body and spirit, her virginity was doubly praised.

760   There is an accursed fornication of the body. For what is so deserving of being cursed as desecrating the "temple of God" and "taking the
members of Christ and making them members of a prostitute" (1 Cor
3:16; 6:15)? Yet far more accursed is that general fornication in
which every kind of sin is contained. General fornication is the situation when the soul which has been taken up into communion with the
WORD of God and united with him in marriage, so to speak, is de-
spoiled and violated by another, enemy man. The husband and
bridegroom of the pure and chaste soul, therefore, is the WORD of
God which is Christ the Lord. . . . As long as the soul clings to her
spouse and listens to his word and embraces it, she doubtless receives

from him the seed of the WORD; and as the prophet said: "From your fear, O Lord, we conceived in our womb" (cf. Isa 26:18 LXX). . . . If the soul thus conceives from Christ and bears sons, because of which it can be said of her that "she will be saved through bearing children, if she continues in faith and love and holiness, with modesty" (1 Tim 2:15). . . . But if the unhappy soul abandons the holy nuptials of the divine Word and, deceived by their seductions, throws herself into the adulterous embraces of the devil and the other demons, she will surely generate sons from this, but only the kind about which scripture says: "But children of adulterers will not come to maturity, and the offspring of an unlawful union will perish" (Wis 3:16). . . . For there is never a time when the soul is not giving birth; it is always doing so.

761   The nearer we were to God and the closer to beatitude, so much farther will we be from it when we sin, so much closer to the terrors of the greatest punishments.

762   O would that Jesus would always hold me captive and take me along as his booty and that I would remain bound by his chains, and that I too might be worthy of being called a "prisoner for Christ Jesus" (Eph 3:1).

THE GREAT CANTICLE

In the Song of Songs and its spiritual interpretation are summed up all the situations of the mystical marriage. Of importance in this is the conscious oscillation between the interpretation of the bride as soul and as church: each interpretation depends on the other, and neither is adequately separable from the other (763–777).

763   Songs are what were once sung by the prophets and angels. For "the law," it is said, "was ordained by angels through an intermediary" (Gal 3:19). Thus all those that were proclaimed by them were preliminary songs by the friends of the bridegroom; but this is the one song which was to be sung in the form of an epithalamium to the bridegroom himself as he was about to receive his spouse. In it the bride does not want to be still sung to by the friends of the spouse, but wants to hear the bridegroom himself already present saying in his own words: "Let him kiss me with the kisses of his mouth" (Cant 1:2). Hence it is rightly preferred to all the other songs. For it seems that the other songs which the law and the prophets sang were sung to a

bride who was still a child and had not yet crossed the threshold into maturity, but that this song is sung for a bride already mature and very strong and already capable of receiving manly power and perfect mystery. It is accordingly said of her that she is "the one, perfect dove" (Cant 6:8).

764   The bridegroom is the Word [*logos*], the bride a *logos*-endowed living being—if, that is, the soul has understanding and the bridegroom accepts the bride. But if this is the WORD, he is not united with just one soul but with many different ones: with one who is brilliant with regal glory—let her be called the perfect dove; then with the royal ones a little lower down, hence the sixty queens; and then with the other souls who are educated through fear of God—these are the concubines (cf. Cant 6:8-9).

765   "For lo, the winter is past, the rain is over and gone. The flowers appear on the earth" (Cant 2:11-12). First I understand the winter of the soul as the time when it is still tossed about by the waves of passions and the storms of vices and is buffeted by the fierce winds of the evil spirits. At this time the WORD of God does not urge her to go "outside," but to gather herself within and fortify herself on all sides and take cover against the pernicious winds of the evil spirits. No "flowers" appear to her then in her scripture reading, nor do any secrets of a deeper wisdom or hidden mysteries echo, so to speak, from the "voice of the turtledove." Nor does her sense of smell perceive anything pleasant so to speak from the "blossoms of the vineyard," nor her sight take delight in the "buds of the fig tree." It is enough that in the storms of temptations she remain safe and protected from falling into sin. If she manages this and remains unharmed, her "winter is past" and spring comes for her. Spring for her is when the soul is granted repose and the mind tranquility. Then the WORD of God comes to her, then he calls her to himself and urges her to "go out" not only outside the house but outside the city, that is, not only to be beyond the vices of the flesh but also beyond everything that is bodily and visible in the world.

766   "Behold, there he stands behind our wall, gazing in at the windows, looking through the lattice. My beloved speaks and says to me . . ." (Cant 2:9-10). The spouse of the WORD, the soul, who lives in her royal house, that is, in the church, is instructed by the WORD of God, her spouse, in all the things which are stored and hidden inside the royal hall and "bedroom" of the king. . . . When she is sufficiently familiar with these she receives in herself him who "was in the beginning with God, the WORD of God" (cf. Jn 1:11), but not as remaining with

her at all times — for this is not possible for human nature —; rather she is at times visited and at other times left alone by him, so that she will desire him the more. But when she is visited by the WORD of God, he is said to come to her, as it is written, "leaping upon the mountains" (Cant 2:8), namely, revealing to her the exalted and sublime meanings of heavenly knowledge so that he might move on to the building up of the "church which is the house of the living God, the pillar and bulwark of the truth" (cf. 1 Tim 3:15), and stand "next to the wall" or "behind the wall" (cf. Cant 2:9) so as to be neither fully hidden nor completely in the open. For the WORD of God and the "utterance of wisdom" (cf. 1 Cor 12:8) is not set out in full public view nor does it become visible "to be tread under foot" (cf. Mt 7:6); but when it is sought, it is found; and it is found not, as we said, set out in the open, but veiled and, as it were, hiding "behind the wall" (Cant 2:9).

But the soul, which is said to be the church, is not to be thought of as set within the structures of walls, but within the fortifications of faith and the houses of wisdom and roofed over by the lofty vaults of charity. Good dispositions and belief in right doctrine make a soul resident in the house of the church; this house has different rooms which are called "bedroom" or "wine cellar," etc., according to the different degrees of graces and spiritual gifts. Thus the "wall" here is a part of this house which could indicate the firmness of the doctrines under which the spouse is said to "stand" and in which he is so great and tall that he towers above the whole building and "gazes in" at the bride, that is, the soul. And he still doesn't show himself to her in complete openness but, "looking through the lattice" as it were, exhorts and encourages her not to sit lazily inside but to "go outside" to him and try to see him no longer "through windows" and "lattices" nor "in a mirror dimly," but coming outside to see him "face to face" (1 Cor 13:12). For now, because she cannot yet look upon him this way, he does not "stand before" but "behind" her and "behind the wall." But he "leans in through the windows" (Cant 2:9 LXX) which doubtless were open to let in light and illuminate the house. Thus the WORD of God "leans in" through them and, looking in, exhorts the soul to "arise" and "come" to him.

We can, however, understand the windows as referring to the bodily senses. . . . If the soul, gazing on the splendor of the world, sees from the beauty of creatures that God is the maker of all and praises him and his works, to this soul LIFE enters in through the windows of the eyes. . . . But when it says that he "looks through the lattice of the windows" (Cant 2:9), this doubtless indicates that as long as the soul lives in the house of this body, it cannot grasp the open and uncovered wisdom of God. Instead it contemplates what is invisible and bodiless through certain examples and indicators and images of visible things.

767   "If you stir up and awaken love as far as it wishes" (Cant 2:7). What this means is that when you have come to the point where you begin to be moved "not" with "the spirit of slavery . . . but the spirit of sonship" (Rom 8:15), and when you have made such progress in this that "perfect love" in you "casts out fear" (1 Jn 4:18), you should then "stir up and awaken love" in you as much as he wants, I mean the "son of love"—yes the very one who is "love born of God" (1 Jn 4:7). You should do this lest, thinking that the measures of human love are sufficient for the love of God, you do something that is something less than worthy of God. For the measure of God's love is this alone, that he be loved every bit as much as he himself wishes. But the will of God is ever the same, ever unchanged. Therefore there is never any change or end in the love of God. Take note that the canticle does not say: if you receive love, but: "if you stir up" (Cant 2:7), as if it were already in you, but lying dormant. And further, it does not say "if you find," but "if you awaken love," as if it were really there but slumbering until it found someone to "awaken" it (Cant 2:7). Paul too, it seems to me, was stirring up this love which was still dormant in some disciples when he said: "Awake, O sleeper, and you will gain Christ" (cf. Eph 5:14).

768   Without ceasing the soul searches after the bridegroom, the WORD, and when it finds him it looks for him again, like an addict, in other things as well. And when it has contemplated those, it longs for the revelation of the rest; and having received this, it begs the bridegroom to come and stay longer.

769   "Arise, my love, my fair one, and come away. O my dove, in the clefts of the rock, in the covert of the cliff, let me see your face" (Cant 2:13–14). He wants the soul to transcend the things of the senses. For he calls the world of sense the "wall and fortifications" of the city. Therefore the soul which is one with reason must dwell "in the clefts of the rock," not just outside the city walls but also beyond the outworks so that, when it has come near, the glory of the Lord might be reflected on its unveiled face. . . . For the "outworks" represent the boundary of corporeal but the beginning of incorporeal things.

770 "Open to me, my sister, my love, . . . for my head is wet with dew" (Cant 5:2). "To me" necessarily follows "Open," in order to make no opening for the enemy powers. . . . After the resurrection he entered through closed doors and invited Thomas, and through him all unbelieving souls, to open their hearts and receive the whole fullness of the resurrection. He invited him to say finally: "My Lord and my God!" (Jn 20:28). But the dew points to the resurrection in the morning when the dew falls.

771 "I am wounded with love" (Cant 2:5). She received her wound from him of whom Isaiah said: "He made me a polished arrow, in his quiver he hid me away" (Isa 49:2). It is fitting for God to inflict souls with such a wound, to pierce them with such darts and projectiles and hurt them with salutary wounds so that they too, since "God is love," might say: "I am wounded with love" (Cant 2:5). . . . A soul which is ardent for the wisdom of God could also say in a similar vein: "I am wounded with" wisdom, namely, with the capacity to gaze upon the beauty of his wisdom. And another soul, looking upon the magnificence of his power and admiring the power of the WORD of God, can say: "I am wounded with" power. That would be a soul like the one which said: "The Lord is my light and my salvation; whom shall I fear?" (Ps 27:1). . . . But common to all these is that wound "of love" with which the bride professes to have been "wounded."

772 How beautiful it is, and how becoming, to be wounded by love! Some are struck by the arrow of fleshly love, others are wounded by earthly greed; but as for you, offer yourself with limbs exposed to that "chosen arrow" (Isa 49:2), that beautifully polished arrow of which God is the archer. . . . It was with this arrow that they were wounded who said to each other: "Did not our hearts burn within us while he talked to us on the road, while he opened to us the scriptures?" (Lk 24:32).

773 Blessed then are those souls who bend their back and take the WORD of God as rider on themselves, and bear his bridle so that he directs them wherever he wills and guides them with the reins of his precepts. For they no longer go about as they wish but in all things are led back and forth by the will of the rider.

774 "Lead me into the wine cellar" (Cant 2:4 LXX). She says this to the friends of the bridegroom, the holy angels or the apostles and prophets, as if to say: Mingle me with the body of Christ!

775   Thus, Paul too says: "The body is not for immorality, but for the Lord, and the Lord for the body" (1 Cor 6:13). For the body is the church, the bride of Christ.

776   "Lo, a bright cloud overshadowed them" (Mt 17:5). A bright cloud overshadows the just, simultaneously covering and illuminating them.

777   Thus the bride says: "I will not let him go until I bring him into my mother's house" (Cant 3:4), so that after she has departed this life she can go with him into the house of the Jerusalem above and there enter into the more common levels of the knowledge of the WORD, and into the more ineffable things in the chamber of her who conceived the bride. That the mother and the conceiver are the same is clear from the fact that in this conception she is the beginning of all things; but after the forming and completing of the one conceived, she is called mother.[1]

DIVINE BIRTH

But the whole nuptial mystery is still grounded in the ultimate mystery of childhood in God himself. The eternal Son is constantly being born of the Father (778–779), and in the Son's being born we are born with him (780). Thus, for the Christian, the road does not lead from youth to age but from the age of sin to the eternal youth of being a child born of God (781–783).

778   "You are my son, today I have begotten you" (Ps 2:7). This is spoken to him by God with whom all time is "today." For, it seems to me, there is no evening or morning with God; instead, the "time" so to speak which is coextensive with his uncreated and eternal life is this "today" in which the Son is begotten. Thus no beginning or day for his birth can be found.

779   It is for human beings who before this were incapable of the WORD, the Son of God, that the WORD comes to be. But with God, the WORD does not come to be as if he were not with him

---

[1] Origen likes to build on the words of Paul which call the heavenly Jerusalem (for Origen, the super-worldly community of souls) our mother. This is where the identity of this heavenly Jerusalem with the earthly church is established; the period of earthly existence seems thereby to be expressed by the image of "pregnancy." Before the fall the church is the conceiver, after the restoration she is the mother of born children, but at the same time she is the bride of the WORD who himself leads her (in so far as the Word has come to perfect understanding in her) into the heavenly kingdom.

before; but because he is always with the Father it is said: "And the WORD was with God" . . . for before all time and eternity, "in the beginning was the WORD" (Jn 1:1).

780   Blessed is the one who is always being born of God. Now I am not saying that the just person is born once of God, but continually, according to each good deed in which God begets the just. If then I associate you with the Savior — because the Father did not generate the Son and then send him away after the generation, but generates him continually — I could do something similar for the just person. But we know which of us is the Savior. He is "the reflection of the glory of God" (cf. Heb 1:3). But the reflection of God's glory did not come about just once and then never again; for as long as the light exists which produces the reflection, so long will the reflection of God's glory also be generated. Our Savior is the wisdom of God (cf. 1 Cor 1:24), but wisdom is "a reflection of eternal light" (Wis 7:26). If then the Savior is continually . . . generated by the Father, so with you also; if you have the spirit of sonship (cf. Rom 8:15), God will continually generate you in the spirit with each good work and each disposition. And thus born, you will be continually born a son of God in Christ Jesus.

781   For you should not think that a renewal of life which is said to be once and for all is enough; but the very newness itself, if I may so speak, must be renewed continually, day by day. For, as the Apostle says: "Though our outer nature is wasting away, our inner nature is being renewed every day" (2 Cor 4:16). For just as the old gets older and older, . . . so too is this new [nature] continually renewed.

782   It is possible, then, to pass over from old age and wrinkles to youth; and what is wondrous in this is that while the body progresses from youth to old age, the soul, if it comes to perfection, changes from old age to youth.

783   All human beings are little children if you compare them to the perfection of the WORD. . . . Since what comes to children is much less than what is given to adults, those among the children who seem to be sharper and quicker in understanding should not get puffed up and proud. All those are called children whom the Savior also referred to when he said: "Behold, I and the children whom the Lord has given me" (Isa 8:18). . . . And you must not think that he who received them does not have them just because he who gave them still has them.

MYSTICAL BODY

ONE BODY

Only after the inner appropriation of the objective "incarnation" of the Word (as grace, inner sense, nourishment and marriage) has been completed can the full meaning of the "incarnation" become visible: the building up of the mystical body of Christ and its inner divine life.

The Holy Spirit is the principle of Unity (784). The sign of the good is unity (785–786). The highest praise of a human being is unity (787). Concretely, this unity is that of the humanity of Christ (788–790), but with this building on a natural unity in Adam (790). Indeed all creation, angels included, belongs to the body of the WORD (791–795). Just as the soul suffers not in itself but in its body, so does Christ suffer in his members (796). The point of contact and, as it were, merging point of Christ and the church is the flesh of Christ (797). Christ and the church are "one flesh" like Adam and Eve; from the beginning of time they are made for each other (798). Thus, whoever persecutes the church persecutes Christ (799). In Christ's death and resurrection is included the fate of the church (800). Christ's life is further completed in the church (801– 802). His life in the flesh was only a symbol of his truer life in the church (803). The suffering of the members in each other (804). Even the saints in heaven suffer still with the suffering church (805). The resurrection is completed step by step, as the life of Jesus shows (806). Saved in hope (807).

784   If the God of all, living in the saints, becomes their God, and thus is called the God of Abraham and the God of Isaac and the God of Jacob, how much more can the Holy Spirit, living in the prophets, be called as it were their Spirit, so that one could speak of the spirit of Elias and the spirit of Isaiah?

785   The sign of evil is the confusion of tongues; the sign of virtue is that all "who believed were of one heart and soul" (Acts 4:32). When you search the scripture this way you will find that where there is plurality in number, where there is schism, division and disharmony, etc., all these are signs of evil. . . . But you will find that unity and harmony are signs of virtue.

785a   For the one WORD consists of many aspects, each of which is a part of the whole WORD. Whatever words are proclaimed outside of this one . . . even if they are words about truth, no one of them, to put it paradoxically, is the Word; they are all words. For nowhere is the monad, nowhere the harmony and the one; because of their dissension and quarreling, the one has abandoned them and they have become numbers, perhaps endless numbers.

786   Where there is sin, there is plurality, schism, heresy, dissension; but where there is virtue, there is single-mindedness and unity, so that all the faithful "were of one heart and soul" (Acts 4:32).

787   "There was one man of Armathem of the hill country of Ephraim" (1 Sam 1:1). . . . "There was," then, "one man." Is not this very thing a reason for praising the just man, that one can say of him: "There was one man"? We who are still sinners cannot acquire that title of praise because each of us is not "one" but many. For looking at me is the face of one who is now angry, and then sad, a little later happy, and then disturbed and then gentle, at times concerned with the things of God and actions leading to eternal life, but shortly after doing things based on greed or the glory of this world. You can see, then, that he who was thought to be one is not one at all; but there seem to be as many persons in him as there are customs, because, as scripture says: "The fool changes like the moon" (Sir 27:11). For the moon too, although it seems to be one in its unchanging substance, is still always changing, always different; and thus in it too it is clear that one is many. . . .

But as for the just, not only is each said to be one but they are, all together, said to be one. And why shouldn't they all be called one, who were described as being of "one heart and soul" (Acts 4:32)? They constantly contemplate one wisdom, are of one affection and disposition, reverence one God, confess one Jesus Christ as Lord, are filled with the one Spirit of God. They are rightly called not just one [thing] but "one person," as the Apostle indicated when he said: "All the runners compete but only one receives the prize" (1 Cor 9:24).

You can clearly see that all the just who "receive the prize" are one person. For the just person truly imitates the "one God" who is just. For when the prophetic voice proclaims: "Hear, O Israel: the Lord your God is one God" (Deut 6:4), it seems to me that not just the number "one" is meant, which is indeed to be regarded as above every number, but rather, he is to be understood as "one" in such a way that he never becomes other than he is. That is, he is never changed, never turns into anything else, just as David professes: "But you are the same and your years have no end" (Ps 102:27). . . . Hence also the imitators of God, the just, who were created in his image (cf. Gen 1:27), are also called "one person" when they come to perfection. . . . Because, then, according to this marvelous unity the just is "one," the many just are also "one." Hence the Apostle is exhorting the whole church when he asks "that all of you may say the same thing and that there be no dissensions among you, but that you be united in the same mind and the same judgment" (1 Cor 1:10).

788   "Do you not know that in a race all the runners compete, but only one receives the prize?" (1 Cor 9:24). Is it indeed so that we all run, and only one takes the prize, and the rest of us lose? . . . All the redeemed are one and one body, for we are all "one bread and partake of the same bread" (1 Cor 10:17); and "you are all the body of Christ" (cf. 1 Cor 12:27). Thus all the saved are the "one," the one who takes the prize, . . . the one man of whom the Apostle says: "until we all attain . . . to mature manhood, to the measure of the stature of the fullness of Christ" (Eph 4:13).

789   "One" is used in many ways . . . in the sense of harmony when it is said that "the company of those who believed were of one heart and soul" (Acts 4:32); but also in the sense of identity when it is said that "by one Spirit we were all baptized into one body" (1 Cor 12:13), according to the similarity of the nature. And just as we are all said to have one body, since we have by nature Adam as the origin and head of our race, so too do we consider Christ as our head through the divine rebirth which has become for us a type of his death and resurrection who arose as "the first-born from the dead" (Col 1:18). We claim him as head, because of the prefiguring of the resurrection, of his body, of which all of us are members (cf. Eph 5:30; 1 Cor 12:27); and as his body, we are reborn to incorruption through the Spirit.

790   Every multitude of things which are alike is one, and the many who are alike are not many bodies but one body, as has been written: "You are the body of Christ and individually members of it" (1 Cor 12:27).

And in the "sacrament" of the ninety-nine sheep who were not lost
and the one that was lost, our Savior came "to seek what was lost" (cf.
Lk 15:4–7; Mt 18:12–14). . . . "One body" are the many bodies,
and one sheep are the many sheep which have gone astray.

791   Thus Christ has the whole human race, and perhaps even the
totality of all creatiort, as his body, and each of us is individually a
member of it (cf. 1 Cor 12:27).

792   "You are all brethren" (Mt 23:8). "All" means the whole creation;
and one and only one is Lord, Jesus Christ.

793   And he is the head itself, a gift from God given to the whole house,
and a wondrous head in our eyes which are able to look upon it.

794   "Or do you think that I cannot appeal to my Father, and he will at
once send me more than twelve legions of angels?" (Mt 26:53). For
the angels have more need of the help of the Son of Man than he has
of them. Hence the text which says: "For he will give his angels charge
of you to guard you in all your ways" (Ps 91:11; cf. Mt 4:6; Lk 4:10)
is not to be understood as spoken of the only-begotten Son of God,
but as spoken either of every just person as represented by Christ, or
of Christ himself according to his human nature.

795   But when John says: "He is the expiation for our sins, and not for
ours only but also for the sins of the whole world" (1 Jn 2:2), there
seems to us to be a certain deepening of the mystery. For it shows that
Jesus is the expiation not only of the believers but of the whole world;
but not first of the world and then of us, but first us and only then of
the whole world. For although all creation awaits the grace of the
Redeemer, all will nevertheless come to salvation in their own particular ways.

796   It was written to the faithful: "You are the body of Christ and individually members of it" (1 Cor 12:27). So then, just as the soul
which dwells in the body does not, since it is a spiritual substance, experience hunger, but still hungers after every bodily food because it is
connected with its body, so too does the Savior suffer whatever his
body the church suffers, although he is incapable of suffering as far as
his divinity is concerned.

797   "Behold you are beautiful, my beloved, truly lovely. Our wedding
couch is shady" (Cant 1:16). . . . The common wedding couch
which [the bride] says she shares with the bridegroom seems to me to
indicate the body of the soul. While still in this body she was considered worthy to advance to meet the Word of God. . . . But
because she calls it "our wedding couch," as if indicating a place in the

body common to herself and her spouse, this is to be understood according to that image in which Paul says that our "bodies are members of Christ" (cf. 1 Cor 6:15). For when he says "our bodies," he shows that he is the "body," as it were, of the bride; but when he says "members of Christ," he is indicating that the same bodies are the body of the bridegroom. . . . Consider too whether the body which Jesus assumed, and which is common to him and the bride, could not also be called wedding couch since, through it, the church seems to be united to Christ and be able to share in the Word of God, according to which he is said to be the "mediator between God and men" (1 Tim 2:5), and according to which the Apostle says: in him "we have access by faith in hope of sharing the glory of God" (cf. Rom 5:2).

798   Then, since it is necessary to hold that the one "who is united to the Lord becomes one spirit with him" (1 Cor 6:17), in the case of those who are joined together by God, after the words: "So they are no longer two" come the words: "but one flesh" (Mt 19:6). It is God who has joined the two into one so that, when the woman is married to the man by God, they are no longer two. And since it is God who does the joining, there is a gift of grace in those so joined. Paul knew this since he . . . called marriage according to God's word a gift of grace (cf. 1 Cor 7:7). . . . But since the Apostle takes the words: "The two shall become one flesh" as applying to Christ and the church (cf. Eph 5:31-32), it must be said that Christ did not dismiss his first (so to speak) wife (the former synagogue) for any other reason—observing the injunction: "What therefore God has joined together, let no man put asunder" (Mt 19:6)—than that this wife committed adultery, after being corrupted by the evil one and plotting with him against her husband and killing him with the words: "Away with such a fellow from the earth!" and "Crucify, crucify him!" (Acts 22:22; Lk 23:18, 21). Thus, instead of him dismissing her, she is the one who herself made off. . . . He who in the beginning made them in his image (cf. Gen 1:27), while he was still "in the form of God" (cf. Phil 2:6) made him male and the church female, giving to both the gift of unity according to his image.

And for the sake of the church, the Lord—the husband—who was with the Father when he was "in the form of God" (Phil 2:6), left also his mother—he himself being the son of the Jerusalem above—and was joined to his wife down here who had already fallen, and the two, down here, became one flesh. For it was for their sakes that he himself became flesh when "the Word became flesh and dwelt among us"

(Jn 1:14). "No longer are they two, but now they are one flesh" (Mt 19:6), since to the woman (the church) is said: "You are the body of Christ and individually members of it" (1 Cor 12:27). For the body of Christ is not something apart or different from the church which, with its individual members, is his body. But both of these, who are now no longer two but have become one flesh, God has joined together, forbidding man to separate the church from the Lord.

799   From this it is clear that anyone who becomes a betrayer of the disciples of Jesus is to be considered a betrayer of Jesus. Hence the words to Saul when he was still a persecutor: "Saul, Saul, why do you persecute me?" (Acts 9:4).

800   "God raised us up together with Christ and made us sit with him in the heavenly places" (Eph 2:6). If you believe that Christ has risen from the dead, believe too that you yourselves will likewise rise with him; and if you believe that he is sitting at the right hand of the Father in heaven, believe too that you yourselves will no longer be on earth but in heaven; and if you believe that you have died with Christ, believe that you will also live with him; and if you believe that Christ has died to sin and lives to God, be you also dead to sin and alive to God.

801   If there had been a mere man in Mary's womb and not the Son of God, how could it have come about that, both then and now, many sicknesses not only of the body but also of the soul are being cured? . . . Which of us was not wandering far astray, while we now, because of the Savior's coming, are no longer tossed about and upset but are actually on the way towards him who said: "I am the way" (Jn 14:6)? We could also bring in all the rest and see that everything that has been written of him . . . his birth and upbringing and power and passion and resurrection do not refer only to that time, but are also active now in us.

802   His death, then, and his resurrection and his circumcision, all took place for our sakes.

803   Both of these, the temple and the body of Jesus, seem to me, according to one interpretation, to be a type of the church signifying that it is built of living stones, a spiritual house for a holy priesthood (1 Pet 2:5). . . . The temple will be rebuilt and the body will rise again on the third day, after the day of evil which threatens it and the day of consummation which comes after (cf. 2 Pet 3:3, 10, 13). For the third day will rise on the new heaven and the new earth (cf. Rev 21:1; 2 Pet 3:13) when these bones—the whole house of Israel—will rise again on the great day of the Lord, victorious over death. Thus it

is that the already completed resurrection of Christ, including his sufferings on the cross, contains the mystery of the resurrection of the whole body of Christ. But as that physical body of Jesus was crucified and buried and then raised up, so the whole body of Christ's saints is crucified with Christ and now lives no longer (cf. Gal 2:20). . . . "All my bones are scattered" (Ps 22:14 LXX). . . . But when the actual resurrection of the true and more perfect body of Christ takes place, then will the members of Christ, which now exist, in comparison with the future, dry bones (cf. Ezek 37:7), be gathered together. . . . Then the many members will be the one body, all the members of the body, though they are many, becoming one body (cf. 1 Cor 12:12). But the distinction between foot and hand and eye and ear and nose, which in one sense fills out the head and in another sense represents the feet and the rest of the members, the weaker and the humbler, the less honorable and the more honorable — this distinction is for God alone to make who will put together the body and, more than he does now, will give "the greater honor to the inferior part,[1] that there may be no discord in the body, but that the members may have the same care for one another, and if one member suffers, all suffer together; if one member is honored, all rejoice together" (1 Cor 12:24–26).

804   "O Lord my God, I cried to you for help, and you have healed me" (Ps 30:2). If these words are attributed to the Savior, see whether they could not be properly explained in this way: Those who believe "are the body of Christ and individually members of it." But "if one member suffers, all suffer together; if one member is honored, all rejoice together" (1 Cor 12:27, 26). This is how the body of Christ suffers and needs healing.

805   Now if the knowledge given to those worthy of it in the present age comes "in a mirror, dimly," but will be revealed "then face to face" (1 Cor 12:12), it is not out of place to think analogously of the other virtues; for what is being prepared for in this life will be made properly perfect only then. The one most sublime of the virtues, according to God's Word, is love of neighbor. We have to think that, in contrast to those still struggling in this life, it is far more strongly present in the saints who have gone before us than with those still in human weakness

---

[1] Behind this lies the idea that in the course of endless aeons, during which the souls ascend to heaven, those who are "backward" and lower down will finally catch up to the perfect so that the original equality will be restored and all the just will shine like one single sun.

and struggling with the lower elements. For it is not just here below that the words: "If one member suffers, all suffer together; if one member is honored, all rejoice together" (1 Cor 12:26) apply to love of sister and brother. For it is also fitting for the love which exists beyond the present life to speak of "the anxiety of all the churches. Who is weak and I am not weak? Who is made to fall, and I am not indignant?" (2 Cor 11:28-29).

806　"Destroy this temple, and in three days I will raise it up" (Jn 2:19). Each one . . . must be destroyed by the zeal [of Jesus] living within him so as to be raised up by Jesus . . . "in three days." For after its destruction the building up of the temple takes place on the first and second days, but the completion of the resurrection involves all the three days. Hence the resurrection both has taken place and is still to take place; indeed we are buried with Christ and are risen with him (cf. Rom 6:4). And because what is meant by "We are risen with him" is not enough for the full resurrection, there is added "In Christ all shall be made alive. But each in his own order: Christ the first fruits, then at his coming those who belong to Christ. Then comes the end" (1 Cor 15:22-24). For it was resurrection to be in God's paradise on the first day (cf. above No. 376), and resurrection when he appeared and said: "Do not hold me, for I have not yet ascended to the Father" (Jn 20:17). But the completion of the resurrection came about when he went to the Father.[1]

807　If, then, we too have been united with the death of Christ (cf. Rom 6:5, 10) in the winter of this world and present life, we will also in the spring to come be found to be bearing fruits of justice from his root (cf. Jn 15:1-2).

ONE SACRIFICE

Christ the Priest

The unity of the mystical body is above all a unity of redemption. Not only the head, but the whole body too, is sacrificed for the salvation of the world, even if only the head is the spotless offering from whose power all the other offerings of his body take their

---

[1] The three stages of the resurrection of Christ are the image of the three stages of the resurrection of the mystical body.

*possibility and effectiveness. The following passages come mostly
from Origen's exegesis of Leviticus, his interpretation of Old Testament priesthood. One must always keep in mind here that for Origen
and his time (as it had been also for the Epistle to the Hebrews), the
application of the name of priest (or high priest) still had very much
the character of a* comparison, *or spiritual "allegory."*

*In a strict sense, Christ is the only priest of the new covenant
(808–809). He is spiritual offering, priest and altar all in one
(810–811). He allowed himself to be killed in a bloody manner for
the benefit of all human beings, but his spiritual sacrificial disposition is also of benefit to the heavenly world (812–813).*

808   Everyone who is a priest among human beings is small and insignificant in relation to that priest of whom God said: "You are a priest
forever after the order of Melchisedek" (Ps 110:4; Heb 5:6; 7:17). But
he is the "great priest" (cf. Lev 21:10) who can "pass through the
heavens" (Heb 4:14) and transcend all creation and ascend to him
who "dwells in unapproachable light" (1 Tim 6:16), the God and
Father of all.

809   There is indeed one great high priest, our Lord Jesus Christ. But
he is not the high priest of priests, but the high priest of high priests,
. . . just as he is not called king of the people but "King of kings" and
not lord of servants but "Lord of lords" (1 Tim 6:15).

810   Who then is it who offers sacrifice "before the Lord" (Lev 6:25)?
The person, I should think, who has not "gone away from the presence
of the Lord" like Cain and become filled with "fear and trembling"
(Gen 4:14, 16). It is, thus, someone who has the confidence to stand
"before the Lord" and does not flee from his face nor, in the consciousness of sin, turn away from his countenance. This is the one who
offers sacrifice "before the Lord." . . . I want to have the courage to
say something more, if you will but listen. What is the "victim" which
is offered for sins and is the "Holy of Holies" if not the "only begotten
Son of God" (cf. Jn 3:18), my Lord Jesus Christ? He alone is the sacrifice "for sin," he himself the offering which is the "Holy of Holies"
(cf. Lev 6:25). But when the text continues: "The priest who offers it
for sin shall eat it" (Lev 6:26) it becomes difficult to understand. For
that which is supposed to be eaten seems to refer to sin, just as in
another place the prophet says that the priests "shall eat the sins of my
people" (Hos 4:8). We have often shown from the holy scriptures that
Christ is both the sacrifice which is offered for sin and the priest which

offers the sacrifice. The Apostle explains this in one phrase when he says: "who offered himself to God" (Heb 9:14). He, then, is the priest who eats and consumes "the sins of the people." . . . How does he eat the sins of the people? Hear what is written: "Our God is a devouring fire" (cf. Deut 4:24). What does this "God-fire" consume? Will we be stupid enough to think that God as fire consumes "wood" or "hay" or "stubble" (cf. 1 Cor 3:12)? Rather, "God-fire" consumes human sins, devours them, gets rid of them and purifies them, as is written in another place: "And I will purify you with fire until you are pure" (Isa 1:25 LXX). . . . While on the other hand, "death" is said "to be the shepherd" (Ps 49:14) of those who remain in their sins.

811   Thus you will find that . . . he himself is the expiation and high priest and sacrifice which is offered for the people (cf. Rom 3:25).

812   But what is the sacrifice of the priest for sin (cf. Lev 4:3)? It is written: "A young bull," as "a burnt offering" (cf. Lev 4:3; 1:3). For the second time we find that "a young bull" is offered by the high priest "as a burnt offering": once for his official duty (Lev 1:3) and once for [his own] sin (Lev 4:3). The one for his official duty is burned "upon the altar of burned offering" (cf. Lev 4:10); but the one "for sin," is burned "outside the camp" (cf. Lev 4:12). . . . See now whether Jesus, whom Paul says "has pacified by his blood" (cf. Col 1:20) "not only what is on earth but also what is in heaven" (cf. Eph 1:10), is not himself the young bull who is offered up "in heaven" not "for sin" but for his official duty, but on earth, where sin "reigned from Adam to Moses" (Rom 5:14), is offered up for sin. And this is what it is to have suffered "outside the camp": outside the heavenly camp of the angels of God which Jacob saw, . . . and at the sight of which Jacob said: "This is the camp of God" (Gen 32:2). Hence every earthly place in which we live and in which Christ suffered in the flesh is outside that heavenly camp.

813   But here too, it is perhaps not without reason that it was already written that he should "offer it at the door of the tent of meeting" (Lev 1:3), but later, in repeating this, it says: "at the altar which is at the door of the tent of meeting" (Lev 1:5). As if it were not enough to have designated the place once in the same account! — except that he perhaps wanted it to be understood that the blood of Jesus is shed not only in Jerusalem, where there was the altar and the base of the altar and the tent of meeting, but that this very same blood is also sprinkled on that altar above which is in heaven and where the "assembly of the first-born" (Heb 12:23) is. As the Apostle says: "All things, whether

on earth or in heaven, he pacified by the blood of his cross" (Col 1:20). He thus rightly mentions a second time the "altar that is at the door of the tent of meeting" (Lev 1:5), because Jesus was offered in sacrifice not only for what is on earth but also for what is in heaven. Here below he poured out for human beings the very bodily material of his blood; but in heaven, by the ministry of priests — if there are any there — he offered up the life-giving power of his body as a kind of spiritual sacrifice. You want to know just why there was a double sacrifice, one suited for what is on earth and the other for what is in heaven? The Apostle, writing to the Hebrews, says: "through the curtain, that is, through his flesh" (Heb 10:20). And then the inner curtain is interpreted as "heaven" (Heb 9:24) which Jesus "has entered . . . to appear in the presence of God on our behalf" (Heb 9:24), "always," he says, "living to make intercession for them" (Heb 7:25). If then these are understood to be two curtains through which Jesus as high priest has entered, the sacrifice also must consequently be understood as double, through which he saved what is on earth and what is in heaven.

Royal Priesthood

If, as far as priesthood is concerned, head and body are one Christ, the priesthood of the body applies radically to all the members. All are "priests," but only some are "presbyters," called by a special ordination to offer the "typical sacrifice" for the community. Each member of the church must, as priest, offer up its sacrifice of praise so that Christ can lay it before the Father (814–815). But there is in the church, apart from the outer, also an inner hierarchy of priests which, according to the outer model of the Mosaic priesthood, has levels of inner priestly disposition (816). The sacrifices of the Christians are their own lives (817), their hearts (818), in which the fire of sacrifice should constantly burn (819), their whole existence (820–821). However, those who are priests do not automatically possess this inner priestly disposition (822). The magnificent example of Abraham in the sacrificing of his son (823). The decisive sacrifice, however, is the offering of his self (824), the "losing" of his soul (825).

814   You have heard of two buildings: the one visible, as it were, and accessible to the priests, the other invisible, as it were, and inaccessible.

Except for the one high priest, the rest remain outside. That first building, I think, can be understood as this church in which we now are in the flesh, in which priests minister at the altar of burnt offerings after lighting that fire of which Jesus said: "I came to cast fire upon the earth; and would that it were already kindled!" (Lk 12:49). And you should not be surprised that this building is only for priests. For all who are anointed with the oil of sacred chrism [baptism] become priests, as Peter says to the whole church: "But you are a chosen race, a royal priesthood, a holy nation" (1 Pet 2:9). You are, therefore, a priestly race; consequently you approach the holy things. But we all have within ourselves our own burnt offering, and we ourselves ignite the altar of our burnt offering so that it will always burn. If I renounce all that I have and take up my cross and follow Christ, I have offered a burnt offering at the altar of God (cf. Lk 14:33; Mk 8:34); or "if I deliver my body to be burned, having love" (cf. 1 Cor 13:3), and if I attain the glory of martyrdom, I have offered myself as a burnt offering at the altar of God. If I love my brothers so that I lay down my life for my brethren (cf. 1 Jn 3:16), "if I strive even to death for justice, for the truth" (cf. Sir 4:28), I have offered a burnt offering at the altar of God. If I "mortify" my "members" from all concupiscence of the flesh (cf. Col 3:5), if "the world is crucified to me and I to the world" (Gal 6:14), I have offered a burnt offering at the altar of God and become myself the priest of my sacrifice. This, then, is how the priestly office is carried out and the sacrifices are offered in the first building. And the high priest, clothed in sacred vestments, goes from this building and enters within the inner curtain, just as in the words of Paul we quoted above which say: "Christ has entered, not into a sanctuary made with hands, . . . but into heaven itself, now to appear in the presence of God on our behalf" (Heb 9:24). It is heaven and the very throne of God that is signified by the figure and image of the inner building.

But consider the marvelous arrangement of the mysteries: The high priest, on entering into the Holy of Holies, carries with him fire from this altar and takes incense from this building. But he also takes his vestments from this place. Do you think that my Lord, the true high priest, will deign to take even from me a part of the "incense beaten small" (Lev 16:12) which he bears with him to the Father? Do you think he will find in me some small spark, and my burnt offering already ignited, from which "to fill his censer with coals" (Lev 16:12) and offer them as a "pleasing odor" (Lev 17:6 and passim) to God the Father? Blessed is the one whose burnt-offering coals he finds so alive and so ignited that he judges them suitable to put on the "altar of incense" (cf. Lev 4:7). Blessed the one in whose heart he will find such a delicate, such a finely tuned and such a spiritual sense . . . that he deigns to fill his hands with it and offer to God the Father the pleasing fragrance of his understanding.

Unhappy, on the other hand, is the soul whose fire of faith is extinguished and whose warmth of love is cooling. For when our heavenly high priest comes to this soul looking for burning and glowing coals on which to offer incense to the Father, he finds in it only meager cinders and cold coals. Such souls are all those who pull back and separate themselves from the WORD of God so that they would not, on hearing the divine words, be ignited to faith, warmed to love, and fired up to mercy. Do you want me to show you how fire comes forth from the words of the Holy Spirit and enkindles the hearts of the faithful? Listen to what David the psalmist says: "Your word fired him up" (Ps 119:140 LXX). And in the gospel, too, it is written, after the Lord spoke to Cleopas: "Did not our hearts burn within us while he opened to us the scriptures?" (Lk 24:32). But you, now: what will make you burn? How shall coals of fire be found in you if you are never ignited with the Lord's WORD, never inflamed with the words of the Holy Spirit?

815   The irrational animals are sacrificed when they are fat, and they are wholly burned up; rational beings, however, become fat only after being offered, for after the purification of holy fire, what has been wholly sanctified by fire is made worthy of understanding.

816   The people from the tribes offer to God tithes and first fruits through the levites and priests, but do not consider everything to be first fruits or tithes (cf. Lev 23:10; 27:30). The levites and priests who receive everything in tithes and first fruits offer tithes to God through the high priest, and first fruits too, I think. Now among us who follow the teachings of Christ, the majority are busy with the many things of this life and dedicate only a few actions to God. . . . But they who devote themselves to the divine word and are given solely to the service of God . . . could even be called our levites and priests. And perhaps those who are the best of all and have, so to speak, the first places in their generations, will be the high priests, but according to the order of Aaron and not according to the order of Melchisedek (cf. Heb 7:11).

817   Or don't you know that to you also, that is, to the whole church of God and to all those who believe, the priesthood has been given?

Listen to how Peter speaks of the faithful: "a chosen race," he says, "royal, priestly, a holy nation, a people for God's possession" (1 Pet 2:9). You have, therefore, the priesthood because you are a "priestly race" and thus "you must offer to God a sacrifice of praise" (cf. Heb 13:15), a sacrifice of prayer, a sacrifice of mercy, a sacrifice of modesty, a sacrifice of justice, and a sacrifice of holiness.

318 The altar, therefore, is the human heart; it is the most important part of the human being. The vows and gifts which are placed on the altar are everything that is placed on the heart. For example, you propose to pray: you place the vow of your prayer on your heart as if on an altar. . . . Thus every vow of a human being turns his heart into something honorable and holy from which the vow is offered to God. Thus there cannot be a vow that is more worthy than the heart of the human being from which the vow is transmitted. . . . For the altar is the heart which sanctifies the vow of the person who is "clean of heart" (cf. Mt 5:8).

319 Take heed: there must always be "fire on the altar" (cf. Lev 6:12–13). And you too, if you are a high priest of God, as is written: "For you shall all be called priests of the Lord" (Isa 61:6); for to you also are spoken the words: "chosen race, royal priesthood, a people for God's possession" (1 Pet 2:9). If therefore you wish to perform the priestly duty of your soul, never let the fire go from your altar.

320 Once, when I was reading in the Apostle where he said: "Pray constantly" (1 Thes 5:17), I asked myself if it were possible to observe this precept. For how can anyone never stop praying, and thus have not time for food or drink? To take care of these needs it would seem that prayer has to be interrupted. . . . But is it not perhaps true that all the actions of those who are in the service of God, and all the deeds and words which they do or say under God, are related to prayer? . . . I think we are also taught this in the Psalms where it says: "Let the lifting up of my hands be as an evening sacrifice" (Ps 141:2). For I do not think that when someone has raised or stretched his "hands" to heaven—as is the custom when praying—that one has automatically offered a "sacrifice" to God. But is it not perhaps true that the meaning of God's word is that "hands" are understood as works? For that person raises his "hands" who raises his actions above the earth and whose "home," even while still on earth, is "in heaven" (Phil 3:20).

321 The precept: "Pray constantly" (1 Thes 5:17) . . . can be understood as taking the entire life of a saint as one great prayer, only part of which is what is normally called prayer.

822   One should note the difference between the lower priests and the higher priestly offices. The lesser priests are not given double robes, nor the "shoulder-cloth" [ephod], nor the "oracular breastplate," nor the "turban" (Lev 8:7–9), but only "girdles" and "caps" to keep their tunic in place (Lev 8:13). They therefore receive the grace of priesthood and exercise that office, but not in the way that he does who is also adorned with the "shoulder-cloth" and "oracular breastplate," resplendent with "manifestation and truth" [the Urim and the Thummim], and bedecked with the "golden plate" and "holy crown" (cf. Lev 8:7–9). Hence I consider it one thing for priests to exercise their office, and another thing to be equipped and adorned in every way. For anyone can carry out a solemn ceremony for the people; but there are few who are adorned with good morals, instructed in doctrine, formed in wisdom and truly suited to represent the truth. . . . The name for priesthood is thus one; but the worthiness that goes with a meritorious life or the virtues of the soul is not one.

823   "God tested Abraham and said to him: . . . Take your son, your dearly beloved [LXX] son Isaac, whom you love" (Gen 22:2). For it wasn't enough to have said "son," but "dearly beloved" is added. Fine, but even beyond this we read: "whom you love"! Just look at the severity of the temptation! With sweet names of endearment repeated again and again, his fatherly affection is aroused so that this awakened memory of love would hold back the right hand of the father from sacrificing the son, and so that the whole armory of the flesh would fight against the faith of the soul. . . . What need was there for you to mention the name of Isaac? Didn't Abraham know that his most dear son, whom he loved, was called Isaac? Why add this — at this time? Simply so that Abraham would be reminded that you had said to him: "Through Isaac shall your descendants be named" (Gen 21:12; cf. Rom 9:7–8; Heb 11:18; Gal 3:16, 18; 4:23). The name is also mentioned so that the doubt would also extend to the promises which were made under this name. All this, however, because God tested Abraham.

What happened then? "Go," said God, "into a high land, to one of the mountains which I will show you, and offer him up there as a burnt offering" (Gen 22:2 LXX). See how the testing is intensified with each detail. . . . Could not Abraham have first been led with his boy to that high land . . . and there been told to offer up his son? But he is first told that he must sacrifice his son and then is commanded to go "into a high land" and climb up a mountain. For what reason?

So that for the entire journey, he would be tortured by his thoughts as he walked along and made his way, so that he would be torn on one side by so urgent a command, but on the other side by the resistance of his love for his only son. That is why a journey was also commanded, and the climbing of a mountain too, so that in all this, emotions and faith, love of God and of the flesh, present grace and future hope, would all have room in which to struggle. He is sent "into a high land." But for the great work the Patriarch was to carry out for the Lord, high land was not enough; he was also ordered to climb a mountain so that, elevated by faith, he would leave behind the things of the earth and ascend to those above.

"So Abraham rose early in the morning" (Gen 22:3). . . . He doesn't argue, doesn't hold back, doesn't take counsel with anyone, but immediately begins the journey. "And he came," it says, "to the place which the Lord had told him, on the third day" (Gen 22:3-4). (. . . For when the people came out of Egypt, they also offered sacrifice on the third day and were purified on the third day; and the day of the Lord's resurrection is the third day. . . .) For there was no mountain in that region, and the whole thing was to take place in mountains. The journey lasted for three days, and for the whole three days the father's heart is subjected to ever-recurring tortures; for the father had to gaze upon his son for so long a time, and eat with him; and for so many nights the boy lay in his father's arms, rested on his breast, slept in his lap. Could the testing be any more intense?

"Abraham took the wood of the burnt offering, and laid it on Isaac his son; and he took in his hand the fire and the knife. So they went both of them together" (Gen 22:6). Since Isaac himself carries "the wood of the burnt offering" he is a figure of the fact that Christ too "bore his own cross" (cf. Jn 19:17). But it is the duty of the priest to carry "the wood of the burnt offering." He thus becomes both sacrifice and priest.

Many of you who are hearing this here in church are fathers. Do you think that any of you might take from the account of these events enough constancy, enough strength of soul, that when perchance a son is lost to the death that is common to and destined for all, even if he is an only son, even if he is dearly loved, you might take Abraham as your model? . . . And yet you will not be asked to have such greatness of soul that you yourself must bind your son, you yourself hold him down, you yourself draw the sword and you yourself strike him dead. All these duties are not asked of you. But be at least firm in resolution, and set in faith. Joyfully offer your son to God. Be the priest of the soul of your son; it is not fitting for the priest who is offering sacrifice to be weeping. Do you want proof that this is required of you? In the gospel the Lord says: "If you were Abraham's children, you would do what Abraham did" (Jn 8:39). Look, this is the work of Abraham. Do what Abraham did, but not with sadness, "for God loves a cheerful giver" (2 Cor 9:7). And if you also are as prompt in obeying God, to you too will be said: "Go into a high land, to one of the mountains which I will show you, and there offer me your son" (Gen 22:2). . . .

But we want now to compare this with what the Apostle says of God: "He who did not spare his own Son but gave him up for us all" (Rom 8:32). See God, with marvelous magnanimity, competing with men! Abraham offered to God his mortal son who was not supposed to die; God gave up his immortal Son to death for the sake of human beings. What will we say to this? "What shall we give to the Lord for all that he has given to us?" . . . Thus we seem to be doing business with the Lord, but to us come the profits of the business. We seem to be offering sacrifices to God, but what we offer is given back to us. For God has need of nothing but wants us to be rich: in all things it is our progress that he desires.

824   For to offer up a son or daughter or cattle or land, all this is outside ourselves. But to offer oneself to God, and to please him not with someone else's work but with one's own, this is more perfect and more sublime than any vow. Whoever does this is an "imitator of Christ" (cf. 1 Cor 4:16). For he gave to human beings "the earth and the sea and all that is in them" (Acts 14:15); he gave also the sky for them, set out the sun and the moon and the stars to serve them, and bestowed on them the rain and the winds and everything that is in the world. But after all this he gave himself: "For God so loved the world that he gave his only son" (Jn 3:16) for the life of this world. What is so great about the deed of those who offer themselves to the God who first offered himself? If then you "take up your cross and follow Christ" (cf. Mt 10:38), if you say: "It is no longer I who live, but Christ who lives in me" (cf. Gal 2:20), if "our soul thirsts and longs to depart and be with Christ" (cf. Ps 41:3; Phil 1:23) . . . then we have offered ourselves, that is, our soul, to God.

825   "Whoever would save his life will lose it" (Mt 16:25). In the first place, the meaning here is double, for it can on the one hand be saying this: If someone is a lover of life and thinks that the present life is

good, and thus is concerned to keep his soul alive in the flesh, and is afraid to die, thinking he would lose it through death, such a person will lose his soul through his very desire to save it because he is putting it outside the limits of blessedness. . . . But we can also understand this *logion* in another way: If someone, considering what salvation really is, wishes to attain the salvation of his soul, such a person, renouncing this world and "denying himself and taking up his cross and following me" (Mt 16:24), would lose his soul in relation to the world. . . . There has to be a certain good end of the soul for Christ's sake as a prelude to its blessed redemption. . . . Each one must lose his soul so that, after he has lost it as sinful, he can regain it as healed for good actions.

Co-Redemption

From the universal priesthood of all Christians comes the active co-redemption of the members with Christ. Origen reserves this first for select souls which, in addition to their own sufferings, also take on sufferings for others (826–827). But in the last analysis, all Christians are sent to their suffering brothers (828–829). Consequently, all must also share in the sufferings of the apostles and prophets (830). Every Christian must become like Christ in his sacrifice (830–835), with the grace of Christ (836). All progress in the Christian life is an increase of suffering and persecutions (837–840), and the vision of God becomes one with death (841). Longing for spiritual death (842). The heroic sacrifice of Paul (843). The "greater" deeds of Christ in his weak members (844). The everyday aspect of Christian martyrdom (845–846).

26   But let us come back to our high priest, "the great high priest who has passed through the heavens, Jesus" (Heb 4:14) our Lord, and let us see how he himself, together with his sons, namely, the apostles and martyrs, takes away the sins of the saints. Indeed everyone who believes in Christ knows that he . . . wipes out our sins by his death. But let us see what we can do to show from the sacred scripture how his sons, the apostles and martyrs, take away the sins of the saints. Hear first what Paul says: "I will most gladly," he says, "spend and be spent for your souls." And in another place he says: "For I am already on the point of being sacrificed, and the time of my departure" — or "dissolution" — "has come" (2 Tim 4:6). Thus the Apostle says that he

is being "spent" and "offered up" for those to whom he is writing. But when a sacrifice is offered it is offered for the purpose of purging the sins of those for whom the victim is killed. The apostle John writes in the Apocalypse about the martyrs that "the souls of those who had been slain because of the name of the Lord Jesus stand at the altar" (cf. Rev 6:9). But whoever stands at the altar is shown thereby to be exercising the priestly office; and the office of a priest is to intercede for the sins of the people.

827   Among the people of God are some, as the Apostle says, who "fight for God" (2 Tim 2:3-4). They are obviously those who do not get involved in worldly affairs; and they are the ones who "go out to battle" (cf. Num 31:27) and fight against the enemy nations and "against the spiritual hosts of wickedness" (Eph 6:12) on behalf of the rest of the people and of those who are weaker. . . . But they fight with prayers and fasts, justice and piety, gentleness and chastity and all the virtues of abnegation, as if armed with so many weapons of war. And when they come back to the camp victorious, even the weak and those not called to be warriors will enjoy the fruits of their labors.

828   "It is good for us to be here" (Mt 17:4). Peter, as one loving the contemplative life and preferring its delights to life among the many with its disturbances, said, wishing to benefit those who desired such a life: "It is good for us to be here." But since love does "not insist on its own way" (cf. 1 Cor 13:5), Jesus did not do that which seemed good to Peter. Accordingly, he came down from the mountain to those unable to ascend it and see his transfiguration, so that they would still see him at least to the extent of their capacity. It is characteristic of the righteous person who possesses the love which does "not insist on its own way," to be "free from all" in order to make himself a servant "to all" here below in order to "win the more" of them (cf. 1 Cor 9:19).

829   Who is it then who has no garment? The one who is totally without God. We must therefore take off our own clothes and give to those who are naked.

830   In our prayers we often say: Almighty God, give us a share in the work of the prophets, give us a share in the work of the apostles of your Christ so that we also might be found to be in the following of Christ himself. When we say these things, we don't realize what we are praying for; for, in effect, this is what we are saying: give us to suffer what the prophets suffered, grant that we be hated as the prophets were hated, put words in our mouths for which we will be hated, make us fall into the kinds of disasters into which the apostles

fell. But to say: give me a share in the work of the prophets, and not suffer what the prophets suffered or be unwilling to suffer, that is wrong! To say: give me a share in the work of the apostles, and not be willing, with the attitude of Paul, to say honestly: "with far greater labors, far more imprisonments, with countless beatings, and often near death" (2 Cor 11:23) and so forth, is the greatest wrong of all! . . . The admirable apostles, abused in countless ways because of the truth, say: "For the sake of Christ, then, I am content with weakness, insults, hardships, persecutions, and calamities" (2 Cor 12:10). We must only make sure that in our tribulations we are abused for no other reason than for Christ's sake . . . that the reason why we suffer is Christ.

31   "They attack me without cause" (Ps 109:3). The just person who is attacked—not in every way, but "without reason"—has a share in the work of Christ. It is a gift of God to be attacked and hated for the sake of Jesus Christ.

32   We, therefore, who read and hear this must make sure of both of these: being chaste in body and true in spirit . . . that we may be found worthy of being conformed to the image of the sacrifice of Christ (cf. Rom 12:1-2).

33   For in him is every sacrifice summed up and repeated.

34   Hence every thought and idea of ours, every word and deed in which we are involved should breathe our self-abnegation as we give witness about Christ and in Christ. For I am convinced that every deed of a perfect person is a witnessing of Jesus Christ, and that every rejection of sin is a denial of self which leads one in the footsteps of Jesus. Such a person is crucified with Christ (Gal 2:20), is someone who "takes up his cross and follows" (Mt 16:24) him who for us takes up his cross, as John records: "They took Jesus, and he went out, bearing his own cross" (Jn 19:17).

35   "They compelled" Simon "to carry the cross" of Christ (Mt 27:32). It was not fitting for the Savior to carry his cross alone; but it was fitting for us, subjected to a salutary compulsion, to carry it too.

36   "I will take up the cup of salvation" (Ps 116:13). It is as if I were answering the question: "Are you able to drink the cup that I am to drink?" (Mt 20:22) and saying: I can, Lord. Thus do I say: I take up the cup of your passion with full free will; but holding on to the grace of your cup, that is, your passion, unto the end, that is beyond my strength; hence "I call on the name of the Lord" (Ps 116:13).

37   As soon as we receive a share in the more perfect things, we have stronger and more numerous adversaries, as the Apostle says: "A

wide door . . . has opened to me, and there are many adversaries"
(1 Cor 16:9).

838   As often as you become hard pressed, so often will you also be given
spiritual food.

839   But when one makes progress and begins to stir up and call the inner human being to see God with the unveiled eye of the spirit, that
person is then attacked by the enemy not just with curses but with
"supercurses"; that is, with an even more intense hurling of curses.

840   The more one progresses to a clearer vision of the Word, the more
will he (because Christ will be more perfectly found in him) be hated
by all who hate Christ, and not so much by all the pagans of flesh and
blood as by the pagans of the "spiritual hosts of Wickedness" (cf. Eph
6:12). For it is precisely the implanted manifestation of the qualities
of Christ in him which is the reason why he is called Christian, and
which makes him be hated by all who have the spirit of the world.

841   "The cloud of the tent of meeting covered them and the congregation rushed at Moses and Aaron and the glory of the Lord appeared"
(Num 16:42). However great in meritorious living were Moses and
Aaron, however strong they were in the virtues of the soul, the glory
of God still could not appear to them except in persecutions, in difficulties, in dangers, and when they were brought practically to the
point of death. Therefore you too are not to think that the glory of the
Lord can appear to you when you are asleep or at rest.

842   "And from Nahaliel we came to Bamoth" (Num 21:19) which
means: coming of death. Of whose death are we to understand this
coming if not that of him by which we die with Christ so as also to live
with him (cf. 2 Tim 2:11; 1 Thes 5:10), and by which we ought to
mortify our members which are on the earth (cf. Col 3:5), and also by
which "we are buried with him by baptism into death" (Rom 6:4)? If
then someone observes the order of this way of salvation . . . he
must also, after a long journey, come to this place which we said
means "coming of death." But as we learn from scripture, there is one
death which is an enemy of Christ and another which is his friend.
Thus we are not talking here about the death inimical to Christ, of
which is said: "The last enemy to be destroyed is death" (1 Cor 15:26),
and who is the devil. Rather we are talking about this death in which
"we die with him so that we might also rise with him" (cf. 2 Tim 2:11;
1 Thes 5:10), and which God had in mind when he said: "I will kill
and I will make alive" (Deut 32:39). . . . It is therefore for us to wish

to come to Bamoth and with all speed prepare for the arrival of this blessed death.

343 "I want you to understand this mystery, brethren: a hardening has come upon part of Israel, until the full number of the Gentiles come in, and so all Israel will be saved" (Rom 11:25-26). You can see that Paul's prayer was heard; and because he put himself forward as a sacrificial offering, he earned salvation for his brethren. And it seems to me that all this has to be presupposed, in particular that there is no force that could separate him from the love of God, so that when he offers himself to be "accursed" (Rom 9:3) for the sake of his brethren, you do not think it is possible for him to be damned. Instead, just as he who is by nature inseparable from the Father both died and descended into hell, so too Paul, imitating the Master, while he could not be separated from the love of Christ, could become "accursed and cut off from Christ for the sake of my brethren" (Rom 9:3), but by dedication and not by transgression.

344 Perhaps this was what was said in the gospels, that "he who believes in" him will not only do the works that he did, but will also "do greater works than these" (cf. Jn 14:12). It truly seems to me to be something greater when a human being, here in the flesh, weak and fragile, armed solely with the faith of Christ and his word, conquers giants and legions of angels. Although he is the one who is victorious in us, he nevertheless calls it something "greater" to be victorious through us than to be victorious by himself.

345 "All who desire to lead a godly life in Christ Jesus will be persecuted" (2 Tim 3:12). But even though persecution always threatens the just person, this persecution doesn't always have to come from outside: "Fighting without and fear within!" (2 Cor 7:5). For it is the enemy powers which persecute and lead to sin, by means of house-companions, or by a quarrelsome and gossiping wife, or by an insubordinate servant, or by a hundred other things. . . . Whenever one considers the battles of the martyrs with the intention of fighting in the same way, one becomes oneself a martyr of God. . . . There is no just person who is not persecuted, no just person who is not a martyr.

346 The sick did not touch him at all, not even his whole garment; it was enough for them to touch just the hem of his garment in order to be healed (cf. Mt 9:20-21 parr). But we, if we want, can have all of him. For even his body lies now before us, not just to touch but to eat and be filled with it. Therefore let everyone who is weak come near with faith.

For if they who touch the hem of his garment draw such power from it, how much more will they who encompass all of him.

ONE MEAL

All that is essentially WORD in this world, that is, everything that has to do with community and dedication, is grounded in a sacrifice. The great total-Eucharist of the mystical body of Christ (as Augustine also understood it) is nothing other than this communication of the members among themselves in Christ, this being of mutual assistance which then, of course, spreads beyond itself to a perfect Eucharist in the world beyond (847–857).

847   "Jesus took bread" (Mt 26:26). Taking it from God who gives it, he gives it to those who are worthy to receive the bread and the cup. . . . "It was not Moses who gave you the bread from heaven; my Father gives you the true bread from heaven" (Jn 6:32).

848   And Jesus is constantly giving this bread to those who celebrate with him when he, "taking the bread" from the Father, "gives thanks and breaks it and gives it to his disciples" according to each one's capacity to receive it, and gives it to them "saying, 'Take and eat,'" (cf. Mt 26:26); and he shows, when he feeds them with this bread, that it is his own body, since he himself is the WORD, which is necessary for us both now and when it will be fulfilled in the kingdom of God (cf. Mt 26:29). Right now, of course, it is not yet fulfilled, but it will be fulfilled then when we too have been prepared to grasp the full paschal feast which he came to fulfill. For he did not come "to abolish the law . . . but to fulfill it" (cf. Mt 5:17), but with a fulfillment that takes place now "in a mirror, dimly," but will take place "then, face to face" (1 Cor 13:12), when perfection has been reached.

849   Something like this is said in Luke about the bread as well: "I have earnestly desired to eat this passover with you. . . . I tell you I shall not eat it again until it is fulfilled in the kingdom of God" (Lk 22:15–16). Therefore the Savior will eat and drink that paschal bread and wine anew "in the kingdom of God," and will eat and drink with his disciples, . . . "when he delivers the kingdom to God the Father" (1 Cor 15:24). Notice that he says "when I drink it new with you" not at any other time but "in my Father's kingdom" (Mt 26:29). But elsewhere it is said "The kingdom of God does not mean food and drink" (Rom 14:17). For it is in a bodily way and after the manner of the

food and drink of this age that "the kingdom of God does not mean food and drink" [gap in the text] to those who have proven worthy of the heavenly bread and of the bread of angels and of that bread of which the Savior says: "My food is to do the will of him who sent me, and to accomplish his work" (Jn 4:34).

But that we will indeed eat and drink "in the kingdom of God" is demonstrable from many passages in scripture, especially where it is written: "Blessed is he who shall eat bread in the kingdom of God" (Lk 4:15). Therefore this paschal feast will be fulfilled in the kingdom of God and Jesus will eat and drink it with his disciples. And what the Apostle says: "Let no one pass judgment on you in questions of food and drink, etc., which are a shadow of what is to come" (Col 2:16–17), is revelatory of the future mysteries of spiritual food and drink of which the food and drink written about in the law were the shadows. But it is clear that "in the kingdom of God" we will eat true food and drink true drink, thereby building up and strengthening that life which is the truest life of all.

350 But he himself who took the chalice and said: "Drink of it, all of you" (Mt 26:27), does not abandon us as we drink, but drinks it with us (since he is in each one), because we are unable alone and without him either to eat of that bread or drink of the fruit of that true vine (cf. Jn 15:1) . . . which is drunk and poured out: it is drunk by the disciples, but "is poured out for the forgiveness of sins" which have been committed by those by whom it is drunk. . . . But if you are also asking how it is poured out, reflect on this statement which is also in scripture: "God's love has been poured into our hearts" (Rom 5:5). . . . So do not be astonished that he himself is the drink of the fruit of the vine and drinks it with us. For all-powerful is the WORD of God; it is called by many names, and innumerable is the multitude of its powers, since all power is [in him] one and the same.

351 Christ too professes that he "stands at the door and knocks" (Rev 3:20) in order to enter in with those who open to him, and to eat with them from what they have.

352 For just as that one well, which is the WORD of God, becomes countless wells and springs and rivers, so too can the soul of the human being which is made "in God's image" (cf. Gen 9:6) have in itself and produce from itself wells and springs and rivers. But in reality, the wells which are in our souls need someone to dig them, . . . so that those veins of the spiritual senses which God has put in them will produce pure and unadulterated streams.

853   Our Lord and Savior says: "Unless you eat my flesh and drink my blood, you will not have life in you. . . . For my flesh is food indeed, and my blood is drink indeed" (cf. Jn 6:53–55). Because, therefore, Jesus is in every way pure, his whole "flesh is food" and his whole "blood is drink," because every work of his is holy and every word of his is true. That is why his "flesh is food indeed" and his "blood is drink indeed." For with the flesh and blood of his WORD he gives drink and refreshment, as if with pure food and drink, to the whole human race. In the second place, after his flesh, Peter and Paul and all the apostles are a pure food; and in third place after that, their disciples. And so each one, according to the measure of his merits or the purity of his senses, becomes pure food for his neighbor. . . . Each human being has some food in himself from which others can take nourishment. If the food is good and "out of the good treasure of his heart produces good things," he is offering pure food to his neighbor. But if he is evil and "produces evil," he is offering impure food to his neighbor (cf. Lk 6:45).

854   But Jesus was constantly hungering in his desire to eat the fruits of the Holy Spirit in the just. And the food, the figs so to speak, which he in his hunger eats (cf. Mt 21:18–19) are the love of that person who bears this fruit. The first is "the fruit of the Spirit," and grace and peace and patience and the rest (cf. Gal 5:22). When we bear them as fruit, we will not "wither away" (Mt 21:19). But if he comes hungry and looking for our fruit and finds nothing but the mere proclamation of the faith without fruit, we will wither up "on the spot" and also lose the appearance of being faithful.

855   He who is "born of a virgin, Immanuel," eats "curds and honey" (cf. Isa 7:14–15) and seeks from each of us curds to eat. . . . For our works of gentleness, our most sweet and helpful words are "honey" which Immanuel eats. . . . But if our words are full of bitterness, anger, animosity, sadness, scandal, vice and contentiousness, this has put "gall in my mouth," and the Savior does not eat of these words. The Savior will eat of the words of human beings when their words are "honey." Let us demonstrate this from the scripture: "Behold, I stand at the door and knock; if anyone opens the door for me, I will come in to him and eat with him, and he with me" (cf. Rev 3:20). Thus he himself promises to eat of our food and with us. But it is certain that we also eat with him when we eat him. When he eats of our good words, he is feeding us in deed and understanding with his own spiritual and divine and better foods. Because it is a blessed thing to

receive the savior, let us, with the doors to the depths of our heart open, prepare for him "honey" and his whole banquet, so that he will lead us to that great banquet of the Father in the kingdom of heaven.

856 Thus God wants first to receive something from us and then bestow his generosity on us so that he would seem to be bestowing his gifts and blessings on those who deserve them rather than on those who do not. But what is it that God wants from us? Listen to the word of scripture: "And now, Israel, what does the Lord your God require of you, but to fear the Lord your God, to walk in all his ways, to love him with all your heart and all your soul and all your strength?" (Deut 10:12; Lk 10:27). . . . Hence I say that if we offer him our righteousness, we will receive from him God's righteousness; and if we offer him our, that is, our body's, chastity, we will receive spiritual chastity from him; and if we offer him our faculty of perception, we will receive from him his, as the Apostle used to say: "We have the mind of Christ" (1 Cor 2:16).

857 "God's love has been poured into our hearts" (Rom 5:5). One has to consider, it seems to me, whether he is talking about that love by which we love God, or that by which we are loved by God. . . . It is certain that love is established as the highest and greatest gift of the Holy Spirit and that we, in first receiving this gift from God, become thereby capable of loving him, because we are loved by God.

ONE LIFE

Thus there is no longer any private life for the members of the life of Christ. Everything is there in the community of love (858–859), and also of guilt: one sin stains the whole body (860). Connectedness in being requires of itself connectedness in love (861). Christ is in all members, and it is for him that all good is done (862–863). In the end, God gathers in all good for himself because he is in the giver as well as in the receiver (864). The longing of the members to help in the building up of the body (865). Only when all is together will the body be brought to completion, for in suffering and in resurrection it has only one fate (866–869).

858 Now we ask what "participation in the Spirit" might be. Listen to the Apostle . . . : "If there is any incentive of love, any participation in the Spirit, any affection and sympathy, complete my joy" (Phil 2:1–2). You can see how the Apostle Paul understood the law of participation.

And listen to how John expresses himself in the very same spirit: "Our fellowship is with the Father and with his Son Jesus Christ" (1 Jn 1:3). Peter too says: "We have become partakers of the divine nature" (cf. 2 Pet 1:4), that is, in fellowship with it. . . .

The Apostle calls us fellow citizens with the saints (cf. Eph 2:19), and no wonder; for if we are said to have fellowship "with the Father and the Son," how then not also with the saints, not just with those on earth but also with those in heaven (cf. Col 1:20)? This is because Christ did reconcile the earthly and the heavenly by his blood, thus bringing the earthly into fellowship with the heavenly.

859   "Ordain love in me" (cf. Cant 2:4 LXX). This order and measure is, for example, of this kind: for loving God there is no mode or measure, there is only this principle, that you expend all you have . . . but to love one's neighbor is already a certain measure. . . . For if, as the Apostle says, "we are members of one another" (Eph 4:25), I think we should have such an attitude towards our neighbors that we love them not as if they were foreign bodies but as our own members. Due to the fact, then, that we are members of each other (cf. Eph 4:25), we should have an equal and similar love towards all. But because some members in the body are "more honorable" and "more presentable," and others "less presentable" and "inferior" (cf. 1 Cor 12:22–24), I still think that the measure of love also has to be weighed according to the merits and honor of the members.

860   Look how far you have come: from an insignificant human being you have truly progressed to become a temple of God in which God is supposed to live; and you who were flesh and blood have come so far as to become a member of Christ (cf. 1 Cor 3:17; 6:15, 19). You are no longer allowed to use the "temple of God" except in sanctity, nor involve the "members of Christ" in anything unworthy. . . . But add also that he who acts impurely "sins against his own body" (cf. 1 Cor 6:18), not just that body which has been made the "temple of God," but also that body of which it is said that the whole church is the body of Christ (cf. Col 1:24); for he who defiles his own body seems to sin against the whole church, because the stain is spread through one member to the whole body.

861   "Again I say to you, if two of you agree on earth about anything they ask, it will be done for them" (Mt 18:19). Strictly speaking, the word "symphony" is used by musicians for the voices of harmony. For among musical tones, some harmonize with each other and others do not. But the gospel is also familiar with this term as applied to music

where it says: "He heard music [*symphōnias*] and dancing " (Lk 15:25). For it was fitting that, at the accord, caused by repentance, of the lost but now found son with his father, a symphony should be heard on the occasion of the rejoicing of the house. . . . Akin to this kind of symphony is what is written in the Second Book of Kings when the brothers of Aminadab "went before the Ark, and David and the sons of Israel were playing before the face of the Lord on well-tuned instruments and in power and in songs" (2 Sam 6:4–5). For the "well-tuned instruments in power and in song" have in them that harmony of tones which is of such power that if only two people bring before the Father in heaven any request with that symphony which is found in divine and spiritual music, the Father grants it to them—which is most remarkable. . . . This is how I understand the apostolic saying: "Do not refuse one another except perhaps by agreement for a season, that you may devote yourselves to prayer" (1 Cor 7:5). For when, in the following text from Proverbs, the term "harmony" is applied to those who marry under God: "Fathers divide up house and substance among their sons, but by God is the wife joined to her husband" (Prov 19:14 LXX), this is due to the harmony related to prayer, which is obvious in the phrase: "except perhaps by agreement" (1 Cor 7:5). Then the WORD, going on to explain that the agreement of two on earth is the same as agreement with Christ, adds: "where two or three are gathered in my name" (Mt 18:19–20). . . .

But if you still wish to see some making harmony on earth, look to those who were exhorted "that you may be united in the same mind and the same judgment" (1 Cor 1:10), and who strove that "the company of those who believed be of one heart and soul" (Acts 4:32), and who became one, as far as this is possible among many, so that there was no discord among them, just as there is no discord among the strings of the ten-stringed harp. . . . For discord dissolves just as concord unites. But discord drives away the Son of God who is "in the midst" only of those in concord. Strictly speaking, concord comes about in two general ways: in the (as the Apostle called it) being united in the same mind, and in having the same attitude to a similar way of life. This is the meaning of "If two of you agree on earth about anything they ask, it will be done for them by my Father in heaven" (Mt 18:19). And it is clear, when the "anything they ask" is not done "by the Father in heaven," that these two "on earth" were not really in concord. And this is the reason why our prayers are not heard: that neither in how we think nor in how we live are we in harmony with each other. And yet, if we are "the body of Christ," and "God arranged the organs in the body, each one of them," so that "the members may have the same care for one another" and be in harmony with each other, and if one member suffers they all suffer, and if one is honored all rejoice together, we ought to practice the symphony of this divine music (cf. 1 Cor 12:18–27). For just as in music there is no pleasure in hearing without harmony of voices, so too in the church; unless it has harmony, God does not take pleasure in it nor listen to their voices. Let us therefore be in harmony so that when we are gathered together in Christ's name, Christ, the WORD of God and the wisdom of God and the power of God, may indeed be in our midst.

862　　"I was hungry and you gave me food" (Mt 25:35). It seems to me that this is saying that not just one kind of righteousness is rewarded, as many think. For it is absurd to think that no other kind of virtue is rewarded than just the sharing of humaneness. But we are not saying this to make us less concerned with humaneness, for this has to be particularly practiced by all the faithful. . . . But whether we understand this as applying to the more simple and bodily benefactions or according to spiritual ones, it is certain that whoever does a good work in one way or the other . . . is giving food and drink to the hungry and thirsty Christ. . . . In the same way we weave a garment for the freezing Christ. . . . And do not think it is blasphemy to call Christ weak. "For he was crucified in weakness" (2 Cor 13:4) out of mercy for us, and he, and all his friends with him, "bears our weaknesses" (Isa 53:4). . . . "Who is weak, and I am not weak? Who is made to fall, and we are not indignant?" (2 Cor 11:29). And if his disciples become weak with the weak, how much more their Savior and Creator? For the greater the compassion one has for weak human beings, the more seriously is one concerned for their weaknesses as well. . . . Finally, everything that is here is a prison of Christ and of those who belong to him. Let us then go to those who live in this house of bondage, as if in prison, and who are inhabitants in this world, held by the necessity of nature as if in a dungeon. When we have done a good work for them, we have visited them in prison and Christ in them.

863　　When the saints are in need of food, he [Christ] also is hungry. When others of his members need medicine, he too, weak as it were, also needs it. And when others are in need of being taken in, he himself, as if a traveler, seeks in them for "where to lay his head" (Mt 8:20). He thus freezes in the one who is naked and is clothed in the one who is clothed. . . . This is why he says: "I was sick and in prison and you did not visit me" (Mt 25:43). For if a member of Christ is in prison, then he himself is not free of prison, for he said of the just person: "I am with him in tribulation" (Ps 91:15 LXX); that is, I suffer with him. For just as those who belong to me are in tribulation with me, so am I in tribulation with them.

864   "You knew that I reap where I have not sowed, and gather where I have not winnowed?" (Mt 25:26). How are we to understand that our Lord actually reaps where he has not sowed, and gathers where he has not winnowed? It seems to me that the meaning of this passage is that the just person "sows to the Spirit" and from that "reaps eternal life" (cf. Gal 6:8). But everything which is sown and reaped by another (that is, by a just person) to eternal life, God reaps. For the just person belongs to God who reaps where not he but the just person has sown. Consequently, we will also say that "he scatters abroad and gives to the poor" (2 Cor 9:9); but the Lord gathers into himself all that the just person "scatters abroad and gives to the poor." But in reaping what he has not sown and gathering where he has not scattered, he reckons as having been given to himself whatever is sown or dispersed to the poor faithful, saying to those who have helped their neighbors: "Come, O blessed of my Father, inherit the kingdom prepared for you . . . for I was hungry and you gave me food," etc. (Mt 25:34–35).

865   I would wish, if it were somehow possible, that there were something of me in that gold of which the mercy seat is made, or with which the ark is covered, or with which the lamps and lampstands are made. Or, if I have no gold, that I would at least be able to offer some silver to be used in the columns or their bases; or that I would in any case have some bronze for use in making the bronze rings in the sanctuary and the other things which the WORD of God describes (cf. Exod 25–27). O, would that it were possible for me to be one of the princes to offer gems for the ornamentation of the high priest (cf. Exod 35:27). But because these things are above me, I would still like to be worthy of supplying some goats' hair for the tabernacle [tent of meeting] of God (cf. Exod 35:6) so that I would not be found empty and unfruitful in everything.

866   "And the Lord spoke to Aaron, saying: 'Drink no wine nor strong drink, you nor your sons with you, when you go into the tent of meeting, or when you approach the altar'" (Lev 10:8–9). For the WORD of God wishes the priests of the Lord to be sober in all things, since they are the ones who, drawing near to the altar of God, must pray

for the people and make intercession for the sins of others (cf. Lev
9:7). . . . But if we consider in how many ways the human mind can
become drunk, we will also find among the inebriated those who to
themselves seem to be sober. Anger intoxicates the soul, but rage
makes it more than drunk, if there can be something beyond drunk-
enness. Passionate desire and greed make people not only drunk but
also raging. And unclean desires intoxicate the soul just as, on the
other hand, holy desires intoxicate it, but with that holy intoxication
of which one of the saints said: "And your inebriating cup, how marvelous it is!" (Ps 23:5 LXX). . . .

Our Lord and Savior is called by Paul: "High priest of the good
things to come" (Heb 9:11). Thus he himself is Aaron and his sons are
the apostles to whom he himself said: "Little children, yet a little while
I am with you" (Jn 13:33). What, then, did the law command "Aaron
and his sons"? To drink no wine nor strong drink when they approach
the altar (cf. Lev 10:8-9). Let us see how we can apply this to the true
high priest, our Lord Jesus Christ, and his priests and sons, our
apostles. First one must take note how this true high priest does indeed drink wine with his priests before he comes to the altar; but
when he begins to draw near to the altar and "go into the tent of
meeting" (Lev 10:9), he abstains from wine. . . . Before he offered
sacrifice, while living in this world, he drank wine. Recall that they
did call him "a glutton and a drunkard, a friend of tax collectors and
sinners" (Mt 11:19). But when the time of his cross arrived and he
was about to "draw near to the altar" (cf. Lev 9:7-8) where he would
offer the sacrifice of his flesh, "taking," it is written, "a cup, and when
he had given thanks he gave it to his disciples, saying, 'Take and
drink of this'" (cf. Mt 26:27). "You drink," he says, you who are not
about to draw near to the altar. But he, as he is about to "draw near to
the altar," says of himself: "I tell you truly, I shall not drink again of
this fruit of the vine until that day when I drink it new with you in my
Father's kingdom" (Mt 26:29). If any of you draw near to hear with
purified ears, you will gaze upon the secret of an inexhaustible mystery.

What does it mean when he says: "I shall not drink again . . ."?
We said above that the saints were promised a holy inebriation. . . .
If, then, we have understood what the inebriation of the saints is
. . . let us now see how our Savior will no longer drink wine until he
drinks it anew with the saints in the kingdom of God (cf. Mt 26:29;
Mk 14:25). My Savior is grieving even now over my sins. My Savior
cannot be glad as long as I persist in iniquity. And why not? Because

he himself is the "advocate with the Father for our sins," as John, his co-worker, explains saying that "if anyone does sin, we have an advocate with the Father, Jesus Christ the righteous; and he is the expiation for our sins" (1 Jn 2:1–2). How then can he who is the "advocate for my sins" drink the wine of gladness when I am saddening him with my sins? How can he who "draws near to the altar" to make expiation for me the sinner be joyful when his sadness for my sins is constantly increasing? "With you," he says, "will I drink it in my Father's kingdom" (Mt 26:29). As long as we do not act so as to ascend to the kingdom, he cannot drink alone the wine he promised to drink with us. He therefore is in grief as long as we persist in error. For if his Apostle "mourns for those who sinned before and have not repented of what they did" (cf. 2 Cor 12:21), what shall I say of him who is called "the Son of love" (cf. Col 1:13), who "emptied himself" for the love he bore for us and "did not seek his own benefit," though he "was in the form of God," but sought what was of benefit to us, and for this reason "poured himself out" (cf. Phil 2:6–7; 1 Cor 13:5)? If, then, in this way he has sought what is to our benefit, will he now no longer seek after us, nor consider what is to our benefit, nor grieve for our errors, nor grieve over our wretchedness and tribulations, he who wept over Jerusalem and said to it: "How often would I have gathered your children together as a hen gathers her brood under her wings, and you would not" (Mt 23:37)? He who bore our wounds (cf. Isa 53:4) and suffered for us as a doctor of souls and bodies, shall he now pay no attention to the decay of our wounds? . . .

He is waiting, therefore, for us to be converted, to imitate his example, to follow his footsteps, and to be able to rejoice with us and "drink wine with us in the kingdom of his Father" (Mt 26:29). . . . We, therefore, are the ones who, neglecting our own life, are delaying his joy. He is waiting for us to drink "of the fruit of this vine." Of what vine? Of that vine of which he himself is the figure: "I am the vine, you are the branches" (Jn 15:1). Hence he can also say that: "My blood is drink indeed, and my flesh is food indeed" (cf. Jn 6:55). For he has truly "washed his vesture in the blood of grapes" (cf. Gen 49:11). What then is this? He is waiting for joy? When does he expect it? "When I have accomplished," he says, "your work" (cf. Jn 17:4). When will he accomplish this work? When he has brought me, the last and worst of all sinners, to fulfillment and perfection, that is, when his work is accomplished. For now, his work is imperfect as long as I am imperfect. Finally, as long as I am not yet "subjected" to the Father, he himself will also not be called "subjected" (cf. 1 Cor 15:28). It is not that he needs to be subjected to the Father; but, for my sake, in whom his work is not yet accomplished, he himself is said to be not yet subjected. Thus we read: we are "the body of Christ and in part members of it" (cf. 1 Cor 12:27).

Let us see what it means when it says: "in part." I am now, for example, subject to God according to the Spirit, that is, in intention and will. For as long as "the desires of the flesh are against the Spirit and the desires of the Spirit are against the flesh" (Gal 5:17) within me, and I have not yet been able to subject the flesh to the Spirit, I am indeed "subject" to God, however not wholly but only "in part." But when I can bring my flesh and all my members in harmony with the Spirit, then I will seem to be in perfect subjection. If you have understood what it means to be subjected "in part" and in full, go back to what we said about the subjection of the Lord and see, since we are all said to be his body and his members, that as long as there are some among us who are not yet subject with a perfect subjection, it cannot be said that he is fully subjected. But when he has accomplished his work and has led all of creation to the fullness of perfection, then is he said to be subjected to those whom he has subjected to the Father and in whom he has "accomplished the work" which the Father gave him (Jn 17:4) so that "God may be everything to every one" (1 Cor 15:28). . . . Then will there be "joy and gladness," then will "the bones which have been broken rejoice" (cf. Ps 51:8), then will the scripture be fulfilled that "sorrow and sighing shall flee away" (Isa 35:10).

But let us not forget that not just of Aaron is it said that "he should drink no wine," but also of his sons when they enter in to the sanctuary (cf. Lev 10:9). Nor have the apostles too yet received their joy; but they too are waiting for me to become a sharer in their joy. Nor do the saints themselves immediately receive the full reward of their merits; they too wait for us, even though we are slow and lazy. For they do not have full joy as long as they grieve for our errant ways and mourn our sins. You will perhaps not want to believe me as I say these things; for where do I get the authority to make such an important statement? But I offer as witness one whom you cannot doubt: the "teacher of the Gentiles in faith and truth" (1 Tim 2:7), the Apostle Paul. In writing to the Hebrews, after he had listed all the holy fathers who were justified by faith, he adds this at the end: "And all these, though well attested by their faith, did not receive what was promised, since God had foreseen something better for us, that apart from us they should not be made perfect" (Heb 11:39-40). You can see, then, that Abraham is still waiting to reach perfection; Isaac and Jacob are waiting and all the prophets are waiting for us, to receive perfect beatitude with us. It is for this reason that the mystery of judgment delayed to the last day is also preserved. For it is "one body" (cf. Rom 12:5) which is awaiting justification, "one body" which will rise for judgment. "For although there are many members, there is still but one body; the eye cannot say to the hand, 'I have no need of you'" (1 Cor 12:20-21). Even if the eye is healthy and sees clearly, . . . if the other members were missing, what joy would the eye have? Or what kind of perfection would it be if the body had no hands, if the feet or the other members were missing? For if there is a particular glory of the eye, it consists especially in being the leader of the body and in there being no deficiency in the duties of the other members.

I think this is what we are being taught by that vision of the prophet Ezekiel where he says: "The bones came together, bone to its bone and joint to joint and sinews and veins and skin" (cf. Ezek 37:7-8). Each part must find its place. . . . For each of these bones was weak and oppressed by the hand of the stronger (cf. Ps 35:10). For it did not have the "joint" of love, nor the "sinews" of patience, nor the "veins" of the living spirit and the power of faith. But when he came "to gather the scattered" (cf. Jn 11:52) and join together the separated, joining "bone to bone and joint to joint," he began to build the holy body of the church. . . . Observe, finally, what the prophet adds: "These bones" — he did not say all men, but said "these bones" — "are the house of Israel" (Ezek 37:11). You will therefore be happy when you leave this life, if you have been holy. But it will then be a full joy when none of your members is missing. For you will also wait for the others just as you yourself were waited for. Because if you, who are a member, do not seem to have perfect joy if another member is missing, how much more will our Lord and Savior, who is the head and originator of the whole body, not consider his joy to be perfect as long as he sees any of the members missing from his body! . . . Therefore he does not wish to come into his perfect glory without you, that is, without his people which is his body and who are his members. For he wishes to dwell in this body of his church and in these members of his people as its soul, so that all its activities and works will proceed according to his will so that in us that prophetic word will be fulfilled: "I will walk among you and will be your God" (Lev 26:12). But now, while we are all not yet "perfect" (cf. Phil 3:15), but "are still sinners" (cf. Rom 5:8), he is "in part" in us and thus "our knowledge is imperfect and our prophecy is imperfect" (1 Cor 13:9), until someone is worthy to come to that measure which the Apostle spoke of: "It is no longer I who live, but Christ who lives in me" (Gal 2:20). "In part," as the Apostle says, we are now "members of his body," and "in part" we are his bones (cf. 1 Cor 12:27; Eph 5:30). But when "bone is joined to bone and joint to joint" (cf. Ezek 37:7–8), as we said above, then will he say over us that prophetic word: "All my bones shall say, 'O Lord, who is like thee?'" (Ps 35:10). For all those bones are speaking and singing praise and giving thanks to God.

867   That we are sons and have been redeemed (cf. Rom 8:16; Gal 3:13), rests on hope. "For now we see in a mirror dimly, but then face to face" (1 Cor 13:12). Through a mirror, therefore, and dimly do we receive adoption and redemption. . . . But when what is perfect has come, then we will receive adoption "face to face." And when it says "the redemption of our bodies" (Rom 8:33), I think that this indicates the body of the whole church. . . . Thus the Apostle hopes that the whole body of the church will be redeemed, and does not think that what is perfect can be given to the individual members unless the whole body has been gathered into one.

868   The praise of God . . . is at first sung by a multitude, but in the end, just by one. Be aware that the church is now a multitude, . . . but that the one is the Lord who gives thanks for the church.

869   Because, as we have explained, he had come to restore the order not only of ruling and reigning but also of obeying (accomplishing first in himself what he wanted to be fulfilled by others), he not only became "obedient" to the Father "unto the death of the cross" (cf. Phil 2:8), but (encompassing in himself at the end of the world all those whom he subjects to the Father and who come to salvation through him) he also is said to be subjected to the Father (cf. 1 Cor 15:28) with them and in them. For "all things are held together in him" (Col 1:17), and "he himself is the head of all," and "in him is the fullness" of those who attain salvation (Eph 1:22–23).

IV

GOD

THE MYSTERY OF GOD

The objective order of salvation (WORD) and its subjective appropriation (Spirit) flow into the eternal and other-worldly mystery of "God" which even with Paul is the very special name of the Father. This rounds off the implicitly trinitarian structure of Origen's thought. Behind all the wisdom of the world rises the impenetrable mystery of God who holds the beginnings ("Peri Archōn") and ends of things in his inscrutable hands (870–874). Human longing for knowledge can only resign itself to this mystery (875). Even through the "opening" which is called Christ, the whole of God never becomes visible (876).

870   "About him stood the seraphim; one had six wings, and the other had six wings" (cf. Isa 6:2). I see two seraphim, each of which has six wings. And now, the arrangement of the wings: "with two wings they covered the face" — not their own but God's — "and with two wings they covered the feet" — not their own but God's — "and with two wings they flew" (cf. Isa 6:2 LXX). What is written seems to be contradictory: if they were standing, they could not be flying. For it is written: "They stood about him; one had six wings, and the other had six wings; and with two they covered the face and with two they covered the feet, and with two they flew; and they called out the one to the other" (Isa 6:2-3 LXX). But these seraphim which stand around God, which only mentally say: "Holy, Holy, Holy!" (Isa 6:3), guard the mystery of the Trinity because they themselves are holy. For among all the things that exist, nothing is more holy than them. And they do not casually cry out one to the other: "Holy, Holy, Holy!", but loudly proclaim to all this saving confession. Who are these two seraphim? My Lord Jesus and the Holy Spirit. . . . They covered the face of God; for what could be understood as the end in our God? Only the middle is visible; what was before this, I do not know. From what now is, I recognize God; what will come about after

317

this, I do not know. . . . . They "stand," therefore, and move themselves; they "stand" with God and move themselves in pointing out
God. For you should understand that in covering his face and in
covering his feet, they do not move what is covered, they do not cover
what they move.

871   "And my eyes have seen the King, the Lord of hosts" (Isa 6:5).
Why should we not mention here a certain tradition of the Jews which,
although not true, has a touch of likelihood to it? . . . They say that
Isaiah was cut off from the people as one who transgressed against the
law and proclaimed things contrary to scripture. For the scripture
says: "Man shall not see me and live" (Exod 33:20), but he says: "I
have seen the Lord of hosts" (Isa 6:5). Moses, they say, did not "see,"
and you "have seen"? For this reason they cut him off and condemned
him as godless; for they did not know that the seraphim covered the
face of God with two wings (cf. Isa 6:2). "I have seen the Lord." If
Isaiah saw the face, Moses did too. Moses saw him from behind, as it
is written (Exod 33:23); but he did "see the Lord," even if he did not
"see" his "face." So here too, although he [Isaiah] "saw," he did not "see
the face."

872   It is impossible to find the origin of God. You will never understand the beginning of movement in God, neither you nor anyone
else nor any other kind of existing being. Only the Savior and the Holy
Spirit, who always were with God, see his "face"; and perhaps the
"angels" who "always behold the face of the Father who is in heaven"
(Mt 18:10), also see the beginnings of things. And so also do the
seraphim hide his feet from human sight (cf. Isa 6:2); for the last
things cannot be related as they are. "Who will tell us of the last
things?" (cf. Isa 41:26) says the scripture. What we see — admitting
that we do see something — are the things in between. What was
before the world, we do not know; and there were indeed certain
things before the world. What will come about after the world, we do
not know for sure; but there will be other things after the world. What
is written: "In the beginning God created the heavens and the earth.
The earth was without form and void, and darkness was upon the
face of the deep; and the Spirit of God was moving over the face of the
waters" (Gen 1:1-2), is understood as follows. These "waters" over
which "the Spirit of God was brooding" belong to the world. But also
the "darkness" which was "upon the face of the deep" is not uncreated;
for both were created out of nothing. Hear God speaking in Isaiah: "I
am the Lord; I form light and create darkness" (Isa 45:7). Listen to

how Wisdom in Proverbs proclaims: "When there were no depths I was brought forth" (Prov 8:24). These things are not uncreated, but when or how they were born, I do not know. For the beginnings of the works of God, that is, "the face of God," are "hidden" by the "seraphim"; and so too are his "feet" (cf. Isa 6:2). For who can describe what will be after the final age in the future age of ages? Some talkative types promise knowledge of these things, unaware that a human being can grasp only the things in between. . . . They did not just veil, they also covered; that is, they veiled in such a way that not the slightest bit of the first things, I mean the "face," would be seen, nor anything at all of the last things, that is, his "feet," would be made known. "And with two wings they flew" (Isa 6:2). The things in between stand open to view.

873 There is a certain "gate" which remains "shut," and "through" which "no one enters" (cf. Ezek 44:1-2). For there are certain things which are hidden from the created world and known only to one; for the Son has not opened all he knows to the world.

874 Darkness, gloom and storm surround God, says the Book of Exodus. . . . For if one considers the fullness of the doctrine and knowledge about God which remains inaccessible to human nature, and perhaps also to all other beings outside of Christ and the Holy Spirit, one will understand why there is darkness around God.

875 "What remains of the flesh of the sacrifice on the third day shall be burned with fire" (Lev 6:17). . . . In these can be understood the two testaments in which every word relating to God—for this is the sacrifice . . . can be examined and discussed, and from them the knowledge of all things be drawn . . . but we should burn with fire, that is, turn over to God, "what remains". . . . Therefore, lest our sacrifice become unacceptable, and lest the very wisdom we desire to take from the sacred scripture turn into sin for us, let us observe those measures which . . . the spiritual law gives us.

876 Moses desired to know God, and God revealed himself to him saying: "Behold, I will put you in a cleft of the rock, and you shall see my back; but my face shall not be visible to you" (Exod 33:22-23). . . . What then was that rock? "The Rock was Christ" (1 Cor 10:4). . . . What was the cleft in the rock? If you see the coming of Jesus and completely understand him as rock, you will see in his coming the cleft through which are seen the things of God. This is what is meant in the words: "You shall see my back."

GOD-FIRE

SPIRITUAL END OF THE WORLD

But the relationship to the Father is not only an eschatological one in the chronological sense. For the tremendous presence of God is even now present behind the veil of the world of appearances (877), and thus, for those to whom this curtain is already raised, the "apo-calypse" (i.e., unveiling) of God can be carried out now. Along with the "teleological," there is also an "axiological" relationship to the last things; this is nothing other than the transcending of what is worldly in one's dying and rising with Christ. For the work of Christ is not only unique, but is also one which is being continually fulfilled throughout all of history (878–879). Its arrival ("parousia") is just as much a daily and hourly as it is an eschatological event (880–886). Hence the attention of the Christian is turned wholly to the mystically coming Christ. This turn to the axiological means, in church history, the true and thorough overcoming of the general eschatologism of primitive Christianity (887). But eschatological and mystical coming do not stand immediately opposed to each other. Instead, Origen goes so far as to interpret the eschatological coming only as the, so to speak, actualization of the general mystical coming in which the world of appearances is, so to speak, at an end and God becomes transparent for all. He does not intend by this to deny the temporal reality of the second parousia and the bodily resurrection, but only to counteract the earlier, strongly materialistic chiliasm of Irenaeus and others (888). Even the judgment is a wholly inner process: one's whole life becoming present in an instant (889). But Christ's second coming will truly reveal his whole divine power (890). It will come about when the world also as a material reality is at an end (891). From God's point of view, the end is already here (892).

877   ". . . as you wait for the revealing of our Lord Jesus Christ" (1 Cor 1:7). He calls it "revealing" (apocalypse), thus indicating that not everything that is and is present is seen. But it will at that time become manifest.

878   Thus, they who keep their lamps lighted, they are the ones waiting for their Lord, the WORD of God. . . . And they light their lamps more or less in the light of the knowledge they each have according to the level of their progress, and they pour in oil through meditation (cf. Mt 25:1-2). . . . But to those who make greater progress and forget what lies behind them, namely, evil, . . . it can be fittingly said: "The night is far gone, the day is at hand" (Rom 13:12).

879   "This generation will not pass away till all these things take place. Heaven and earth will pass away, but my words will not pass away" (Mt 24:34-35). This generation will indeed pass away when not only "the earth" but also "the heavens" will pass away; that is, not only those whose life is earthly and thus are called "earth," but also those whose "activity is in heaven" (cf. Phil 3:20) and thus are called "heaven." But they and everything with them will pass over to the future things in order to come to what is higher and better. Creation (since they are sons of God) is awaiting the fulfillment of these things, and "all creation is groaning and in travail together" (Rom 8:22) until, conceiving in the womb from the fear of the Lord, they bring forth the "Spirit of salvation" (cf. Isa 26:18 LXX). Then will the "generation" of which Christ spoke pass away, and the "heaven" as we have explained it, and the "earth" as we have interpreted it. But "the words" spoken by the Savior "will not pass away," because they are both now doing and will always be doing their work. For they are perfect and do not receive anything that makes them any better, nor do they change from what they are to come to what they are not. Rather, "Heaven and earth will pass away," but his words remain as the words of him "through whom all things were made" (cf. Jn 1:3).

But when he says: "My words will not pass away" (Mt 24:35), we must, I think, ask whether perhaps the words of Moses and the prophets do pass away, but the words of Christ do not pass away; since what was prophesied by them has been fulfilled, but the words of Christ are always full, and are always in the act of being fulfilled, and are daily fulfilled and never overfilled. For they are what were fulfilled in the saints, and are being fulfilled and are still to be fulfilled. Or perhaps we should not say that the words of Moses and the prophets have been completely fulfilled; for, strictly speaking, they too are the words of the Son of God and are constantly being fulfilled. It is therefore good to expound the sublimity of the divine words in simple words. Yet, for the sake of the few, we want to make our analyses and understand at least this much: that the WORD, which is human in the WORD of God, from the creation of the world to its consummation does not pass away. For it is present and working, since it has no beginning of its work before the beginning of time, but it began with creation and with creation will pass away. But the WORD, which was before creation, will not pass away with creation.

880   "Therefore you must also be ready; for you do not know at what hour your Lord will come" (cf. Mt 24:42). The simpler Christians might say that he [Christ] is here talking about his second coming. But others might say that he was speaking of the future, spiritual coming of the WORD to the mind of the disciples, for he had not yet come into their spirit as he would later. . . . But among those who are watching and ready, he brings about the day of his coming in the soul of those illuminated by the true light of him who comes into their souls.

881   As long as the church, which is the body of Christ, does not know that day or hour (cf. Eph 1:23; Mt 24:36), so long is the Son himself said not to know that day and hour; but he is then said to know when all his members know.

And perhaps everything that is perceivable by the senses, right up to heaven itself and what is in it, are fields white for the harvest, waiting for those who lift up their eyes (Jn 4:35).

882   Perhaps each individual virtue is a kingdom of heaven, and all of them together are the kingdom of heaven. According to this, whoever lives a virtuous life is already in the kingdom of heaven; and the words: "Repent, for the kingdom of heaven is at hand" (Mt 3:2; 4:17) do not refer to time but to deeds and the inner disposition that goes with them. For Christ, who is every virtue, has completed his coming and speaks; consequently, the kingdom of God is within his disciples, and not "here" or "there" (cf. Lk 17:21).

883   There is a twofold resurrection: the one by which we in spirit, will and faith rise with Christ from what is earthly so as to turn our minds to what is heavenly and seek out the things to come; and the other one which will be the general resurrection of all in the flesh.

884   "The night is far gone, the day is at hand" (Rom 13:12). One must know that the coming of this light and this day is to be understood in two ways. . . . The light and the day that is general to all will come about when the time of the future age has come, in comparison to which the space of this present world is called darkness. This time comes nearer and nearer with each passing day, and what belongs to the past is increased, and what goes with the future is decreased. This is why Paul says that our "salvation is nearer to us than we first

believed" (Rom 13:11), and it is getting nearer every day, as our Lord said when he was interpreting the signs of the end of the age: "When these things begin to take place, look up and raise your heads, because your redemption is drawing near" (Lk 21:28). But the coming of this day also takes place in each one. For Christ makes this day for us too, if he is in our heart.

885 And there is another way of understanding the twofold coming of Christ, namely, as the coming of the Word into the soul. For at first the simple faithful and those just beginning to know Christ, because they cannot see the transparency of his beauty, say: "We saw him and there was no beauty or comeliness in him" (Isa 53:2 LXX). . . . But there is a second coming of Christ in the mature, of whom the dispenser of this Word says: "Among the mature we do impart wisdom" (1 Cor 2:6). They have become accomplished lovers of his beauty. . . . Connected with this second coming is the end of the world in the one who is coming to perfection and saying: "Far be it from me to glory except in the cross of our Lord Jesus Christ, through whom the world has been crucified to me, and I to the world" (Gal 6:14). For if the world is crucified to the just, this has also become for them the end of the world.

886 According to the historically recorded coming of our Lord Jesus Christ, his coming in the flesh had a certain universal quality to it, one which illumined the whole world. . . . However, one must be aware that he also came before this, although it was not in the body but in each one of the saints, and that after this visible coming of his he will come again.

887 They who listen to the gospel more deeply . . . do not worry much about the general end of the world, whether it will come suddenly and all at once, or only bit by bit; rather, they think only about this: that the end of each individual comes without him or her knowing either the day or the hour of his death. . . . I also know another end of the just person . . . for the one to whom the world is crucified, a certain end of the world has already come about; and for the one who is dead to worldly things, the weekdays have been skipped and the day of the Lord has come, on which the coming of the Son of Man to his soul takes place.

888 We must also consider whether our Savior's coming "in glory" (cf. Mt 25:31–32) will happen in a place, or whether we have to look for another explanation. For where is the place big enough to hold all at once both "all" the angels coming with Christ and "all the nations"

being gathered there? . . . . I believe that the time of Christ's coming will come about when there is such a revelation of Christ and his divinity that not only none of the just but also none of the sinners will fail to see Christ "as he is" (cf. 1 Jn 3:2), and when both the sinners will recognize their own sins in his face and the just will see clearly to what end the seeds of their righteousness has led them. This is the meaning of "Before him will be gathered all the nations" (Mt 25:32). For if now, when "all" do not recognize Christ "as he is," and they who do seem to recognize him do not seem to recognize him openly, but only in faith come before his face when they come to knowledge of him through faith—as it is written: "Come into his presence with singing" (Ps 100:2)—how much more truly will it be said that all the nations are to be gathered and arranged before him when he will be made visible to all, the good as well as the bad, the faithful as well as the unfaithful, discovered before their mind's eye not because of their faith and efforts to find him, but simply set before them by the manifestation of his divinity!

The Son of God will not yet appear in any particular place "when he comes in his glory" . . . but . . . "the coming of the Son of Man will be like the lightning which comes from the east and shines as far as the west" (cf. Mt 24:27). . . . Hence he will be everywhere, and he will be everywhere in the sight of all, and all, everywhere, will be in his sight. . . . Therefore—as long as the wicked are confused and know neither themselves nor Christ, but are clouded over in errors, and as long as the just see "in a mirror, dimly" and recognize themselves only "in part" (1 Cor 13:12) and not according to what they truly are—the good are not separated from the wicked. But when, through the revelation of the Son of God, all have come to self-understanding, then the Savior will separate the good from the wicked.

889   For when God wants to remind each one quickly of all the good and bad things they are conscious of having done over a long period of time, he does so with unspeakable power. . . . And should one not believe in the speed of God's power in doing this, such a person has yet no notion of God the Creator of all who did not need any time at all to bring about the creation of something so great as the heavens and the earth and everything in them. For although he seems to have done this in six days, one has to have the understanding to know what is meant by this.

890   Jesus comes with the power and glory (cf. Mt 24:30) with which the Father glorified him (cf. Jn 17:5), with which power "he did great

wonders and signs among the people" (Acts 6:8) and healed "every disease and every infirmity" (Mt 4:23). This is why he said: "Someone touched me; for I perceive that power has gone forth from me" (Lk 8:46). But all this power, in comparison with that great power with which he will come at the end, is small; for it was the power of someone emptying himself.

891 "There will be famines and earthquakes in various places: all this is but the beginning of the sufferings" (Mt 24:7-8). For just as bodies take sick before they die, that is, when they do not suffer violence from without; and just as in all cases, sickness is part of the process that leads to the separation of the soul from the body, so too this great and powerful created reality, the world, when it — since it has a beginning and end — begins to decay, must also become sick before its dissolution. . . . For the heavens "will pass away" (cf. Mt 24:35) because they "wear out like a garment" (Ps 102:26), and "what is becoming obsolete and growing old is ready to vanish away" (Heb 8:13).

892 "Hereafter you will see the Son of Man seated at the right hand of power" (Mt 26:64). Let us see whether it is possible to measure the hours and the days not according to the brevity of human hours and days but according to the length which applies to the eternal Lord for whom there is but one day from the foundation of the world to its consummation. This is proven in the parable which talks about those hired to work in the vineyard in the morning, and at the third hour and sixth hour right up to the eleventh hour. It is no wonder then that the Savior here speaks of "hereafter" as a very small length of time up to the point he was speaking of when he said: "You will see the Son of Man seated at the right hand of power."

FIRE

Passing through the world to God, whether the passage be finite or mystical, is in any case a dying. For world as such cannot "see God's face and live." The fire that must consume them is the fire of God himself. This truth, that God is "consuming fire" and "fiery sword," Origen thought through to the end with a consuming passion. The fire of God is either the mystical, purifying fire in those who commit themselves to him, or the punishing fire in sinners (893–895). But even the first of these is fearsome, more fearsome than all material fire (896); it is already the anticipated, inner fire of judgment (897–899). Good and evil mingle in every human being (900), and so there is no one who does not have to go through the fire (901), who does not have to be torn away (902), who does not need the fiery sword (903). For sin is quickly committed, but a fracture heals only very slowly and painfully (904–905). The many ways of God in this purification (906). After God as fire has burned out a soul, he remains only light for it (907–908).

893   "Then flew one of the seraphim to me, having in his hand a burning coal which he had taken with tongs from the altar" (Isa 6:6). The prophet is not purified with any old fire, but with fire that comes from the altar of God. If you are not purified with fire from the altar, you will be the one of whom it is said: "Depart from me into the eternal fire which was prepared for the devil and his angels" (cf. Mt 25:41). That is not fire "from the altar." All must be handed over to fire, but not all to the same fire. . . . Thus, may the chastising WORD touch the "lips" of our mind and soul so that we too may say: "And he touched my mouth" (Isa 6:7). . . . May the divine WORD sink its teeth into us and burn out our souls, so that as we listen we might say: "Did not our hearts burn within us?" (Lk 24:32).

894   "And he shall take a censer full of coals of fire" (Lev 16:12). Not all are purified by that fire which is taken "from the altar." Aaron is purified by that fire, as well as Isaiah and whoever is like them. But others who are not like them, among whom I also count myself, we will be purified with a different fire; and I fear it is that fire of which it is written: "A stream of fire issued and came forth from before him" (Dan 7:10). This fire is not "from the altar." The fire "from the altar" is the fire of the Lord; but what is not from the altar is not of the Lord; it is instead the fire proper to each sinner and of which is said: "Their worm shall not die, and their fire shall not be quenched" (Isa 66:24). It is therefore the fire of their very selves which has ignited them, just as is written in another place: "Walk by the light of your fire and by the brands which you have kindled" (Isa 50:11).

895   That fire which attacks sinners and burns within them is invisible. It is spiritual and punishing. If you want an image of that fire, then think of someone who has a massive fever and is being consumed by it. With your eye you will find no fire in him; but it is there, inside, burning out his innards. It is no different when someone is being consumed by the fire of sin.

896   "If I say, 'I will not mention him, or speak any more in his name,' there is in my heart as it were a burning fire shut up in my bones, and

I am weary with holding it in, and I cannot bear it" (Jer 20:9). The WORD of the Lord became fire consuming his heart. . . . He confessed his sins with the words: "I will not mention the name of the Lord, or speak any more in his name." And Jeremiah confessed his sin as soon as he said this. Would that I too, at the moment that I sin and speak a sinful word, might perceive that there is fire in my heart, burning and consuming so that I cannot bear it. . . . He said that there is a kind of fire, of non-sensible fire, which hurts those being punished so much that they cannot bear it, . . . I fear that the kind of fire that is awaiting us is like the fire there was in the heart of Jeremiah. But we have not yet experienced it. If we had experienced and were given the choice of two fires, this fire and the external fire which we see in those put to the fire by the leaders of the pagans, we would indeed choose that external fire rather than this one. For that fire burns the surface, while this one burns the heart, and beginning from the heart is spread to all the bones, and from the bones goes to every part of the one being burned, and thus it comes about that the one being burned cannot bear it. . . . This is the fire which the Savior is enkindling when he says: "I came to cast fire upon the earth" (Lk 12:49). . . . Is there anyone who is now worthy to receive this fire in his heart? . . . Because each of us must be punished for sin, let each one pray to God that this fire, which was in Jeremiah, will come over him . . ., so as not to be destroyed by another fire.

897   "And devouring fire came from his mouth" (Ps 18:8). So did it once burn the tax-collector, Matthew, and the persecutor and blasphemer, Paul.

898   "And the books were opened" (Dan 7:10). That is, those which are now wrapped up and hidden in the heart, and which contain in writing and in certain characters engraved on our consciences what we have done, and which are known to no one but God alone. And so these books of our soul or these pages of our heart will be opened "before the face of the throne of fiery flames and the wheels of burning fire and the stream of fire which came forth from before the ancient of days" (cf. Dan 7:9–10).

899   "You have tested my heart, you have visited me by night, you have tried me with fire, and there was found no wickedness in me" (Ps 17:3 LXX). David was tempted and left without help so that he could see what human weakness is capable of.

900   But because we who are not perfect in every way do not speak in such a way as to be always "justified," but have some "words by which

we will be justified" and others "by which we will be condemned,"
God puts both on his scales and carefully weighs and judges that in
which I am just and in what words I am to be condemned (cf. Mt
12:37). And what he does with our words he does also with our deeds.

901   "Our God is a consuming fire" (Heb 12:29). What does this fire
consume? Not "word" or "hay" that can be seen or felt, not visible
"straw," but if you "build on the foundation of Jesus Christ" with the
"wood" of sinful works, the "hay" of sinful works, the "straw" of the
lower sinful works, this fire comes and "tests" all that (cf. 1 Cor
3:12–15). What is this fire which proclaims the law and is not silent
about the gospel? "The fire will test what sort of work each one has
done" (1 Cor 3:13). What is, O Apostle, this fire which tests our
works? What is this fire so wise that it guards my "gold" and shows
forth my "silver" more brilliantly, that it leaves undamaged that
"precious stone" in me and "burns up" only the evil I have done, the
"word, hay and straw" which I have built over it (cf. 1 Cor 3:12–15).
What is this fire? "I came to cast fire upon the earth; and would that it
were already kindled!" (Lk 12:49). Jesus Christ says: "How I wish
that it were already kindled!" For he is good, and he knows that if this
fire is enkindled, wickedness will be consumed. For it is written in the
prophets: "He sanctified him in burning fire and devoured the forest
like straw" (cf. Isa 10:17 LXX), and again: "The Lord of Hosts will
send forth contumely in his honor, and to his glory will a burning fire
be kindled" (cf. Isa 10:16 LXX). This means, that fire is sent forth
upon your sinful works so that you will be glorified.

902   And it is quite proper for the Lord to consume such and to eliminate
the bad. While this is happening, there is suffering and pain, but not
from any bodily contact, in the higher parts of the soul, precisely
where that structure stands which needs to be torn down.

903   What then is this "sword" which we need to fear lest it be "brought
upon" our "land". . . . lest we have to pass through the "sword," but
a sword that punishes in two ways? For it is of the nature of a sword to
divide and cut what it is applied to; but if, in addition to the sharpness
of the point, its very touch also inflicts pain, the one being punished
by this sword is doubly hurt. For it is written: "He placed the
cherubim, and a flaming sword . . . to guard the way to the tree of
life" (Gen 3:24). And just as, when a sharp and red-hot sword is
thrust into a body, it causes a double pain, burning and cutting, so
also does the sword which was set up to guard paradise . . . inflict a
twofold pain [on the soul]; it burns and cuts.

04   Just as bodily wounds are often inflicted very quickly, but the healing of the wounds involves tremendous suffering and is not measured according to the amount of time it took to inflict them but according to the method of the cure (for example, the breaking of a hand or the spraining of a foot takes place in an instant; but what happens in a very short time is hardly cured in three months or longer), so too sinful pleasure which cuts through the nerves of the soul, and impurity and all the other sins, although they seduce the unhappy soul and lead it to vice in a short time, they afterwards cause it to go through long periods of pain and punishment.

05   When a wound is inflicted on the body or a bone broken or a nerve center disrupted, these things usually happen to a body in less than an hour, and then are barely healed with great pain and suffering over a long period of time. How many swellings and pains come from the wounded spot! And if it should happen that someone is repeatedly wounded in the same place, or the same bone repeatedly broken, what tremendous pain and torment can be required for the treatment and cure! . . . Switch now from bodily wounds to the wounds of the soul. . . . Oh, if we could only see how with each sin our inner human being is wounded, how a bad word causes a wound! . . . If we could see all this and feel the scars of the wounded soul, we would certainly resist sin unto death. But now, just as the possessed or the insane do not feel it when they are wounded because of their lack of natural feelings, so is it with us: crazed by the desires of the world or intoxicated with vice, we are deprived of our spiritual senses.

06   And it will be necessary for fire to be sent to such a soul to seek out the thorns, and approach them with its divine power, and not also burn up the grain and the plants of the field. But many are the ways, beginning with his own killing, of the Lamb which takes away the sin of the world. . . . What need is there to count how many ways there are for a human being to come to faith, since all those who are still in the body can see that for themselves? But one of the ways to faith and the forgiveness of sin is through chastisements, spiritual sufferings, painful diseases and serious weaknesses.

07   But fire has a twofold power: to illuminate, and to burn. . . . When we come to the spiritual meaning, there too fire is twofold: there is a fire in this world and there is one in the future world. The Lord Jesus says: "I came to cast fire upon the earth" (Lk 12:49): this fire illuminates. The same Jesus says in the future world to the "workers of iniquity" (cf. Lk 13:27): "Depart into the eternal fire which

my Father has prepared for the devil and his angels": this fire burns.
But this fire which Jesus came to cast upon the earth really does "en-
lighten every man coming into the world" (cf. Jn 1:9), and yet it also
has a burning quality to it, as they profess who say: "Did not our
hearts burn within us while he opened to us the scriptures?" (Lk
24:32). Thus, he both ignited and enlightened as he "opened the
scriptures." But I do not know whether that fire in the future world
which burns also has an illuminating quality to it.

908   But remember that it is written: "Whoever draws near to me draws
near to fire."[1] . . . Blessed therefore are those who are near, and who
are so near that the fire enlightens but does not burn them.

THE SALVIFIC SIGNIFICANCE OF PUNISHMENT

*It is inconceivable for Origen that God's fire in a soul should
only punish and not also purify. With this idea (which has already
been touched on several times, as in the "universal salvation" of the
world through the suffering of the WORD) Origen expresses his
doctrine of the universality of salvation. He knows that in doing
this he is reaching out into the secretum regis [royal secret], the
mystery reserved to God alone. But this doctrine seems to him to be
so unmistakably transparent in so many places in scripture that he
does not hesitate to express it openly for the purified, i.e., for those
who, because of their respect for the mystery of God's love, are in no
danger of misusing it. But with this doctrine he is drawn still more
deeply into the mystery of providence; because now, sin appears as
an episode in the mystery of love. And although it comes about purely
and solely from human freedom, because of the goodness of God it
still works for the salvation of sinners to the extent that it teaches
them by experience what it is to be turned away from God and then,
after turning back again, to be implanted with a deeper and more
lasting love for God than they had in the beginning.*

*For sinners, then, God is punishment (909–910). They sink by
their weight into the depth of fire (911), whose pains are unimag-
inably horrible (912). But suffering is already grace (913–917),*

---

[1] This is one of the more famous sayings which are attributed to Christ but
are not found in the canonical gospels. It is quoted again by Origen in Jer h
20, 3 and later also by Didymus.

and suffering here below saves from suffering hereafter (918). And all suffering is purifying (919–924).

909 "There came forth a shoot from the stump of Jesse, and a branch grew out of his roots" (cf. Isa 11:1). What is the "branch" and what is the "root" [or "rod"]? For both are the same in the one subject; the difference is only one of activity. For if you are a sinner, the shoot is not for you, nor will you see the shoot from Jesse's roots. For the "rod" will come to you in the way that the disciple [Paul] speaks of the "rod" and the "shoot" ["spirit of gentleness"—cf. 1 Cor 4:21]. Speaking of the "rod," he says: "What do you wish? Shall I come to you with a rod?" But of the "shoot," he says: "Or with God's love in a spirit of gentleness?" Thus "there comes forth from the root of Jesse a rod" for the one who is inflicted with punishment, . . . But a "shoot" . . . for the one who already has knowledge . . . and can already begin to bloom on the way towards becoming perfect fruit.

910 The sun seems to have a twofold power: one by which it illuminates, another by which it burns; and it depends on the things and materials under its rays whether it illuminates with its light or darkens and burns with its heat. It is in this sense, perhaps, that God is said to have "hardened the heart of Pharaoh" (Exod 9:12): namely, that the matter of his heart was such as to take in the presence of the "sun of justice" not from its illuminating side but from its burning and hardening side. . . . But where there is no sin, neither is the sun said to burn or darken. As the psalm says of the just: "The sun shall not smite you by day, nor the moon by night" (Ps 121:6). . . . But it burns the sinners, since they hate the light because of their evil deeds (cf. Jn 3:20).

911 "They [Pharaoh's army] went down into the depths like a stone" (Exod 15:5). For they were not the kind of stones from which children of Abraham could be raised up, but the kind that love the deep and liquid element, that is, who grasp after the bitter and passing pleasure of the things of the present. Hence they are said to have "sunk like lead in the mighty waters" (Exod 15:10). The saints, however, do not sink in but walk over the waters because they are light. . . . Thus did our Lord and Savior walk over the waters (cf. Mt 14:15, 29), for he is the one who truly knows no sin. His disciple, Peter, also walked on the waters, although with some trepidation; for he was not so great and so holy as not to have a bit of lead mixed in with him. . . . Thus, they who are to be saved are to be saved by fire, so that if they do have

any lead mixed in with them, the fire will melt and separate it so that they all can become pure gold. For "the gold of that land" where the saints are to live is said to be "good" (Gen 2:12); and just as the furnace tests gold, so does temptation test the just. For all must come to the fire, all come to the melting oven, . . . and should there be any there who are nothing but lead, it will happen to them as is written: they will "sink into the depths like lead in the mighty waters" (Exod 15:5, 10).

912   If then in the present life there are such unbearably painful punishments, what must it be when the soul no longer has on this heavier garment, but gets it back after it has been made spiritual by the resurrection, and then, because it is more refined, all the more fiercely feels the power of pain? For as great as the difference is in this world between whipping someone who is naked and someone who is clothed, . . . so great, I think, will be the difference in pain hereafter when the human body is stripped of the crassness of this garment and begins to suffer torments like a naked body.

913   It is a [sign of even] great[er] wrath to suffer no punishment at all from God. For they who are punished, even though they are being chastised by the so-called wrath of God, are being punished for their own improvement. . . . As you consider this, you can see that the person who keeps sinning without being punished is not even worthy of punishment. For the visitation of God is made manifest by the sufferings of the one visited.

914   It happens sometimes that bodily members die and dry up, . . . and often such dead members do not feel the pain when painful things are done to them. . . . What you see in the body you can transfer to the soul and see that a soul can also have parts that are so dead that they feel nothing even when inflicted with the painful blows of a scourge. Terrible things are inflicted, but the soul will not feel them; but a different soul would feel them. And perhaps those who do not feel the pain inflicted on them will regret this more than the feeling of pain, wishing rather to feel the pain of what is painful, since that is a sign of life.

915   But even if one could, one should not, I think, want to escape the judgment of God.

916   "The Lord answer you in the day of trouble" (Ps 20:1). They who travel the straight and narrow path which leads to life are constantly in tribulation and for that reason receive the blessing of being heard. Those who walk the broad and easy path do not have this blessing.

917   It is a terrible thing, indeed the worst thing of all, when we are no longer punished for our sins, when we are no longer corrected for our faults.

918   "In judgment he will not punish twice for the same thing" (cf. Nah 1:9 LXX). He punished once in judgment by the flood (cf. Gen 7–8), he punished once in judgment over Sodom and Gomorrah (cf. Gen 18:20–19:28). He punished once in judgment over Egypt and the six hundred thousand Israelites (cf. Exod 12:37). You are not to think that this is only the punishment in this world for their sins, and that after this suffering and death they are to be subjected to new punishment. They are punished in the present life so as not to be punished in the same way in the future. Look at the story of the poor man in the gospel: he suffers squalor and poverty, and afterwards rests "in Abraham's bosom." He received bad things in his lifetime (cf. Lk 16:19–31). How do you know that they who were killed in the flood might not have already received in this life the bad things due them? How do you know that Sodom and Gomorrah might not have already paid in this life their debt of suffering? Listen to the testimony of scripture. Do you want to hear what the Old Testament says? "Sodom shall return to its former estate" (Ezek 16:55); and you still have doubts whether the Lord is good in punishing the Sodomites? "It shall be more tolerable on the day of judgment for the land of Sodom and Gomorrah," says the Lord, having mercy on the Sodomites (Mt 10:15). For the Lord is full of goodness and mercy: "He makes his sun rise on the evil and on the good" (Mt 5:45), . . . not just this sun which we see with our eyes but also that sun which is seen with the eyes of the spirit.

919   Thus the good and merciful God in his love for human beings arranged it so that along with the pains with which he punishes sinners would also be mixed the gift of his visitation, and so that the poor sufferers would not be subjected to an immoderate punishment. For God always acts in this way: he torments the wicked, but like a devoted father, he mitigates the torment with mildness.

920   Pharaoh too, you can see, is very hard; but once punished, he makes progress. Before being punished he does not know the Lord. But when punished, he asks that they pray to the Lord for him. It is progress to recognize in the punishment why one has deserved it.

921   "Cast him out into the outer darkness" (Mt 22:13) so that, living out there in the outer darkness he may become thirsty for the light and cry out to God who can help him and liberate him.

922   God gathers together the just, but the sinners he scatters. . . .
When the people of Israel did not sin, they were in Judaea; but when
they sinned they were scattered from there and strewn across the
whole face of the earth. A similar thing happens to us all. There is a
"church of the first-born who are enrolled in heaven" where "Mount
Sion and the city of the living God, the heavenly Jerusalem" is (Heb
12:23, 22). The blessed are gathered there in order to be together.
But the sinners are punished by the fact that they cannot be with each
other. . . . Therefore, to increase the pain that chastises, those being
punished are separated from each other.

923   Therefore, since a rapid and too brief healing process causes some
to think of the diseases into which they had fallen as easy to heal, so
that they fall into them a second time after being healed, God will not
without reason overlook the growth of such disease up to a certain
point, and disregard it even to the point of incurability in them. He
does this so that they will become surfeited with evil, and by being filled
with the sin which they desire, will perceive the harm that has befallen
them. Then, hating what they previously welcomed, and being healed
more thoroughly, they can profit from the health of soul which comes
from the healing.

924   You chastise every son whom you accept (cf. Prov 3:12). I beg you,
then, chastise me too, and do not put me with those who are not chastised. . . . I am ready for chastisement. That is, if you want to inflict
poor health on me and send me sickness, I will bear it patiently. For I
know that I am not only worthy to pay for my sins through sickness,
but I desire to be purified by every affliction as long as I am preserved
from eternal sufferings and punishment. . . . If it is your pleasure
that I lose all my faculties, let them go, as long as I do not lose my soul
in your sight.

UNJUDGEABLE GUILT

The church has never declared any human being to be damned
with certainty. Human beings can not and should not judge.
Origen is tireless in pointing out mitigating reasons for sinners; and
if he has found one grain of good in a soul, he believes that eternal
punishment has already been averted (925–933).

925   But what are the kinds of sins unto death (cf. 1 Jn 5:16), and what
are those not unto death but to "loss" [as the Apostle says: "If any

man's work is burned up, he will suffer loss, though he himself will be saved, but only as through fire" (1 Cor 3:15)], this, I think, cannot be easily decided by any human being. For it is written: "Who can discern sins?" (Ps 19:12 LXX).

926   Consider Cain: although he was obviously a sinner, he was still doing something right; for this reason the Lord said to him: "If you offer correctly" (Gen 4:7 LXX). And when Pharaoh said: "The Lord is in the right, and I and my people are in the wrong" (Exod 9:27), he was doing something right. But this was not sufficient reason to call him just.

927   When some try to refer the saying: "A bad tree cannot bear good fruit" (Mt 7:18) to a necessity of nature, they are suggesting to us that there may be a breath of goodness in Judas, even though it is not perfect or sufficient for his conversion. They are thinking of the fact that "he brought back the thirty pieces of silver" and said, acknowledging his sin: "I have sinned in betraying innocent blood" (Mt 27:3–4). Where does this come from if not from the good planting of the Spirit and the seed of virtue which is sown in every spiritual soul?

928   If he had driven every inkling of good out of his soul, he would not have felt regret when he saw that Jesus was condemned.

929   It was a sign of reverence in Pilate that he washed his hands and said: "I am innocent of this man's blood; see to it yourselves" (Mt 27:24).

930   One should note that the foolish maidens were sent to buy oil, but it is not mentioned whether they actually bought or obtained any; this is passed over in silence. Then we read: "Afterward the other maidens came also, saying, 'Lord, lord, open to us'" (Mt 25:11). Although it could have said: "Afterwards they came too, after obtaining or buying some oil," there is fittingly no mention of this. This is so that the words: "I do not know you" (Mt 25:12) would not be said to those who have oil or were trimming their lamps at the last minute.

931   Since, then, "it is the Lord who judges" (1 Cor 4:4) . . ., and his is the only true judgment . . ., let us make sure that we judge no one, lest we ourselves be judged (cf. Mt 7:1). For we do not know the extent to which other persons have sinned; we do not know their state of mind in sinning, or whether they have excusing reasons for their sin. If, then, we would be prudent, we will "not pronounce judgment before the time" (1 Cor 4:5). Rather we will learn all things in the judgment of God through our Savior Jesus Christ.

932   Therefore, let us not anticipate the judgment of God and say that so-and-so is already damned, or, rejoicing, say that so-and-so is clearly saved; for we do not know how to weigh and judge one deed against another.

933   "You stretched out your right hand; the earth swallowed them" (Exod 15:12). But one should not completely despair. For it is possible that, if those swallowed should perhaps repent, they could be vomited forth again like Jonah. But it seems to me that the earth has at times kept all of us swallowed up in the bowels of the deep. Hence our Lord descended not only to the earth but also to the depths of the earth.

THE SALVIFIC SIGNIFICANCE OF GUILT

It is in this context that the meaning and the role of evil in the world is understood: it has the task of providing opportunity for battle and perseverance (934–935), and in God's hand it is changed into a means of good (936–939). Thus, within this (contingent) world order, one can call it "Not-wendig" [necessary for the transformation of evil] (940). God's pedagogy (941–946). Putting to death and bringing to life (947–949). Light and darkness (950–951).

934   But someone might ask why the great whales and dragons are seen as bad and the birds are seen as good? For it is said of all of them together: "And God saw that it was good" (Gen 1:21). For the saints, the things that oppose them are good, because they can overcome them and in overcoming them gain more glory before God. When, for example, the devil asked to be given power over Job, the adversary attacking him became the cause of double glory for him after his victory. This is shown in the fact that he received back double what he had lost in the present world, whereby he will surely be rewarded similarly in heaven. The Apostle says that no one "is crowned unless he competes according to the rules" (2 Tim 2:5). And truly, how can there be a struggle unless there is someone who resists? How bright and beautiful the light is would not be recognized if the darkness of night did not intervene. How could some be praised for chastity unless others were condemned for impurity? How could the strong and the brave be praised if there were none who were weak and cowardly? Take something bitter, and the sweet will be that much nicer. Look into the dark, and what is bright will seem more pleasing to you. In other words, reflection on evil highlights more brightly the beauty of the good. Hence, it is of everything that the scripture says: "And God saw that it was good" (Gen 1:21).

935   It is my opinion that temptations can be understood as wind which, from the mixed pile of believers, reveals that some are straw and

others are wheat. For when your soul has been overcome by some temptation, it is not temptation turning you into straw but, since you were already straw, . . . the temptation only reveals you as being what you already were in secret.

936   What seemed at first to be an evil, the Egyptian famine, became the starting point of the best decisions the Hebrews could make. Indeed, whatever is regarded as evil, even if it really is evil, is later turned into something good.

937   An untested and unexamined virtue is no virtue at all. . . . Take Joseph, for example. Take away the evil of his brothers, take away the envy, take away all the parricidal lying with which they vented their rage against their brother until they sold him into slavery (cf. Gen 37:18–36); if you take all this away, look at how much of the divine plan of redemption you would eliminate: you would be cutting away everything that happened in Egypt through Joseph for the salvation of all. . . . No one would have understood what God had revealed to the king, no one would have stored up grain (Gen 41:1–49), . . . Egypt would have perished and also the neighboring regions would have perished in the famine. Israel too would have died and his seed would not have gone to Egypt in search of bread (Gen 42:1–5), nor would the children of Israel have left Egypt under the wondrous deeds of the Lord (Exod 6–15). . . . No one would have walked through the Red Sea with dry feet (Exod 14); mortal life would not have come to know the nourishment of the manna (Exod 16); no flowing water would have gushed forth from the "following rock" (cf. Exod 17:6; 1 Cor 10:4), the law would not have been given to human beings by God. . . .

If you take away the perversity of Judas and eliminate his betrayal, you are at the same time taking away the cross of Christ and his passion; and if there is no cross, there is no "disarming of the principalities and powers," or "triumphing in the wood of the cross" (cf. Col 2:15). If there had been no death of Christ, neither would there have been any resurrection, nor would anyone have become "the first-born from the dead" (Col 1:18). And if there had been no "first-born of the dead," we would have no hope of resurrection.

Let us suppose the same thing with regard to the devil. If, for example, he had been prevented by some necessity from sinning, or if his desire for evil had been taken away from him after his sin, this would have eliminated our battle against the trickery of the devil, nor would there be any hope of a crown of victory for those who legitimately fought for it (cf. 2 Tim 2:5; 4:7-8). . . . From all this one gathers that God not only uses good things for his good work, but also evil things — and that is truly marvelous! . . . For in the "great house" of this world "there are not only vessels of gold and silver but also of wood and earthenware, and some for noble use, some for ignoble" (2 Tim 2:20), but both kinds are necessary. . . . Now the creator did not make them to be this way, but by the justice and, as it were, ineffable wisdom of his providence, he makes use of these spirits in accordance with their own free decisions. In the great cities, for example, just as those who are the less worthy, the people of low life and despicable conduct, are condemned to perform the lowest and most difficult tasks, works that are nevertheless necessary for a city of this kind — they serve, for example, as fire-tenders in the furnaces of the baths so that you can have your comfort and pleasure, or they clean the latrines and perform other services of this kind so that your life in the city will be pleasant, and whether they do these things willingly or because condemned to do so, their work is of service to those for whose benefit these good and useful things are done — so too is it in the point we have been discussing. God, of course, did not make evil; but having found it in the deliberate intention of those who deviated from the right path, he had no intention of eliminating it because he foresaw that even if it were of no benefit to those who did the evil, he could still make it useful for those against whom it was applied.

938   "How unsearchable are his judgments!" (Rom 11:33). How could a mere human mind have come to such a thought: that with the free will of each individual preserved, what is a work of evil for one is turned into a work of salvation for another!

939   Just as smoke is a result of there being fire and light, so are sinners a consequence of there being righteous people.

940   After this, one has to examine carefully the word "necessary" in the saying: "It is necessary that scandals should come" (Lk 17:1). . . . Just as it is necessary for a mortal being to die, . . .[1] just as it is necessary for a bodily being to be nourished, . . . so is it "necessary" and unavoidable "that scandals should come," since it is necessary for

---

[1] In the same measure that, within a descriptive philosophy of essence, the human being appears as "being unto death" and cannot appear otherwise, to the same degree, then, evil appears as "necessary." That this necessity can, to a higher theological consideration, appear as contingent, this cannot be determined, nor even be suspected, by philosophy.

there to be evil before there is virtue among human beings, from which evil come scandals. For it is impossible to find a completely sinless human being, one who has attained virtue without sinning. . . . But do not think that the scandals are in reality some nature, or being, when they happen to the people through whom they come; for just as "God did not make death" (Wis 1:13), he did not create scandals either—instead, it was human freedom, in certain ones who were unwilling to accept the burden of virtue, that created scandal.

941   This is why he did not deprive the devil of his dominion over this world. It is because there is still need of his works for the perfection of those who are to be crowned; there is still need of his works for the battle-training and victories of the blessed.

942   Hence it is said that God permits, and indeed practically incites, the contrary powers to take us on in battle, so that we will have the opportunity to be victorious.

943   But knowing the future and how strenuously Paul would work for the true religion [the Lord said to himself]: In the beginning I will lead him on in youthful zeal caused by ignorance to persecute under the guise of devotion those who believe in my Christ . . . so that when he has grown older, made a new start and turned to what is best, he will not boast in my presence (cf. 1 Cor 1:29) but say: "By the grace of God I am what I am" (1 Cor 15:10).

944   For we do not, once we have decided to obey, manage to obey immediately; for just as one still needs time for the healing of wounds, so too is it with conversion until one turns to God completely and purely.

945   "God gave them up in the lusts of their hearts to impurity" (Rom 1:24). How can it be just that someone, even when given up because of his own sins, is given up to impurity? . . . Just as, for example, someone given over to darkness cannot be held responsible for the fact that he is in darkness, and someone given over to the fire cannot be blamed for the fact that he is burned, so too it does not seem to be right to hold those who are given over to lust and impurity responsible for doing shameful things with their bodies.

946   "I will send famine upon them [the land], and cut off from them man and beast" (Ezek 14:13). How can I bring such hidden things forth into the open? Where can I get the power to explain why famine and why fruitfulness happen to the earth? Why abundance? Why need? "O the depths of the riches and wisdom and knowledge of God!" (Rom 11:33).

947   One might say that the words to the effect that Jesus was not sent to judge (condemn) the world now (cf. Jn 3:17) are not fully understandable

when one sets beside them the following: "This is the judgment, that the light has come into the world" (Jn 3:19). And in this same gospel Jesus says: "For judgment I came into this world" (Jn 9:39). Let us try to solve the difficulty this way. Jesus, by his coming, brings about both: judging the world and saving it, but the one by means of the other. For he came into the world to judge it in order to save it (for he does not save it in order to judge it), and like a doctor comes to the sick in order to heal them. . . . "He who believes in him is not judged (condemned)" (Jn 3:18). For they who through faith come to the fullness of salvation are not subject to judgment. But they who do not believe are "self-condemned" (cf. Tit 3:11); they are already condemned.

948   The words of God do first what is necessary: the uprooting and the tearing down and the destroying, then the building up and the planting. And we have noticed that in the scripture the unpleasant-seeming things are, as it were, mentioned first, then in second place the things that seem to be happy. "I kill and I make alive" (Deut 32:39). . . . Whom do I kill? Paul the betrayer, Paul the persecutor. "And I make alive," so that he becomes "Paul, the apostle of Jesus Christ" (2 Cor 1:1 and passim in Paul). If the poor heretics[1] could only understand this, they would not be constantly repeating to us: Do you see how the God of the law is savage and inhuman, since he says: "I kill and I make alive" (Deut 32:39)? Don't you see in the scriptures the message of the resurrection of the dead? Or don't you see that the resurrection of the dead has already begun in each one? "We were buried" unto Christ "through baptism" and we have risen with him (cf. Rom 6:4; Col 2:12; 3:1). . . . Evil must be torn out by its deepest roots, the structure of evil in our souls must be destroyed so that after this the words [of God] can build [and grow], . . . so that, with that idolatrous structure torn down, the temple of God might be built, and the glory of God might be found in the rebuilt temple.

949   The good rain also fell on the bad earth, but because the ground was uncultivated and untended, it brought forth "thorns and thistles" (cf. Heb 6:8). In the same way, the wonderful things done by God are like rain; but the different human dispositions are, as it were, the cultivated and neglected earth; and they are in one nature, like the earth. And just as if the sun were to speak up and say: "I melt and I

---

[1] The Marcionites.

dry out," it would not be speaking falsely of the subject at hand, even though melting and drying out are opposites, because it is by one and the same heat that the wax is melted and the clay dried out. Thus the same operation carried out by Moses demonstrated the hardness of Pharaoh because of his wickedness, but also the obedience of those Egyptians who, mixed in with the Hebrews, went out with them.

950   "The light shone in the darkness, and the darkness has not over-taken it" (Jn 1:15). In two ways the darkness has not overtaken the light: either it was left far behind and because of its own slowness was unable to keep up with the rapid speed of the light; or the light planned to set an ambush for the darkness and, according to its plan, waited for it to catch up. In this case the darkness, upon approaching the light, was dispelled. But in neither way did the darkness overtake or overcome the light.

951   The light that is called God dissolves all darkness and ignorance of sin. Hence, when it shines in such great darkness, it is not overcome by it. For this light is the wisdom and justice of God. As wisdom it dispels the ignorance of the mind; as justice it sets straight the foot-steps of the soul. This is what it means to shine in the darkness, namely, to send its own rays without hindrance to those who are being enlightened. This is why it is not overcome by the darkness which is dissolved and dispersed at the coming of the light. For it is not as something subsisting and acting that it does not overcome the light, but as something being dissolved and no longer existing. Thus it was that Paul, when he did not know Christ, persecuted him, spurred on to this by his former ignorance which we have called darkness. But when the persecuted light sent forth its rays over it, this darkness was dissolved and made incapable of overcoming the light it was persecut-ing. So it was with the repentant thief on the cross: blinded by this darkness, he persecuted the light; but the darkness in the thief was dissolved and thus did not overcome the light here either.

To express this idea more clearly: the light is the truth. When un-truth and every kind of deceit — this is the darkness — persecutes the light, it is dissolved and dispersed when it approaches what it perse-cutes. For when the truth appears, untruth and deceit is dissolved. This is paradoxical, for when the darkness is distant it persecutes the light, but when it approaches in order to overcome the light, it dis-appears. For it is only as long as it keeps its distance from the truth that untruth has any power or room to operate in human beings to drive truth from their minds. As soon as it draws near, its complete nothingness is revealed. It is from this necessity that God has permitted evil to exist, that the greatness of virtue might be demonstrated.

THE CUNNING OF LOVE

This is how the mystery of purifying punishment flows into the ultimate mystery of the superior power of love over evil. Even human freedom is not so absolute that it can remain impervious to God's more absolute love (952–953). But this mystery remains veiled, and must remain so (954–959). For only when life is an absolute choice does it maintain its seriousness and its tension (960). The human being must remain under God (961). Jeremiah's reproachful and still more deeply loving complaint against God's deception: both the suffering which God keeps to himself and the good he draws from it must remain hidden because of their greatness (962–963). The concept of the "wrath" of God is part of the same character of "concealing" which the whole economy (order of salvation) has in the Alexandrian view (964–966). The real and comprehensive judgment is the cross (966a).

952   Hence the God of all could have brought about in us something that was only an apparent good: that we would give alms out of necessity and be prudent out of necessity, but he did not choose to do that. He thus orders us not to perform what we do grudgingly or because we are forced to, so that what is done will be done freely. He [Paul] is thus looking for a way in which a person will do freely what God wills.[1]

953   Because the WORD and its healing power is stronger than all the evils in the soul, he applies this power to each one according to God's will; and the end of all things is the elimination of evil.

954   These things should remain hidden and not be brought out into the open—although the heretics force us to bring out in public what should remain hidden—because it is helpful to keep them hidden from those who are still "infants" according to the age of the soul and still need the fear of teachers, . . . so that they will not disrespect the goodness of God.

---

[1] Cf. below, Nos. 1019–1020.

955   But in this purification which is obtained through the punishment of fire, how much time and how many ages of punishment may be required of sinners, only he can know to whom "the Father has given all judgment" (Jn 5:22), who so loves his creation that for it "he emptied himself" of the "form of God, taking the form of a servant, humbling himself unto death" (cf. Phil 2:6–8), desiring "all men to be saved and to come to the knowledge of the truth" (2 Tim 2:4). But yet we must ever keep in mind that the Apostle wanted this passage to be treated as a mystery, in that the faithful and the mature should keep meanings of this kind covered in silence among themselves as the mystery of God and not lay them indiscriminately before the immature and less capable. For "it is good," says the scripture, "to keep secret the mystery of the king" (Tob 12:7).

956   It is customary with the Apostle Paul, when making something known about the mildness of God and his indescribable goodness, to express himself a bit harshly, as it were, because of the more neglectful among his hearers, and to inject fear into the lax, as when in his discussion of the end of all things with the Corinthians he says: "Just as in Adam all die, so also in Christ shall all be made alive"; and shortly afterwards: "Then comes the end, when he delivers the kingdom to God the Father," etc. (1 Cor 15:22, 24). But for those from whom he fears someone might "presume upon the riches of the kindness and forbearance and patience of God . . . in his hard and impenitent heart storing up wrath for himself on the day of wrath when God's righteous judgment will be revealed" (Rom 2:4–5), he adds afterwards what he said about the end: "Do not be deceived: 'Bad company ruins good morals.' Come to your right mind and sin no more. For some have no knowledge of God. I say this to your shame" (1 Cor 15:33–34).

957   Although the Holy Spirit did want something written about these things, it was not according to his good pleasure that they should be laid out in the open and trod upon so to speak by the feet of the inexperienced. Instead he so arranged it that, even though they would seem to be treated openly, they would nevertheless, hidden by the obscurity of speech, remain protected in secret and mystery.

958   "I have laid up your word in my heart that I may not sin against you" (Ps 119:11). They sin against God who are considered worthy of the more ineffable or secret words . . . and do not keep them hidden from those from whom they should.

959   Even to speak truly of God is dangerous. For not only are those things dangerous which are said falsely of him, but also the things that are true and not said at the right time bring danger to the one saying them. It is a true "pearl," but if it is "thrown before swine," then it is to the judgment of the one who cast it before their feet (cf. Mt 7:6).

960   In Jeremiah it says: "Perhaps they will listen and do penance" (Jer 26:3). Now God does not say this because he does not know whether they will listen or not . . . but to demonstrate the, so to speak, equality of the possibilities. This is so that the event being foretold, though it has the appearance of necessity, would not discourage the hearers into thinking that conversion was not in their power and that the event was the cause of their sins. It is also so that, for those who, in ignorance of the good which is to come, can fight against evil and strive to lead a good life, this foreknowledge would not cause them to relax and no longer resist sin the way they should, since what was foretold would be happening in any case. The foreknowledge would thus become an obstacle to the future good. And since God does a superb job in arranging the whole order of the universe, he has quite rightly made us blind with regard to the things to come, for knowledge of them would hinder us in our struggle against evil. Otherwise it would happen that someone who was struggling for the good and the beautiful would have already come to the foreknowledge that he would be good. For in addition to what we naturally have, we need to have great vehemence and tension to attain to moral goodness. But the foreknowledge that we will all turn out to be good in any case would cripple our efforts. Thus it is fitting for us not to know whether we will turn out good or bad.[1]

961   "I harden the heart of Pharaoh and multiply my signs. . . . And Pharaoh's heart became hardened" (Exod 7:3; 9:13 and passim). Now if we really believe that these writings are divine and written by the Holy Spirit, I do not think that we would think so poorly of the divine Spirit as to attribute it to chance that there is this variety in so great a work as this: that at one time God is said to have hardened Pharaoh's heart, but at another it is said to have been hardened not by God but as if by itself. And indeed I profess myself as not particularly suited or

---

[1] With this is expressed a principle which does not explain this whole theory of salvation as something false, but does indeed remove it from the grasp of human beings and of any theology (which is necessarily objective and, as doctrine, itself never "existential").

qualified to examine the secrets of divine wisdom in variations such as this. But I see Paul the Apostle who, because of the Spirit of God dwelling in him, dared to say with confidence: "God has revealed to us through the Spirit. For the Spirit searches everything, even the depths of God" (1 Cor 2:10). For I see Paul as one who understands the difference between "the heart of Pharaoh became hardened" and "the Lord hardened the heart of Pharaoh," for he said in another place: "Or do you presume upon the riches of his kindness and forbearance and patience? Do you not know that God's kindness is meant to lead you to repentance? But by your hard and impenitent heart you are stirring up wrath for yourself on the day of wrath when God's righteous judgment will be revealed" (Rom 2:4–5). By this he is obviously casting blame on those who have become hardened of their own accord. But elsewhere, he expresses himself on this matter in a kind of question when he says: "So then he has mercy on whomever he wills, and he hardens the heart of whomever he wills. You will say to me then, 'Why does he still find fault? For who can resist his will?'" He also adds this: "But who are you, a man, to answer back to God?" (Rom 9:18–20). With these words he gives his answer with regard to him whose heart is said to be hardened by the Lord, responding not so much with a solution of the problem as with apostolic authority, and judging, I think, that it is not right, in view of the inability of his hearers, to commit the solution of this kind of secret to "paper and ink" (cf. 2 Jn 12), just as in another place he says of certain words that he has "heard" things "which man may not utter" (2 Cor 12:4). As a consequence of this, it is less the person with a laudable eagerness to know than the one with a greed for knowledge who indulges his curiosity in the most secret questions that he rebuffs with the severity of a magisterial teacher when he says: "Who are you, a man, to answer back to God? Will what is molded say to its molder, 'Why have you made me thus?'" (Rom 9:20), etc. Hence let it be enough for us to have observed and examined this much and to have shown our hearers what great things are hidden in the mysterious depths of the divine law, for the sake of which we must say in prayer: "Out of the depths I cry to you, O Lord" (Ps 130:1).

962   "O Lord, you have deceived me and I was deceived" (Jer 20:7). God—deceives? I do not know how I can explain this. For if I see something in this text in relation to God and his WORD, what will be said must be of elevated meaning. . . . Thus it is necessary to conceive of God's "deception" in a different way than the deception which

we commit. What then is this deception of God which the prophet became aware of when it was already done, and of which he said, recognizing the benefit of being deceived: "O Lord, you have deceived me and I was deceived"? . . . I pray that my examination will find something true in this passage. Is it not like the situation of a father who, in his desire to help his son, deceives him when he is still a child, unable to help the child in any other way except by deceiving him, just as the physician tries to deceive the sick person who cannot be healed except by deceiving words? So too does the God of all in his desire to help the human race. Should the doctor tell the patient: you must be cut open, you must be cauterized, you must suffer other terrible things, the sick person would never entrust himself to the doctor. But sometimes he says something else and hides under a sponge that cutting and separating steel. Another time he disguises under honey the bitter and unpleasant medicine with the intention not of hurting but of healing the patient. The whole of sacred scripture is filled with such medicines. Sometimes good things are concealed, and sometimes it is the bitter which is hidden. When you see a father casting out his son as if in hatred, and threatening him, and not showing his son his affection but hiding his love from him, you will know that his intention is to deceive the child. For it is not always good for the son to know the love of the father and his concerned tenderness; he would only take advantage of it and not become educated. Thus the father conceals the sweetness of his affection and shows the bitterness of threats.

Now God acts somewhat like a father and a doctor. There are certain bitter things which bring healing even to the most just and most wise . . . [gap in text]. For all sinners must be punished for their sins. "Do not be deceived; God is not mocked" (Gal 6:7). "Neither the immoral, nor idolaters, nor adulterers, nor homosexuals, nor thieves, nor the greedy, nor drunkards, nor revilers, nor robbers will inherit the kingdom of God" (1 Cor 6:9-10). If this were known and clearly understood by those who are unable to see the healing steel under the sponge, and unable to comprehend the bitter medicine under the honey, they would lose heart. For who of us can claim never to have drunk immoderately or been intoxicated? Which of us is innocent of theft or of having been forced by necessity to steal what we needed? But see what the word of God says: "Do not be deceived; these will not inherit the kingdom of God" (cf. 1 Cor 6:10). The mystery in this passage must be concealed so that the many will not lose heart, so that they will not, upon learning the facts, think of the outcome as a punishment instead of peaceful tranquility. For who can be like Paul, able to say: "My desire is to be dissolved and be with Christ" (cf. Phil 1:23)? I am not capable of saying this. . . . Just as with the good and the just, "the heart of man has not conceived what God has prepared for those who love him" (cf. 1 Cor 2:9), so too has it not been conceived in the heart of man what he has prepared for those who sin by impurity and adultery. For if this were conceived in the heart of the one who said to his brother: "You fool!" (Mt 5:22), it is clear that something worse than what is conceived in the heart is prepared for those who have committed worse sins. I cannot think of anything worse than hell, but I believe that something worse than hell is what is prepared for the impure. . . . What else does the Apostle say? "A man who has violated the law of Moses dies without mercy at the testimony of two or three witnesses. How much worse punishment do you think will be deserved by the man who has trampled on the Son of God?" (Heb 10:28–29). Name it, O Paul! Say what the punishment is! I will not mention it, he says. More than anything that can be expressed is the punishment of those who sin against the gospel. . . . Do you see how all this is hidden from the majority of the faithful? — and rightly hidden! And each one of us, since we have not committed adultery or impurity (O may we be sinless at least in these things!) has the idea that, on departing this life, he will be saved. We do not see before us the fact that "we must all appear before the judgment seat of Christ, so that each one may receive good or evil, according to what he has done in the body" (2 Cor 5:10).

Therefore, since the physician sometimes conceals the healing steel beneath the soft and delicate sponge, and the father conceals his tenderness with threatening words, . . . the prophet understood in mystery that God acts in a similar way; and seeing that he has been deceived by God unto good, says: "O Lord, you have deceived me and I was deceived" (Jer 20:7). God set him in such an ecstasy that he even said to God: Deceive me, if this is helpful. For being deceived by God is not the same thing as being deceived by the serpent. See what the woman says to God: "The serpent beguiled me and I ate" (Gen 3:13). And the deceit of the serpent cast Adam and his wife out of God's paradise. But the deception practiced on the prophet, . . . gave him such a high gift of prophecy that its power in him was increased, he was brought to perfection, and became able to obey, without fear of other men, the will of the WORD of God. . . . If the serpent says anything to me, whether he is telling me something true or only trying to deceive me, I am suspicious of his words, sure that, whether he is deceiving me or speaking the truth, he is doing injury to me. For even the serpent's truth is harmful. Nothing helpful comes from the serpent since "a bad tree cannot bear good fruit" (Mt 7:18). But if God says something to me and I am sure that it is God who is speaking, I am ready to put myself at his disposition. He speaks the truth, I accept. He wishes to deceive me, I am willing to be deceived; but let God alone be the one to deceive me. And when I have put myself at his disposition, sure that it is God who is speaking, and I am deceived, it doesn't bother me. . . . Hence I say not only that you have performed a deception, but also that I know that you have deceived me, and thus I say: "O Lord, you have deceived me and I was deceived" (Jer 20:7). . . . We deceive children who have childish fears, so that they may grow out of the uneducated state. . . . We are all children with respect to God and we need the education of children. Therefore God, in his consideration for us, deceives us (even if we are not aware of the deception ahead of time). This is to keep us from skipping over childhood, as it were, and, instead of by deception, having to be educated just by the bare facts.

963   Even when he comes at me with great power and many threats, I still know that the truth lies with him.

964   God wills, and the wrath causes what God wills to be done. For should someone not wish to come to be in the will of the Word of God, the wrath will be sent upon that person.

965   For truly, wrath is something other than God, so that it is not connected to him as something internal. This is why it is said of sinners: "You send forth your wrath and it consumes them" (cf. Exod 15:7). No one can "send forth" what is connected to himself as an integral part.

966   But there might well be someone who, offended by the very name of wrath, objects to it in God. To this we respond that the wrath of God is not so much wrath as a necessary part of his plan of salvation.

966a   The suffering on the cross was the judgment over this whole world, for, "having made peace by the blood of his cross, both for the things on earth as for those in heaven" (Col 1:20), and after triumphing on the cross, he disarmed the principalities and powers (cf. Col 2:15) and took his seat in the heavenly places (Eph 2:6) ordering each individual thing according to its fitting and proper end. Since, therefore, that which contained the judgment of each individual thing was the order of salvation on the cross, he said, as the time of this suffering drew near: "Now is the judgment of this world" (Jn 12:31).

FEAR AND LOVE

For those who have been brought into these mysteries, there re-
mains as final attitude only the tension between fear and love: in
fear nailed with Christ to the cross, in love rising with Christ from
the dead. But even if their (servile) fear is overcome by love, their at-
titude of praising service is not (967–974).

967   Just as he is both sacrificial victim and priest, and is both in "the form of a servant" and in "the form of God" (Phil 2:6–7), so too is he our advocate and judge.

968   For neither is he kind without being severe, nor is he severe without being benevolent (cf. Rom 11:22). For if he were only benevolent and not also severe, we would for the most part abuse his kindness (cf. Rom 2:4). If he were only severe and not also kind, we would perhaps despair in our sins. But as it is, he is, as God, both kind and severe.

969   "Blessed is the one who fears the Lord" (Ps 112:1). Whoever does not fear is not blessed.

970   "Rejoice in him with trembling" (Ps 2:11 LXX), having constantly before one's eyes, so to speak, the possibility of falling, should God's assistance abandon the one who is doing something praiseworthy.

971   "And they were very sorrowful, and began to say to him one after another, 'Is it I, Lord?'" (Mt 26:22). But I think that each of the disciples knew from what Jesus had taught that human nature is changeable and prone to evil. . . . In our weakness we have to be afraid of all future things, we who have not yet received the wisdom of perfection which the Apostle spoke of: "For I am sure that neither death, nor life," etc., "will be able to separate us from the love of God in Christ Jesus our Lord" (Rom 8:38–39). They who are not yet perfect have doubts about themselves since they are capable of falling. Writing about this human weakness to the Corinthians, Paul said: "I pommel my body and subdue it, lest after preaching to others I myself should be disqualified" (1 Cor 9:27).

972   "Nail my flesh with your fear, for I am fearful of your judgments" (Ps 119:120 LXX). Whoever is nailed is crucified. I am therefore searching for the cross and ask if perchance the cross is the fear of God. For the Savior said: "He who does not take his cross and follow me is not worthy of me" (Mt 10:38). We have often made distinctions between fear and love, and said that the one who loves is more perfect than the one who fears, and that fear is necessary in the beginning.

But where "perfect love" has come in, "it casts out fear" (1 Jn 4:13). Since then the just person is nailed to the cross by God with fear, I ask whether the one who is crucified and nailed with fear is indeed afraid so that he will mortify his earthly members (cf. Col 3:5); but when "perfect love" comes, he is taken down from the cross, buried and raised from the dead that he might "walk in newness of life" (Rom 6:4), no longer in fear but in the love which is in Christ Jesus.

973   Just as he is not a "God of the dead but of the living" (Mt 22:32; Mk 12:27; Lk 20:38), so too is he not Lord of lowly slaves but of those who in the beginning were in fear because of their childishness but, after being educated, entered under love into a more blessed service than they had in fear.

974   A son too can serve. But then fear alone is not the cause of his serving but also love.

GOD, ALL IN ALL

THE SACRAMENTS OF TRUTH

The basic constitution of being, its double aspect as both truth and image, is maintained in the eschatological for one last time. It had already been intimated before this that, just as the Old Testament was an image of the New, so the New, and indeed all of scripture, is an image of the eternal gospel. Everything that takes place in the earthly order of salvation is sign and sacrament, mirror and mystery of what is completed in the eternal order of salvation. So it is with the life of grace (975–976), with resurrection (977–980), with knowledge of God (981), with faith (982) and virtue (983). But even the sacraments of the church are, in all their true effectiveness, only shadows of the eternal sacrament: baptism is only the image of that eternal baptism of fire (984–988), marriage the image of the eternal marriage (989), eucharist the image of the heavenly banquet (990), the liturgical sacrifice image of the eternal sacrifice (991). But the recollection of the event of earthly death will remain (992). And earthly freedom of will is only an image of the heavenly freedom of love and grace (993). In the beyond, the creature will be completely swept up into God (994), and then the great sabbath will begin (995–996).

975   For if we say, and this seems to make sense, that life reigns when death has been destroyed (cf. 1 Cor 15:26), the objection could be raised: How then does sin take place? And it is clear that death reigns through sin. But if we wanted to say that in some Christ reigns, that is, life, and in others death, would we find any, and where would we find them, in whom life reigns in such a way that the reign of death has no power in them, that is, who are totally without sin? . . . And the Lord himself at the beginning of his preaching does not say: "The kingdom of heaven has come," but: "The kingdom of heaven has drawn near" (Mt 3:12).

976   "If you would enter life, keep the commandments" (Mt 20:17). Take note that this was said as to someone who was still outside of life. . . . Is not therefore that person outside of life who happens to be outside of (and also a stranger to) the one who says: "I am the life" (Jn 11:25; 14:6)? But in another way, everyone on earth (even the most just) can be in the shadow of life and say: . . . "Under his shadow we shall live among the nations" (Lam 4:20), and not in life itself. . . . Thus Paul says: "Your life is hid with Christ in God" (Col 3:3).

977   Now then let this "perishable" nature of ours put on sanctity in holiness and all purity and "imperishability"; and, when death has been destroyed, let this mortal nature of ours put on the "immortality" of the Father (cf. 1 Cor 15:53–54), so that, in being ruled over by God, we may enjoy the good things of regeneration and resurrection (cf. Mt 19:28).

978   Or don't you see that the resurrection of the dead has already begun in each one?

979   Already, it is said, has the Lord raised us, as if, according to this, the resurrection has already taken place. But it is perhaps a resurrection "in part," just as the knowledge which Christians have is "in part" (cf. 1 Cor 13:12).

980   "He raised us up with him and made us sit with him in the heavenly places in Christ Jesus" (Eph 2:6). Those who take this "being raised up with him" and "made to sit with him" according to its simpler meaning will say that these things are spoken, according to God's foreknowledge and predetermination, as if the future has already come. But they who have insight into the spiritual kingdom of Christ will not hesitate to say that, just as the holy is not now in the flesh, even if it is said to be by the more simple, so too is it not on the earth, even if it seems to be according to the senses.

981   "In Judah God is known" (Ps 76:1). In the Judaea above, God is known, there where the true God is and not just his imaged glory. For now God is known "in a mirror dimly" (1 Cor 13:12).

982   In comparison with "the perfect" which, "when it comes will abolish what is imperfect" (1 Cor 13:9–10), all our faith here below is little faith; and, in regard to that perfection, we who know only in part do not yet know nor remember, for we are simply not able to acquire a memory which is sufficient and suitable for the depth of the nature of these objects of contemplation.

983   Now, while we are in the body in this present life, and "this earthly tent burdens the thoughtful mind" (Wis 9:15), we have the likeness of

knowledge but not knowledge itself, as the Apostle said in another place: "Now we see in a mirror dimly" (1 Cor 13:12). . . . Hence in the present life too, it is my opinion that we can attain to the image and shadow of the virtues, but to the virtues themselves only when what is perfect has come. And thus the just person, as I see it, lives more in the shadow of the virtues than in the virtues themselves.

984   They, then, who "have followed" the Savior "will sit on twelve thrones, judging the twelve tribes of Israel," and they will receive this power at the resurrection of the dead. And this is that "regeneration" (Mt 19:28) which really is a new birth, when "a new heaven and a new earth" (Rev 21:1) is created for those who have renewed themselves, and a new testament and its cup is handed on. A prelude of that regeneration is what Paul calls the "washing of regeneration" (Tit 3:5) and [the symbol] of that newness, [the Spirit which] after the "washing of regeneration" hovered over [the waters], in the [washing] of the renewal of the Spirit.[1] And perhaps because of birth "no one is free from filth, even if he has only lived for one day" (Job 14:4–5 LXX) because of the mystery of our birth concerning which every individual who has been born can say what was said thus by David in the fiftieth Psalm: "I was brought forth in iniquity, and in sin did my mother conceive me" (Ps 51:5). Through the rebirth that comes from the washing everyone is "free from filth" (Job 14:4) who has been born "from above" "of water and the Spirit" (Jn 3:3, 5); but, to speak daringly, he is pure only "in a mirror" and "darkly" (1 Cor 13:12). It is only through that other rebirth "when the Son of Man shall sit on his glorious throne" (Mt 19:28), that each one who has come to that rebirth in Christ will be completely pure from filth and see "face to face" (1 Cor 13:12). Indeed he comes to this rebirth only through the "washing of regeneration." If you want to understand that washing, consider how John, baptizing "with water for repentance," said of the Savior: "He will baptize you with the Holy Spirit and with fire" (Mt 3:11). Thus, in the rebirth through the washing (Tit 3:5), we have been buried with Christ: "For we were buried with him," according to the Apostle, "by baptism" (Rom 6:4). In the rebirth of washing through fire and the spirit we become "like unto the glorious body" of Christ (Phil 3:21), . . . if "we have left everything and followed" Christ (Mt 19:27).

---

[1] This is how we interpret this elliptical text, basing our interpretation on what Origen says in Jo Co 6, 17 (P 4, 143, line 15).

985   "When the days of their purification had been fulfilled" (Lk 2:22). These days are also fulfilled in a mystical way, for a soul is not purified immediately at its birth, nor does it come to perfect purity right from the beginning, but, as is written in the law: "If a woman bears a male child, then she shall be unclean seven days. . . . Then she shall continue for thirty-three days in the blood of her purifying, she and her child" (cf. Lev 12:2-4). Thus, because "the law" is spiritual and "has but a shadow of the good things to come" (Heb 10:1), we can understand that full purification will come to us only in time. Perhaps even after we rise from the dead we will need a sacrament that washes and purifies us. . . . In this rebirth, therefore, there will be a sacrament of purification like that which Jesus went through at his birth.

986   Hear how the Savior explains in two places the meanings of "fire" and "sword." In one place he says: "I have not come to bring peace, but a sword" (Mt 10:34). But in another place: "I came to cast fire upon the earth; and would that it were already kindled" (Lk 12:49). Thus the Savior brings both "sword" and "fire" and baptizes you "in sword" and "in fire." For those who have not been healed by the baptism of the Holy Spirit he baptizes "with fire". . . . These are divine sacraments [mysteries] which transcend human words and are known to God alone. But they consist more in the conferring of graces than in different kinds of torments.

987   Just as John stood by the Jordan waiting for those who came for baptism, some of whom he sent away with the words: "You brood of vipers," but the rest, who confessed their sins and vices, he accepted, so too will the Lord Jesus Christ stand in the river of fire by the "flaming sword"; and all those who, after departing this life, want to cross over into paradise but need purification, he will baptize them in this stream and bring them across to what they desire. But they who do not bear the sign of the prior baptisms, he will not baptize in this washing with fire. For it is necessary first to be baptized "with water and the Spirit" (Jn 3:5) so that, when arriving at the river of fire, one can show that one has undergone the washings of water and the Spirit and so is worthy also to receive the baptism of fire in Christ Jesus.

988   We must all, I think, come to that fire. Even if one is a Paul or a Peter, he must still come to that fire. But they who are like them hear the words: "When you walk through fire you shall not be burned" (Isa 43:2). But should there be any who are like me, a sinner, they will indeed come to that fire like Peter and Paul, but they will not pass through it like Peter and Paul.

989 At the resurrection of the dead, the son of the king will celebrate a marriage feast (cf. Mt 22:2) surpassing every marriage feast which any "eye has seen or ear heard or the heart of man conceived" (cf. 1 Cor 2:9); and that sacred and divine and spiritual marriage will take place in words of mystery "which man may not utter" (2 Cor 12:4). Someone may ask whether in the resurrection of the dead there will be other similar marriages like the marriage of the bridegroom, or whether in the resurrection of the dead the bridegroom will dissolve every other marriage and alone celebrate his marriage, where there will be not "two in one flesh" (cf. Mt 19:5), but where it will be more fitting to say that the bridegroom and the bride are one spirit (cf. 1 Cor 6:17). (But when you hear such things make sure that you aren't deceived into accepting that myth of the male and female aeons according to the teaching of those who invent their syzygies [double essences] which do not exist nor are mentioned anywhere in the sacred scripture.) . . . If someone, then, in searching through the law and going through the texts which speak of the marriage of women and men thinks that there is nothing more there than the literal meaning, that person is in error, and knows "neither the scriptures nor the power of God" (Mt 22:29).

990 But be aware of this: As long as one remains in this life, one looks "through a mirror, darkly" (1 Cor 13:12) and is a little sheep which is led around by the shepherd. But when one passes over into the world to come, one comes "face to face" before the truth and takes one's seat at the spiritual banquet, according to the words: "And I will prepare for you a covenant so that you may eat and drink at the table of my Father in truth" (cf. Lk 22:29-30).

991 Then will the never-ending sacrifice . . . also be better offered. For then will the soul be better able to stand unceasingly before God and offer a "sacrifice of praise" through the high priest who is "priest for ever after the order of Melshisedek" (Heb 6:20).

992 But the WORD of God riding on a white horse in John's vision is not naked, but clothed in a robe sprinkled with blood (cf. Rev 19:11-13). For the WORD who became flesh, and because of that becoming flesh died, is covered with the marks of the fact that his blood flowed out onto the earth when the soldier pierced his side. But even if we should one day come to that highest and most sublime contemplation of the WORD and the Truth, we will never completely forget what has come about by his entering into our body.

993 But this too, it seems, we should also add at this point: that just as the knowledge given to the saints in this world is given through a

mirror and darkly (cf. 1 Cor 13:12), . . . so too the liberty which is now given to the saints is not yet a full liberty but is, so to speak, "through a mirror, darkly." That is why the saints call themselves servants; it is in contrast to that liberty which is given face to face.

994   The "sun of righteousness" is Christ. When the moon, that is, his church which is filled with his light, is joined and thoroughly united with him (so that, as the Apostle says, "whoever is united to the Lord becomes one spirit with him" — 1 Cor 6:17), then it celebrates the feast of the new moon (cf. Num 28:11); for then it becomes new. . . . And that, finally, is when it can no longer be seen or understood by human viewers. For when the soul has completely united itself to the Lord and has totally given itself up to the splendor of his light, . . . how can it be seen by human beings or grasped by human insight?

995   For we can see that what was written in Genesis, that "God rested on the seventh day from all his work" (Gen 2:2), has been fulfilled neither then nor now. For we see that God is working continually, and there is no sabbath on which God does not work, in which he does not "make his sun rise on the evil and on the good and send his rain on the just and on the unjust" (Mt 5:45), on which he does not "make hay grow upon the hills, and grass for the benefit of men" (Ps 147:8 LXX), on which he does not "wound and heal," go down into the nether world and back up again, on which he does not "kill and make alive" (Deut 32:39). . . . So too did the Lord in the gospels express himself: "My Father is working still, and I am working" (Jn 5:17). . . . But it will be a true sabbath on which God will "rest from all his work" . . . when God "will be all in all" (Col 3:11).

996   God made the works of the world in six days and rested on the sabbath. But he rested from the works of the world which he had undertaken. The works of justice, however, he performs and will perform continually without beginning and without end.

SUPER-WORLD

The law of sublation (as surviving, but only through annihilating death by fire) applies ultimately to the totality of the world. Hence, not one of the things now visible is, as such, the eternal (997–1000). Even the human being will have to become the superhuman being in order to enter into the super-world (1001). There, everything evil is destroyed (1002–1004); the super-heavenly place (i.e., the place above the changeability of the heavenly spheres)

becomes our dwelling place (1005). Installation of the members of
Christ as his co-heirs (1006–1008).

997   Friends learn not by riddles but by seeing (cf. 1 Cor 13:12), or by
the bare wisdom of sounds and words and symbols and types, as they
encounter the nature of intelligible things and the beauty of truth.

998   Consider, then, how great and of what nature are the things which
not only could no one see or hear, but which could not even be conceived in the heart, that is, in human thinking (1 Cor 2:9). Therefore,
whether you mention the earth or the sky or this sun and the brightness of this visible light, all these the eye sees and the ear hears, and
thus they cannot be those things which "no eye has seen, nor ear
heard, nor the heart of man conceived" (1 Cor 2:9). Therefore pass
through all these things and transcend everything that you see, that
you hear, yes even that you can think, and know that to those who
love God is given what could not even be conceived in your heart (cf.
1 Cor 2:9). Hence I consider that in promises of this kind, nothing
can be thought of as applying to corporeal things. The essence of
bodily matter is not wholly beyond the comprehension of human
thought, but those things cannot be conceived in any mind or in any
heart, since they are contained in the unique wisdom of God.

999   Therefore, of these things which are seen, nothing at all is to be hoped
for in the future. For "no eye has seen . . . what God has prepared for
those who love him" (1 Cor 2:9). But the eye sees the heaven and the
earth; therefore it should not be believed that this which is seen has been
prepared by God for those who love him. Indeed there must be a heaven,
indeed there must rather be heavens which are much more sublime and
elevated than this firmament that can be seen by the eyes.

1000   For since "the WORD of God is living and active, sharper than any
two-edged sword, piercing to the division of soul and spirit" (Heb
4:12) . . ., God drew the sword between the "image of the man of
dust" and the "image of the man of heaven" (1 Cor 15:49) in order that,
receiving the heavenly part from us now, he might in the future make
us become super-heavenly after we have become worthy of not being
cut in two.

1001   "There shall be no man there when the high priest enters within the
veil in the tent of meeting" (cf. Lev 16:17). What is the meaning of this
"There shall be no man"? I take it to mean that the person who is able
to follow Christ and enter with him inside the tent and climb to the
heights of heaven shall no longer be man but, according to his word,
will be "like an angel of God" (cf. Mt 22:30). Or perhaps there will be

fulfilled in him also that word which the Lord himself spoke: "I say, 'You are gods, sons of the Most High, all of you'" (Ps 82:6). Thus, whether in becoming spiritual he becomes one spirit with the Lord (cf. 1 Cor 6:17), or through the glory of the resurrection passes over to the ranks of the angels, he shall certainly no longer be man. But each individual is personally responsible for either going beyond this human name or continuing to be classified under this human condition. For if the human being "made from the beginning" (Mk 10:6) had lived according to what the scripture says to him: "See, I have set before you death and life; choose life" (cf. Deut 30:15), and followed this advice, mortality would never have gotten its hold on the human race. But because he abandoned life and chose death, man became a human being; and not just a human being, but also earth. This is why it is said that he will "return to the ground" (Gen 3:19). . . . And I am convinced that the human soul in itself cannot be called either mortal or immortal. Rather, if it has chosen life, it will be immortal through its participation in life (for death has no place in life); however, if it turns away from life and makes common cause with death, it makes itself mortal. Thus the prophet says: "The soul that sins shall die" (Ezek 18:4) — although we do not understand this death as the end of existence, but rather as saying that whoever is a stranger to or exiled from God, who is true life, is believed to be dead.

1002   "He must reign until . . . the last enemy, death, has been destroyed" (1 Cor 15:25-26). And when he has been destroyed, death will no longer stand before the face of those being saved, but only the life that is believed in. For as long as death stands before their face, life is not believed in by any of those over whom death has power; but when death has been destroyed, life is believed in by all.

1003   Now indeed, "my soul cleaves to the dust" (Ps 119:25) and has become flesh. In the resurrection, however, the flesh will cleave to the soul and will become a soul which, in the general resurrection, will cleave to the Lord and become "one spirit with him" (1 Cor 6:17), and become a "spiritual body" (1 Cor 15:44).

1004   But when the perfection of all things has come and the bride has been made perfect — which is to say: when the totality of rational creation has been united to him because "he has brought peace by his blood not only to what is on earth but also to what is in heaven" (Col 1:20) — then he will be called simply Solomon "when he has delivered the kingdom to God the Father after destroying every rule and every authority and power" (1 Cor 15:24). When thus all things have been made peaceful and subject to the Father, when God will be "all in all" (cf. Col 3:11), then will he be called simply Solomon, that is, Prince of Peace.

)05   The bride in the Song of Songs has made such progress that she is now something more than the kingdom of Jerusalem. For the Apostle says that there is a "heavenly Jerusalem" and exhorts the faithful to "draw near" to it (cf. Heb 12:18–24). Now this bridegroom to whom the bride now hurries is the same whom Paul calls "a great high priest," and writes of him as if he is not in heaven but had entered into and passed through all the heavens (cf. Heb 4:14), and as if his perfect bride had followed him there, or rather, joined and united to him, had ascended there with him, for she has become "one spirit" with him (cf. 1 Cor 6:17).

)06   "Well done, good and faithful servant." His faith is reckoned as justification for him who was "faithful over a little" (Mt 25:21, 23). The "little," however, are all the things of this life, so that he might be entrusted with the whole mystery of the resurrection. . . . But notice that the Lord did not speak any differently to the second servant than he did to the first, saying: "Well done, good and faithful servant; you have been faithful over a little, I will set you over much" (Mt 25:21, 23). I ask myself why the same thing is said to both. Is not perhaps this the answer: that they who have less capability and have used all that they had precisely as they were supposed to use it, that they will receive no less from God than those who had a greater capability, so that in them would be fulfilled what was written: "He who gathered much had nothing over, and he who gathered little had no lack" (2 Cor 8:15; Exod 16:18)? Something like this is also found in the command of love for God and neighbor . . . for clearly when someone has loved God with his whole heart and with his whole soul and with his whole strength (cf. Mt 22:37), that person will have the same reward of love as the one who had a larger heart or had a more exalted soul or received a greater capability. For only this is demanded, that whatever we have from God, we use wholly for the glory of God.

)07   " 'Show me a coin.' And when he had received it he said: 'Whose likeness and inscription has it?' They said: 'Caesar's.' He said to them: 'Then render to Caesar the things that are Caesar's, and to God the things that are God's' " (Lk 20:24–25 parr). Paul also draws this same conclusion when he says: "Just as we have borne the image of the man of dust, let us also bear the image of the man of heaven" (1 Cor 15:49). . . . God demands back from us. What does he demand back?

Read Moses: "And now, what does the Lord your God require of you, but to fear the Lord your God, to walk in all his ways . . .," etc. (Deut 10:12-13). Therefore, God demands and asks of us, not because he has need of anything we might give him, but that, after we have given to him, he might give back to us for our salvation. . . . God makes demands and requests of us so that he himself will have the opportunity to give, so that he will be able to give back what he has asked for. Let us then rise up and pray to God that we might be worthy to offer him gifts which he will give back to us as heavenly gifts in exchange for our earthly ones, in Christ Jesus.

1008   To be placed over all the household of the master (cf. Mt 24:45), what does this say if not to be "heirs of God and fellow heirs with Christ" (Rom 8:17) and co-rulers with Christ to whom he had given all that was his, as he himself says: "All authority in heaven and on earth has been given to me" (Mt 28:18)? And, as Son of the good Father . . . he shares this dignity and glory with his faithful and prudent stewards that they too might be above every creature and power, that they too might be with Christ (cf. Rom 8:38-39).

UNION IN AND WITH GOD

The inheritance prepared by God (1009-1010). God himself the eternal inheritance of the soul (1011-1012). Christ as the eternal peace (1013), as the eternal Gospel (1014). The individual soul as "kingdom of heaven," the communion of all souls as "kingdom of heaven" (1015-1017). Divinization (1018). Subjection of all creation under Christ and handing over of the kingdom to the Father (1018-1025). Ascent to the trinitarian co-vision of the Father with the Son (1026-1029). With this vision there is no further possibility of defection (1030-1031). God all in all (1032-1033).

1009   "In the place, O Lord, which you have made for your abode" (Exod 15:17). See the goodness of the merciful Lord! He doesn't want to force work on you, he doesn't want you to have to build a house for yourself; he is leading you to an already prepared house. Listen to the Lord speaking in the gospel: "Others have labored, and you have entered into their labor" (Jn 4:38). . . . How does this happen? For your benefit God both plants and builds; he becomes a farmer, he becomes a builder, so that you will lack for nothing.

)10   Blessed indeed it is to inherit in this way eternal life which has so many fields to inherit and so many trees cultivated by God and houses "of living stones" (1 Pet 2:5) in which all who have "left brothers and sisters," etc. (cf. Mt 19:29) will take their repose.

)11   You will ask if it is not also God himself who is the inheritance of the saints (cf. Eph 1:18), so that one can thus speak of heirs of God. . . . It was something like this that the law had in mind when it said: "The sons of Levi have no inheritance with their brothers, for I will be their inheritance, says the Lord" (cf. Deut 10:9; Num 18:20; 26:62), and in another place: "The Lord is their inheritance" (cf. Jos 18:7).

)12   "The salvation of the righteous is from the Lord" (Ps 37:39). He does not say that the salvation of the righteous is in heaven, for this too will pass away (cf. Mt 24:35). Nor is it from any creature, because nothing is unshakable or unchangeable; but "the salvation of the righteous is from the Lord" who is always there, is always the same, is always unshakable; nor can our salvation ever be more secure than when it is from the Lord. May he be my ground, he my house, he my mansion, he my repose, may he be the place where I dwell.

)13   "For he is our peace" (Eph 2:14). Just as Christ is the WORD and wisdom and power and life, so too must it be asked whether he is also our peace. For all of his names must be brought together from the whole of scripture so that we might know him more clearly. Thus, just as the one who possesses him possesses the WORD, after seeking and finding him as WORD (and the same holds also for wisdom and righteousness), so too should we also seek him as peace so that we will also possess him precisely in the way that he is peace itself and is the peace of all rational beings. For whoever does not have peace does not have Christ.

)14   And this too must be looked into, whether it is not true, because Christ is called the power of God (1 Cor 1:24) and the gospel is called the power of God (Rom 1:16), that he ought, among other things, also to be understood as gospel; and perhaps what is called the eternal gospel is to be understood as applying to Christ himself.

)15   "Woe to you, scribes" (Mt 23:13). This is said to everyone who understands nothing but the letter. Hence you might ask if, just as there is a scribe of the law, there is not also a scribe of the gospel, so that just as there is one who reads the law and listens to it and tells its allegorical meanings (cf. Gal 4:24), so too is there someone for the gospel who (while preserving the historical meaning) knows the sure way up to the spiritual. . . . A "scribe is trained for the kingdom of heaven" (cf. Mt 13:52). This takes place according to the simpler sense when, coming from Judaism, one accepts the church's teaching on Jesus Christ; but it takes place according to the deeper sense when, grasping the introductory things which come from the letter of the scriptures, one ascends to the spiritual things called "the kingdom of heaven." It is also according to each of the meanings one encounters (when understood, compared and grounded in their upward-looking sense) that the kingdom of heaven is to be understood. Thus, whoever is in possession of unerring knowledge comes into the kingdom of the many heavens thus understood. Hence, one can understand the words: "Repent, for the kingdom of heaven is at hand" (Mt 4:17) metaphorically in such a way that the scribes, who before had been satisfied with the bare letter, turn away from this interpretation and are trained through Jesus Christ, the Spirit-filled WORD, in the spiritual teaching which is called the kingdom of heaven. Accordingly, as long as Jesus Christ who, as God the WORD, "was in the beginning with God" (Jn 1:2) does not dwell in a soul, the kingdom of heaven is not in that soul. But when someone has come close to understanding the WORD, the kingdom of heaven has drawn near to that person.

But if in reality, if not in concept, the kingdom of heaven and the kingdom of God are the same, then it is clear that those to whom is said: "The kingdom of God is in the midst of you" (Lk 17:21) are the same ones to hear: "The kingdom of heaven is within you" (cf. Lk 11:20; Mt 12:38), especially because of the change of meaning from the letter to the spirit. Because "when a man turns to the Lord the veil" which covers the letter "is removed. Now the Lord is the Spirit" (2 Cor 3:16–17).

1016   If the will of God is "done on earth as it is in heaven" (Mt 6:10), the earth does not remain earth, . . . and thus we will all become heaven.

1017   The Son of God is king of heaven. And just as he is wisdom itself and righteousness itself and truth itself, so too is he also the kingdom itself [autobasileia]. But it is not a kingdom over the things below or over a part of the things above, but over all the things above which have been called heaven. And if you are searching for the meaning of "theirs is the kingdom of heaven" (Mt 5:3), you can say that theirs is Christ since he is the kingdom itself, ruling as king over every thought of those who are no longer ruled by sin which reigns "in the mortal bodies" of those who subject themselves to it (cf. Rom 6:12). By this ruling over all their thoughts I mean his becoming heaven (by bearing "the image of the man of heaven" — 1 Cor 15:49), since he is righteousness and wisdom and truth and the other virtues.

018   If you, when tempted, imitate that man who was tempted on your behalf (cf. Heb 2:18), and you overcome every temptation, you will have hope together with him who once was man but has now ceased to be man. . . . But if he is God who once was man, and it is necessary for you to become like him since "we shall be like him and see him as he is" (cf. 1 Jn 3:12), it will also be necessary for you to become God in Christ Jesus.

019   If "every knee bows" before Jesus (cf. Phil 2:10), it is without doubt Jesus to whom "all things are put in subjection" . . . through whom "all things are subjected to the Father" (cf. 1 Cor 15:24-28). For it is through wisdom, that is, by the WORD and by reason, not by force and necessity, that they are put in subjection. Hence it is the manner in which he obtains everything that is his glory; and this is the purest and most limpid glory of omnipotence, that all things are put in subjection by WORD and wisdom and not by force and necessity.

020   All things must be subjected to Christ and then he himself must be subjected (cf. 1 Cor 15:27-28), but with that subjection which it is worthy to think of taking place in a spiritual being.

021   It is fitting, then, for him to reign (cf. 1 Cor 15:24-26) so that he might carry out the mystery of salvation which he had undertaken in the flesh, and make known the good, while the guilty will all be received according to their works. But when "he delivers the kingdom to God the Father" (1 Cor 15:24), that is, offers to God all those who have been converted and corrected, and has carried out to the full the mystery of the reconciliation of the world, that is when all will stand before the judgment seat of God so that the following words might be fulfilled: "As I live, says the Lord, every knee shall bow to me, and every tongue shall give praise to God" (Isa 46:23; cf. Phil 2:10-11).

022   If indeed "all nations" are to "come" and worship the name of the Lord (cf. Ps 86:9), then clearly those "peoples who delight in war" (Ps 68:30) will also come. That means, then, that the whole of rational creation will bow down before the Lord and worship.

023   And truly, if the eternity of death is taken as the same as that of life, death will no longer be the opposite of life but its equal. For the eternal is not the contrary of the eternal but its equal.

024   It was the intention of the Apostle to show what "the first Adam" who "became a living being" brought on the human race; but also to show what "the second Adam" who "became a life-giving spirit" did

(cf. 1 Cor 15:45). . . . And he wants to show that life is much more powerful than death, and righteousness much more powerful than sin.

1025   It is my considered opinion that the text where God is said to be "all in all" (1 Cor 15:28) means also that he is everything in each individual. But he will be everything to each individual in such a way that whatever the rational spirit, when purged of all filth of sin . . ., can feel or understand or think, this "all" is God, and that this spirit does not do anything other than feel God, think God, see God, hold God, and that God is the mode and measure of its every movement; and in that way God will be "everything" to it. . . . Nor does someone who constantly leads a good life desire any longer to eat of "the tree of the knowledge of good and evil" (Gen 2:17).

1026   Now if the Creator himself is given to us, how is it that all creation is not given to us along with him? However, this phrase: "He will give us all things with him" (Rom 8:32), can be understood in two ways. For it can apparently mean, if we have Christ in us, in as much as he is WORD and wisdom and truth and righteousness and peace and all the other things written of him, that with this fullness of virtue everything else is given to us. We are, consequently, not just one among all the creatures, nor do we have just this small piece of earth which we seem to occupy, but have together with Christ everything that God has created, visible and invisible, hidden and open, temporal and eternal. But this text which says: "He will give us all things with him" (Rom 8:32) can also be understood another way: namely, that to him as heir will indeed be given the whole created world to enjoy, but also to us as co-heirs together with him.

1027   When someone in seeing the Son has also seen the Father who sent him, that person has seen the Father in the Son. But when someone sees the Father and the things of the Father as the Son does, he will be, just as the Son is, a witness of the Father and the things of the Father, no longer recognizing just from an image the things in him which are thus imaged. This, I think, will be the end, when the Son "delivers the kingdom to God the Father" (1 Cor 15:24) and when God will be "all in all" (1 Cor 15:28).

1028   Then will there be but one activity for those who come to God on account of the WORD which is with him (cf. Jn 1:1), that of knowing God so that they might thus all become formed in the knowledge of the Father . . . just as the Son alone now is . . . and they will become one as the Son and the Father are one (cf. Jn 10:30).

029   The vision of all created things is limited. Only the knowledge of
the Holy Three is unlimited, for this is wisdom itself.

030   "I am sure that neither death, nor life, nor angels, nor principalities,
nor things present, nor things to come, nor powers, nor height, nor
depth, nor any other creation will be able to separate us from the love
of God in Christ Jesus our Lord" (Rom 8:38–39). Consider whether
these words: "I am convinced that nothing can separate us," are not
indeed well said. . . . The death that wishes to separate us . . . is
not the ordinary death of which it was said earlier: "For thy sake we
are being killed all the day long" (Rom 8:36; cf. Ps 44:22), but the
enemy of Christ, "the last enemy to be destroyed" (1 Cor 15:26). This
enemy will want to separate, for example, Paul; but he will be unable
to do so, since he is destroyed by the Christ within Paul. And the life
[that would separate us] is not the life that is opposed to this death, for
things that are opposed to each other cannot want one and the same
thing; it is rather the life by which one lives to sin and deception in its
various forms. . . . But it will not be able to do this, but will be destroyed, whether by the death by which one dies to sin, or by the life
which "is hid with Christ in God" (Col 3:3). Even angels will want to
separate us from the love of God in Christ Jesus. They are the ones
standing on the left, to whom is said: "Depart . . . into the eternal
fire prepared for the devil and his angels" (Mt 25:41).

But someone might say that the "things present" refer to visible and
temporal things. Let us see, then, what the "things to come" (Rom 8:38)
are. Do they refer to the things which in the future will be struggling
against the Apostle in this life, in the days after the writing of this epistle
[to the Romans]? Do they not rather refer to what is to be expected immediately after one's departure from the present age when "the prince of
this world" (Jn 12:31) and the powers under him will try to overpower us
as we are leaving this world, but will have no power over those who have
previously received the love of God in Christ Jesus? Continuing on,
Paul says "nor powers." These seem to be a kind of spiritual being
without mortal body. For the human soul will never be plotted against
by any "height," namely, "the spiritual hosts of wickedness in the
heavenly places" (Eph 6:12), nor by any "depth," namely, those "under
the earth" (Phil 2:10), in such a way that even one of those fighting in the
love of the Lord will be able to be separated from it.

But if in addition to this visible creation there is another creation,
essentially visible but at present not yet seen, one might ask if this

is what is referred to with the words: "nor any other creation will be able to separate us from the love of God" (Rom 8:39).[1]

1031   "See Lord, you know all things, the last and the first" (cf. Rev 1:17; 2:8; 22:13). What is between will be passed over in silence because it is the evil which occupies the space in between. For in the beginning it was not, nor will it be any longer at the end.

1032   "From him and through him and to him are all things" (Rom 11:36). "From him" signifies the first creation of all things, and the fact that whatever is, takes its existence from God. "Through him" means that the things which were first made are ruled and guided by him from whom they took the origin of their being. "In him" means that those who are already corrected and brought to what is good are grounded in his perfection.

1033   "One God and Father of us all, who is above all and through all and in all" (Eph 4:6). One must use a bodily image for this. The sun, by its position, is "above all things" which are on earth; by its rays it can be said to shine "through all"; but when the power of its light has pierced into every depth, it is said to be "in all." In this way, then, it seems to us that according to the spiritual understanding, pre-eminence is indicated by the "above all," sufficiency for everyone in the "through all," and the coming of the power of God in the "in all." The result is that no one is found to be empty because of God's being "in all."

---

[1] This Greek text from Cramer's *Catena* has until now not received the attention it deserves. For it gives witness to the genuineness of Rufinus's translation of the *Commentary on the Epistle to the Romans* (Rom Co VII, 12) whose genuineness is constantly under suspicion. The definitiveness of salvation is here expressed in all clarity. That apparently contradictory expressions do not really create any difficulty, cf. our Introduction above, p. 17.

EPILOGUE[1]

1034   For the wise, it is enough to have given them the opportunity (cf. Prov 9:9 LXX), for it is not desirable for the understanding of the hearers to remain completely idle and lazy. Therefore, from its study of these things, may the understanding draw still more benefit and come to the contemplation of something more profound and more divine. "For it is not by measure that God gives the Spirit" (Jn 3:34). But because "the Lord is Spirit" (2 Cor 3:17), he "blows where he wills" (Jn 3:8). And we hope and pray that he may also blow on you, so that as you make your way through the things we have described in our limited way, you may come to perceive in the words of the Lord better and higher things than these. And we also pray that we too might walk with you in that better and higher life, led by our Lord Jesus Christ himself who is "the way and the truth and the life" (Jn 14:6), until we come to the Father "when he delivers the kingdom to God the Father and makes every rule and authority and power subject to him" (cf. 1 Cor 15:24-28), "to him be glory and dominion for ever and ever" (1 Pet 5:11).

---

[1] In the epilogue to the second edition (1956) von Balthasar remarks: "This second edition does not represent a major change from the first. There are some stylistic improvements, and a small number of new texts were added (406a, 681a, 718a, 966a). A few unimportant texts on the doctrine of the discernment of spirits (569-573, perhaps also 590) really should have been deleted because, as I myself have indicated (*Zeitschrift für katholische Theologie*, 1939, 86-106, 181-206), along with a whole series of similar texts found among the works of Origen, they come from Evagrius of Pontus. I left them there, however, in order to avoid changing the numbering."

APPENDIX: THE PASCHAL MYSTERY

All of sacred scripture signifies or points to the living reality, Jesus Christ, the WORD. Thus the words and events of the Old Testament are not images and types of historical or bodily realities which, once they take place, are past or "dead" realities. In particular, the first passover in Egypt does not refer to the passion of Christ, as some say who erroneously think that the word for passover (Hebrew: pesah; Greek: pascha) means suffering (from the Greek word paschein, to suffer). For the Hebrew word means "passage" or "passing over." And this refers not just to Christ's "passage," but also to our own still ongoing passage in Christ (1035–1039). This sums up Origen's central theological insight and his overriding hermeneutical principle.

1035   One should not think that historical events are types of [other] historical events, and that bodily things are types of bodily things, but that bodily things are types of spiritual things, and that historical events are types of intelligible events.

1036   Before beginning our exegesis of the passover, a few remarks about the very word "passover" are in order. Most of the brethren, indeed perhaps all, take the word "passover" as referring to the passion of the Savior. But among the Hebrews, the feast in question is not called *pascha* but *phas*, . . . which, translated, means "passage" [*diabasis*]. . . . And if one of us in discussion with the Hebrews should rashly say that the passover is so named because of the passion of the Savior, they will laugh at him as one ignorant of the meaning of the word.

1037   That the passover still takes place today, that the sheep is sacrificed and the people come out of Egypt, this is what the Apostle is teaching us when he says: "For Christ, our paschal lamb, has been sacrificed. Let us, therefore, celebrate the festival, not with the old leaven, the leaven of malice and evil, but with the unleavened bread of sincerity and truth" (1 Cor 5:7–8). If "our pasch has been sacrificed," Jesus "Christ," those who sacrifice Christ come up out of Egypt, cross the

Red Sea and will see Pharaoh engulfed. And if there are any among
you who would like to return to Egypt, they will not enter the holy land.

1038   It is necessary for us to sacrifice the true lamb—if we have been ordained priests, or like priests have offered sacrifice—and it is necessary
for us to cook and eat its flesh (cf. Exod 12:8-9). But if this does not
take place in the passion of the Savior, then the antitype of the passover is not his suffering; rather the passover becomes the type of
Christ himself sacrificed for us. . . . To show that the passover is
something spiritual and not the sensible passover, he himself says:
"Unless you eat my flesh and drink my blood, you have no life in you"
(cf. Jn 6:53). Are we then to eat his flesh and drink his blood in a
physical manner? But if this is said spiritually, then the passover is
spiritual, not physical.

1039   Since the sacred ceremony and sacrifice of the passover was already
carried out in mystery [*mystēriōdōs*] in the time of Moses according to
God's orders for the salvation of the first-born of the sons of Israel
because "of the wrath of God inflicted" (cf. Rom 3:5) on Pharaoh and
on those who under his leadership disobey the WORD of God, we
now raise the question whether it is only in that time of its concrete
celebration that it is carried out, or whether we might not have to admit that it is also carried out in a different manner in our own time,
the time of fulfillment—"upon whom the end of the ages has come" (1
Cor 10:11). In answer to this we have found that the sacred and inspired scriptures are not silent; we find that they oblige us to fulfill the
commands which have been given, and that they have been fulfilled
up to our time, according to the word: "Search the scriptures in which
you have life, and they give witness of me" (cf. Jn 5:39). And their
witness does not consist only in words of prophecy, but in the very
acts themselves knowledge is written. This is what the great
prophet, in full understanding, ordains for the Hebrew nation when
he envisions the taking and the preserving of the lamb, and then its
sacrificing and its eating after being roasted, and the manner of
clothing, and the haste in consuming what had been sacrificed, and
the burning up of the remains, and the fulfillment of the commandment that this should be done "forever in the generations" to come as
a memorial for them "and their sons" (cf. Exod 12:14, 24); for he
recognizes there not only the historical but also the anagogical meaning, as it is written: "interpreting spiritual truths to those who possess
the Spirit" (1 Cor 2:13).

I will therefore try, with the grace of God, to expound the spiritual meaning in order that the power of the salvation accomplished in Christ may become manifest to those who love instruction, as it is written: "To all who received him, he gave power to become children of God, who were born, not of blood nor of the will of man, but of God" (Jn 1:12-13). For adoption in Christ has given us the power of so tremendous a salvation, we who are not born of the blood and the will of man and woman, and whom he [Christ] recognizes as his brothers when he says: "I will proclaim thy name to my brethren" (Heb 2:13; Ps 21:23).

For these, salvation has been brought about by the blood of Christ himself "like a lamb without blemish" (Isa 53:7; cf. Lev 23:12, etc.). For the word reads: "Like a lamb he was led to the slaughter, and like a sheep that before its shearers is dumb, so he opened not his mouth. Who will recount his generation, that he is cut off out of the land of the living, and led to his death for the transgression of his people. And I will give the poor in exchange for his death and the wealthy in exchange for his grave because he committed no sin and there was no deceit in his mouth" (Isa 53:7-8; cf. Acts 8:32-33). For it was not because "of sin" that his death came about, but "he himself bears our sins and suffers for us and by his bruises we have all been healed" (Isa 53:4-5).

For just as they were prefigured in a *male* lamb (cf. Exod 12:5), so are we in the "man like a lamb" (cf. Isa 53:7); just as they were prefigured in a "perfect" lamb (cf. Exod 12:5), so are we in the "fullness" (cf. Jn 1:16) of him who has carried out his Father's will; just as they were prefigured in a one-year-old lamb, so are we at the end of the ages (1 Cor 10:11)—for just as the year is the fulfillment of the months, so is the fulfillment of the law and the prophets—just as they in a lamb "without blemish" (cf. Exod 12:5, etc.), so we in a man without sin; just as they in the first month (cf. Lev 23:5), so we in the beginning of all creation, in which all things were made (cf. Rev 3:14; Col 1:15-16); [there] "in the tenth month" (cf. Exod 12:3), here in the fullness of the unicity [of God].

TRANSLATOR'S EPILOGUE

I. RECENT ORIGEN STUDIES

Although there has been nothing in Origen studies comparable to the massive external impact on New Testament studies of such things as the Dead Sea Scrolls, increased access to the religious life and writings of early rabbinic Judaism and the discovery and publication of the Nag Hammadi gnostic texts, to say nothing of the internal impact of the movements from form criticism to redaction criticism, and then on to structural criticism and sociological analysis, there has nevertheless been an impressive amount of movement and progress in Origen studies over the past four and one-half decades since the first German edition of *Spirit and Fire* in 1938. At that time, Origen scholars were just beginning to come to terms with Walther Völker's recent insistence that all Origen texts, even those available only in the reputedly suspect Latin translations from the end of the fourth century and later, had to be taken into consideration if one was to do justice to the full range of Origen's thought.[1] This ran counter to the prevailing scholarly opinion which tended to see Origen much more as a philosopher and systematician than as a Christian biblical theologian. Eliminating all the Latin translations (which included most of the extant homilies as well as the commentaries on Romans and on the Song of Songs, and much of that on Matthew) left the speculatively oriented *Peri Archōn — On First Principles —* in a much more central position and made it easier to read Origen as a primarily philosophical figure.

This interpretative principle of giving due, if cautious, attention to the writings extant only in Latin was readily welcomed by Henri de Lubac, the theological mentor who introduced von Balthasar to Origen and the Fathers in the mid 1930s. These two theologians, together with Jean Daniélou, led the charge which eventually restored,

---

[1] W. Völker, *Das Vollkommenheitsideal des Origenes* (BHT 7; Tübingen: Mohr-Siebeck, 1931).

at least to the consciousness of scholars, the reputation of Origen as the towering figure of early Christian spiritual and biblical theology. By the time of the second edition of *Spirit and Fire* (1956), all three had made major contributions to Origen studies,[2] and the modern revival in the study of Origen was well under way. However, the more dominant earlier view which saw Origen as primarily a philosopher also had its defenders, and it was too early to tell which view would eventually dominate. The long series of books and articles by scores of authors which would eventually give massive support to the portrait of Origen as a biblical and spiritual theologian had only begun to appear.

However, to say simply that the biblical and theological view eventually won the day does not do justice either to the complexity of Origen studies or to the many-sidedness of the great Alexandrian himself. And as the decades passed, the debate took place in a more and more irenic and "ecumenical" atmosphere. Emphasizing one facet of Origen carried with it less and less a diminution of other facets. Greatly contributing to this process have doubtless been the meetings of patristics scholars every four years at the Oxford Patristic Congresses and, in 1973, 1977 and 1981 (at midpoint between the Oxford meetings) the international Origen congresses held at Montserrat, Bari and Manchester. Reading through the proceedings of the Origen congresses and the relevant papers from the Oxford congresses is a good way to step into the flow of the current course of Origen studies.[3]

---

[2] H. Urs von Balthasar, "Le mystérion d'Origène," *Recherches de science religieuse* 26 (1936), 513-62; 27 (1937), 38-64; reprinted as *Parole et mystère chez Origène* (Paris: Cerf, 1957); J. Daniélou, *Origène* (Paris: La Table Ronde, 1948); Engl. tr., *Origen* (New York: Sheed and Ward, 1955); H. de Lubac, *Histoire et esprit: L'intelligence de l'Ecriture d'après Origène* (Théologie 16; Paris: Aubier, 1950).

[3] The proceedings of the second to the sixth Oxford Patristic Conferences have been published as Studia Patristica 1-14 within the Texte und Untersuchungen series as follows: Oxford 2 (1955): SP 1-2 = TU 63-64; Oxford 3 (1959): SP 3-6 = TU 78-81; Oxford 4 (1963): SP 7-9 = TU 92-94; Oxford 5 (1967): SP 10-11 = TU 107-108; Oxford 6 (1971): SP 12-14 = TU 115-117. The proceedings of Oxford 7 (1975) are also scheduled to appear in the SP/TU series. The proceedings of Oxford 8 (1979) have been published by Pergamon Press, Oxford, as SP 17 (1982).

The proceedings of the first Origen congress (Montserrat, 1973) appeared as: H. Crouzel, G. Lomiento, J. Ruis-Camps, eds., *Origeniana* (Quaderni di "Vetera christianorum" 12; Bari: Istituto di Letteratura Cristiana Antica,

But probably the most helpful place to begin is with the magisterial survey provided by Henri Crouzel in the "Origen" article in the *New Catholic Encyclopedia*. The next step might best be three recent review articles by myself, Lothar Lies, S.J., and Joseph Trigg which summarize the recent course of Origen studies.[4] Moving on from there, the obvious key tool is the great critical bibliography on Origen studies produced by the patriarch of current Origen scholars, Henri Crouzel, S.J.[5]

II. THIS TRANSLATION

In a modest way, this translation amounts to a new (i.e., third) edition. However, apart from the few instances where minor errors or inadequacies were discovered and corrected, no liberties whatsoever were taken with von Balthasar's work. My occasional additional remarks (in the footnotes) have all been clearly indicated as additions by my initials: R.J.D. Beyond that, the "newness" of this edition consists in the following. (1) The texts have been freshly translated from the original Greek and Latin.[6] (2) There is an additional Translator's Foreword in which I try to make Origen's way of doing theology and

---

1975). The second Origen congress (Bari, 1977) proceedings appeared as H. Crouzel, A. Quacquarelli, *Origeniana Secunda* (Quaderni di "Vetera christianorum" 15; Rome: Edizioni dell'Ateneo, 1980). The proceedings of the third Origen congress (Manchester, 1981) are still in the press.

[4] R. Daly, "Origen Studies and Pierre Nautin's *Origène*," *Theological Studies* 39 (1978), 508-519. Nautin's *Origène: Sa vie et son oeuvre* (Christianisme antique 1; Paris: Beauchesne, 1977) was the first comprehensive study of Origen's life and work to appear since E. de Faye, *Origène: Sa vie, son oeuvre, sa pensée* (3 vols.; Paris: Leroux, 1923-1928). L. Lies, "Zum Stand heutiger Origenesforschung," *Zeitschrift für katholische Theologie* (now *Innsbrucker theologische Zeitschrift*) 102 (1980), 61-75, 190-205; J. W. Trigg, "A Decade of Origen Studies," *Religious Studies Review* 7 (1981), 21-27.

[5] H. Crouzel, *Bibliographie critique d'Origène* (Instrumenta Patristica 8; The Hague: Nijhoff, 1971). This is somewhat complemented by R. Farina, *Bibliographia Origeniana 1960-1970* (Biblioteca del "Salesianum" 77; Turin: Società Editrice Internazionale, 1971). Since 1967, Crouzel has published annually in the *Bulletin de Litterature Ecclésiastique* under the title "Chronique Origénienne" a review of the new Origen books of the previous year.

[6] With the exception of 38 mostly very brief texts on the Psalms from J. B. Pitra, *Analecta sacra* 2 (Tusculanis, 1884) and 3 (Venice, 1883), and 3 from R. Cadiou, *Commentaires inédits des Psaumes: Etude sur les textes d'Origène contenus dans le manuscrit Vindobonensis 8* (Paris, 1936). These editions were not

interpreting scripture more understandable and helpful to the modern reader. (3) In the first part of this Translator's Epilogue (above), under the title "Recent Origen Studies," the reader with scholarly inclinations is provided with the key concepts and bibliographic information needed to gain a solid overview of Origen studies in recent decades. (4) From the recently published Origen texts not yet available when von Balthasar produced the second edition, I have added a new section: "Appendix: The Paschal Mystery" with the additional texts 1035–1039. The final four of these are from the *Peri Pascha*, Origen's treatise on the passover which was among the 1941 Toura papyrus discoveries, but only recently edited and published. (5) In the hope of making this translation more helpful to the reader, and of drawing the reader's attention more forcefully to the unmistakable center of Origen's writings, the WORD incarnated in the scriptures, I have traced down and parenthetically inserted in the translations the references to the scripture texts which Origen quoted, paraphrased, or obviously alluded to. For the sake of consistency, all the references are made according to the chapter and verse numbering as found in the RSV. Where appropriate, the RSV wording has been followed. This was often not appropriate, as when Origen was paraphrasing, quoting freely and at times inexactly from memory, or following the Septuagint or some other translation or version of the Old Testament. In those cases where the differences in wording or numbering seemed to be due to Origen following the Septuagint, this has been indicated by the abbreviation "LXX" after the text reference. (6) An index of biblical references has been provided.[7]

In the translation itself, I have chosen, where necessary, to be faithful and precise rather then elegant or literary. This corresponds to Origen's own attitude which was far more concerned with content

---

available to me during the time I was working on this translation. I simply translated these texts from von Balthasar's German, after checking to make sure that none of them represented a critical or unique witness to important points in Origen's thought.

[7] Since this is an index to an inevitably somewhat arbitrary and, relative to the whole work of Origen, small *selection* of Origen's writings, this index has no precise statistical value in relation to Origen's work as a whole. Those interested in such precise information should consult the comprehensive index of scripture quotations in Origen contained in *Biblia Patristica. Index des citations et allusions bibliques dans la littérature patristique 3: Origène* (Paris: Éditions du Centre National de la Recherche Scientifique, 1980).

and meaning than with expression and style. I have also tried to reproduce in good English the thought structure reflected in Origen's sometimes involuted prose. Origen's mind was tireless in noting the rich panoply of the connectedness and interconnectedness of things. Language and sentence structure was often simply inadequate to express what was in his mind. Thus, in our translation, some of the occasional "strangeness" or "roughness" is due not merely to the limitations of the translator; it is sometimes a calculated reflection of the text being translated. However, I have consciously allowed such roughness to remain in the translation only when it seemed needed to reflect Origen's own thought and expression. Otherwise, it has been my constant effort to produce as smooth and readable a translation as would be commensurate with texts which are important theological sources. I have tried to eliminate exclusive language, but without full success. And in any case I stopped short whenever I sensed that my efforts might endanger the meaning of the text in hand.

Many, sometimes difficult, hours have gone into this translation. But in the end, it will all have been worth it if it succeeds in making more effectively accessible to the reader of modern English one of the greatest minds ever to serve the church of God.

INDEX OF ABBREVIATIONS

I. EDITIONS AND EDITORS

B = Baehrens (Berlin Edition of Origen = *Die griechischen christlichen Schriftsteller der ersten drei Jahrhunderte*, vols. 6–8)

Cad = Cadiou, *Commentaires inédits des Psaumes* [see Introduction] (Paris, 1936)

Cramer = Cramer: *Catena Graecorum Patrum* (Oxford: 1838–1844, 8 vols.)

G-N = Guéraud and Nautin, *Origène sur la Paque* (*Christianisme antique* 2; Paris, 1979)

Gregg = Edition of the Fragments of the *Commentary on the Letter to the Ephesians* (*Journal of Theological Studies*, 1902)

K = Koetschau (Berlin Edition, vols. 1-2, 5)

Kl = Klostermann (Berlin Edition, vol. 3)

KlB = Klostermann and Benz (Berlin Edition, vols. 10–12)

M = Migne (*Patrologia Graeca,* vols. 11–17)

P = Preuschen (Berlin Edition, vol. 4)

PitAn. = Pitra (*Analecta sacra*, vols. 2-3, 1884, 1883)

R = Rauer (Berlin Edition, vol. 9; 2nd ed., 1959)

TU = Texte und Untersuchungen, ed. von Harnack, vols. 17 and 38

II. WORKS OF ORIGEN

1. Homilies, Commentaries, Scholia and Fragments on the Bible

Act = Acts of the Apostles
Apoc = Book of Revelation (Apocalypse)
Cant = Song of Songs
Col = Letter to the Colossians
Cor = Letter to the Corinthians
Eph = Letter to the Ephesians
Ex = Exodus

Ez   = Ezekiel
Ga   = Letter to the Galatians
Gen = Genesis
Hebr = Letter to the Hebrews
Is   = Isaiah
Jer = Jeremiah
Jes Nav = Joshua
Jo   = Gospel of John
Job = Book of Job
Jud = Judges
Lev = Leviticus
Luc = Gospel of Luke
Mt   = Gospel of Matthew
Num = Numbers
Os   = Hosea
Prov = Proverbs
Ps   = Psalms
Reg = Kings
Rom = Letter to the Romans
Ser = "Commentariorum Series" (ancient Latin translation of the
        Commentary on Matthew)
Th   = Letter to the Thessalonians

2. Other Works of Origen

C Cels   = *Contra Celsum* (*Against Celsus, Eight Books*)
Ep ad Greg = *Letter to Gregory Thaumaturgos*
Mart   = *Exhortation to Martyrdom*
PA   = *Peri Archōn* (*On First Principles*)
PE   = *Peri Euchēs* (*On Prayer*)
PP   = *Peri Pascha* (*On the Passover*)
Resurr   = *On the Resurrection*

h   = Homily
Co   = Commentary
frag = Fragment
schol = Scholion

INDEX OF PASSAGES TRANSLATED

1	Num h, 17, 4	B 7, 159–160	
2	C Cels 6, 15	K 2, 85	M 11, 1312D–1313A
3	PA 4, 25	K 5, 345–347	M 11, 399B–400C
4	Ps Co 118, 114		PitAn. 3, 294
5	Ps Co 118, 147		PitAn. 3, 304
6	Ps Co 70, 14		PitAn. 3, 91
7	Gen h 13, 1-4	B 6, 113–121	
8	Gen h 12, 5	B 6, 112	
9	Gen h 13, 4	B 6, 121	
10	Jud h 8, 5	B 7, 514–515	
11	Jer h 18, 9	KlB 3, 163–164	M 13, 481B–484A
12	Ps Co 117, 14		M 12, 1581A
13	PA 2, 11, 4	K 5, 187	M 11, 243BC
14	Cant Co 2	B 8, 146–149	
15	Cant Co 2	B 8, 141–142	
16	Lev h 5, 2	B 6, 336–337	
17	Luc h 21	R 9, 130–131	
18	Lev h 12, 4	B 6, 462	
19	Lev h 13, 5	B 6, 476	
20	Lev h 3, 3	B 6, 318	
21	PA 3, 6, 7	K 5, 289	M 11, 340AB
22	Ps Co 1		M 12, 1089C
23	PA 2, 2, 2	K 5, 112	M 11, 187B
24	PE 16, 2	K 2, 337	M 11, 469AB
25	PE 17, 1	K 2, 338	M 11, 472AB
26	Cant Co 2	B 8, 160	
27	Jes Nav h 14, 2	B 7, 378–379	
28	PE 21, 2	K 2, 345	M 11, 481A
29	Os frag		M 13, 828C
30	Jo Co 1, 24	P 4, 31	M 14, 69A
31	C Cels 4, 74	K 1, 344	M 11, 1145A
32	Jo Co 19, 5	P 4, 323–324	
33	Cant Co 3	B 8, 208–210	
34	Cant Co 4	B 8, 238	
35	Is h 5, 3	B 8, 266	
36	Rom Co 4, 9		M 14, 995AB
37	C Cels 7, 63	K 2, 213	M 11, 512A
38	Rom Co 4, 9		M 14, 994AB
39	Jo Co 20, 31	P 4, 380–381	M 14, 665AB
40	Gen h 15, 3	B 6, 129	
41	PA 1, 5, 5	K 5, 77	M 11, 164C
42	Lev h 12, 2	B 6, 457	

42a	Ez h 1, 3	B 8, 326	
43	Lev h 2, 2	B 6, 292–293	
44	Rom Co 4, 14		M 14, 1101C
45	1 Cor frag		Cramer V, 112
46	Gen h 1, 12	B 6, 14	
47	Gen h 2, 6	B 6, 38	
48	Ps Co 145, 8		PitAn. 3, 357
49	Gen h 1, 14–15	B 6, 19–21	
50	Mt Co 13, 2	KlB 10, 183–184	M 13, 1079B
51	Mt Co 13, 2	KlB 10, 180	M 13, 1093AB
52	PA 2, 8, 1–3	K 5, 152–156. 161	M 11, 219–223
53	Ser 57, 62	KlB 11, 144	
54	PA 4, 36–37	K 5, 361–364	M 11, 411–413
55	PA 3, 6, 5	K 5, 287	M 11, 338B
56	1 Reg h 1, 11	B 8, 20–21	
57	Rom Co 4, 5		M 14, 978C
58	PA 4, 4, 5	K 5, 356	M 11, 407A
59	Jo Co 2, 12	P 4, 75	M 14, 145C
60	Ps Co 114, 4		M 12, 1573D
61	Jo Co 2, 4	P 4, 61	M 14, 120C
62	Ps Co 24		PitAn. 2, 483
63	Ps Co 118, 156		M 12, 1621C
64	Rom Co 10, 38		M 14, 1287C
65	Gen h 1, 2	B 6, 3–4	
66	Gen h 2, 4	B 6, 33	
67	Rom Co 4, 1		M 14, 965AB
68	Gen h 1, 2	B 6, 3	
69	Gen h 1, 13	B 6, 15	
70	Ps Co 4, 3		M 12, 1140B
71	Luc h 39	R 9, 219–220	
72	Gen h 1, 13	B 6, 17–18	
73	Jes Nav h 22, 4	B 7, 436	
74	Ex h 6, 5	B 6, 196–197	
75	PA 3, 6, 1	K 5, 280–281	M 11, 333–334
76	Gen h 1, 13	B 6, 16–17	
77	Jo Co 1, 28	P 4, 34–35	
78	PA 2, 6, 3	K 5, 141–142	M 11, 211B
79	Jer h 14, 10	Kl 3, 114	M 13, 416AB
80	1 Th frag		M 14, 1299B
81	Jo Co 2, 11	P 4, 74	M 14, 144B
82	Jo Co 2, 9	P 4, 72	M 14, 141
83	Jo Co 2, 9	P 4, 71–72	M 14, 140BD
84	Jo Co 2, 3	P 4, 55–56	M 14, 109D-112B
85	Num h 21, 2	B 7, 202	
86	Jo Co 2, 7	P 4, 69	M 14, 136AB
87	Ps Co 1, 6		M 12, 1100A
88	Gen h 4, 6	B 6, 56–57	
89	Gen h 15, 2	B 6, 128–129	
90	Mt Co 13, 9	KlB 10, 203	M 13, 116C-117A
91	Jo Co 20, 22	P 4, 363–364	M 14, 636AD
92	C Cels 4, 40	K 1, 313–314	M 11, 1093A-1196A
93	Jo Co 20, 21	P 4, 361	M 14, 632BC
94	Jer h 8, 1	Kl 3, 56	M 13, 337AB

95	PA 3, 1, 21	K 5, 239	M 11, 297BC
96	Ez h 1, 5	B 8, 330	
97	Is h 3, 2	B 8, 255	
98	Ex h 4, 8	B 6, 181	
99	Rom Co 3, 2		M 14, 931BC
100	Ex h 6, 9	B 6, 200	
101	PA 3, 1, 12	K 5, 215–216	M 11, 269B–272A
102	Gen h 9, 1	B 6, 88–89	
103	Jer h lat 3, 4	B 8, 314	
104	Ex h 3, 3	B 6, 165	
105	Cant Co	B 8, 212	
106	Num h 26, 4	B 7, 249–250	
107	Jes Nav h 5, 1	B 7, 314	
108	Ex h 5, 4	B 6, 189	
109	Num h 1, 4	B 7, 163–164	
110	Cant Co 1	B 8, 106	
111	Cant Co 4	B 8, 223	
112	Num h 20, 3	B 7, 195	
113	Ez h 13, 2	B 8, 444	
114	Num 27, 4–12	B 7, 260–279	
115	Cant Co Prol	B 8, 79	
116	Jo Co 32, 6	P 4, 437	M 14, 760BC
117	Jo Co 1, 26	P 4, 34	M 14, 73A
118	Ps Co 118, 1		PitAn. 3, 251
119	Jo Co 32, 19	P 4, 478	M 14, 825C
120	Ps Co 118, 109		M 12, 1609C
121	Ps Co 46, 7		PitAn. 3, 45
122	Ps Co 144, 1		M 12, 1672CD
123	Hebr frag 1, 8		Cramer VII, 361–362
124	Gen h 1, 1	B 6, 1	
125	Jer h lat 3, 4	B 8, 313	
126	Jer h 8, 2	Kl 3, 57	M 11, 337
127	Jo Co 1, 22	P 4, 23	M 14, 56B
128	Jo Co 19, 5	P 4, 324	M 14, 568BD
129	PA 1, 2, 2–4	K 5, 30–31	M 11, 131–132
130	Apoc schol 20		TU 38, 3, p 29
131	Jo Co 6, 3	P 4, 114–115	M 14, 209D–212C
132	Jo Co 1, 24	P 4, 30–31	M 14, 68B
133	Jo Co 20, 31	P 4, 382	M 14, 668A
134	Jer h 19, 1	Kl 3, 176	M 13, 500C
135	Jo Co 1, 23	P 4, 29–30	M 14, 65C
136	Jo Co 1, 39	P 4, 43	M 14, 89BD
137	PA 1, 2, 4	K 5, 31–32	M 11, 133A
138	Jo Co 1, 11	P 4, 14	M 14, 40C–41A
139	PA 1, 1, 5–6	K 5, 20–21	M 11, 124A–125A
140	C Cels 6, 65	K 2, 135–136	M 11, 1397B
141	C Cels 6, 65	K 2, 135	M 11, 1397A
142	Jo Co 2, 3	P 4, 57	M 14, 113
143	Mt Co 16, 23	KlB 10, 555	M 13, 1453B
144	Mt Co 10, 2	KlB 10, 2	M 13, 840A
145	PA 2, 1, 3	K 5, 108	M 11, 184BA
146	C Cels 7, 37	K 2, 188	M 11, 1473A
147	C Cels 7, 44	K 2, 194–195	M 11, 1484C

148	C Cels 7, 42	K 2, 192-193	M 11, 1481A-C
149	C Cels	K 2, 195-196	M 11, 1484D-1485B
150	Jo Co 1, 42	P 4, 48-49	M 14, 97B-100B
151	Col frag		M 14, 1297C
152	Luc h 15		
153	Mt Co frag	R 9, 105	M 17, 289AB
154	Mt Co frag		M 13, 832C
155	Jo Co 13, 46	P 4, 272	M 14, 481A
156	Jer h frag	Kl 13, 197	M 13, 544C
157	Jo Co 2, 4	P 4, 61	M 14, 121A
158	Jo Co 19, 2	P 4, 309	M 14, 544A
159	Jo Co 2, 4	P 4, 60	M 14, 117D-120A
160	Jo Co 10, 18	P 4, 201	M 14, 357BC
161	Lev h 3, 8	B 6, 314	
162	PA 1, Prooem 8	K 5, 14	M 11, 119B
163	Ex h 1, 4	B 6, 149	
164	Lev h 8, 1	B 6, 394	
165	C Cels 4, 50	K 1, 323	M 11, 1109A
166	Ps Co 1, 3		M 12, 1081AB
167	Gen h 9, 1	B 6, 86-87	
168	Jes Nav h 23, 4	B 7, 446	
169	PA 4, anaceph.	K 5, 347	M 11, 402A
170	Rom Co 5, 1		M 14, 1007C-1008C
171	PA 4, 10	K 5, 310-311	M 11, 361BC
172	Mt Co 14, 12	KlB 10, 304	M 13, 1212C-1213A
173	C Cels 4, 38	K 1, 310-311	M 11, 1089B
174	Ez h 9, 1	B 8, 424	
175	Jo Co 13, 42	P 4, 269	M 14, 476A
176	Jo Co 13, 46	P 4, 272	M 14, 481A
177	C Cels 3, 33	K 1, 229-230	M 11, 961C
178	Jo Co 10, 2	P 4, 173	M 14, 312AB
179	Jo Co 10, 4	P 4, 175	M 14, 313C
180	Ps Co 38, 6		M 12, 1389A
181	Prov Co 23		M 17, 221CD-224A
182	Prov Co 5, 15		M 17, 173CD
183	Jer h 39 frag	Kl 3, 196-197	M 13, 541C
184	Luc h frag c 8	R 9 (1st ed.), 240	M 17, 340AB
185	Ps Co 36, 23		M 17, 133B
186	Ep ad Greg		M 11, 92A
187	Ps Co 104, 19		PitAn. 3, 207
188	Mt Co 10, 2	KlB 10, 13-14	M 13, 861B-864A
189	Mt Co 10, 8-9	KlB 10, 9-10	M 13, 853A-857B
190	Jer h 5, 15	Kl 3, 44	M 13, 317C
191	Jer h 39 frag	Kl 13, 197-198	M 13, 544A-C
192	Ser 18	KlB 11, 32-33	
193	Lev h 4, 1	B 6, 316	
194	Ser 40	KlB 11, 78	
195	Mt Co 14, 6	KlB 10, 288	M 13 1197BC
196	C Cels 6, 2	K 2, 71-72	M 11, 1289CD
197	C Cels 6, 5	K 2, 75	M 11, 1296D-1297A
198	Mt Co 10, 5	KlB 10, 5	M 13, 845A
199	Jo Co 2, 4	P 4, 58	M 14, 116C
200	Jo Co 5 frag	P 4, 102-103	M 14, 189B-192D

201	Ps Co frag 39, 8		PitAn. 3, 36
202	Ex h 1, 1	B 6, 145	
203	Gen h 12, 5	B 6, 112	
204	Ex h 5, 1	B 6, 184	
205	Mt Co 12, 3	KlB 10, 73	M 13, 980C–981A
206	Rom Co 4, 2		M 14, 968AD–969A
207	PA 4, 14, 15	K 5, 318–321	M 11, 372A–373C
208	Num h 9, 1	B 7, 77	
209	Lev h 5, 5	B 6, 344	
210	Num h 9, 7	B 7, 63–64	
211	Gen h 2, 6	B 6, 36–37	
212	Cant Co Prol	B 8, 77–79	
213	Lev h 5, 1	B 6, 333–334	
214	Is h 6, 3	B 8, 272	
215	Mt Co 10, 13	KlB 10, 15	M 13, 865B
216	Cant Co 3	B 8, 216	
217	Ser 38	KlB 11, 72	
218	Jo Co frag 9, 6	P 4, 534	
219	Ps Co frag 80, 1		PitAn. 3, 135
220	Jo Co 1, 6	P 4, 8–9	M 13, 29B–32B
221	Is h 1, 5	B 8, 247–248	
222	Cant Co 3	B 8, 201	
223	Lev h 1, 1	B 6, 280	
224	Ser 139	KlB 11, 289	
225	Cant Co 3	B 8, 204–205	
226	Gen h 7, 5	B 6, 75–76	
227	Jo Co 13, 60	P 4, 294–295	M 14, 517CD
228	Ser 79	KlB 11, 190–191	
229	Ser 10	KlB 11, 19–20	
230	Ser 4	KlB 11, 7–8	
231	Gen h 7, 4	B 6, 74	
232	Num h 9, 4	B 7, 59	
233	Jo Co 13, 5	P 4, 229–230	M 14, 405B–D
234	Rom Co 3, 1		M 14, 924BC
235	Rom Co 3, 7		M 14, 942C
236	Ex h 12, 3	B 6, 264	
237	Lev h 10, 1	B 6, 441	
238	Mt Co frag 12, 1		Cramer I, 89
239	Ser 101	KlB 11, 221	
240	Luc h 20	R 9, 121	
241	Lev h 10, 1	B 6, 442	
242	Jer h 14, 12	Kl 3, 117	M 13, 417BC
243	Ser 27	KlB 11, 45–46	
244	Num h 7, 4	B 7, 44	
245	Lev h 2, 2	B 6, 292	
246	Rom Co 8, 6		M 14, 1174C–1175A
247	Ser 31	KlB 11, 56, 57	
248	Num h 23, 1	B 7, 210–211	
249	Lev h 4, 10	B 6, 331	
250	Rom Co 1, 15		M 14, 861BC
251	Mt Co 10, 10	KlB 10, 11	M 13, 857BC
252	Mt Co 11, 14	KlB 10, 57	M 13, 947B
253	Rom Co 6, 11		M 14, 1092C–1093A

254	Mt Co 11, 5–6	KlB 10, 41–43	M 13, 913C. 916B. C. 920B
255	Jes Nav h 20, 5	B 7 424	
256	Lev h 6, 2	B 6, 361	
257	Mt Co 12, 43	KlB 10, 168	M 13, 1084AB
258	Rom Co 4, 7		M 14, 985A
259	Gen h 14, 1	B 6, 121–122	
260	Jes Nav h 24, 3	B 7, 461–462	
261	Jo Co 20, 12	P 4, 342	M 14, 600BC
262	Rom Co 2, 11		M 14, 896D
263	Col frag		M 14, 1297–1298
264	Ser 28	KlB 11, 53	
265	Rom Co 8, 11		M 14, 1193C
266	PA 2, 6, 2	K 5, 140–141	M 11, 210–211
267	Ps Co 117, 27		M 12, 1584D–1585A
268	C Cels 4, 69	Kl 338–339	M 11, 1137BC
269	Ez h 6, 6	B 8, 384–385	
270	Jer h 8, 8	Kl 3, 61–62	M 13, 345A
271	PA 1, 2, 8	K 5, 38	M 11, 136C
272	Cor Co frag		Cramer V, 30
273	Ps Co frag 69, 5–6		PitAn. 3, 88
274	PE 23, 2	K 2, 350	M 11, 488B
275	Ps Co 118, 151		M 12, 1620D
276	C Cels 3, 28	K 1, 226	M 11, 956CD
277	C Cels 4, 17	K 1, 268	M 11, 1048D
278	Jer h 7, 3	Kl 3, 54	M 13, 333B–334A
279	Ps Co 131, 7		PitAn. 3, 330
280	Luc h 39	R 9 (1st ed.), 201–202	
281	Mt Co 16, 20	KlB 10, 545	M 13, 1443B
282	Jer h 1, 8	Kl 3, 8	M 13, 265AB
283	Ez h 1, 4	B 8, 328	
284	Luc h 8	R 9, 54–55	
285	Mt Co 10, 17	KlB 10, 22	M 13, 877A
286	Luc h 11	R 9, 81–82	
287	Luc h 14	R 9, 97–98	
288	Luc h 27	R 9, 159–160	
289	Ez h 1, 6	B 8, 331	
290	C Cels 1, 62	K 1, 113–114	M 11, 776AB
291	Jo Co 13, 28	P 4, 252	M 14, 448A
292	Jo Co 1, 37	P 4, 41	M 14, 85C
293	Ser 113	KlB 11, 235	
294	Ps Co 19, 6		M 12, 1248B
295	Eph Co frag		Gregg 411–412
296	Ser 75. 97	KlB 11, 176. 216	
297	Ser 92	KlB 11, 208	
298	Ser 92	KlB 11, 209	
299	Lev h, 1, 2	B 6, 283	
300	Luc h 17	R 9, 104–105	
301	Rom Co 4, 2		M 14, 968AB
302	Jer h 11, 2	Kl 3, 79–80	M 13, 369A
303	Ex h 11, 2	B 6, 254	
304	Ps Co 77, 31		M 17, 141D
305	Prov Co 13, 16		M 17, 252A

306	Ser 125	KlB 11, 261-262		
307	Rom Co 5, 10			M 14, 1051AB
308	Jes Nav h 8, 6	B 7, 338-342		
309	Ser 138	KlB 11, 284		
310	C Cels 6, 68	K 2, 138		M 11, 1401BC
311	C Cels 4, 15	K 1, 285		M 11, 1048AB
312	Gen h 8, 9	B 6, 84-85		
313	Lev h, 1, 4	B 6, 286-287		
314	Rom Co 1, 6			M 14, 852AB
315	Ps Co 15, 9			M 12, 1215-1216
316	Jo Co 32, 17	P 4, 470		M 14, 813A
317	Ps Co 2, 8			M 12, 1108A
318	Ser 50	KlB 11, 109		
319	C Cels 7, 34	K 2, 184		M 11, 1468C
320	PA 4, 31	K 5, 353		M 11, 405
321	Jo Co 4, 15	P 4, 140		M 14, 252C
322	PA 2, 11, 6	K 5, 190-191		M 11, 246
323	Ser 65	KlB 11, 151-153		
324	Jo Co 10, 4	P 4, 176		M 14, 316C
325	Ser 33	KlB 11, 63-64		
326	Jo Co 13, 64	P 4, 296-297		M 14, 521CD
327	Rom Co 5, 10			M 14, 1048C
328	C Cels 2, 63	K 1, 185		M 11, 896B
329	C Cels 2, 65	K 1, 187		M 11, 897D-900A
330	C Cels 2, 67	K 1, 189		M 11, 901B
331	Ser 28	KlB 11, 54		
332	Ser 35	KlB 11, 65		
333	Luc h 3	R 9, 19-22		
334	Luc h 6	R 9, 38-39		
335	Ps Co 64, 3			M 12, 1494B
336	Jo Co 13, 21	P 4, 245		M 14, 436
337	Rom Co 5, 9			M 14, 1047AB
338	Rom Co 5, 9			M 14, 1046BC
339	Gal frag			M 14, 1295BC
340	C Cels 2, 16	K 1, 145		M 11, 828A
341	Rom Co 5, 9			M 14, 1044
342	Mt Co 17, 29	Kl 10, 665-668		M 13, 1561C-1564AB. 1565AC
343	C Cels 5, 22. 23	K 2, 23-24		M 11, 1216AC
344	Luc frag	R 9, 227*		
345	PA 2, 10, 3	K 5, 175-176		M 11, 235B-236B
346	De Resurr frag			M 11, 97D-98A-C
347	Jo Co 13, 59	P 4, 293		M 14, 516CD
348	C Cels 7, 32	K 2, 183		M 11, 1465D
349	Rom Co 2, 13			M 14, 913BC
350	C Cels 8, 50	K 2, M 11, 1589C		
351	Ps Co 23, 6			M 12, 1268B
352	Jer h 15, 6	Kl 3, 130		M 13, 438CD
353	Ser 83	KlB 11, 195		
354	Jo Co 1, 37	P 4, 42		M 14, 88AB

*This reference is erroneous. I have been unable to find the correct one. —R.J.D.

355	Mt Co 15, 24	KlB 10, 419-420	M 13, 1324B
356	Rom Co 3, 6		M 14, 939C
357	Rom Co frag		Cramer IV, 20
358	Mt Co 12, 4	Kl 10, 73-74	M 13, 981A-D
359	Jo Co 2, 15	P 4, 77-78	M 14, 149D-152A
	PE 9, 2	K 2, 319	M 11, 444D
360	Jo Co 1, 34	P 4, 40	M 14, 84B
361	Gen h 8, 8	B 6, 83	
362	Jo Co 1, 34	P 4, 38	M 14, 81AB
363	Hebr frag 2, 9		Cramer VII, 147
364	Jo Co 13, 37	P 4, 263	M 14, 464D-465A
365	Jo Co 1, 40	P 4, 45	M 14, 93A
366	Jo Co 19, 1	P 4, 305	M 14, 536CD
367	Mt Co 16, 5		M 13, 1380A
368	Cant Co 2	B 8, 157-158	
369	Gen h 2, 3	B 6, 30	
370	Rom Co 4, 4		M 14, 971BC
371	Gen h 6, 3	B 6, 69	
372	Jud h 5, 5	B 7, 495	
373	Cant Co 1	B 8, 90	
374	Cant Co 1	B 8, 98	
375	Cant Co 1	B 8, 118-121	
376	Gen frag		M 12, 100B
377	Ps Co 48, 1-2		M 12, 1441D
378	Gen h 1, 5	B 6, 7	
379	Gen h 1, 6	B 6, 8	
380	Luc h 32	R 9, 182	
381	Cant Co schol 4, 9		M 17, 272D
382	Mt Co 11, 2	KlB 10, 35	M 13, 905A
383	Is h 6, 4	B 8, 274	
384	Rom Co 8, 5		M 14, 1167AB
385	Rom Co 6, 13		M 14, 1100C-1101A
386	Ez h 6, 2	B 8, 378-379	
387	Luc h 32	R 9, 195	
388	Lev h 7, 4	B 6, 383	
389	Luc h 16	R 9, 97-98	
390	Jes Nav h 7, 6	B 7, 334	
391	Ser 47	KlB 11, 95-96	
392	Ser 47	KlB 11, 98	
393	Mt Co 12, 4	KlB 10, 75	M 13, 984B-985A
394	Ser 8	B 11, 13	
395	Jes Nav h 3, 3-5	B 7, 304-307	
396	Jer h 5, 16	Kl 3, 46	M 13, 320D-321A
397	Ser 35	KlB 11, 68	
398	1 Cor frag		Cramer V, 11
399	Jes Nav h 21	B 7, 428-429	
400	Ps Co 73, 3		M 12, 1529C
401	Jer h 15, 3	Kl 3, 127	M 13, 431BC
402	Luc h 38	R 9, 213-214	
403	Mt Co 16, 21		M 13, 1445BA
404	Jer h 15, 3	Kl 3, 128	M 13, 431CD
405	Luc h 2	R 9, 13	
406	Mt Co 11, 18	KlB 10, 65-66	M 13, 965CD

406a	Ez h 6–10	B 8, 378–423	
407	Jer h 18, 12	Kl 3, 168	M 13, 488AB
408	Jo Co 20, 29	P 4, 378	M 14, 661B
409	Ser 129	KlB 11, 266–267	
410	Jo Co 20, 6	P 4, 334	M 14, 585B
411	Jer h 10, 2	Kl 3, 72	M 13, 360BC
412	Num h 9, 1	B 7, 55	
413	Jo Co frag 3, 31	P 4, 522	
414	Jo Co 13, 13	P 4, 237–238	M 14, 417D–420A
415	C Cels 3, 12–13	K 1, 211–213	M 11, 933–936B
416	Ps Co 17, 44		M 12, 1240A
417	Job frag 20, 15		M 12, 1036A
418	Rom Co 6, 1		M 14, 1055C
419	Ps Co 82, 19		PitAn. 3, 142
420	Ser 38	KlB 11, 72	
421	Ps Co frag 67, 6		PitAn. 3, 82
422	Ps Co 44, 11		M 12, 1432B
423	Lev h 11, 3	B 6, 452–453	
424	Mt Co 17, 13	Kl 10, 619–622	M 13, 1516AC. 1517A
425	1 Cor frag		Cramer V, 48
426	Ps Co 21, 19		M 12, 1257B
427	Cant Co 4	B 8, 232	
428	Cant Co 4	B 8, 234–235	
429	Mt Co 12, 37–38	KlB 10, 152–155	M 13, 1068B–1069C
430	Ser 138	KlB 11, 284–286	
431	Jo Co 1, 9	P 4, 12	M 14, 36CD
432	Rom Co 5, 1		M 14, 1020BC
433	Rom Co 3, 2		M 14, 958AD–959A
434	Ser 113	KlB 11, 236	
435	Jo Co 32, 17	P 4, 472, 473	M 14, 816D–817A
436	Jo Co frag 3, 29	P 4, 520–521	
437	Rom Co 4, 8		M 14, 992BC
438	Jo Co 32, 18	P 4, 474–475	M 14, 820BD
439	C Cels 6, 71	K 2, 141	M 11, 1405BC
440	PA 1, 3, 1	K 5, 49	M 11, 145–146
441	Jo Co frag 3, 8	P 4, 513	
442	Rom Co 7, 6		M 14, 1120C–1121
443	Jo Co 2, 6	P 4, 65	M 14, 129A
444	C Cels 8, 54	K 2, 270	M 11, 1597BC
445	C Cels 4, 6	K 1, 278–279	M 11, 1036CD
446	Jo Co 13, 23	P 4, 247	M 14, 437C
447	PE 2, 4	K 2, 301–302	M 11, 421A
448	1 Cor frag		Cramer V, 43
449	1 Cor frag		Cramer V, 46–47
450	Jo Co 1, 30	P 4, 35–36	M 14, 76C–77A
451	Rom Co 6, 7		M 14, 1070C
452	Jer h 9, 1	Kl 3, 64	M 13, 347CD
453	Gen h 9, 3	B 6, 92	
454	Gen h 9, 2	B 6, 89	
455	1 Cor frag		Cramer V, 66
456	Is h 2, 1	B 8, 248–249	
457	Gen h 3, 7	B 6, 49–50	
458	Luc h 22	R 9, 144	

459	Cant Co 4	B 8, 227	
460	Ex h 13, 2	B 6, 271	
461	Lev h 3, 3	B 6, 305	
462	Luc h 21	R 9, 130	
463	Ps Co 76, 19		M 12, 1539CD
464	Luc h 1	R 9, 7	
465	Jo Co 2, 26	P 4, 89-90	M 14, 169D-172B
466	Jo Co 6, 10	P 4, 126-127	M 14, 229B-232C
467	Luc h 4	R 9, 29-30	
468	Luc h 21	R 9, 128	
469	Jo Co frag 9, 35	P 4, 539	
470	Ps Co 47, 9		M 12, 1440C
471	Ser 63-64	KlB 11, 145-150	
472	Rom Co 8, 5		M 14, 1166A-1167A
473	Jer h 16	Kl 3, 132-133	M 13, 437D-440C
474	Rom Co 9, 3		M 14, 1215AB
475	Jo Co 20, 18	P 4, 351-352	M 14, 616B
476	Jo Co 20, 18	P 4, 352	M 14, 616C
477	Mt Co 11, 16	Kl 10, 60	M 13, 957A
478	Jo Co 20, 4	P 4, 367, 368	M 14, 641B-644C
479	Mt Co 10, 19	Kl 10, 25-26	M 13, 884A-885B
480	Jes Nav 13, 4	B 7, 374	
481	Rom Co 3, 6		M 14, 938CD-939A
482	Jo Co 19, 2	P 4, 307-308	M 14, 540B-541A
483	PA 3, 1, 18-19	K 5, 229-235	M 11, 288A-293B
484	Rom Co 4, 1		M 14, 963C-964A
485	Rom Co frag		Cramer IV, 28
486	Rom Co 4, 5		M 14, 974CD
487	Rom Co frag		Cramer IV, 24
488	Rom Co 9, 3		M 14, 1213B-1214A
489	Rom Co 8, 7		M 14, 1178C-1197A
490	Rom Co 4, 3		M 14, 970C
491	Rom Co 3, 9		M 14, 953CD
492	Rom Co 3, 7		M 14, 943AB. 944C
493	Rom Co 2, 7		M 14, 887A-888AC. 889BC
494	Rom Co 1, 12		M 14, 857CD
495	Mt Co 15, 10	Kl 10, 376-377	M 13, 1281B-1284A
496	Ser 69	KlB 11, 162-163	
497	Ser 77	KlB 11, 185-186	
498	Num h 11, 7	B 7, 88	
499	Rom Co 9, 4		M 14, 1218AB
500	Rom Co 9, 31		M 14, 1232B
501	Mt Co 12, 25	Kl 10, 125-126	M 13, 1040AB
502	Rom Co 9, 2		M 14, 1208BC
503	Num h 12, 3	B 7, 101	
504	C Cels 1, 10-11	K 1, 62-64	M 11, 673C-677A
505	C Cels 3, 39	K 1, 235-236	M 11, 969C-972A
506	PA 3, 3, 2	K 5, 257-258	M 11, 314C-315C
507	Rom Co 4, 9		M 14, 994CD
508	PE 1	K 2, 297	M 11, 416A
509	Rom Co 2, 14		M 11, 919ABC
510	Ps Co 11, 7		M 12, 1201CD

511	Jes Nav h 7	B 7, 334-335	
512	Ex h 9	B 6, 260	
513	Gen h 14, 3	B 6, 123-124	
514	Lev h, 7, 6	B 6, 391	
515	Lev h 5, 7	B 6, 347	
516	Jer h 19(20), 5	Kl 3, 184-185	M 13, 512BC
517	Ps Co 115, 2		PitAn. 3, 236
518	Jo Co 20, 23	P 4, 367	M 14, 641B
519	Ez h 3, 8	B 8, 355, 356	
520	Rom Co 2, 13		M 14, 912D-913AB
521	Luc h 11	R 9, 66-67	
522	Ex h 8, 2	B 6, 218-219	
523	Iudic h 2, 3	B 7, 476-477	
524	Jer h 7, 3	Kl 3, 53	M 13, 332D-333A
525	Is h 8, 1	B 8, 286	
526	Jer h 16, 9	Kl 3, 141	M 13, 449C
527	Jer 5, 2	Kl 32, 33	M 13, 300A
528	C Cels 8, 17-18	K 2, 234-236	M 11, 1540C-1545C
529	Luc h 16 + 17	R 9, 97. 102	
530	Luc h 17	R 9, 103	
531	Ex h 3, 3	B 6, 169	
532	Ex h 7, 6	B 6, 212-213	
533	Gen h 6, 3	B 6, 68	
534	Ps Co frag 74, 2		PitAn. 3, 102-103
535	Cant Co Prol	B 8, 63-67; 72(11-15); 69(20-26); 70(12-32); 71(13-20); 74(21-30)	
536	Gen h 3, 2	B 6, 40-41	
537	Num h 2, 2	B 7, 10-12	
538	Job frag 22, 2		M 12, 1036D-1037A
539	Num h 9, 9	B 7, 67	
540	Cant Co 2	B 8, 167-168	
541	Cant Co 1	B 8, 103-104	
542	Ser 66	KlB 11, 154	
543	C Cels 1, 48	K 1, 98	M 11, 749B
544	Jo Co 20, 33	P 4, 386	M 14, 676AB
545	Jo Co 20, 33	P 4, 386-388	
546	Rom Co 4, 5		M 14, 977D-978A
547	Cant Co 1	B 8, 105	
548	Ex h 3, 1-2	B 6, 161-163	
549	PA 3, 2, 1-2	K 5, 246-247	M 11, 305B-306A
550	Jes Nav h 5, 2	B 7, 316	
551	Iudic h 4	B 7, 484-485	
552	PE 29	K 2, 391	M 11, 544CD
553	PA 3, 2, 2	K 5, 247	M 11, 306BC
554	Luc h 8	R 9, 47. 49	
555	Jes Nav h 11	B 7, 363	
556	Mt Co 17, 2	Kl 10, 580	M 13, 1478BC
557	Ps Co 118, 157		M 12, 1621D
558	Jes Nav 15, 5	B 7, 390	
559	Iudic h 9, 1	B 7, 517-518	
560	C Cels 8, 23	K 2, 240	M 11, 1552C
561	Luc h 12	R 9, 75	

562	Iudic h 1, 1	B 7, 466	
563	Ez h 15, 2	B 8, 435	
564	PA 3, 2, 4	K 5, 251	M 11, 309C
565	Luc h 35	R 9, 199	
566	PA 3, 3, 4	K 5, 260–261	M 11, 317AB
567	Ps Co 65, 12		PitAn. 3, 77
568	Ser 35	KlB 11, 66. 68	
569	Ps Co 123, 6		PitAn. 3, 322
570	Ps Co 118, 28		M 12, 1593AB
571	Ps Co 118, 82		M 12, 1601B
572	Ps Co 93, 19		M 12, 1553D
573	Ps Co frag 36, 11		PitAn. 3, 10
574	Rom Co 7, 6		M 14, 1119B–1120
575	Ps Co 88, 13		PitAn. 3, 161
576	Ps 36 h, 5, 5		M 12, 1346B
577	Ps Co 118, 55		M 12, 1597D
578	Ps Co 17, 19. 20		M 12, 1232BC
579	Jes Nav h 16, 1	B 7, 395	
580	Ps Co 147, 16		M 12, 1677C
581	Jer h 14, 16	Kl 3, 122	M 13, 425A
582	Ser 117	KlB 11, 247	
583	Rom Co 2, 6		M 14, 885CD–886A
584	Ps Co 118, 45		M 12, 1596CD
585	Jo Co 28, 4	P 4, 392–393	M 14, 685BC
586	Ez h 2, 3	B 8, 344	
587	PA 3, 4, 3	K 5, 267–268	M 11, 322C–323A
588	Rom Co 2, 4		M 14, 875A
589	Ps Co 17, 2–3		M 12, 1224CD
590	Ps Co frag 100, 5		PitAn. 3, 191
591	Jer h 18, 10	Kl 3, 164	M 13, 484A
592	PA 3, 2, 5	K 5, 253	M 11, 311C
593	Jer h 8, 1	Kl 3, 55	M 13, 336C
594	Ser 29	KlB 11, 55	
595	Rom Co 2, 5		M 14, 882B
596	Ps Co 4, 7		M 12, 1164BC
597	Num h 6, 2	B 7, 32–33	
598	Rom Co 1, 13		M 14, 859CD–860A
599	Jer h 8, 5–6	Kl 3, 60–61	M 13, 341D–344C
600	Rom Co 7, 5		M 14, 1115A
601	PE 30, 1–2	K 2, 393–394	M 11, 545C–548A
602	Ps Co 4, 1		M 12, 1133B
603	Ps Co 68, 5		M 12, 1512D–1513A
604	Ps 4, 4		M 12, 1142BC
605	Ex h 5, 4	B 6, 189	
606	Is 6, 1	B 8, 270	
607	Gen h, 3, 2	B 6, 41	
608	Luc h 18	R 9, 124	
609	Mt Co 10, 14	Kl 10, 16	M 13, 866D
610	Ps 37 h 2, 3		M 12, 1384B
611	Is h 6, 6	B 8, 277	
612	Jo Co 19, 3	P 4, 311–312	M 14, 548BC
613	Ps Co 27, 1		M 12, 1284B
614	Ex h 3, 3	B 6, 167	

615	Rom Co 7, 6		M 14, 1121A
616	Jer h 12, 13	KlB 3, 99	M 13, 396BC
617	Jo Co 20, 27	P 4, 372	M 14, 652B
618	Ps Co 27, 1		M 17, 116D–117A
619	Gen h 2, 6	B 6, 38–39	
620	Luc h 16	R 9, 98	
621	C Cels 7, 39	K 2, 189–190	M 11, 1476C
622	Num h 17, 3	B 7, 158	
623	Ez h 3, 1	B 8, 348–349	
624	Luc h 22	R 9, 138	
625	Mt Co 11, 18	Kl 10, 66	M 13, 967
626	Cant Co 3	B 8, 215–216	
627	Luc h 1	R 9, 7	
628	Jo Co 28, 21	P 4, 424	M 14, 737CD
629	C Cels 6, 77	K 2, 146	M 11, 1413D–1416A
630	Gen h 15, 7	B 6, 135	
631	Mt Co 16:11	Kl 10, 508–509	M 13, 1407BC
632	Lev h 1, 1	B 6, 281	
633	Jer h 5, 8–9	Kl 3, 37–39	M 13, 305B–308C
634	Luc h 22	R 9, 145	
635	Gen h 9, 3	B 6, 104–105	
636	Cant Co 2	B 8, 140	
637	C Cels 3, 69	K 1, 262	M 11, 1012C
638	Cant Co 2	B 8, 162. 164	
639	Cant Co 3	B 8, 182–183	
640	Jo Co 6, 11	P 4, 127–128	M 14, 232D–233C
641	Ser 33	KlB 11, 61–62	
642	Jo Co 2, 20	P 4, 81–82	M 14, 158B
643	C Cels 7, 46	K 2, 198	M 11, 1488D–1489A
644	C Cels 8, 6	K 2, 225	M 11, 1528A
645	Ps Co 4, 1		M 12, 1136C
646	Iudic h 1, 4	B 7, 471	
647	Ps Co 103, 13		PitAn. 3, 204
648	Jer h 10, 1	Kl 3, 72	
649	Rom Co 7, 13		M 14, 1137CD
650	Jo Co 20, 31	P 4, 382	M 14, 668CD
651	Rom Co 3, 2		M 14, 932C
652	Lev h 5, 12	B 6, 355	
653	Jo Co 2, 18	P 4, 80	M 14, 156AB
654	Rom Co 6, 14		M 14, 1102C
655	Rom Co 6, 9		M 14, 1088B
656	Rom Co 4, 6		M 14, 980BC–981A
657	Rom Co frag		Cramer IV, 34
658	Prov Co 6, 3		M 17, 176D
659	Mt Co 16, 9	Kl 10, 503	M 13, 1401BC
660	Jo Co 10, 28	P 4, 222–223	M 14, 393C–396B
661	C Cels 1, 9	K 1, 62	M 11, 673AB
662	Mt Co 12, 15	Kl 10, 103	M 13, 1017AC
663	Jo Co 13, 52	P 4, 281–282	M 14, 496D–497A
663a	Jo Co 10, 27	P 4, 221–222	M 14, 392A–393B
664	Gen h 1, 7	B 6, 9–10	
665	Jo Co 19, 3–4	P 4, 301–303	M 14, 529A–532C
666	Luc h 15	R 9, 105	

667	Ps Co frag 49, 3		PitAn. 3, 50
668	Jo Co 20, 26	P 4, 369	M 14, 645D
669	Mt Co 12, 14	Kl 10, 96-97	M 13, 1012BC
670	Rom Co 4, 6		M 14, 981C
671	Mt Co 12, 43	Kl 10, 167	M 13, 1083D-1084A
672	Mt Co 17, 19	Kl 10, 640	M 13, 1537AB
673	Cant Co 2	B 8, 136	
674	Lev h 16, 7	B 6, 505	
675	Mt Co 15, 6-7	Kl 10, 364-366	M 13, 1269A-1272A
676	Mt Co 15, 8	Kl 10, 371	M 13, 1276BC
677	C Cels 1, 48	K 1, 98-99	M 11, 749C
678	Lev h, 3, 3	B 6, 303-304	
679	Lev h 4, 8	B 6, 326-327	
680	Ps Co 118, 169		M 12, 1625BC
681	Jo Co 6, 22	P 4, 146-147	M 14, 264C-265B
681a	Jo Co frag 1, 26	P 4, 566	
682	Jo Co 32, 19	P 4, 477	M 14, 824D
683	Rom Co 8, 2		M 14, 1163AB
684	Jo Co 2, 19	P 4, 81	M 14, 156C-157A
685	Jo Co 10, 8	P 4, 179-180	M 14, 321BC
686	Cant Co 1	B 8, 90-92	
687	Luc h 15	R 9, 92-94	
688	Cant Co schol		M 17, 282D
688a	Gen frag		M 12, 124B
689	Cant Co 1	B 8, 107-108. 102-103	
690	Cant Co 2	B 8, 165-167	
691	Ez h 12, 1	B 8, 432-433	
692	Ez h 12, 1	B 8, 434	
693	Ps Co 104, 28		PitAn. 3, 209
694	Ps Co 22, 1		M 12, 1259C
695	Gen h 1, 17	B 6, 20-21	
696	Ps Co 106, 18		M 12, 1567A
697	Ps Co 106, 17		Cad p 93
698	Ps Co 106, 9		Cad p 92-93
699	Jo Co 13, 34	P 4, 259-260	M 14, 457C-460C
700	PE 27	K 2, 363-364. 367	M 11, 505AC. 509C
701	Ps Co 77, 31		M 17, 144A-145C
702	Ps Co 77, 31		M 17, 148C
703	PE 27, 9	K 2, 369	M 11, 512CD
704	Num h 27, 1	B 7, 255-256	
705	Ps Co 118, 50		PitAn. 3, 272
706	PE 27, 2	K 2, 364	M 11, 505D-505A
707	PE 27, 9. 13	K 2, 369. 371-372	M 11, 513A. 516D
708	Num h 11, 6	B 7, 88	
709	Jo Co 13, 33	P 4, 259	M 14, 457B
710	Jo Co 13, 7	P 4, 231-232	M 14, 409A
711	Ps Co 64, 10		M 12, 1495C
712	Ps Co 77, 25		M 12, 1541BC
713	Luc schol 11, 3		M 17, 353C
714	Gen h 10, 3	B 6, 97	
715	Ser 85	KlB 11, 196-197	
716	Ps Co 80, 17		PitAn. 3, 139
717	Ps Co 77, 19-20		PitAn. 3, 117-118
718	Num h 16, 9	B 7, 151-152	

718a	Prov Co 9, 2		M 17, 185B
719	Rom Co 10, 11		M 14, 1268BC
720	Cant Co schol 4, 3		M 17, 269D-272A
721	Ex h 13, 3	B 6, 274	
722	Jo Co 1, 33	P 4, 37	M 14, 77D-80A
723	Ser 86	KlB 11, 199	
724	Ser 27	KlB 11, 48	
725	Luc schol 9, 27		M 17, 341A
726	Gen h 1, 17	B 6, 22	
727	Ser 22-23	KlB 11, 38-39	
728	Ex h, 7, 8	B 6, 216	
729	C Cels 4, 18	K 1, 287	M 11, 1049CD
730	Ps Co 77, 31		M 17, 144DA
731	Lev h 16, 2	B 6, 496	
732	Gen h 1, 2	B 6, 5	
733	Jo Co 13, 3	P 4, 228	M 14, 404AC
734	Cant Co 2	B 8, 171	
735	Cant Co 3	B 8, 185	
736	Cant Co 3	B 8, 186	
737	Ps Co 16, 15		M 12, 1224BC
738	Mart 47	K 1, 43	M 11, 629B-632A
739	Luc h 36	R 9, 207	
740	Num h 10, 7	B 7, 73	
741	Cant Co 2, 16		M 17, 265C
742	Ps Co 112, 9		M 12, 1571C
743	PE 8	K 2, 316	M 11, 441A
744	Mt Co 17, 21	Kl 10, 643	M 13, 1539CD-1542A
745	Ser 43	KlB 11, 87	
746	Gen h 6, 1	B 6, 66-67	
747	Ex h 1, 3	B 6, 148	
748	Jo Co frag 3, 29	P 4, 519-520	
749	Lev h 12, 7	B 6, 466-467	
750	Ex h 10, 3-4	B 6, 248. 250	
751	Cant h 2, 6	B 8, 51	
752	Rom Co 4, 6		M 14, 983CD
753	Mt Co frag 12, 48		Cramer I, 99
754	Ps Co 105, 3		Cad p 91
755	Ez h 7, 6	B 8, 396	
756	Ez h 8, 1	B 8, 401	
757	Jes Nav h 13, 2	B 7, 372	
758	Ex h 8, 5	B 6, 227-228	
759	Gen h 10, 4	B 6, 97-98	
760	Num h 20, 1-2	B 7, 187-189	
761	Ez h 10, 2	B 8, 419	
762	Num h 18, 4	B 7, 175	
763	Cant Co Prol	B 8, 80	
764	Cant Co schol 6, 7-8		M 17, 277CD
765	Cant Co 4	B 8, 223. 229-230	
766	Cant Co 3	B 8, 218-220	
767	Cant Co 3	B 8, 198-199	
768	Cant Co schol c 5, 6		M 17, 273CD
769	Cant Co schol c 2, 13-14		M 17, 264-265
770	Cant Co schol c 5, 2		M 17, 273BC

771	Cant Co 3	B 8, 194–195	
772	Cant h 2	B 8, 53–54	
773	Cant Co 2	B 8, 153	
774	Cant Co schol c 2, 4		M 17, 261C
775	Cant Co schol c 2, 16		M 17, 265C
776	Mt Co 12, 42		M 13, 1081A
777	Cant Co schol c 3, 1–4		M 17, 269C
778	Jo Co 1, 32	P 4, 37	M 14, 78CD
779	Jo Co 2, 1	P 4, 53	M 14, 106C
780	Jer h 9, 4	Kl 3, 70	M 13, 355D–358A
781	Rom Co 5, 8		M 14, 1042A
782	Ez h 13, 2	M 8, 447	
783	Is h 7, 1	B 8, 280–281	
784	Jo Co 6, 7	P 4, 120	M 14, 221A
785	Act frag 4, 32		Cramer III, 82
785a	Jo Co frag	P 4, 102–103	
786	Ez h 9, 1	B 8, 406	
787	1 Reg h 1, 4	B 8, 5–7	
788	1 Cor frag		Cramer V, 182
789	Jo Co frag 17, 11	P 4, 574	
790	Ez h 4, 6	B 8, 367	
791	Ps 36 h 2, 1		M 12, 1330A
792	Rom Co 9, 36		M 14, 1237A
793	Mt Co 17, 12		M 13, 1511C
794	Ser 102	KlB 11, 223	
795	Rom Co 3, 8		M 14, 951AB
796	Ser 73	KlB 11, 172	
797	Cant Co 3	B 8, 174–176	
798	Mt Co 14, 16–17	Kl 10, 323–326	M 13, 1229A–1232B
799	Jo Co 1, 12	P 4, 17	M 14, 43D–45A
800	Rom Co 4, 7		M 14, 985BC
801	Luc h 7	R 9, 45–46	
802	Luc h 14	R 9, 95	
803	Jo Co 10, 20	P 4, 209–211	M 14, 369D–372B. 373AB
804	Ps Co 29, 3		M 12, 1291D–1294A
805	PE 11	K 2, 322	M 11, 450A
806	Jo Co 19, 21	P 4, 211–212	M 14, 373D–376A
807	Rom Co 5, 9		M 14, 1044C
808	Lev h 12, 1	B 6, 454–455	
809	Lev h 6, 2	B 6, 362	
810	Lev h 5, 3	B 6, 338–339	
811	Rom Co 3, 8		M 14, 950BC
812	Lev h 2, 3	B 6, 294	
813	Lev h 1, 3	B 6, 284–285	
814	Lev h 9, 9	B 6, 436–437	
815	Ps Co 19, 4		M 12, 1247A
816	Jo Co 1, 3	P 4, 5	M 13, 24D–25B
817	Lev h 9, 1	B 6, 418–419	
818	Ser 18	KlB 11, 33	
819	Lev h 4, 6	B 6, 323–324	
820	1 Reg h 1, 9	B 8, 15–16	

821	PE 12, 2	K 2, 325	
822	Lev h 6, 6	B 6, 367–368	
823	Gen h 8, 2–10	B 6, 78–86	
824	Num h 24, 2	B 7, 229–230	
825	Mt Co 12, 26–27	Kl 10, 127–128	M 13, 1042–1043
826	Num h 10, 2	B 7, 71–72	
827	Num h 25, 4	B 7, 238	
828	Mt Co 12, 41	Kl 10, 163–164	M 13, 1079
829	Luc h 23	R 9, 143	
830	Jer h 14, 14	Kl 3, 119, 120	M 13, 422AD
831	Ps Co 108, 3		Cad p 95
832	Lev h 1, 5	B 6, 288	
833	Lev h 3, 5	B 6, 309	
834	Mt Co 12, 24	KlB 10, 124–125	M 13, 1038
835	Ser 126	KlB 11, 263	
836	Rom Co 2, 14		M 14, 919D–920A
837	Ps Co 22		PitAn. 2, 480
838	Ps Co 22		PitAn. 2, 480
839	Num h 15, 2	B 7, 132	
840	Ser 39	KlB 11, 77	
841	Num h 9, 2	B 7, 57	
842	Num h 12, 3	B 7, 102–103	
843	Rom Co 7, 13		M 14, 1139AB
844	Num h 7, 6	B 7, 48	
845	Ps Co 118, 157		PitAn. 3, 307–308
846	Mt Co frag 14, 28		Cramer I, 119, 120
847	Ser 86	KlB 11, 198	
848	Ser 86	KlB 11, 198–199	
849	Ser 86	KlB 11, 197–198	
850	Ser 86	KlB 11, 199	
851	PE 27, 12	K 2, 370	M 11, 514D
852	Num h 12, 1	B 7, 96	
853	Lev h 7, 5	B 6, 386–387	
854	Mt Co 16, 27	Kl 10, 565. 567	M 13, 1464A–1465A
855	Is h 2, 2	B 8, 252	
856	Num h 24, 2	B 7, 228–229	
857	Rom Co 4, 9		M 14, 997B
858	Lev h 4, 4	B 6, 319–320	
859	Cant Co 3	B 8, 186–187	
860	Jes Nav h 5, 6	B 7, 319–320	
861	Mt Co 14, 1–2	KlB 10, 271–277	M 13, 1182–1190
862	Ser 72	KlB 11, 168–170	
863	Ser 73	KlB 11, 172- 173	
864	Ser 68	KlB 11, 159–160	
865	Ex h 13, 3	B 6, 273–274	
866	Lev h 7, 1–2	B 6, 370–380	
867	Rom Co 7, 5		M 14, 1116C–1117A
868	Ps Co frag 74, 1		PitAn. 3, 102
869	PA 3, 5, 6	K 5, 277	M 11, 331
870	Is h 1, 2	B 8, 244–245	
871	Is h 1, 5	B 8, 247	
872	Is h 4, 1	B 8, 257–258	
873	Ez h 14, 2	B 8, 452–453	

874	Jo Co 2, 23	P 4, 85	
875	Lev h 5, 9	B 6, 350–351	
876	Jer h 16, 2	Kl 3, 134	M 13, 441A
877	1 Cor frag		Cramer V, 10
878	Ser 59	KlB 11, 136	
879	Ser 54	KlB 11, 122–124	
880	Ser 59	KlB 11, 133	
881	Ser 55	KlB 11, 126–127	
	Jo Co 13, 42	P 4, 268	M 14, 473C
882	Mt Co 12, 14		M 13, 1012C–1013A
883	Rom Co 5, 9		M 14, 1047CD
884	Rom Co 9, 32		M 14, 1233AC
885	Ser 32	KlB 11, 58–59	
886	Jer h 9, 1	Kl 3, 63	M 13, 348BC
887	Ser 56	KlB 11, 130–131	
888	Ser 70	KlB 11, 164–166	
889	Mt Co 14, 9		M 13, 1205BC
890	Ser 50	KlB 11, 110	
891	Ser 36	KlB 11, 68–69	
892	Ser 111	KlB 11, 232	
893	Is h 4, 5–6	B 8, 262	
894	Lev h 9, 8	B 6, 432	
895	Job schol 20, 25		M 17, 75AB
896	Jer h 19, 8–9	Kl 3, 190–192	M 13, 519B–D. 522
897	Ps Co 17, 8–9		M 12, 1228B
898	Rom Co 9, 41		M 14, 1242C
899	Ez h 9, 5	B 8, 415	
900	Ez h 2, 3	B 8, 343	
901	Ez h 1, 3	B 8, 324	
902	Jo Co 13, 23		M 14, 437A
903	Ez h 5, 1	B 8, 371	
904	Ez h 10, 4	B 8, 421–422	
905	Num h 8, 1	B 7, 51–52	
906	Jo Co 6, 38	P 4, 166–167	M 14, 301AB
907	Ex h 13, 4	B 6, 275–276	
908	Jes Nav h 4, 3	B 7, 311–312	
909	Is h 3, 1	B 8, 254	
910	Cant Co 2	B 8, 128–129	
911	Ex h 4, 4	B 6, 195–196	
912	Ps Co 6		M 12, 1177–1178
913	Jer h lat 2, 5	B 8, 294–295	
914	Jer h 6, 2	Kl 3, 49	M 13, 325AB
915	Rom Co 2, 2		M 14, 874A
916	Ps Co 19, 23		M 12, 1245D
917	Ex h 8, 5	B 6, 230	
918	Ez h 1, 2	B 8, 322–323	
919	Ez 1, 1	B 8, 319	
920	Ex h 3, 3	B 6, 167	
921	Mt Co 17, 24		M 13, 1548B
922	Jer h 12, 3	Kl 3, 90–91	M 13, 384AC
923	PE 29, 13	K 2, 388	M 11, 540AB
924	Ps 37 h 2, 5		M 12, 1385CD
925	Ex h 10, 3	B 6, 249	

926	Rom Co 5, 5		M 14, 1031C
927	Ser 117	KlB 11, 244	
928	Jo Co 32, 12	P 4, 458	
929	Ser 118	KlB 11, 251	
930	Ser 64	KlB 11, 151	
931	1 Cor frag		Cramer V, 73
932	1 Cor frag		Cramer V, 74
933	Ex h 6, 6	B 6, 197–198	
934	Gen h 1, 10	B 6, 11–12	
935	Luc h 24	R 9, 166	
936	Ps Co 104, 16		PitAn. 3, 207
937	Num h 14, 2	B 7, 121–124	
938	Rom Co 8, 13		M 14, 1200C
939	Ps Co 67, 3		PitAn. 3, 78
940	Mt Co 13, 23	Kl 10, 241–243	M 13, 1156–1157A
941	Num h 13, 7	B 7, 117	
942	Jes Nav h 15, 5	B 7, 389	
943	PE 6, 5	K 2, 315	M 11, 440AB
944	Jer h 5, 10	Kl 3, 39–40	M 13, 310B
945	Rom Co 1, 18		M 14, 865BC
946	Ez 4, 2	B 8, 363	
947	Jo Co frag 3, 18–19	P 4, 516	
948	Jer h 1, 16	Kl 3, 14–16	M 13, 273D–276C
949	PA 3, 1, 10–11	K 5, 211–212	M 11, 267
950	Jo Co 2, 22	P 4, 84	M 14, 161C
951	Jo Co frag 3	P 4, 486–487	
952	Jer h 19, 2	Kl 3, 178	M 13, 501D–504A
953	C Cels 8, 72	K 2, 289	M 11, 1625A
954	Ez h 1, 3	B 8, 325	
955	Rom Co 8, 12		M 14, 1198BC
956	Rom Co 5, 1		M 14, 1006D–1007A
957	Num h 18, 4	B 7, 175	
958	Ps Co 118, 11		M 12, 1589C
959	Ez h 1, 11	B 8, 334	
960	Gen Co frag 3, 7		M 12, 68B–D
961	Ex h 4, 1–2	B 6, 172–173	
962	Jer h 19–20	Kl 3, 173. 178. 180. 175. 181. 183–184. 173–174	M 13, 495B. 502C. 503D–506D. 498CD– 499A. 506D–507B 510BC. 495CD
963	Job schol 23, 6		PitAn. 2, 373
964	Jer frag 30, 21	Kl 3, 225	M 13, 580C
965	Ez h 10, 2	B 8, 420	
966	Ez h 1, 2	B 8, 321	
966a	Jo Co frag 12, 31	P 4, 552–553	
967	Rom Co 7, 10		M 14, 1131A
968	Jer h 4, 4	Kl 3, 26	M 13, 289B
969	Ps Co 118, 128		M 12, 1616B
970	Ps Co 2, 11		M 12, 1116B
971	Ser 81	KlB 11, 192–193	
972	Ps Co 118, 120		M 12, 1613CD
973	PE 16, 1	K 2, 336	M 11, 468C
974	Ps Co 2, 11		M 12, 1113D

975	Rom Co 5, 3		M 14, 1028AB
976	Mt Co 15, 12	Kl 10, 380–381	M 13, 1285BC
977	PE 25, 3	K 2, 359	M 11, 499A
978	Jer h 1, 16	Kl 3, 15	M 13, 175A
979	1 Cor Co frag 1		TU 17, 4; p 62
980	Eph Co frag		Gregg 405
981	Ps Co 74, 2		M 12, 1536B
982	Mt Co 12, 6	KlB 10, 78	M 13, 989C
983	Rom Co 6, 3		M 14, 1061C–1062A
984	Mt Co 15, 22–23	Kl 10, 416–418	M 13, 1320B–1321B
985	Luc h 14	R 9, 88–89	
986	Ez h 5, 2	B 8, 372	
987	Luc h 24	R 9, 148	
988	Ps 36 h 3, 1		M 12, 1337BC
989	Mt Co 17, 33–34	Kl 10, 692. 696	M 13, 1589AB. 1593A
990	Ps Co 22, 5		PitAn. 2, 480
991	Num h 23, 4	B 7, 217	
992	Jo Co 2, 4	P 4, 62	M 14, 121D–124A
993	Rom Co 1, 1		M 14, 839C–840A
994	Num h 23, 5	B 7, 217–218	
995	Num h 23, 4	B 7, 216	
996	Ser 45	KlB 11, 90	
997	Mart 13	Kl 1, 13	M 11, 579C
998	Num h 9, 8	B 7, 65–66	
999	Rom Co 7, 5		M 14, 1117C
1000	Mart 37	K 1, 35	M 11, 611C
1001	Lev h 9, 11	B 6, 438–440	
1002	Mt Co 15, 23	Kl 10, 418–419	M 13, 1321C–1324A
1003	Ps Co 118, 25		M 12, 1591D
1004	Cant Co Prol	B 8, 84–85	
1005	Cant Co Prol	B 8, 85	
1006	Ser 67	KlB 11, 158	
1007	Luc h 39	R 9, 220–222	
1008	Ser 62	KlB 11, 143	
1009	Ex h 6, 11–12	B 6, 202	
1010	Mt Co 15, 25	Kl 10, 425	M 13, 1328C–1329A
1011	Eph Co frag		Gregg 399
1012	Ps 36 h 5, 7		M 12, 1365C-D
1013	Eph Co frag		Gregg 406
1014	Rom Co 1, 14		M 14, 860–861
1015	Mt Co 10, 14	KlB 10, 17–18	M 13, 868C–869B
1016	PE 26, 6	K 2, 363	M 11, 503C–506A
1017	Mt Co 14, 7	KlB 10, 289–290	M 13, 1197BC
1018	Luc h 39	R 9, 171	
1019	PA 1, 2, 10	K 5, 44	M 11, 142A
1020	Ps 36 h 2, 1		M 12, 1329C
1021	Rom Co 9, 41		M 14, 1243BC
1022	Ps Co 85, 9		PitAn. 3, 148–149
1023	Rom Co 5, 7		M 14, 1037A
1024	Rom Co 5, 2		M 14, 1022BC
1025	PA 3, 6, 3	K 5, 283–284	M 11, 335C–336B
1026	Rom Co 7, 9		M 14, 1129C–1130A
1027	Jo Co 20, 7	P 4, 334	M 14, 587A

1028	Jo Co 1, 16	P 4, 20	M 14, 50D. 51A
1029	Ps Co 144, 3		PitAn. 3, 354
1030	Rom Co frag		Cramer IV, 155–157
1031	Ps Co 135, 8		PitAn. 3, 341
1032	Rom Co 3, 10		M 14, 956AB
1033	Eph Co frag		Gregg 412–413
1034	Num h 27, 13	B 7, 280	
1035	Jo Co 10, 18	P 4, 189	M 14, 337D
1036	PP 1–2	G-N 154–156	
1037	PP 3	G-N 158	
1038	PP 13	G-N 178	
1039	PP 39–42	G-N 230–236	

INDEX OF BIBLICAL REFERENCES

Note: The references are not to page numbers but to the individual passage numbers. For the sake of consistency and usefulness to the reader, the most commonly used system of dividing biblical chapters and verses (as found, e.g., in the RSV) is followed. In cases where, because Origen worked from the Septuagint (LXX), the chapter and verse numbering, or even the wording of the text itself, is different, the reader is alerted to this by the abbreviation "LXX" added to the biblical reference.

OLD TESTAMENT

Genesis				
1:1	124	4:16	810	
1:1–2	872	5:1	7	
1:7	65	5:24	114	
1:14	378	7–8	918	
1:21	934	9:6	852	
1:26	7, 54, 93, 535,	12:1	370	
	755	12:2	231	
1:26–27	20, 700	15:5	16, 102, 113	
1:26–28	75	15:7	103	
1:27	15, 33, 49, 69,	17:13	457	
	76, 787, 799	18:1	636	
1:28	521	18:20–19:28	918	
1:29–30	695	20:5	371	
2:2	995	21:12	746	
2:7	69, 71, 535	22:1–18	823	
2:8	480	22:12	259	
2:9	253, 308	22:16–17	259	
2:12	911	22:17	102, 453	
2:23	665	24:16	759	
2:17	1025	25:11	635	
2:24	368	26:12–22	7	
3:4	89	26:13	521	
3:6–7	620	26:19	9	
3:7	621	28:12	212	
3:13	962	28:17	212	
3:19	1001	32:2	812	
3:21	92	37:18–36	937	
3:24	903	38:17	373	
4:1	665	41:1–49	937	
4:7	926	42:1–5	937	
4:10	724	46:4	630	
4:14	810	49:10	430	
		49:11	734, 866	

Exodus

3:2–4	114
3:5	640
3:6	212
3:14	57, 86
4:6	236
4:10	548, 606
4:11	620
5:23	531
6–15	937
7:3	961
9:12	910
9:13	961
12:3	1039
12:5	1039
12:8–9	1038
12:14	1039
12:24	1039
12:37	918
13:21	114
14	937
14:15	605
14:22	114
15:5	911
15:7	965
15:10	911
15:11	74
15:12	932
15:17	1009
15:22–25	717
15:25	411
16	937
16:18	1006
16:20	532
17:6	937
20:3–6	522
20:5	758
21:23	750
25–27	865
30:22–33	374
33:20	351, 871
33:22–23	876
34:34–35	633
35:6	865
35:27	865

Leviticus

1:2–3	299
1:3	812, 813
1:5	813
1:9	375
1:13	375
1:17	375

2:13	114
2:14	245
4:3	812
4:7	814
4:10	812
5:2	678
6:12–13	819
5:18	679
6:1	193
6:17	679, 875
6:25	810
6:26	810
7:20	652
8:7–9	822
8:13	822
9:7–8	866
10:8–9	866
12:2–4	164, 985
13:48	211
14:34	211
16:12	814, 894
16:17	1001
17:6	814
20:9	423
20:26	56
21:10	808
21:12	823
23:5	1039
23:10	816
23:12	1039
24:9	19
26:9	674
26:12	7, 866
26:23	691
27:30	816

Numbers

11:25	597
12:14	244
16:15	665
16:42	841
18:30	1011
21:19	842
23:4	718
24:5	1
26:62	1011
28:2	503
28:11	994
31:27	827
33:6–48	114

Deuteronomy

1:31	269

4:24	810	4:1	578, 583
5:32	118	4:6	640
6:4	787	4:7	387, 633
8:15	105	8:1	404
10:9	1011	11:7	131, 640
10:12	856	12:6	158, 510
10:12–13	1007	17:1	406a
16:6	229	17:3	406a, 899
16:16	229	18:8	897
28:14	118	18:43	416
30:15	1001	19:4	295, 334, 395
32:6	423	19:7	118
32:39	529, 842, 948,	20:1	916
	995	21:23	1039
		22:14	803
Joshua		22:16	420
2:1	395	22:18	426
2:1–24	393	22:22	406a
2:9	395	23:5	866
2:18–20	395	24:1	7
4:10	127	24:4–5	641
6:17–25	393	25:1	359
7:21	511	25:7	98
8:29	308	27:1	592
18:7	1011	28:1	618
		30:2	804
Judges		30:9	403
2:7	646	30:24	131
7:3	559	32:11	728
9:4	372	33:6	16
		33:15	291
1 Samuel		34:8	544
1:1	787	34:14	495
2:2	56	35:10	7, 866
		36:8	731
2 Samuel		37:8	728
6:4–5	861	37:11	573
		37:39	1012
1 Chronicles		38:4	611
29:15	639	38:5	545, 688a
		40:7	200, 201
Job		40:8	201
1:9–12	601	41:3	824
1:22	601	41:5	114
3:8	307	42:1	11
10:10–11	113	42:4	114
14:4	287, 984	43:16	633
14:4–5	97, 984	44:22	1030
19:25–26	342	46:4	106
		46:10	14
Psalms		48:8	470
1:6	87	49:14	810
2:2	506	50:2–3	667
2:7	406a, 778		
2:11	970		

Psalms (continued)

50:4–5	548
50:6	434
51:5	984
51:17	728
55:6	611
65:9	711
66:12	567
67:12	535
68:18	288
68:30	1022
71:14	6
72:1	450
73:2	91
73:9	428
73:22	548
73:27	11
73:28	388
74:2	368
74:3	400
75:1	534
76:1	981
77:25	109
78:14	114
78:25	712
81:16	716
82:6	352, 1001
83:6	613
84:2	695
84:7	114
86:9	1022
91:11	794
91:15	863
94:10	538
94:10–11	509
100:2	888
102:26	891
102:27	787
103:1	114
103:3	728
103:3–4	114
103:8	269
103:15	715
104:15	375, 722, 734
104:24	33, 126, 508, 680
105:28	693
107:9	698
107:18	697
107:20	700
109:3	831
110:1	217, 394
110:4	312, 808
112:1	969

113:7	728
115:2	91
116:7	114
116:10	509
116:11	509, 517, 518
116:13	836
118:131	606
119:1	118
119:11	958
119:18	165, 632
119:25	1003
119:31	686
119:55	577
119:103	691
119:120	972
119:140	814
119:151	275
119:157	557
120:6	114
121:6	910
124:5	569
127:1	483
128:2	114
130:1	961
131:1	2
132:7	279
137:1–3	96
137:4	278
139:8	334
141:2	528, 820
143:2	406a, 495
145:2	122
145:15	217
147:8	995

Proverbs

1:24	200
2:3	542
2:5	471, 542
3:12	923
3:18	308
3:19	126
4:27	640
5:15	7
5:15–16	226
5:17	7
7:4	746
8:22	127, 129, 136, 158
8:24	872
8:30	123
9:1	375
9:2	718a
9:9	1034

9:14	861		7:14-15	855
10:19	200		7:15	98
19:14	494		8:18	783
20:9	641		9:6	150
26:9	211		10:10-11	525
27:1	406a		10:16-17	901
			11:1	909
Qoheleth			11:2	626
1:2	212		11:2-3	599
3:1	251		26:18	760, 889
7:20	97		40:5	342, 634
12:7	53		40:6	349
12:12	200		41:26	872
1:2	373, 686, 763		42:18	625
			43:2	988
			44:22	7
Canticle			45:7	872
1:2	373, 686, 763		46:23	1021
1:3	374, 540		49:2	535, 771, 772
1:3-4	689		49:20-21	395
1:4	540, 688		50:1	758
1:5	375		50:2-7	293
1:8	14, 15		50:6	407
1:11	26, 638		50:11	894
1:12	540, 690		53:2	629, 885
1:16	797		53:4	116, 862, 866
2:4	774, 859		53:4-8	1039
2:5	771		54:2	395
2:7	767		61:6	819
2:8	222, 225, 766		63:1	315
2:9	766		65:1-2	246
2:9-10	766		66:1	68
2:11-12	765		66:24	894
2:13	459			
2:13-14	769		*Jeremiah*	
2:14	428, 535		1:5	291
3:4	777		2:13	7
4:13-14	690		3:25	633
5:2	770		4:19	542
5:2-3	10		6:16	640
6:7-8	14		9:23	479
6:8	763		10:12	94
			11:19	411
			13:11	11
Isaiah			16:16	473
1:19	603		17:5	352
1:21	393		17:13	616
1:25	810		18:14	11
6:2	871, 872		20:7	962
6:2-3	870		20:9	896
6:5	871		23:23	11, 664
6:7	893		23:24	16
6:9	214		26:3	960
7:11	456		50:1	535

Lamentations			*Nahum*	
4:20	308, 639, 976		1:9	918
Ezekiel			*Habakkuk*	
1:1	96		2:4	250
13:2-3	586			
14:4	519		*Zechariah*	
14:13	946		1:3	664
16:2-3	386		2:4-5	396
16:2-63	406a		3:3	287
16:25	755		9:9	160
16:55	918		13:7	303
17:12	563, 691			
18:4	347, 1001		*Malachi*	
28:1	506		1:11	7, 149, 278
37:7	803		4:2	579
37:11	866			
44:1-2	873		*Tobit*	
			12:7	955
Daniel				
2:21	494		*Judith*	
4:27	497		9:11	291
7:9-10	898			
7:10	894		*Wisdom*	
9:5	94		1:2	246, 333
10:13	506		1:13	42a, 940
10:20	506		3:16	760
			6:5	406a
Hosea			6:6	406a
1:2	393, 395		7:7	626
1:2-3	395		7:17-21	33
4:8	810		7:22	626
10:12	642		7:26	780
12:10	259		8:2	544
			8:17-18	14
Joel			9:6	474, 479, 496
2:28	16		9:15	738, 983
2:32	534		13:5	625
			16:20-21	730
Amos			16:26	715
8:11	303			
			Sirach	
Jonah			1:26	212
1:4-17	386		3:18	406a
3:4	386		4:28	814
			14:26	427
Micah			27:11	787
7:1	401			

NEW TESTAMENT

Matthew			4:6	794
3:2	882		4:17	882, 1015
3:11	984		4:23	890
3:12	976		5:3	1017
3:16	111		5:3-9	107

5:6	210	13:16-17	663a
5:8	597, 631, 641,	13:25	759
	818	13:29-30	399
5:13	406a	13:31-32	33
5:14	16, 113	13:38	144
5:16	471	13:43	535
5:17	188, 433, 848	13:44	198
5:18	163	13:45	189
5:22	962	13:45-46	598
5:28	678	13:46	599
5:30	390	13:51	609
5:35	453	13:52	1015
5:45	918, 995	13:58	479
5:48	56	14:15	911
6:1	492	14:16	382
6:3	492	14:22	254
6:10	1016	14:24-25	254
6:11	700, 713	14:29	911
6:13	601	15:22	477
7:1	931	16:17	325
7:2	485	16:24	501, 825, 834
7:6	766, 959	16:25	825
7:12	374	16:28	545
7:14	581, 660	17:1-2	429
7:18	927, 962	17:1-8	671
7:21	645	17:2	429
7:22	660	17:3	257
7:23	88	17:4	828
7:24	528	17:5	776
8:13	728	17:6	629
8:20	863	17:8	257
8:21-22	112	18:10	638, 872
9:20	164	18:12	453
9:20-21	846	18:12-14	790
10:10	116	18:19-20	861
10:14	214	18:20	323
10:15	918	19:5	989
10:28	718a	19:6	798, 799
10:34	986	19:13	675
10:34-36	302	19:13-15	676
10:38	559, 824, 972	19:27-28	984
10:42	231	19:28	355
11:12	640	20:17	976
11:19	866	20:22	836
11:27	123, 147, 150,	20:29-34	631
	438, 535, 626	21:18-19	854
11:29	291	21:31	395
12:1	238	21:43	242
12:25-26	420	21:46	424
12:37	900	22:2	989
12:38	1015	22:13	921
12:39-40	205	22:29	989
12:40	307	22:30	1001
12:50	752	22:32	261, 973

Matthew (continued)

22:37	1006
22:40	230
22:44	394
23:2-3	406a
23:3	229
23:8	792
23:13	7, 626, 1015
23:31-32	243
23:35	724
23:37	221, 264, 331, 866
23:38	7, 240
23:39	331
24:1	240
24:6	568
24:6-7	420
24:7-8	890
24:25	1008
24:26	392
24:27	391, 392, 888
24:30	890
24:34-35	879
24:35	889, 891, 1012
24:36	881
24:42	880
24:50	53
25:1-2	471, 878
25:1-13	471
25:4	197
25:11-12	930
25:14	323
25:15	664
25:21	640, 1006
25:23	1006
25:31-32	888
25:34-35	864
25:35	862
25:41	893, 1030
25:43	863
26:22	971
26:26	715, 847, 848, 864
26:27	850, 866
26:28	723
26:29	228, 734, 736, 848, 849, 866
26:38	266
26:39	297, 298
26:45	296
26:51	239
26:53	794
26:64	892

27:24	928
27:28-29	306
27:31	306
27:32	835
27:40	246
27:42	246
27:50	309
27:50-51	430
27:51	224, 430
28:18	1008
28:19	7
28:20	16, 112, 323, 392

Mark

3:32	753
4:14	749
4:34	664
5:25	164, 679
5:25-29	678
5:25-34	687
6:5	479
6:45-51	575
7:34	475
8:34	814
9:2	310, 429
9:2-6	256
9:2-8	664
10:6	1001
10:13	675
12:27	973
14:6	690
14:13	228
14:24-25	734
14:25	866
14:33-34	323

Luke

1:17	467
1:35	308, 338, 751
1:46	554
2:22	985
2:28-29	687
2:30	666
2:34	300, 529
2:37	497
2:40	521
2:44	416
2:47	608
2:49	240
2:52	79, 282, 638
3:3	468
3:4	17, 468
3:6	349, 634
3:8	406a

3:32	288	20:24–25	1007
4:10	794	20:38	973
4:15	380, 849	20:41–43	402
4:20	387	20:43	217
6:47	528	21:3	482
7:37–38	394	21:28	884
7:50	487	22:4	548
8:20	753	22:10	228
8:42–48	626	22:15–16	849
8:46	890	22:29–30	990
8:48	184	23:18	799
9:31	257	23:21	626, 799
9:62	112, 118	23:43	106
10:16	384	24:32	7, 772, 814, 893,
10:18	113		907
10:22	438		
10:23	223	*John*	
10:27	535, 856	1:1	84, 127, 141,
10:30	280		150, 158, 540,
10:30–37	535		707, 779, 1028
10:41–42	664	1:1–2	355, 548
11:13	700	1:1–3	123, 124
11:20	1015	1:2	148, 207, 358,
11:46	229		1015
11:52	7	1:3	681, 889
12:46	53	1:4	133, 136, 151,
12:49	814, 896, 901,		642
	907, 986	1:5	406a
12:51–53	302	1:6	323
13:11	444	1:9	79, 114, 136,
13:27	907		392, 468, 562,
14:27	559		907
14:33	559, 814	1:10	438
15:4	246	1:11	681, 766
15:4–5	453	1:12–13	1039
15:4–7	790	1:13	338
15:8	7, 246	1:14	150, 267, 310,
15:10	299		312, 332, 358,
15:13	299		437, 452, 541,
15:23–24	299		653, 689, 799
15:25	861	1:15	436, 950
16:16	640	1:16	392, 1039
16:19–31	918	1:19–21	681
16:32	106	1:23	466, 640
17:1	940	1:16	321, 681
17:10	495	1:29	312, 318, 354
17:21	7, 882, 1015	1:45	437
17:33	739	2:19	806
18:11–14	406a	2:22	663a
18:13	585	2:23–25	660
18:18	213	3:3	493, 984
18:31	213	3:5	204, 493, 984
19:10	52, 469	3:8	441, 1034

John (continued)

3:16	824
3:17-19	947
3:18	810
3:20	910
3:29	436
3:30	436
3:32	413
3:34	1034
4:10	229
4:14	65, 535, 710, 733
4:20-23	7
4:24	193
4:32	699
4:34	375, 849
4:35	175, 881
4:38	1009
4:42	663
4:47	326
4:54	318
5:17	42a, 995
5:22	955
5:35	468
5:39	177, 200, 1039
5:46	262
6:12	203
6:28	700
6:31-33	703
6:32	847
6:32-33	700
6:33	456, 535, 540
6:35	540, 716
6:41	535
6:44	112
6:48-58	411
6:49-51	204
6:51	535, 544
6:52-58	541
6:53	1038
6:53-55	853
6:55	616, 866
6:63	193, 718
7:6	371
7:37	11, 466, 681
7:38	7, 65, 540, 731
8:12	136, 378
8:31-32	661, 665
8:32	478
8:32-33	1039
8:39	823
8:43	475
8:44	91, 406a
8:45	478

8:49	408
8:51	545
8:56	258
9:35	469
9:39	529, 947
10:8	150
10:9	136
10:11	453
10:14	246
10:15	123
10:16	260
10:27	384
10:28-29	665
10:30	1028
11:25	39, 90, 136, 976
11:41	585
11:41-42	610
11:52	866
11:57	628
12:3	690
12:24	343, 715, 716
12:27	323
12:31	71, 278. 966a
12:32	112
13:1	274
13:2	548
13:3-15	10
13:4	116
13:5-8	214
13:13-14	10
13:27	548
13:31	438
13:33	866
13:35	316
14:2	114
14:6	87, 90, 116, 117, 131, 136, 214, 639, 640, 801, 976, 1034
14:9	626
14:10-11	282
14:12	383, 844
14:23	528, 593
14:30	308
15:1	715, 722, 734, 735, 736, 850, 866
15:1-2	807
15:2-4	735
15:22	83, 150, 532
15:26	535
16:11	453
16:16-21	575
16:27-28	535

17:4	866	4:4–5	484
17:5	890	4:5	67
17:21	75, 689	4:11	205
17:21–22	72	4:12	206
17:24	75	4:16	102
18:10	239	4:17	57, 86
19:1	626	4:18	657
19:17	823, 834	5:2	797
19:26	220	5:5	850, 857
19:30	309	5:8	293, 718a, 866
19:34	303, 716, 717	5:14	92, 812
20:17	806	6:4	806, 842, 948,
20:28	770		972, 984
20:29	663a	6:5	457, 807
21:15	172	6:6	454
		6:9	307, 314
Acts		6:10	807
2:21	534	6:12	1017
2:35	394	6:15	639
2:38	287	7:1–2	358
3:12	493	7:3	757
3:21	672	7:6	451
4:32	785, 786, 787,	7:9	99
	789, 861	7:14	252, 358
6:8	890	7:22	535, 680
8:13	406a	7:23	358, 453
8:17	406a	7:24	338
8:20	406a	8:3	207, 278, 338
9:4	799	8:7	1008
10:44	385	8:8–9	50
13:46	7	8:11	342
14:15	824	8:14–16	644
15:14	395	8:15	767, 780
16:16–18	649	8:16	51, 867
17:23	18	8:22	879
17:28	145	8:26–27	605
22:22	798	8:32	296, 1026
		8:33	867
Romans		8:35	535
1:16	1014	8:36	1030
1:17	250	8:38	1030
1:20	33, 146	8:38–39	592, 971, 1030
1:24	945	8:39	535, 1030
2:4	968	9:3	843
2:4–5	956, 961	9:4	298
2:5	588	9:5	527
2:10	493	9:7–8	823
3:5	1039	9:16	483
3:20	236	9:18–20	961
3:20–21	235	9:20	961
3:21	492	9:21	95
3:25	811	9:32	183
3:31	433	9:33	183, 207

Romans (continued)
10:6   334
10:6-8   82, 456
10:8   150
10:13   534
10:14   384, 472
10:18   334, 395
11:16-24   298
11:22   968
11:25-26   206, 843
11:33   3, 938, 946
11:36   1032
12:1-2   832
12:2   449
12:3   488
12:5   866
12:6   24
12:9   499
12:16   477
13:11   884
13:12   878, 884
13:14   406a
14:1   241, 731
14:13   207
14:17   849
15:16   719

1 Corinthians
1:2   472
1:7   877
1:10   398, 787, 861
1:23   246
1:24   136, 780, 1014
1:27   149
1:29   943
1:30   508, 595
1:31   507
2:4   169
2:4-5   196
2:5   290
2:6   885
2:6-8   506
2:7   198
2:9   962, 989, 998,
            999
2:10   447, 448, 961
2:11   51, 195, 535
2:12   171
2:13   171, 1039
2:14   52, 428, 439
2:14-15   359
2:15   114, 425, 428,
            690
2:15-16   424, 449

2:16   171, 424, 856
3:1   535
3:2   731
3:12   810, 981
3:12-15   901
3:15   925
3:16   760
3:17   860
3:19   157
3:20   455
4:4-5   931
4:6   101
4:12-13   643
4:15   747
4:14   824
4:20   727
4:21   909
5:1   582
5:3   323
5:4   334
5:7   229, 616, 679
5:7-8   1037
5:8   229
6:9-10   962
6:11   680
6:13   775
6:15   45, 760, 797, 860
6:16-17   665
6:17   57, 316, 323,
            355, 356, 689,
            739, 798, 989,
            994, 1001,
            1003, 1005
6:18-19   860
7:1   678
7:5   861
7:7   798
8:1   101
8:5-6   84
9:10   433
9:19   355, 828
9:20   358
9:22   362
9:24   689, 787, 788
9:27   971
10:1-4   204
10:3   708
10:4   716, 876, 937
10:11   1039
10:14   471
10:17   788
11:19   412, 415
12:1   24
12:4   24

12:7	24, 488	15:36	345
12:8	14, 230, 766	15:37	343
12:8-9	665	15:37-38	345
12:8-11	486	15:42	312
12:9	668	15:44	287, 346, 1003
12:10	548	15:45	308, 1024
12:11	24, 441, 488	15:47-49	529
12:12	803, 805	15:49	7, 454, 701,
12:13	789		1000, 1007,
12:18-27	861		1017
12:20-21	806	15:50	738
12:22-24	859	15:51	345
12:24-26	803	15:53	348
12:26	805	15:53-54	977
12:26-27	804	16:9	837
12:27	788, 789, 790,		
	791, 796, 799,	*2 Corinthians*	
	866	1:1	948
13:2	33	2:7-8	582
13:3	814	2:11	582
13:4	101	2:15	688a
13:5	828, 866	2:16	7
13:7	5	3:1	633
13:8	232	3:3	172
13:9	170, 866	3:6	210
13:9-10	189, 982	3:7	252
13:10	430	3:7-8	433
13:10-13	663a	3:10	189
13:12	170, 639, 766,	3:14	225
	848, 867, 888,	3:15	633
	979, 983, 984,	3:16	225
	990, 993, 997	3:16-17	632, 1015
13:13	657	3:17	193, 1034
14:37-38	88	3:18	435, 437, 438,
15:9	168		623, 633
15:10	489, 943	4:2	633
15:19	342	4:7	228
15:22	92, 93, 94, 308,	4:10	80, 457
	956	4:16	54, 72, 111, 519,
15:24	354, 849, 956,		781
	1004, 1021,	4:18	33, 110, 213, 254
	1027	5:5	451
15:24-26	1020	5:7	663
15:24-28	278, 1019, 1034	5:10	962
15:25-26	1002	5:16	310, 313, 352,
15:26	307, 842, 975,		429
	1030	6:6	528
15:27-28	1020	6:16	16
15:28	75, 360, 866,	6:18	16
	869, 1025,	7:5	845
	1027	7:9-10	582
15:33	347	8:15	1006
15:33-34	956	9:7	823

2 Corinthians (continued)
9:9   864
10:10   727
11:2   748, 758
11:3   755
11:6   727
11:14   114, 562
11:23   830
11:28-29   805
11:29   862
12:2   603
12:4   961, 989
12:7   114, 406a
12:10   830
12:21   866
13:4   308, 862

Galatians
1:8   66
2:19   261
2:20   45, 261, 295,
           358, 457, 458,
           685, 803, 824,
           834, 866
2:29   501
3:6   453
3:13   867
3:16   823
3:18   823
3:19   373, 763
3:27   375
4:2   637
4:3   471
4:4   189, 374
4:6   644
4:9   665
4:16   605
4:19   747, 749, 752
4:22   231
4:23   190, 823
4:24   1015
4:26   423
4:28   226
5:7   560
5:17   114, 276, 302,
           587, 866
5:19-22   598
5:22   854
6:1   406a
6:7   962
6:8   43, 864
6:14   308, 685, 814,
           885
6:17   457

Ephesians
1:4-5   368
1:10   812
1:18   3, 1011
1:22-23   869
1:23   274, 881
2:6   308, 800, 966a,
           980
2:8-9   485
2:14   375, 450, 1013
2:19   858
2:20   368
3:1   762
3:10   128, 372
3:18   295
4:4   111
4:6   136, 527, 1033
4:8   266
4:8-9   295
4:10   334, 456
4:13   535, 788
4:22   405
4:25   859
4:27   19
5:14   767
5:22   748
5:23   416
5:25-26   368
5:27   374, 405
5:30   789, 866
5:31-32   798
5:32   368, 665
6:12   556, 827, 840,
           1030

Philippians
1:22   358
1:23   738, 824, 962
2:1-2   858
2:6   316, 799
2:6-7   271, 689, 866,
           967
2:6-8   318, 429, 955
2:7   270, 274, 307
2:8   292, 361, 869
2:9   318
2:10   334, 1030
2:10-11   1021
2:13   483
2:18   471
3:3   205, 229
3:8   189
3:13   118

3:14	1, 3, 483
3:15	866
3:19	7, 524, 527
3:20	820, 879
3:21	72, 338, 346, 984

Colossians

1:9	274
1:13	298, 866
1:15	76, 77, 123, 124, 128, 266, 282, 373, 450, 528, 535
1:15-16	1039
1:16	54
1:17	869
1:18	789, 937
1:20	812, 813, 858, 966a, 1004
1:24	860
2:3	198, 210, 599
2:9	271, 274, 371
2:12	948
2:14-15	308
2:15	298, 937, 966a
2:16-17	849
2:18	418, 620
3:1	948
3:3	39, 976, 1030
3:4	131
3:5	814, 842, 972
3:9	405
3:9-10	700
3:11	995, 1004
3:12-13	406a
3:15	457
4:6	177, 406a

1 Thessalonians

5:10	718a, 842
5:17	820, 821
5:19	40
5:21	512

2 Thessalonians

1:4	396
2:3	298
2:10	13

1 Timothy

1:7	229
1:9	356
2:5	374, 797

2:7	866
2:8	149
2:15	535, 745, 760
3:15	392, 766
3:16	334
4:10	124
6:16	59, 689, 808, 809
6:20	20

2 Timothy

1:4	7
1:7	599
2:3-4	827
2:4	955
2:5	934, 937
2:11	114, 842
2:12	457
2:19	665
2:20	87, 937
3:12	845
4:6	826
4:7-8	937

Titus

1:14	7, 204
3:5	984
3:6	3
3:8	3
3:11	947

Hebrews

1:3	123, 780
1:13	394
2:9	363
2:13	1039
2:18	1018
4:12	80, 681a, 1000
4:14	808, 826, 1005
4:15	365
5:1	358
5:6	808
5:7	312
5:12	638
5:13	241
5:14	363, 540, 542, 547
6:1	189, 251
6:5	541, 546
6:8	949
6:20	991
7:11	816
7:17	808
7:25	813

Hebrews (continued)

8:5	213, 432, 663a
8:13	891
9:1-5	430
9:7	363
9:10	237
9:14	810
9:24	26, 33, 813, 814
9:26	282
9:26-28	363
9:28	365
10:1	237, 431, 432, 985
10:13	394
10:20	813
10:28-29	962
11:1	656
11:18	823
11:39-40	866
12:18-24	1005
12:22	423
12:22-23	922
12:23	813
12:29	901
13:15	817

James

1:22	619

1 Peter

2:5	803, 1010
2:9	814, 817, 819
2:21	308
2:22	288
3:15	177
5:6	2, 496, 671
5:8	308
5:11	1034

2 Peter

1:4	858
3:3	803
3:10	803
3:13	803

1 John

1:1	279, 541
1:3	858
1:5	123
2:1-2	866
2:2	795
2:8	232, 540
3:2	74, 75, 672, 888
3:8	406a
3:12	1018
3:16	814
3:23	232
4:1	548
4:3	323
4:7	767
4:7-8	535
4:9	374
4:13	972
4:18	231, 767
5:16	925

2 John

12	961

Revelation

1:17	1031
2:8	1031
3:7	130
3:14	1039
3:20	851, 855
5:8	528
6:9	826
14:6	431
14:16	599
17:19	599
19:11	150, 159, 992
19:12	157
19:13	992
20:15	286
21:1	803, 984
21:6	716
22:1	716
22:13	1031